CHRIST
ON
EARTH

Other Titles by the Author

CHRIST ON EARTH

The Gospel Narratives as History

Jakob van Bruggen

Translated by
Nancy Forest-Flier

Baker Books

A Division of Baker Book House Co
Grand Rapids, Michigan 49516

Originally published as *Christus op aarde: Zijn levensbeschrijving door leerlingen en tijd-genoten*

© 1987 by Uitgeversmaatschappij J. H. Kok B. V., Kampen, Netherlands

English translation © 1998 by Baker Book House Company

Published by Baker Books
a division of Baker Book House Company
P.O. Box 6287, Grand Rapids, MI 49516-6287

Printed in the United States of America

Library of Congress Cataloging-in-Publication Data

Bruggen, J. van, 1936–
    [Christus op aarde. English]
    Christ on earth : the Gospel narratives as history / Jakob van Bruggen ; translated by Nancy Forest-Flier.
      p. cm.
    Includes bibliographical references (p.) and indexes.
    ISBN 0-8010-2186-3 (pbk.)
    1. Jesus Christ—Biography. 2. Jesus Christ—Historicity. 3. Bible. N.T. Gospels—Criticism, interpretation, etc. I. Title.
    BT301.2.B76513   1998
    232.9′01—dc21
    [b]   98-45972

For information about academic books, resources for Christian leaders, and all new releases available from Baker Book House, visit our web site:
http://www.bakerbooks.com

Contents

Introduction

This book is about the life of Jesus Christ on earth. In order to trace the course of his ministry, we must closely examine the four main sources for our knowledge of Jesus' life on earth: the Gospels according to Matthew, Mark, Luke, and John. How do these sources relate to each other? Does having four Gospels make it difficult to get a clear picture of Jesus' life, or do the four complement each other, so that our knowledge in fact is deepened? These questions are important. The Christian faith can survive without a complete biography of Christ, but its firm foundation would be seriously threatened if we had to live with a permanent uncertainty about the validity of the narratives provided to us by the writers of the four Gospels. The focal points of this book therefore are: (1) How do the evangelists inform us about Jesus' life on earth? What is the nature of their descriptions? (2) What kind of (incomplete) picture of his life on earth can we establish on the basis of the four Gospels?

Readers may rightly ask, "Another book on the historical Jesus? Don't we already have enough books on the subject?" Although lots of books have been written on this subject, many of these studies have resulted in a fading away of the historical Jesus, leaving only the smoking ruins of the Gospels as mostly unhistorical testimonies of the believing Christian community.

But what if we start with the supposition that the Gospels are reliable witnesses? "Don't they contradict each other too much?" you might ask. Is it really possible to read the four Gospels honestly and without prejudice and find a clear picture of the historical Jesus? The answer is yes, and this book gives the proof. Without devaluing the evangelists' testimonies or being blindly uncritical, this study compares the biblical and extra-biblical sources, analyzes the differences, and offers a plausible historical reconstruction of the key events of Jesus' life. The cumulative weight of plausible interpretations (including explanations that are psychologically and sociologically plausible) creates a solid argument for the essential historicity of the four Gospels. We discover that these early witnesses can withstand rigorous historical investigation. The result is a portrait of Jesus in deeper and richer colors with clearer and more lifelike details.

This book serves two functions. It can be used as an introduction to the Gospels. It can also be used as a survey of Jesus' earthly ministry. Although this book is an independent work that can be read on its own, its companion volume on the person and teaching of Jesus (first published in Dutch in 1996), will be published in English by Baker Book House in the near future. Both of these, in turn, are introductory volumes to a set of commentaries[1] on the four Gospels, published in Dutch between 1988 and 1997 (the first three written by me, the fourth by Dr. P. H. R. van Houwelingen). In a few places in this book I refer the reader to more extensive discussions in the companion commentaries. These references can easily be skipped; they have been retained in the English edition as optional connections with possible future translations of the commentary volumes.

There is much discussion today about what is called "the historical Jesus." Time after time, this discussion has led to a diminishing emphasis on faith in the living Lord Jesus Christ in heaven. In the title of this book, the name *Christ* was deliberately chosen to express the fact that any investigation into the earthly life of Jesus can never be isolated from our faith in his life and work as God's Messiah that continued after his resurrection and ascension. Taking a closer look at the way our Savior lived his earthly life can stimulate our reverence for the heavenly King in our own day.

Jakob van Bruggen
Kampen, Netherlands
Ascension Day 1998

---

1. Commentaar op het Nieuwe Testament, 3d series (Kampen: Kok).

Abbreviations

CCSL   Corpus Christianorum, Series Latina

CSEL   Corpus Scriptorum Ecclesiasticorum Latinorum

GCS   Griechischen Christlichen Schriftsteller der Ersten Jahrhunderte

MPG   *Patrologiae Cursus Completus, Series Graeca*, edited by J.-P. Migne, 161 vols. (Paris, 1857–66)

MPL   *Patrologiae Cursus Completus, Series Latina*, edited by J.-P. Migne, 221 vols. (Paris, 1844–55)

1

The Sources for a History of Jesus' Life

This chapter deals with the sources that are available to us for tracing the course of Jesus' life on earth. First we will look at how the choice of sources affects the final picture. Then we will discuss the extrabiblical data—what are they and of what value are they? The third question is whether there are earlier sources *behind* the familiar Gospel accounts. The answer to this last question determines whether we can accept the Gospels as they are, or whether we must view the Gospels as repainted canvas that requires laborious attempts on the part of a restorer to uncover the original image.

1.1 Source and Image

It is a rarely disputed fact that at the beginning of our era there lived in Palestine a Jew called Joshua (Jesus), who was crucified by the Romans.[1] But from this minimal and rather unhelpful starting point the paths immediately diverge when it comes to describing his life or his teachings. This great divergence in the images of the "historical Jesus" is a direct result of (1) subjectively determined selections from the available sources, and (2) vast differences in the evaluation of the historical sources. All too often it seems that the sources are selected and reworked on the basis of (or in the direction of) an already established image. Often, in spite of such bias, the results then are nevertheless emphatically presented as if a critical investigation of the sources *of necessity* has led to this particular image of Jesus. Obviously, the wide

1. Bruno Bauer, in his book *Christus und die Cäsaren* (Berlin: Grosser, 1877), was not the first scholar to deny the historicity of Jesus outright, but for a long time his explanation of the rise of Christianity on the basis of social and religious factors enjoyed quite a following. See, for example, A. Kalthoff, *Das Christus-Problem: Grundlinien zu einer Sozialtheologie* (Leipzig: Diederichs, 1902). For the discussion on this topic between Bauer and Wilhelm Bousset, see A. F. Verheule, *Wilhelm Bousset, Leben und Werk: Ein theologiegeschichtlicher Versuch* (Amsterdam: Ton Bolland, 1973), 172–73. A survey of the writers who have denied the earthly existence of Jesus is found in A. Drews, *Die Leugnung der Geschichtlichkeit Jesu in Vergangenheit und Gegenwart*, Wissen und Wirken 33 (Karlsruhe: Braun, 1926).

range of perceptions of Jesus' life and work today will necessarily lead to even greater theological divergence within Christendom. After all, it makes quite a difference whether one sees Jesus as a failed idealist or as the Son of God come to earth!

1.1.1 Diversity of Images

Ever since the very first centuries A.D. there have been differences of opinion within the Christian church concerning a number of *details* about Jesus' life—whether, for example, Judas was still present when the Lord's Supper was instituted, or what the exact time of Jesus' resurrection was: early evening or sunrise? The exegesis and comparison of the Gospels resulted in problematic questions about the details of the great events, questions that were often difficult to answer. But these questions did not prevent an essentially uniform understanding of Jesus' life on earth. For centuries, the image that people formed of the life of Christ among his contemporaries was as harmonious as the four Gospels themselves. Only to the extent that the Gospels were unclear or seemed to contradict one another did the otherwise distinct portrait exhibit vague or controversial spots.

But this essential unanimity within Christianity has changed drastically during the past few centuries. We are now confronted with an abundance of images. The differences between these images are vast, even to the point that at times Jesus as he is perceived by one school is the exact opposite of Jesus as seen by another. The search for the "historical Jesus" has become so broad and entangled that the search has become a topic of study in its own right. Late in the nineteenth century Albert Schweitzer carried out such a study.[2] For a while, at the beginning of the twentieth century, the "life of Jesus" research seemed to have peaked as, under the influence of dialectic theology, interest in the historical Jesus declined in favor of the preached kerygmatic Christ. But it soon became apparent that a (mythologizing) Christology ends up suspended in midair if no attention is paid to the historical Jesus, with whom it all began.[3] Thus the pendulum began to swing back, and

2. A. Schweitzer, *The Quest of the Historical Jesus: A Critical Study of Its Progress from Reimarus to Wrede*, trans. W. Montgomery (London: Black, 1948); originally published in 1906 under the title *Von Reimarus zu Wrede*. For Schweitzer's own viewpoint, see also H. B. Kossen, *Op zoek naar de historische Jezus: Een studie over Albert Schweitzers visie op Jezus' leven* (Assen: Van Gorcum, 1960).

3. For reflections on this topic, see the collections of essays *Der historische Jesus und der kerygmatische Christus: Beiträge zum Christusverständnis in Forschung und Verkündigung*, 3d ed., ed. H. Ristow and K. Matthiae (Berlin: Evangelische Verlagsanstalt, 1964), and *Jesus Christus in Historie und Theologie: Festschrift für H. Conzelmann*, ed. G. Strecker (Tübingen: Mohr, 1975).

a survey by W. G. Kümmel and H. Merklein of the Jesus research done during the period 1950–1990 resulted in a book of almost seven hundred pages! Kümmel had to conclude not only that the number of publications on this topic has reached horrendous and barely manageable proportions, but that all the contradictory perceptions give the impression that the research on the historical Jesus is in virtual gridlock.[4]

This can easily be illustrated by taking a brief look at a few noted authors from diverse backgrounds who have devoted much time and attention to describing Jesus' life on earth.

In modern European Protestantism, Herbert Braun's *Jesus: Der Mann aus Nazareth und seine Zeit* is well known. This study appeared in a new edition in 1984, with so many chapters added to the original that the book doubled in size. For Braun, whom this topic has occupied for many years, the heart of Jesus' ministry can be found in the fact that he was a radical who made uncompromising demands. He also accepted other people unconditionally.[5] The stories of his birth and resurrection are later elaborations that seek to convey this essential core, a core that can be found in the most ancient layer of the first three Gospels. The events the church celebrates on Christmas and Easter did not happen as the evangelists later described them. Modern Christians celebrate in these feasts the acceptance of a failed humanity, and in doing so they do justice to the historical Jesus.[6]

E. Schillebeeckx writes from a modernistic Roman Catholic background. In his first book on the subject, *Jesus: An Experiment in Christology,* he pays a great deal of attention to the historical Jesus—to the extent that he can be distinguished from the experiential reflections and projections of the church's proclamation of the Christ.[7] Like Braun, Schillebeeckx sees in Jesus the preacher who unconditionally joins the concerns of God and the concerns of humanity. An oppressive (legalistic) image of God was dismantled and sinners experienced acceptance. But for Schillebeeckx, none of this would have meaning without the historical element of a unique "Abba experience" in Jesus' life. It is in connectedness with this historical Abba experience, which is accepted

---

4. W. G. Kümmel, *Vierzig Jahre Jesusforschung (1950–1990)*, 2d ed., ed. H. Merklein, Bonner Biblische Beiträge 91 (Weinheim: Beltz Athenäum, 1994). Cf. A. E. McGrath, *The Making of Modern German Christology: From the Enlightenment to Pannenberg* (Oxford: Blackwell, 1986). J. Pelikan, *Jesus through the Centuries: His Place in the History of Culture* (New Haven: Yale University Press, 1985).

5. H. Braun, *Jesus: Der Mann aus Nazareth und seine Zeit,* Um 12 Kapitel erweiterte Studienausgabe (Stuttgart: Kreuz, 1984), 246–47.

6. Ibid., 239–53.

7. E. Schillebeeckx, *Jesus: An Experiment in Christology,* trans. H. Hoskins (London: Collins, 1979).

in faith, that the church develops its Christology. Schillebeeckx devoted a second book to the subject, *Christ: The Experience of Jesus as Lord,* as well as a volume of later reflections on both works.[8]

Another image of Jesus was developed by the Jewish New Testament scholar David Flusser. His interest in the person and teaching of Jesus is closely linked to his work on behalf of the dialogue between Christians and Jews. His study stands within a tradition of twentieth-century Jewish books about Jesus that attempt to present a historical picture of Jesus that is acceptable to Jews.[9] Schalom Ben-Chorin, taking his lead from Martin Buber, even went so far as to refer to Jesus as "brother," and H. Falk is of the opinion that Jesus, as an adherent of the school of Hillel, was a victim of the followers of Shammai.[10] Flusser made the rise of Christianity the focus of his study for many years. In his book about Jesus, he portrays him as a law-abiding Jew who proclaimed the message of love. An important element in understanding his ministry was the Essene community, from which he, like John the Baptist, borrowed many ideas. The motive behind his ministry is to be found in his unique interpretation of the gift of the Spirit that took place at the time of John's baptism. Because of this he regarded himself as a Called One of Israel.[11]

Finally, we turn to the image of the historical Jesus in Latin American liberation theology, especially that of Jon Sobrino.[12] In contrast to

8. E. Schillebeeckx, *Christ: The Experience of Jesus as Lord*, trans. J. Bowden (New York: Seabury, 1980). Idem, *Interim Report on the Books* Jesus *and* Christ, trans. J. Bowden (New York: Crossroad, 1981).

9. For an overview, see G. Lindeskog, *Die Jesusfrage im neuzeitlichen Judentum: Ein Beitrag zur Geschichte der Leben-Jesu-Forschung,* Mit einem Nachwort (Darmstadt: Wissenschaftliche Buchgesellschaft, 1973; original edition: Uppsala, 1938).

10. S. Ben-Chorin, *Broeder Jezus: De Nazarener door een Jood gezien* (Baarn: Ten Have, 1971); translation of the German edition of 1967. H. Falk, in *Jesus the Pharisee: A New Look at the Jewishness of Jesus* (New York: Paulist Press, 1985), went so far as to reduce the conflict between Jesus and the Pharisees to a conflict between a follower of Hillel and the then-dominant followers of Shammai.

11. D. Flusser, *Jesus*, trans. R. Walls (New York: Herder & Herder, 1969). Cf. also his *De Joodse oorsprong van het Christendom: Twee essays* (Amsterdam: Moussault, 1964).

12. J. Sobrino, *Christology at the Crossroads: A Latin American Approach* (Maryknoll, N.Y.: Orbis, 1978; original Spanish edition 1976). It is significant that Sobrino is a Jesuit. In an appendix to his book he examines the "Spiritual Exercises" of Ignatius Loyola, the founder of the order, in light of today's issues. Sobrino's work is in line with that of other South American theologians, such as Assman, Gutiérrez, and Ellacuría. For a comparable theological development in Africa, see T. A. Mokofeng, *The Crucified among the Crossbearers: Towards a Black Christology* (Kampen: Kok, 1983). In Asia we find the Minjung Theology of South Korea: Byung-Mu Ahn sees Jesus as the man who addressed the disenfranchised (Minjung), and he views the traditions about Jesus as having arisen from the "suppressed rumors" that circulated among the poor and gave them hope (Byung-Mu Ahn, *Draussen vor dem Tor: Kirche und Minjung in Korea* [Göttingen: Vandenhoek & Ruprecht, 1986]).

classical Chalcedonian Christology, Sobrino argues for a Christology that proceeds entirely from the Jesus who became man and entered history. The faith of Jesus, which we are called to imitate, was a historical faith. It developed from an initial phase, in which Jesus as preacher of God's kingdom stayed within the bounds of familiar religious ideas, to a second phase, in which he pointed to a kind of alternative to the harsh social criticism of the Zealots. It was the Galilean crisis that caused Jesus to become disillusioned and to face up to the apparent invincibility of society's unjust and unfeeling structures. His uncompromising loyalty to God put him on the road to rejection by the existing powers, both religious and social.

Considering what has happened since 1990, this gridlock of the Jesus research is unlikely to be resolved any time soon. Some rather massive books have been published in Germany dealing with the question of who Jesus really was, but there certainly is no agreement among them![13] In the English language, a great many books about Jesus have been published since 1990. They form part of what is called "The Third Quest for the Historical Jesus." The most voluminous are J. P. Meier's three books about Jesus, viewed as a "marginal Jew" (the first two volumes comprise about fifteen hundred pages!).[14] The Jesus Seminar in the United States formed one of the challenges to this Third Quest.[15] A firm defense of the Jesus of the Gospels and against the Jesus Seminar has been offered in the book *Jesus under Fire*.[16] (These and other recent publications are described in B. Witherington's *The Jesus Quest*.)[17] In the meantime, this quest, like the earlier ones, has become a subject of discussion and evaluation in its own right;[18] the focus now is no longer on the diminishing figure of Jesus but on the participants in the debate and on the debate itself. In the end, we are stalled in gridlock and go nowhere!

Even in this brief, highly selective overview we catch a glimpse of the diversity that exists. Was Jesus just an uncompromising preacher

13. G. Theissen and A. Merz, *Der historische Jesus: Ein Lehrbuch* (Göttingen: Vandenhoeck & Ruprecht, 1996); J. Becker, *Jesus von Nazareth*, De Gruyter Lehrbuch (Berlin: De Gruyter, 1996); K. Berger, *Wer war Jesus wirklich?* (Stuttgart: Quell Verlag, 1995).

14. J. P. Meier, *A Marginal Jew: Rethinking the Historical Jesus*, vol. 1, *The Roots of the Problem and the Person* (New York: Doubleday, 1991); vol. 2, *Mentor, Message, and Miracles* (New York: Doubleday, 1994).

15. R. W. Funk and R. W. Hoover, eds., *The Five Gospels: The Search for the Authentic Words of Jesus* (New York: Macmillan, 1993).

16. M. J. Wilkins and J. P. Moreland, *Jesus under Fire: Modern Scholarship Reinvents the Historical Jesus* (Grand Rapids: Zondervan, 1995).

17. B. Witherington III, *The Jesus Quest: The Third Search for the Jew of Nazareth* (Downers Grove, Ill.: InterVarsity, 1995).

18. C. Marsh, "Quests of the Historical Jesus in New Historicist Perspective," *Biblical Interpretation* 5 (1997): 403–37.

(Braun), or is he marked by unique divine experiences? And if so, what are they? His baptism (Flusser), his Abba experience (Schillebeeckx), or his disillusionment in Galilee (Sobrino)? Everyone provides answers to these or other questions, according to his or her own beliefs, by appealing to what can be known about Jesus' life story. The question is, Are the historical sources really so obscure that they leave room for such great diversity of opinion?

1.1.2 Detachment from the Gospels

Even though most modern images of the historical Jesus are diametrically opposed to the clear portrayal in the four Gospels, this is by no means considered a problem. In fact, there is virtual unanimity among scholars today that we must distance ourselves from the four Gospels if we really want to get to know Jesus. The Gospels are never completely dismissed, since there would then be hardly any material left for a description of Jesus' life, but they are used with critical detachment. The Gospels are regarded as valid historical sources *insofar as they still qualify as such* in the opinion of modern historical and literary criticism. The Gospels are not accepted by the historian as they stand but are examined in terms of what they should have been and of what they perhaps originally were. Today, any description of Jesus' life must be preceded by an ostracizing of the four Gospels.

This was true even in the eighteenth century, when *historical* criticism was dominant. Although the English deists of the early eighteenth century had developed a critical attitude toward the Gospels, this attitude became influential in the second half of that century through the work of Hermann Samuel Reimarus.[19] A storm of criticism erupted when G. E. Lessing published Reimarus's work anonymously and posthumously in 1774–78, but Reimarus's ideas nevertheless began to have an impact on the development of German biblical scholarship. Reimarus was of the opinion that Jesus had wanted to be a political liberator (messiah), and that his message of liberation with its religious overtones came to nothing. Afterward his disciples developed the concept of a *spiritual* kingdom and a *heavenly* Messiah. So the Gospels are nothing more than stories written in the light of the disciples' later concepts that are projected back onto Jesus. Sometimes memories of the actual events are dimly visible in the Gospels, for instance when the men on the road to Emmaus say that they had hoped Jesus would liberate Israel, or when the disciples on Holy Saturday do not seem to know anything about an announced resurrection from the dead on the third

---

19. See G. W. Buchanan's introduction in H. S. Reimarus, *The Goal of Jesus and His Disciples*, trans. G. W. Buchanan (Leiden: Brill, 1970), 1–32.

day.[20] Reimarus's image of an almost Zealot-like Jesus will later recur more than once.[21] It is important to note that for Reimarus, who is often seen as the father of the modern portrayals of Jesus, everything is based on a historical-critical approach to the four Gospels. For the historian, the point of departure is not what the Gospels describe but rather the disciples' shortsightedness or their lack of faith as it is honestly reported in the Gospels. This lack of faith now becomes the yardstick for determining the "historical Jesus"—not the Christ of the Gospels, but Jesus as people sometimes misunderstood him! But what is the objective reason for assuming that the shortsighted ideas of the crowds or the disciples (contrary to the way things are presented in the Gospels) give us a picture of the "real" Jesus?

It was David Friedrich Strauss who, in his book *The Life of Jesus Critically Examined* (1835–36), hoped to lay a foundation for this critical rewriting of Jesus' life story.[22] He elaborated on the previously developed idea that the New as well as the Old Testament must be read with the assumption that they contain myths. The earliest histories of all peoples are written in the form of myths, and the tendency for later myths to be woven around historically influential persons is a familiar phenomenon. Granted, the New Testament was written during a period when people were already completely familiar with objective, written historical accounts, but the evangelists were not eyewitnesses, and they could easily have recorded in their writings the myths that had gradually been formed within the circle of the uneducated disciples. Thus Strauss reads the Gospels in a manner very different from that intended by their authors. This becomes especially clear when he deals with the introduction to Luke's Gospel. Strauss discusses the proposition that Luke did not write myths but carefully edited historical reports upon which he was willing and able to base the reliability of the gospel that had been preached to Theophilus. Strauss's response is revealing. He claims that Luke was not aware of writing myths. In other words, Luke was under the impression that he

---

20. Ibid., 81–84.

21. See R. Eisler, *Ièsous Basileus ou basileusas: Die messianische Unabhängigkeitsbewegung vom Auftreten Johannes des Täufers bis zum Untergang Jakobs des Gerechten usw.* (Heidelberg: Winter, 1929–30); S. G. F. Brandon, *Jesus and the Zealots: A Study of the Political Factor in Primitive Christianity* (Manchester: Manchester University Press, 1967), a critical reaction to this book is found in O. Cullmann, *Jesus and the Revolutionaries*, trans. G. Putnam (New York: Harper & Row, 1970); G. W. Buchanan, *The Consequences of the Covenant* (Leiden: Brill, 1970) and *Jesus: The King and His Kingdom* (Macon, Ga.: Mercer University Press, 1984).

22. D. F. Strauss, *The Life of Jesus Critically Examined*, trans. G. Eliot (Philadelphia: Fortress, 1973). For Strauss, see also E. G. Lawler, *David Friedrich Strauss and His Critics: The Life of Jesus Debate in Early Nineteenth-Century German Journals* (New York: Lang, 1986).

was writing history, and that is how his book is intended. So what is the objective reason for assuming that this Gospel might contain myths (contrary to Luke's own way of presenting things)? For Strauss, in fact, all is decided by his conviction that any supernatural intervention by God in this world is out of the question. Thus a deistic, mechanical image of God controls the reading of the Gospels and results in a distancing from the Gospels based on extratextual and ahistorical assumptions.

It is understandable that nineteenth-century New Testament scholars had difficulty sustaining this kind of criticism in the face of the transparent clarity of the Gospels. And thus we see that in the course of the nineteenth century, historical criticism came to travel under the passport of *literary* criticism. Literary criteria, derived from the text of the Gospels themselves, now must form an objective and workable basis for any attempt to use the Gospels as historical sources. It is not possible within the scope of this book to provide a complete sketch of the jumble of opinions that has gradually emerged on this point.[23] The basic premise is rather simple: the first three Gospels reveal a striking combination of similarities and differences. Doesn't this suggest that each of the evangelists worked individually with one or more sources, and that by investigating these sources we end up with an older and more reliable historical layer?

One might envision a written or orally transmitted primitive Gospel, or part of one—a collection of sayings or miracles, for example. One can also imagine one of the evangelists making use of the work of one or two of the other evangelists. A hybrid of these two possibilities, known as the two-source hypothesis, has gained so many adherents that for almost a hundred years it has been accepted as the main achievement of modern Gospel criticism. On the one hand there is the primitive gospel or the primitive collection of the spoken words of Jesus (called L or Q). On the other hand, Matthew and Luke used, in addition to Q, the work of the evangelist Mark (or the historical source behind Mark). This hypothesis, which contains at least one and perhaps two unknown elements (Q and possibly primitive Mark), leaves room for many variations. But what all the variations have in common is that at least Matthew and Luke must be read as *secondary* sources.[24] Now the challenge is to try to see through

23. Every textbook on New Testament introduction provides an overview of the Synoptic problem and the proposed solutions. More detailed than most is W. Schmithals, *Einleitung in die drei ersten Evangelien* (Berlin: De Gruyter, 1985).

24. The four-source hypothesis that was developed in England (associated in particular with the work of B. H. Streeter) is not in conflict with the two-source theory but can be seen as a more detailed variant. The problems that often lead to postulating a primitive Mark are here solved by assuming that separate sources existed for Matthew and Luke in addition to Mark and Q.

these Gospels something of the older layer (Jesus's own words in Q). From a historical standpoint Mark is of primary importance, but even Mark cannot have final historical say because it in turn must also have been based on older traditions (possibly a primitive Mark). The modern image of Jesus is built on a totally unknown "historical" foundation: Q and an unknown earlier version of Mark. Because these sources are more mythical than historical in nature, they do not have definitive, fixed, historical content, and the diversity of images of Jesus has understandably grown exceedingly large over the past century and a half.

This is all the more true because historical criticism does not stop at the "older" layers of tradition found by means of literary analysis. After it was almost generally accepted that Mark must have been the oldest of the three Gospels, William Wrede subjected this Gospel to the same historical criticism that Reimarus had applied.[25] According to Wrede, Jesus himself did not preach as the Messiah; his disciples were the ones who placed him within the framework of messianic expectation. They then had to create a plausible explanation for the fact that later the Christian community preached Jesus as the Christ, even though he himself had never mentioned any messianic titles. Mark's solution was to write a largely fictional Gospel, or at any rate to *rewrite* history from the perspective of a later idea. By describing in his book various scenes in which Jesus forbids people and evil spirits from using the title "Messiah," Mark "explains" the fact that Jesus himself did not talk about his messiahship—which he wanted to keep a secret—while his disciples now had every (fictive) right to do so.

The smaller units of the Gospel tradition (Jesus' sayings or deeds) that can be recognized behind the larger pericopes of the evangelists cannot escape historical criticism either. In the twentieth century, form criticism has raised questions about the historical origins of such sayings or narratives. Those origins are mostly to be found, not in the original events that took place around Jesus, but in the later Christian community. Out of the needs that developed in the areas of mission, catechism, canon law, and community formation, stories or commands emerged that with varying degrees of justification were made part of the core of Jesus' own life and teaching. Thus it turns out that the two unknowns (Q and primitive Mark) do not lead us directly into the history of Jesus' life either, but at best merely reflect that history via the later development of tradition within the community.[26] All this explains why

25. W. Wrede, *The Messianic Secret*, trans. J. C. G. Greig (Cambridge: Clarke, 1971).

26. R. Bultmann, *History of the Synoptic Tradition*, trans. J. Marsh, rev. ed. (Peabody, Mass.: Hendrickson, 1994); K. Berger, *Formgeschichte des Neuen Testaments* (Heidelberg: Quelle & Meyer, 1984).

the diversity of images of Jesus in the twentieth century is almost un-limited. The detachment from the Gospels has become so profound that the methodological-historical underpinnings of many modern images of Jesus are no longer derived from the Gospels but rather from one of the many hypothetical reconstructions of sources *behind* the Gospels.

This can easily be illustrated by looking at the four authors men-tioned earlier. Herbert Braun bases his studies of Jesus on the following premises: (1) John is of no historical importance. (2) Form criticism shows that for their "life of Jesus" Matthew, Mark, and Luke used smaller units of tradition from the oldest Christian communities and reworked them to fit within a subsequently developed historical frame-work. (3) Short pronouncements attributed to Jesus can be considered genuine if they are Palestinian-Jewish in form. (4) When such a saying of Jesus deviates from common Jewish thinking, it can be regarded as typical for Jesus if it fits into our overall picture of him.[27] Braun then adds his own evaluation to this last point: "Of course the observant reader . . . will be immediately aware how unstable the methodological ground is upon which we find ourselves; by being formed in this way, the overall picture is based on the sum total of conclusions concerning specific [statements], yet this overall picture must also serve as the cri-terion for each separate statement [of Jesus]."[28]

Schillebeeckx uses the criterion of "consistency of content" as well: the overall picture of Jesus is the yardstick for the details, while the de-tails, in turn, are the building blocks for the overall picture. There are two other criteria he also considers quite effective: when a tradition concerning Jesus deviates from the editorial trend of a Gospel and/or when it deviates from the Jewish milieu *and* the later Christian commu-nity, it can confidently be considered a stubborn, genuine tradition.[29] In discussing whether John preserves old traditions, Schillebeeckx is less abruptly dismissive than Braun, but he shares with him the com-mon understanding of the Synoptic problem (Q and Mark are channels between the community's tradition and the church's Gospels).[30]

David Flusser, on the other hand, chooses a different source-critical variant. He pays less attention to tradition-formation in the oldest Christian communities.[31] The authentic Jesus tradition did undergo all

27. Braun, *Jesus*, 25–31.
28. Ibid., 29.
29. Schillebeeckx, *Jesus*.
30. Schillebeeckx, *Interim Report*.
31. R. L. Lindsey, "A Modified Two-Document Theory of the Synoptic Dependence and Interdependence," *Novum Testamentum* 6 (1963): 239–63. PN (Proto-Narrative) and Q are first used by Luke (!), and only then by Mark, who already knew Luke. Finally Mat-thew uses them; he, in turn, knew Mark. See Flusser, *Jesus*. For Flusser's "philological

sorts of distortions as it was passed down, which must be tracked by means of a philological analysis of the Gospels. The Gospels all hark back to Q and some kind of primitive Mark, but their mutual dependence does not revolve around Mark. In fact, it is Luke who is most directly related to the two older sources—so that we can conclude that Mark used Luke! In turn, Matthew used Mark (and thus only indirectly Luke). What this all means is that information from the Gospel of Luke is assigned a higher value than is customary.

Although Sobrino is not explicitly concerned with the criteria for finding the "historical Jesus," his work seems to provide sufficient evidence that—through the work of Karl Rahner, Wolfhart Pannenberg, and Jürgen Moltmann—he does lean on the accomplishments, though imprecisely defined, of modern biblical scholarship, which as a matter of course accepts the hypothetical sources behind the familiar Gospels. Books such as Sobrino's illustrate how detachment from the four Gospels has become a kind of dogma. It may well be the only dogma that goes unchallenged in modern theology.

1.1.3 The Importance of the Sources

In moving away from the Gospels, appeals are often made to the contradictions they are supposed to contain. But it should be pointed out that the research, by distancing itself from the Gospels, has given rise to far greater contrasts and contradictions than any that exist between the Gospels themselves. It is easier to live with four evangelists than with four randomly chosen modern theologians when it comes to forming a picture of the historical Jesus. Kümmel is right in his opinion that the modern search for "Jesus as he really is" has resulted in gridlock. But if we want to break out of this gridlock we must come to a decision: either we must finally admit that we cannot form a clear picture of the origins of Christianity (which raises the question, How then can Christianity legitimate itself in today's world?), or we must revisit the place where the problems began: the move away from the traditional sources, the Gospels. Usually the choice is avoided. On the one hand it seems too conservative to even reconsider the abandoned position (if only because someone might accuse us of trying to "harmonize" the Gospels—an opprobrium that keeps us from going back). Yet on the other hand it also seems too radical to abandon Christianity after getting rid of Jesus as the Christ of God. Although a later generation of ordinary churchgoers, having listened to all this, will undoubtedly make this sec-

---

method," see his essay on "De consequente filologie en Jezus' eigen woorden" in D. Flusser, *Tussen oorsprong en schisma: Artikelen over Jezus, het Jodendom en het vroege Christendom*, 2d ed. (Hilversum: Folkertsma Stichting voor Talmudica, 1984), 142–67.

ond choice, many theologians continue to stumble around in the mists of uncertainty, writing books about, in the words of Braun, the "historical Jesus" as he *probably* was.

Because of its ecclesiastical (Schillebeeckx), social (Sobrino), and religious (Flusser) importance, however, the research must not be left to founder. Although the previously inhabited territory was not without its problems, we do well to look back from the far greater confusion of voluntary exile away from the Gospels to what was left behind. In the wilderness of modern christological scholarship, there should be at least some openness toward a rethinking of *why* the departure was made in the first place. Are there really any decisive reasons for turning one's back on the Gospels in the search for Jesus? Is it a distaste for the Christ who, as the Son of God, died for our sins and will come again on clouds of glory? Surely that cannot be the reason. What if it is all true (and why shouldn't it be)? Can we be so sure that our modern worldview is any more credible than the one handed down to us in the Gospels? If we answer this question in the affirmative, we have withdrawn ourselves into a locked room. But if we concede that the truth may also be found outside ourselves, and in ways we did not expect, we are at least open to the *possibility* that the Gospels are reliable sources. Can this possibility stand the test of an open-minded, historical investigation into these and other sources in the quest to learn how Jesus lived and what he said? In order to answer this question we now turn to the extrabiblical as well as the biblical sources for the life of Christ on earth.

1.2 Extrabiblical Sources?

Now that the reputation of the Gospels as reliable historical sources has declined in the eyes of many, interest in other sources is increasing.[32] Morton Smith has written a book, *Jesus the Magician*, in which he systematically bases his image of Jesus on non-Christian sources. In doing so he believes he can track down the real historical Jesus as observed by outsiders. Jesus' followers, as well as outsiders, regarded him as a miracle worker, but according to Smith their Gospel accounts are bent on retouching and embellishing their portrait of a magician. So the extrabiblical material becomes the criterion for assessing the Gospels.[33]

---

32. R. J. Hoffmann, *Jesus outside the Gospels* (Buffalo: Prometheus, 1984). A very low view of the Gospels as historical literature can also be found in the book by R. Helms, *Gospel Fictions* (New York: Prometheus, 1988).

33. M. Smith, *Jesus the Magician*, 2d ed. (Wellingborough: Aquarian Press, 1985; 1st ed., New York: Harper & Row, 1978). This book is a logical sequel to *The Secret Gospel: The Discovery and Interpretation of the Secret Gospel according to Mark* (New York: Harper

But even for those who refuse to adopt Smith's extreme methodological position, the extrabiblical material raises questions about the validity of the Gospels. If Jesus really gave such an impressive performance as the Son of God, why is it that we read so little about him in ancient non-Christian sources?

The fact is that very little information about Jesus can be found in sources outside the Gospels, and what little information there is, is highly varied in character. The only way Smith can conjure up his picture of Jesus as a magician is by emphasizing one element and downplaying the rest. Had he not done so, he would have been left with no other conclusion than that we cannot establish a definitive picture of Jesus without the help of the Gospels. The established facts are at most that Jesus lived, was crucified under Pilate, and became a controversial figure.

Since the disproportionally small amount of extrabiblical data may raise questions about the validity of the Gospels, we will survey those data first with an eye to determining what the reasons for this disproportion in source materials might be.[34]

Because the extrabiblical data are not interrelated, we arrange them by source: (1) pagan, (2) Jewish, and (3) Christian.

1.2.1 Pagan Authors

The Gospels present the story of Jesus as an event of supreme importance for the whole world. Luke dates the coming of God's word to John the Baptist "in the fifteenth year of the reign of Tiberius Caesar" (3:1). Already the beginning of the story is placed on the imperial calendar! And the Gospels end with the preaching of Jesus' life and teaching to all nations, as far away as Rome (Matt. 28:19; Mark 16:15–20; Acts 1:8; 28:28–31).

So at first glance it is rather surprising that the writings of pagan authors from the first century or shortly thereafter contain not the slightest echo of any of this. Didn't the Good News reach them, or do the Gospels give us an exaggerated impression? Some of these questions are easy to answer: the imperial archives, which included documents such as Pilate's reports, have been lost. We lack first-century documentation.[35] There is a lengthy first-century work by Pliny the Elder that deals

---

& Row, 1973), as Smith himself declares in the afterword written for the second edition (*Jesus the Magician*, 153–54).

34. F. F. Bruce provides a good and somewhat broader discussion in *Jesus and Christian Origins outside the New Testament* (London: Hodder & Stoughton, 1974). See also D. Wenham and C. L. Blomberg, eds., *The Jesus Tradition outside the Gospels*, Gospel Perspectives 5 (Sheffield: JSOT Press, 1985); and R. H. Stein, *Jesus the Messiah: A Survey of the Life of Christ* (Downers Grove, Ill.: InterVarsity, 1996).

35. Justin Martyr (*First Apology* 34.2) and Tertullian (*Against Marcion* 4.7.7; 4.19.10) both appeal to the possibility of searching for records of Jesus' birth in the Roman archives

with many countries, but his *Natural History* focuses more on geographic and physical conditions than on the historical aspects of ancient Palestine. We should not expect such a book to provide information about Jesus. For a historical description of the first century, we must turn to two authors from the early second century. And in so doing the question takes on even sharper contours: why don't they have more to tell us?

Both Suetonius and Tacitus write about Roman history. Because Rome had become a world empire, almost the entire world is featured in their work, but always from the viewpoint of imperial politics (Suetonius) or the Roman republic (Tacitus). This limits the writers' interest. Tacitus knew that Jesus had been killed under Pontius Pilate in Palestine, but he does not mention this fact when he writes about Palestine under the rule of Emperor Tiberius. He is very succinct and makes only one comment about this part of the empire: "Peace under Tiberius!"—which means that the Jews of Palestine presented few problems during Tiberius's reign.[36] Considering the fact that they were often quite troublesome and would cause the Romans considerable problems during the Jewish War (A.D. 66–70), we detect in Tacitus's note a hint of relief: those Jews have not always been a source of trouble! Anyone writing history from this vantage point has absolutely no reason to throw in a story about Jesus, for his appearance did not interrupt that period of political tranquillity. Tacitus's characterization of this period implies that Jesus was not even a source of agitation for the *Jews*. In his terseness, Tacitus indirectly refutes the ideas of Reimarus and his successors, who claim that Jesus had political aspirations and that he was active on the periphery of a kind of Zealotry. "Peace under Tiberius": this is the political assessment of Christ's historic ministry that was characterized by his own words, "Learn from me; for I am gentle and humble in heart." Tacitus unintentionally confirms the truth of those words.

---

via the documents from the census taken under Quirinius (Justin Martyr) or Sentius Saturninus (Tertullian). Bruce (*Jesus and Christian Origins*, 20) also refers to Justin Martyr (*First Apology* 48.3) for a reference to documents drawn up during the reign of Pontius Pilate. I think that this is an incorrect interpretation of this passage, however. Justin discusses the fact that Jesus' miracles were *predicted* by the prophets, e.g., Isaiah. The emperor can find out for himself that these predicted events really came to pass by looking into the reports of "what happened under Pontius Pilate"—meaning the Gospels. They are the documents confirming the fulfilled prophecies, and what they describe (in accordance with the ancient words of Isaiah) took place in recent times. Pontius Pilate's name is used to designate a specific time period in the history of Palestine.

36. *Histories* 5.11: "Sub Tiberio quies." The political unrest and the party of the Zealots date from the time after the death of Herod Agrippa I in A.D. 44. See, for example, H. Guevara, *La resistencia judia contra Roma en la epoca de Jesus* (Meitingen: Meitingen, 1981). See also the companion volume to this book, *Het evangelie van Gods zoon* (Kampen: Kok, 1996; English translation forthcoming), sec. 1.2.3.

The Roman historians had no particular interest in Jesus' life. Their attitude with regard to Christ (a name they were familiar with!) was the same as that of Seneca's brother Gallio in Corinth. As proconsul of Achaia under Emperor Claudius, Gallio was confronted with Paul, the Christian. He might have learned a great deal about Jesus from him (Acts 18:14a), but he was not interested because no criminal or wrongful act had been committed within the jurisdiction of Rome. As far as he was concerned, these were "questions about words and names and your own law," matters the Jews had to fight out among themselves (Acts 18:14–17).

That is why the name *Christ* does not appear in the annals of political history. It *is* mentioned, however, whenever the Christians become a source of social unrest. According to some sources, such incidents took place in Rome under Claudius (A.D. 41–54). Suetonius's remark about the expulsion of the Jews from Rome because of disturbances that took place under Chrestus is sometimes taken as an indication of the social unrest in the Jewish quarter of Rome as a result of the preaching of Christ.[37] But the context in which Suetonius makes this comment indicates that it is more likely that he is referring to increasing insurrections in *Palestine* in which a certain Chrestus played a role; the Jews were then driven from Rome for a time in retaliation.[38]

Although the city of Rome was not confronted by the new religion of the Christians under Claudius, it certainly was under Nero (A.D. 54–68). Nero blamed the Christians for the fire of Rome in A.D. 64. Tacitus, in his description of the affair, applauds the elimination of the Christians because he feels that they are driven by an antisocial mentality ("hatred against humanity"), but he deplores the fact that Nero persecuted them *on account of the fire*.[39] His reason is that as a result of the persecution, many Roman citizens, out of distrust of Nero, became more sympathetic toward the unjustly accused Christians. In his description of this matter, which was of importance to Roman society, Tacitus mentions in passing Christ, after whom the Christians are named.

---

37. *Claudius* 25 §4: "Judaeos impulsore Chresto assidue tumultuantes Roma expulit."

38. For a more detailed discussion, see my *De oorsprong van de kerk te Rome* (Groningen: De Vuurbaak, 1967). For this contextual interpretation of Suetonius, see also Thomas Levin, *Fasti Sacri or a Key to the Chronology of the New Testament* (London: Longmans, Green, & Co., 1865), lxii–lxiv.

39. For the persecution of the Christians under Nero and Tacitus's description, see my "Na vele jaren: Stadhouder Felix en de jaren van Paulus," in *Almanak Fides Quadrat Intellectum* (Kampen: Kok, 1979), 119–54, esp. 145–48. See also D. Lührmann, "Superstitio—die Beurteilung des frühen Christentums durch die Römer," *Theologische Zeitschrift* 42 (1986): 192–213. S. Benko, *Pagan Rome and the Early Christians* (Bloomington: Indiana University Press, 1984), 1–29.

Therefore, to scotch the rumour [that he had started the fire], Nero sub-
stituted as culprits, and punished with the utmost refinements of cruelty,
a class of men, loathed for their vices, whom the crowd styled Christians.
Christus, the founder of the name, had undergone the death penalty in
the reign of Tiberius, by sentence of the procurator Pontius Pilatus, and
the pernicious superstition was checked for a moment, only to break out
once more, not merely in Judaea, the home of the disease, but in the capital itself, where all things horrible or shameful in the world collect and
find a vogue.[40]

Despite Tacitus's extremely negative attitude toward all non-Roman
religions and his dislike of Christians, he does provide several facts that
provide external confirmation of biblical data.

1. Already during his life on earth Christ had become an object of religious veneration (Tacitus calls it "superstition"). So the later
   veneration was not a new development within the Christian community, as is all too often suggested, but a continuation of what
   had already begun in Palestine. Tacitus calls this "the rekindling
   of superstition."
2. The Christian gospel had spread over the civilized world from
   Palestine to Rome well before the fire of Rome in A.D. 64. By that
   time the Christians were already being distinguished from the
   Jews, and their way of life was provoking reactions. This shows
   that Christianity did not, as is sometimes thought, remain for
   many years merely a variant of the Judaism of that period.
3. Jesus did exist, and he was killed under Pontius Pilate. The latter
   fact seems not to have been derived from the Christians themselves, since Tacitus would have been more likely to use the term
   crucified if he had taken his information from the Christians' creed.
   In addition, his animosity toward the Christians was such that he
   would not have indiscriminately copied their own claims. Finally,
   Tacitus was a historian who had access to the state archives. It
   would not have been difficult for him to consult the reports that
   Pontius Pilate had sent to Rome. If those reports had given a completely different, nonreligious picture of Jesus, Tacitus would certainly not have failed to use this against the Christians. But the historian who was vehemently opposed to these followers of a new
   religion accepted as a given fact that their founder, Christ, was
   killed by the Roman governor Pontius Pilate and that at that time
   he had already become the object of superstitious veneration.

40. Tacitus, *The Annals*, bks. 13–16, trans. John Jackson, Loeb Classical Library 322
(London: Heinemann, 1969), 15.44.

Under Emperor Trajan (A.D. 98–117), the persecution of the Christians appears to have been raging in full force in Bithynia (northwestern Turkey) when the governor, Pliny the Younger, addressed the situation in a letter to the emperor in A.D. 111. As interesting as the letter may be for the information it provides about Christians, it contains absolutely no information about Christ himself.[41] Again, it appears that the pagan Romans came up against the social phenomenon known as "the Christians" and even displayed a certain curiosity about their activities, but they showed no interest in the life of the founder, Christ of Palestine. This makes the scarcity of information understandable, and it makes Tacitus's single remark all the more valuable. These pagan sources do not supplement history as it is presented in the Gospels—but neither do they contradict it. And the sources corroborate the Gospels on several points: Jesus' death under Pontius Pilate, the religious veneration of Jesus by his earthly followers, and the rapid spread of the Christian religion throughout the known world. On the other hand, they do not corroborate Morton Smith's idea ("Jesus the Magician"), nor do they support the notion that Jesus had political aspirations. Indeed, Christian behavior was not noted for its magic or its political aspirations, but for quite different things. The Christians formed their own religious community with a unique lifestyle. Their refusal to serve idols or to follow a decadent way of life disturbed many of their contemporaries. This negative assessment of the followers of the new religion quelled any desire the pagans may have had to learn more about the story of Christ. With such weak acoustics for the word of God in the world, the echo of his earthly ministry was hardly noticeable at all.

1.2.2 Jewish Sources

We would sooner expect to find information about Jesus' ministry in Palestine in Jewish than in pagan sources. Because Jesus was born in Israel and worked among the Jews in Galilee and Judea, it seems obvious that his life and work would be less likely to escape their notice than that of the faraway Romans.

Our expectations here focus on two sources in particular: Josephus and the rabbinic traditions. The Jewish historian Flavius Josephus wrote about the Jewish War during the late first century A.D. and also produced an extensive work covering the entire history of the Jewish people up to the destruction of Herod's temple. His books were intended to foster understanding for the Jewish people, who had evoked a great deal of antipathy among the Romans following their rebellion

---

41. See R. L. Wilken, *The Christians as the Romans Saw Them* (New Haven and London: Yale University Press, 1984), 1–30.

in A.D. 66–70. Christianity and its origins fall outside Josephus's direct notice. On the other hand, he treats the first century in great detail and from the Jewish point of view, so that we might expect him to devote some attention to John the prophet and Jesus the teacher. Josephus does not disappoint us. His are the oldest extrabiblical attestations of John the Baptist and Jesus.

When we come to the rabbinic traditions, we would expect the confrontation with Christianity to have resulted in information about Jesus in the writings of the rabbis. But the harvest here is not as abundant as we would expect, although we do find traces of traditions about Jesus.

Because the context of Josephus's information is radically different from the context of information in the Talmud, we will discuss the Jewish sources in two separate sections.

1.2.2.1 JOSEPHUS

In our discussion of Josephus, we will momentarily pass over the section in which he refers to the great impression the prophet John the Baptist made on the local populace[42] and limit ourselves to both passages in which he mentions the name of Jesus. In one he refers to him in passing, in the other he discusses him briefly.

The incidental mention occurs in Josephus's description of the stoning of James. He was "the brother of Jesus, who is called Christ" (*Antiquities* 20.9.1 §200). This passage confirms a detail from the Gospels: one of Jesus' brothers was called James (Mark 6:3; Matt. 13:55). It also seems to indicate that those within the circle of Josephus's readership knew the brother of James by the name "Christ," not by the name "Jesus." But because of the family relationship with James, the Jewish historian begins with the *Jewish* proper name (Joshua/Jesus), which he then clarifies for his readers by adding the name by which this Jesus is known in the Greek and Roman world. This information is not unimportant for the other longer passage to which we will now turn.

In narrating the events that took place during the time of Pontius Pilate, Josephus also briefly mentions Jesus' ministry (*Antiquities* 18.3.3 §§63–64). The text reads as follows:

> At this time Jesus appeared—a wise man, at least if he can be so described. He was someone who performed wondrous deeds, a teacher of people who were eager for the truth. He brought many Jews together as well as many Greek people; he was Christ. Based on reports from some of our prominent members (the Jews), Pilate sentenced him to the cross, but those who had grown to love him did not cease in their affections, because

---

42. For an extensive discussion see H. W. Hoehner, *Herod Antipas* (Cambridge: Cambridge University Press, 1972). See also section 6.5 below.

he appeared alive before them on the third day (the divine prophets had mentioned this and many thousands of other wondrous things about him). The tribe of Christians who are named after him still exists.

This oldest non-Christian witness about Jesus (often referred to as the *Testimonium Flavianum*) was quoted by Eusebius as early as the fourth century.[43] During the past two centuries it has been the subject of many studies,[44] for the unquestioned acceptance of Josephus's testimony has been replaced by doubts about the authenticity of all or parts of the text.[45] Because we are dealing with the *oldest* attestation outside the Bible, we must go into this question in somewhat more detail.

More than once the idea has been put forward that the entire passage was added to Josephus (before the time of Eusebius) by Christians, but most scholars now agree that the report is far too neutral. More positive statements about Jesus could have been put in Josephus's mouth as long as material was being inserted anyway. In addition, the passage shows strong similarities with Josephus's style, as well as some small differences. This combination would suggest a forger highly capable of imitating Josephus's style who nevertheless refrained from following it completely. It is more likely that Josephus wrote the passage himself and that we are simply faced with the normal variations in an author's style.

More widely accepted is the idea, suggested by Eisler and supported not only by Winter[46] but also by Bruce,[47] that something has been *removed* from Josephus's report. The assumption is that Josephus had wanted to talk about disturbances during the time of Jesus that were in some way linked to him. Later this note about riots or social unrest must have been stripped from the passage. But this hypothesis does not hold up when the design of Josephus's narrative is carefully scrutinized.

Winter proceeds from the assumption that Josephus wanted on the one hand to relate the history of disturbances under Pilate, while on the other hand attempting to integrate a source with material about events

---

43. Eusebius, *Ecclesiastical History* 1.11.7–8; *Proof of the Gospel* 3.5.124.

44. See section 17 in the bibliography of H. Schreckenberg, *Bibliographie zu Flavius Josephus* (Leiden: Brill, 1968); idem, *Supplementband mit Gesamtregister* (Leiden: Brill, 1979); and in L. H. Feldman, *Josephus: A Supplementary Bibliography* (New York: Garland, 1986).

45. See also J. N. Birdsall, "The Continuing Enigma of Josephus's Testimony about Jesus," *Bulletin of the John Rylands Library* 67 (1984–85): 609–22. This article has not yet been added to Feldman's bibliography on Josephus.

46. P. Winter, "Josephus on Jesus and James," in E. Schürer, *The History of the Jewish People in the Age of Jesus Christ: 175 B.C.–A.D. 135*, new English ed., rev. and ed. G. Vermes, F. Millar, M. Black, and M. Goodman (Edinburgh: Clark, 1973–87), 1:428–41.

47. F. F. Bruce, *Jesus and Christian Origins*, 32–41.

in Rome into the narrative. The original, unabridged story line would have run as follows:

1. The incident with the military standards in Jerusalem at Pilate's arrival (18.3.1 §§55–59).
2. The riot in Jerusalem sparked by Pilate's intended sacrilegious use of temple money (18.3.2 §§60–62).
3. The revolt against Pilate in Samaria (18.4.1 §§85–87).

The report about Jesus falls between the second and the third sections. Within this sequence about riots and revolts, the report about Jesus should also be an account of disturbances! According to Winter, this is apparent from the line that follows the pericope about Jesus, which reads, "And during the same period, another atrocity occurred which caused turmoil among the Jews" (18.3.4 §65). If by this Josephus means that he is now going to report *another* atrocity, it then follows that he has also spoken of an atrocity in the previous passage. So the preceding passage about Jesus must originally have had quite a different tone than it does now.

But Winter's argument can be disputed on several points. His grouping of the passages is contrary to the intention of Josephus himself. The flow of Josephus's narrative is as follows:

1. Disasters among the Jews in *Jerusalem* under Pontius Pilate (first in response to the standards and later because of the assault on the temple money: 18.3.1–2 §§55–62).
2. Disasters among the Jews in *Rome* during the same period (18.3.5 §§81–84).

This means that the *other* atrocity that Josephus intends to discuss after the passage about Jesus (18.3.4 §65) is the disaster that befell the Jews of *Rome*. And it is no wonder that in his mind he made a connection between the temple-money riots that broke out in Palestine under Pilate and the problems suffered by the Jews in Rome. Four dishonest Jews in Rome had absconded with money that had been collected for the temple. This incident made the Jews unpopular in Rome and caused them to be temporarily driven from the city. Thus temple money is at the heart of the issue both in Palestine and in Rome.

From Winter's point of view, the *other* atrocity the Jews encountered would have been some kind of trouble that, like the problems surrounding Jesus, also occurred in Palestine. Winter suggests that this is found in the later passage that deals with Pilate and his attitude toward the Samaritans (18.4.1 §§85–87). But how can a Jewish scholar such as

Winter interpret a disaster that affects the *Samaritans* as a calamity for the *Jews?*

When we focus on the pattern of the narrative, we must also take into account the fact that Josephus often inserts other stories that took place at the same time or that serve as background material. Thus we can summarize the events he covers in 18.3.1–4.1 §§55–87 as follows:

I. Disasters suffered by the Jews in Jerusalem under Pontius Pilate.
   A. Introductory history: disturbance sparked by military standards bearing the likeness of the emperor, which the Romans threaten to carry into Jerusalem. Pilate refrains from acting (18.3.1 §§55–59).
   B. Victims fall when a Jewish riot breaks out, caused by the improper use of temple money by Pilate. This time he presses ahead (18.3.2 §§60–62).
   C. Appendix: this is also the period when Christ makes his appearance (18.3.3 §§63–64).
II. Disasters suffered by the Jews of Rome during the same period.
   A. Introductory history: a scandal in the Isis temple puts non-Roman religions in a bad light and explains why the Jews will later be treated with special severity (18.3.4 §§65–80).
   B. A case of dishonesty involving four Jews who collect money for the temple and abscond with it causes the Jews to be driven from Rome (18.3.5 §§81–84).
III. Supplement: the Samaritans also had to endure abuse under Pontius Pilate during this period (18.4.1 §§85–87).

The structure of Josephus's story is obvious and disproves the idea that he had intended to include his report of Jesus in a series of three disasters or disturbances. The fact that Josephus includes as *another atrocity* (18.3.4 §65) a story that is linked to the temple-money incident strongly suggests that the passage about Jesus should be interpreted as an interlude. In addition, Josephus's dominant theme is not disturbances *caused by* Jews but disasters *suffered by* the Jews. In this context the *Testimonium Flavianum* is more incidental: not a passage that originally must have dealt with disturbances, but possibly a contemporaneous interlude that Josephus himself viewed in a negative light. Despite his restrained tone, as a Jew Josephus would not have been overjoyed to state that many Jews had become followers of Christ.

We have addressed the notion that the *Testimonium Flavianum* must have been a later insertion, as well as the theory that it is genuine but greatly abridged and no longer fits in Josephus's original structure. There is yet a third way to approach this passage: it is genuine but has undergone light *Christian editing.* By introducing a number of additions, the original, neutral text would thus have been given a Christian tinge. Only by removing this Christian varnish can we find the authentic *Testimonium Flavianum* of Josephus, the Jew. We will discuss the various details that are considered inauthentic to see if this theory holds up.

1. "At least if he can be so described [as 'a man']." With these words Josephus suggests that Jesus did such superhuman things that the question arises whether he was an ordinary person, an ordinary man. But this phrase does not necessarily have to be a Christian addition. A Christian formulation would not have been so hesitant and tentative. Furthermore, Josephus writes for an audience that is familiar with the notion of demigods, and he also knows that Christians regard Jesus as more than a human being. His formulation can in no way be interpreted as a reference to the Christian confession of Jesus as the only-begotten Son of God. His statement is explained in the text by the remark that he "performed wondrous deeds." Can someone who does abnormal or paranormal things really be called an ordinary man? For Josephus it is not an issue. He is convinced that Jesus—whoever he may have been—has long been dead. And let us not forget that the Jewish religious leaders did not regard him as an ordinary man either: he was supposed to have been empowered by Beelzebub, the ruler over the evil spirits. Josephus's statement even allows for this negative interpretation!

2. "A teacher of people who were eager for the truth." The characterization "eager" (*hēdonē*) here sounds somewhat ironic. For that reason alone it is not likely that Josephus would be referring to Christianity as the truth here. Nor does he say that Jesus' teaching is the truth, but only that he was a teacher with a serious audience bent on discovering "the true things." His audience was radically different from the masses who are more interested in profit or excitement than truth. People who pursue "true things" may very well choose a teacher who is not recognized by others as teaching truth, but such people can nevertheless be respected as serious lovers of truth. Josephus thus characterizes the kind of people who followed Jesus and their motivation. They came to be taught, but how the content of his teaching should be judged remains undecided. Thus there is no reason to interpret this phrase as a Christian insertion.

3. "Because he appeared alive before them on the third day (the divine prophets had mentioned this and many thousands of other wondrous things about him)." Many take this as a Christian passage par excellence. How could Josephus as non-Christian Jew ever accept Jesus' resurrection and refer to him as the fulfillment

of the prophets? The answer is that he did not—that is not what he is saying here. The entire phrase is an explanation for the fact that "those who had grown to love him did not cease in their affections." To Josephus this seems quite strange. There was every reason to stop loving Jesus: he had been killed by Pilate. How can his disciples maintain a posthumous attachment to him? The explanation is that he appeared to them again, alive, on the third day and that they see in him the fulfillment of the prophets. Josephus does not say that Jesus was physically resurrected. He only says that he "appeared alive" on the third day. He is silent about anything that may have happened *after* the third day. He only points to those elements from the Christian experience ("appearance") and Christian beliefs ("fulfillment of the prophets") that provide an explanation as to why their devotion to Jesus did not end with his death. Josephus then concludes with the remark that this is why there continued to be *Christians* until that very day. This is not a confession of any continued existence of Jesus, but rather an explanation of the undeniable continued existence of his followers. This final sentence reveals Josephus's point of view.

4. "He was Christ." These words are considered the most important proof for the hypothesis that one or more Christian additions were made to Josephus's text. It seems quite evident, certainly when it is translated "He was *the* Christ." How could the non-Christian Jew Josephus possibly have written that Jesus was the Messiah? Again, this is not what he did. We must not forget that in the Greek-speaking world Jesus was known as (*ho*) *Christos*— used as a proper name rather than as a title. The founder of the new religion of Christians was called Christ! The name by which people referred to the followers of this new religion made it easy to remember the name of its founder. Outside Christian circles it was hardly known that in Palestine his name had been *Jesus*. Josephus begins his interlude about the founder of the Christian movement by using his Jewish name Joshua or Jesus. Then he has to explain to his readers what significance his excursus about this Jesus has for them. He does this a few sentences later by announcing that this Jesus is the Christ that the Christians are always talking about. In the same way one might imagine someone writing a history of India choosing an appropriate moment to tell about the appearance of Siddhartha Gautama, and then adding, for the sake of clarity, "This was the Buddha." It is not the author's intention to make a statement of faith about Siddhartha's Buddha experience. Rather, he or she is simply explaining the

connection between the story about Siddhartha Gautama and the well-known person from whose title the name of the Buddhist religion was derived. Josephus is doing much the same thing. The misunderstanding among modern readers results from the idea that the Jews of that time expected *one* Messiah and that they would have called him *ho Christos* in Greek. But neither the facts nor the texts support this idea.[48] Josephus, by following the customary practice of referring to Jesus simply as *ho Christos* (cf. *Antiquities* 20.9.1 §200, where he refers to James as "the brother of Jesus, who is called Christ"), proves instead that in his day there was no uniform, clearly delineated messianic expectation or messianic terminology, since that would have made *ho Christos* a term so charged with religious and political overtones that Josephus would not have used it in a neutral report.

We may conclude that Josephus's excursus about Jesus can be read as a meaningful passage that is an integral part of the design of the eighteenth book of his *Jewish Antiquities* and as balanced information from a Jewish perspective about the historical background of the founder of the by then well-known group called Christians.[49]

The witness of Josephus does not contradict the Gospels and even confirms them on several points. Jesus worked at the time of Pilate and was crucified by him, an event in which the Jewish leaders played an active role. His ministry was characterized by his miracles and his teaching. His followers were serious people who were not after making money or stirring up a revolution, but who chose Jesus out of their love for truth. There is no question of Zealotry or revolt. For outsiders it is a well-known fact that the followers of Jesus say that they saw him on the third day after his death and that they regard him as the fulfillment of the prophets. Jesus' followers, known as Christians, have spread

48. For this point, see my companion volume, *Het evangelie van Gods zoon*, sec. 5.3.

49. I have not discussed the passages that are found in an old-Russian version of Josephus's *Jewish War* (the so-called Slavic Josephus). This version of Josephus contains interpolations that may provide interesting insights into ancient traditions but are generally not considered genuine. See Bruce, *Jesus and Christian Origins*, 42–53. Birdsall is of the opinion that the Russian Josephus has more to tell us about "old Russia and possibly about Byzantium than about Jesus and early Christianity" ("Continuing Enigma," 622). The idea of finding an original, more extensive version of the *Testimonium Flavianum* was recently revived with the publication of an Arabic version (S. Pines, *An Arabic Version of the Testimonium Flavianum and Its Implications* [Jerusalem: Israel Academy of Sciences and Humanities, 1971]). See A. M. Dubarle, "Le témoignage de Josèphe sur Jésus d'après la tradition indirect," *Revue Biblique* 80 (1973): 481–513. In contrast to these authors, E. Noder argues for the originality of the Greek text, which he regards as authentic ("Jésus et Jean Baptiste selon Josèphe," *Revue Biblique* 92 [1985]: 321–48; 497–524).

throughout the whole world, and among the Greek-speaking readers of Josephus, Jesus is known as "Christ."

1.2.2.2 RABBINIC LITERATURE

The books that contain ancient as well as more recent rabbinic traditions—the Mishnah and Gemara, which together form the Talmud, and the Tosefta—were written after the second century. The interval between Jesus' life on earth and the oldest of these writings is thus almost two centuries, so they are even farther removed from the historical events than Josephus. Nevertheless, it is in principle possible for extremely old memories to be preserved in documents written much later. This is certainly true for the rabbinic writings, which were written to preserve older traditions. Since the Jewish rabbis knew of Jesus' ministry in Israel, this seems an obvious place to search for material about the history of his work on earth.

But we will be disappointed if we expect to find a great deal of material. This is not altogether surprising—why would we expect to find much about the history of Jesus among the rabbis? Their intent was to preserve doctrinal debates about issues in Jewish life so that they could be used in teaching. Historical information might be carried along on the stream of the tradition, but such incidental historical facts were subordinate to the primary educational aims. By the time the rabbinic traditions were put down in writing (from the third to the fifth or sixth centuries A.D.), Christianity had long since become an independent entity, entirely separate from the synagogue. The synagogue was not concerned with the church after their separation, and the teachings of the church were irrelevant in the schools of the rabbis. The only occasion for non-Christian Jews to mention the person and teachings of Jesus was in discussions with Christians who claim to be the true heirs of the promises given to Abraham. These discussions certainly took place during the third and fourth centuries (as reflected in the Christian writings from this period), but they had no value for the preservation and development of the non-Christian Jewish lifestyle based on law and tradition. Therefore we find little or no trace of these discussions in the rabbinic literature.

An additional factor is that during these centuries the Christian governing authorities were putting more and more pressure on the non-Christian Jews. It became dangerous for Jews to make negative statements about Jesus. Lapide, a Jew, bitterly remarks that an anti-Judaic Christendom added many scapegoats from his own people to Jesus, the "Lamb of God"—which is why he thinks it understandable that only fifteen of the fifteen thousand pages of Talmudic literature (or .1 percent) make mention of Jesus and the Christian Jews. He calls this a "dignified silence" in the face of aggression. Later censorship, a result of both external pressure and internal precautionary measures, should also be taken into account: passages about Jesus were simply suppressed![50]

What then is the value of the little that remains? What we find are incidental and scattered indirect remarks about *Jeshu* (Jesus?) as well as texts that do not mention the name *Jeshu* but that may refer to him. The latter are passages that refer to a certain Ben Stada or Ben Pandera (Panthera) or to a person not mentioned by name. All these texts from the Jewish tradition were brought together as source material relating to Jesus. An early-medieval anti-Gospel, *Toledot Jeshu*, summarized this material and was sometimes used by Christians in the Middle Ages as justification for persecuting Jews who dared to write and to teach so derogatorily about the Savior.[51]

But to what extent is this conceptualization of Jesus within Judaism, as seen in the *Toledot Jeshu*, a reflection of much older traditions and to what extent is it a later development in reaction to an increasingly aggressive Christian government? Johann Maier subjected the rabbinic passages to a scrupulously detailed study and came to the conclusion that there are no rabbinic statements about Jesus that have their origins in the first two centuries A.D.[52] The statements that date from the third to the fifth centuries were not seen as interconnected until the period of Islamic domination, and it was only then that the reactionary Jewish picture of Jesus began to crystallize. Maier regards the results of his study as an element that might play a role in the Jewish-Christian dialogue.

Exactly the opposite approach is taken by scholars who in their search for the "real, historical Jesus" have moved away from the Gospels as primary sources and give priority to extrabiblical material, especially non-Christian Jewish sources. R. J. Hoffmann is an extreme example.[53] He is of the opinion that on the basis of the rabbinic writings we can confidently establish how the learned Jews of the year A.D. 100 regarded Jesus. The Gospels were written to refute and to replace this erroneous Jewish image. Thus Matthew 1–2 (the virgin birth and the flight to Egypt) would have been a reaction to the factual description that was commonly known among the Jews (Jesus was reportedly an illegitimate child, the son of Pandera, a Roman soldier, and was thought to have learned magic during his stay in Egypt).

50. P. Lapide, *Israelis, Jews, and Jesus*, trans. P. Heinegg (Garden City, N.Y.: Doubleday, 1979).

51. Cf. Lindeskog, *Die Jesusfrage im neuzeitlichen Judentum*, 196–98, and Hoffmann, *Jesus outside the Gospels*, 50–53.

52. J. Maier, *Jesus von Nazareth in der talmudischen Überlieferung* (Darmstadt: Wissenschaftliche Buchgesellschaft, 1978), 268–75.

53. Hoffmann, *Jesus outside the Gospels*, 36–53.

We find two focal points in these differences of opinion: the *age* of the rabbinic materials and their *quality*. Contra Maier, note that the rabbinic tradition concerning Jesus is older than he is willing to admit. Even in the work of the Christian apologist Justin Martyr (ca. A.D. 150) and that of the pagan opponent of Christianity Celsus (ca. A.D. 180) we find an echo and even a replication of Jewish descriptions (and distortions) of Jesus' life. This brings us to a period even earlier than the oldest written rabbinic sources. According to Justin Martyr,[54] non-Christian Jews claimed that Jesus was a magician and a deceiver of the people whose disciples made him the center of a sect after his body had been robbed from the grave. Granted, Justin could have constructed this view himself on the basis of data from the Gospels, in which case it would not support the earlier existence of the third-century rabbinic tradition. But we cannot use this argument against the statements made by Celsus, which still survive to a significant extent in Origen's work.[55] Celsus writes that he heard from non-Christian Jews that Jesus was an illegitimate child, and he mentions in this connection the name of the soldier Panthera. Celsus's report that Jesus had been a migrant worker in Egypt and learned the art of magic there also came from a Jewish source. When Maier observes that some features of the rabbinic tradition are absent in Celsus and that therefore Celsus's informant was not familiar with later rabbinic tradition, he is correct[56]—but this does not alter the fact that there is complete continuity between the elements we find in Celsus and the same elements found in the rabbinic literature. Furthermore, what is involved here is specific information that is found nowhere else. Maier's hypothesis that the rabbis were not yet referring to Jesus in their so-called Ben Pandera statements of the third century is on shaky ground. It seems much more likely that the core of the rabbinic statements about Jesus goes back to the second-century non-Christian Jewish view of Jesus—which takes us back close to the time of Josephus.

But what is the *quality* of this information? Was the original picture of the "historical Jesus" painted over by later Christians in a Hellenistic manner and enveloped in all sorts of myths? The available information does provide us with an answer to this question. Hoffmann's model moves from the Jewish data to the Gospels, but in the process it creates insurmountable difficulties. A story about learning magic in Egypt could never have been "refuted" or "neutralized" by the story of the flight to Egypt of Joseph and Mary with the *child* Jesus. And if grave

---

54. *Dialogue with Trypho*, 69, 108.
55. Origen, *Against Celsus*, 1.28, 32–33, 69; 2.5, 8–9, etc.
56. Maier, *Jesus von Nazareth*, 253–55.

robbery by the disciples had been the basis for founding the Christian sect, how could this event have been "neutralized" by a story about the guarding of the grave by soldiers, something that could easily have been verified at the time? It was with good reason that Rabbi Gamaliel in the first century was not able to deny the preaching of the resurrection with a counter-story about grave robbery (Acts 5:30–40). Such a story could serve to quiet those who knew nothing of the case, and it might have some effect at a later date (Matt. 28:11–15), but we cannot ignore the fact that historically the story obviously was of no use in the encounter between the Sanhedrin and the apostles. The historical accounts in the Gospels cannot be explained by an attempt to rewrite the "original" story that has presumably been preserved in the rabbinic tradition.

But an explanation that moves in the opposite direction—from the Gospels to the Jewish sources—works well. If a person had been involved in Jesus' birth who could later still be identified by name and rank, the story of Jesus' birth in the Gospels would have been too transparent a lie for the Jewish readers of Matthew to swallow. When the Gospels state that Jesus was conceived by the Holy Spirit, it would have been easy to counter the story by insinuating that a natural cause was much more likely. The name that is mentioned in connection with Jesus' birth has the earmarks of slanderous counterpropaganda: Pandera or Panthera is a mutilation of the Christian confession that Jesus was born of the *Virgin* Mary; the Greek word for virgin is *parthenos*.

More important is that while the non-Christian Jewish comments about Jesus are indeed at odds with the view of him presented in the Gospels, they are completely in agreement with what these biblical books tell us about *how the leaders reacted to Jesus*. They called him a demoniac and a Samaritan. His miracles were ascribed to Beelzebub and thus reduced to black magic. He is accused of misleading the people. Insinuations are even made that nothing is known of any unusual origin. And a cover story is contrived for the soldiers who fled from the grave.[57] This continuity shows that the rabbinic picture of Jesus is not inconsistent with the Gospels. In fact, it confirms the historical correctness of the Gospels in its rendering of the negative reactions to Jesus.

We do not have to make a choice between the Gospels and the rabbinic data. The rabbinic sources supplement the Gospels to the extent that the Gospels already contain the historical basis for the distorted picture of Jesus created by his opponents among the Jewish scribes and Pharisees. Those who decide to distance themselves from the Gospels in preference to sources from the rabbinic tradition are not choosing a

---

57. John 8:48; Mark 3:22; John 7:12 and Matt. 27:63–64; John 7:27; Matt. 28:11–15.

different historical *source* but a different *party affiliation*. Thus, with many scholars distancing themselves from the Christology of the Gospels, it is understandable that the Christian theology of the past two centuries is characterized by a disproportionately increased interest in the Jewish views of Jesus.

1.2.3 *The Christian Tradition*

1.2.3.1 THE FOUR GOSPELS

It goes without saying that we can expect to find historical information about Christ's life on earth within the Christian community. From the very beginning, the Christians' faith has been based on the deeds of the LORD as manifest in the appearance of Jesus Christ in world history. Even as the records of the acts of the LORD under the Old Covenant were read in the oldest Christian communities, so the most recent acts of this God in the sending of his Son, through whom he performed miracles and deeds of power (Acts 2:22), were also a focus of attention.[58]

We thus find no fewer than *four* biographies of Jesus Christ that have been preserved in the Christian church throughout the world. A pagan such as Celsus, in the second half of the second century, was already astonished at the fact that there were multiple Gospel accounts.[59] It was his opinion that a religion that proclaims one truth should also have one document to contain that truth; pure truth is always obscured by a multiplicity of writings. But Christians have regarded the four Gospels as a precious possession from the very beginning. The four Gospels provided an abundance of information, as well as confirmation of that information among themselves. The fact that four Gospel accounts were preserved shows how much value was attached to historical events.

These four documents describing Jesus' earthly life occupy a rather lonely position, like four high mountains of information surrounded by virtually empty plains. As soon as we begin searching outside the Gospels for traditional information about Christ's life on earth, we find almost nothing. Yet originally there must have been an entire delta region of streams and rivulets of tradition. In the first place there were many primary witnesses. Second, there was for a long time a demand for information from those who had seen and heard Jesus. As late as the beginning of the second century, Papias did his best to question apostles (and their disciples) to find out as much as he could from them about

---

58. Justin Martyr refers to the Gospels to be read at the meetings of Christians on the first day of the week as "memorial books" (*apomnēmoneumata*); *First Apology* 66.3; 67.3.
    59. Origen, *Against Celsus* 2.26–27.

Jesus' teaching and deeds.[60] And third, many people apparently had already put together coherent narratives before Luke embarked on his own Gospel (Luke 1:1). Isn't it strange then that those many voices have died away and that all we are left with are the four soloists?

More than once it has been suggested that this puts the Gospels in a dubious position. Is it not possible that their survival is due to the fact that other sources and other information of a different nature, not in harmony with the four Gospels, were suppressed? If so, then the four main sources are of questionable integrity. These questions must be considered in some detail before we can use without reservation the tradition that has been preserved in the Gospels.

1.2.3.2 TRADITION

Materials that might be considered "ancient tradition" are not plentiful. Sometimes we find in early Christian writings quotes from Jesus that are not included in the four Gospels. The same is true of a number of papyrus fragments published in the past hundred years: in addition to fragments from the four familiar Gospels they also contain a few unknown sayings of Jesus, and in a few cases they report deeds performed by Jesus that are unknown to us or that have parallels only in extrabiblical material.

This dearth of information is less strange than it seems at first glance.

a. Although there were many eyewitnesses, they all belonged to one generation. By the time Paul wrote his first letter to the Corinthians, some of them had already died (1 Cor. 15:6). The persecution of the oldest Christian community in Jerusalem quickly reduced the number of surviving eyewitnesses.

b. The remembered, oral tradition is only kept alive if it is written down, published, and preserved. Theophilus had learned of Christ's teaching and work, but all we know about what was passed on to him orally is what Luke wrote down for him on paper. In addition, not all private notations or diaries were published and circulated.

c. The oral tradition quickly began to show signs of wear and tear. Already in the Gospel of John we find a firsthand correction of a

---

60. Eusebius, *Ecclesiastical History* 3.39.3–4: "And whenever anyone came who had been a follower of the presbyters, I inquired into the words of the presbyters, what Andrew or Peter had said, or Philip or Thomas or James or John or Matthew, or any other disciple of the Lord, and what Aristion and the presbyter John, disciples of the Lord, were still saying. For I did not imagine that things out of books [i.e., commentaries on Jesus' words] would help me as much as the utterances of a living and abiding voice [i.e., that of the Lord himself]." Papias collected this information for his commentary on the Gospels.

popular tradition (Jesus did not say that John would not die, but, "If I *want* him to remain alive until I return" (John 21:22–23). The Gospel of John was written late, and in this correction we find something like a certificate of authenticity by a third party: "This is the disciple who testifies to these things and who wrote them down. We know that his testimony is true" (John 21:24).

d. Because of this wear and tear, anything that had not been established in the oldest sources or that could not be traced to the apostles or their disciples was regarded with a critical eye. Origen believed that it was possible that the ancient *Kerygmata Petri* contained historically reliable pronouncements of Peter, but he offers no opinion as to whether this can actually be established with certainty.[61] And Eusebius was suspicious of some of the stories passed on by Papias.[62]

e. This critical attitude was stimulated in the second and third centuries with the rise of legends and heretical gospels or other kinds of writings that contained traditions about Jesus. It is possible that the apocryphal Gospels, which were written at a later date and generally supplement the material in the four familiar Gospels (giving, for instance, further details about Jesus' youth or about his resurrection), may indeed contain true elements, but it is impossible to separate historical elements from the clearly legendary stories that are interwoven. This applies also to sectarian literature, of which the Coptic-Gnostic Gospel of Thomas (a collection of individual pronouncements of Jesus) is the best known. The entire work is clearly Gnostic, but some of the statements may well be authentic. The chance of authenticity increases if the material is also found on papyrus fragments and/or is cited in early Christian literature. All in all, we must conclude that for a variety of reasons the scarcity of traditional material outside the four Gospels is understandable.[63]

The little that can be found consists mostly of *sayings* of Jesus. These sayings are known as the *agrapha* (lit. "not written," i.e., in the Gos-

---

61. Origen, *Commentary on John* 13.17 (Sources chrétiennes 222.84–88).

62. Eusebius, *Ecclesiastical History* 3.39.8–14. Here Eusebius mentions a few strange parables, some sayings, and in particular the teaching of the millennial kingdom of peace. In 3.39.17 he notes that Papias borrowed another story from the Gospel of the Hebrews, that of the woman accused before Jesus of many sins.

63. For an overview of the material, see W. Schneemelcher, *New Testament Apocrypha*, rev. ed., trans. A. J. B. Higgins et al., Eng. trans. ed. R. McL. Wilson (Cambridge: Clarke, 1991–92). J. B. Bauer provides a short introduction in *Die neutestamentlichen Apokryphen* (Düsseldorf: Patmos, 1968).

pels).[64] Even in the New Testament we come across such sayings, for example, "It is more blessed to give than to receive" (Acts 20:35).

Another well-known saying can be found in Luke 6:4 in a Greek manuscript, the codex Bezae:

> When on the same day he saw a man working on the Sabbath, he said to him, "Man, if you know what you are doing, you are happy. If you do not know what you are doing, you are cursed and a trespasser of the law."

A saying quoted in Origen that can also be found in the Gospel of Thomas reads:[65]

> He who is close to me is close to the fire;
> He who is far from me is far from the kingdom.

Clement of Alexandria quotes a saying of Jesus that closely resembles sayings that are familiar to us:[66]

> Ask for the small things,
> And God will give you the great things as well.

In general, these and the few other possibly ancient quotations are difficult to explain without a historical context, which is precisely what is missing in the "unwritten sayings of Jesus," the *agrapha*. The historical context is hardly ever included in the extrabiblical tradition. The only source that really gives us unfamiliar historical information is a papyrus fragment whose historical reliability (or at least accuracy) has been demonstrated by Jeremias on the basis of details in the description.[67] It concerns a visit to the temple:

> And he took them [the disciples] with him to the clean part of the temple and walked with them across the temple square. And there he met a chief priest, one of the Pharisees named Levi, who said to the Savior, "How can you enter this clean part of the temple and observe these holy things when you have not bathed and your disciples have not even washed their feet? Defiled, you have entered the temple square, this clean place, while no one may come here and dare to observe these holy things without first washing himself and putting on clean clothes." But the Savior stood right where he was with his disciples and answered, "Then what about yourself, for you also are here on the temple square. Are you clean?" "Yes," he said, "I am clean, for I have washed myself in the pond of David. I went

64. J. Jeremias, *Unknown Sayings of Jesus*, 2d English ed. (London: S.P.C.K., 1964).
65. Ibid, 66–73.
66. Ibid, 98–100.
67. Ibid, 47–60.

down one step and up the other, and I put on clean, white clothes. Only then did I come here and observe these holy things." Then the Savior said to him, "Woe to you, blind man who does not see. You have washed yourself in drainage water in which dogs and pigs lay about day and night, and you washed yourself and wiped dry the outer layer of your skin, which harlots and flute-players also anoint, wash, rub and paint in order to arouse men's desire, but inside they are full of scorpions and all manner of wickedness. I and my disciples, however . . . have been immersed in the living water. . . . But woe to them. . . ."

1.2.3.3 MORE GREEK GOSPELS?

This last papyrus fragment leads Jeremias to suspect that there must have been a lost Gospel in the style of the Synoptics to which this fragment belonged. Other fragments may point to an unknown Gospel with Johannine characteristics.[68]

The fact is that we have no knowledge of the existence of such Gospels, written in Greek. We are not talking about the later apocryphal Gospels or the sectarian Gnostic literature, which also includes Gospel-like documents. Early Christian writers give us direct or indirect information about such material, but they make no mention of Greek Gospels whose age and style would suggest a direct parallel with the four Gospels we have. So it is a precarious undertaking to propose on the basis of a few papyrus fragments that such ancient, lost Gospels existed. This is all the more true because it would appear more likely that the fragments belong to noncanonical works we are familiar with, such as the collection of sayings known as the Gospel of Thomas. This is not to say that historically correct information may not have found its way into these fragments and into the sectarian or apocryphal texts. The issue here is strictly whether or not we may responsibly conclude that more Greek Gospels once existed that dated from the time of Matthew, Mark, Luke, and John.

The matter would seem clearer when we turn to the prologue of Luke's Gospel. He begins his book as follows (Luke 1:1):

> Many have undertaken to draw up an account of the things that have been fulfilled among us.

Does this not suggest that *many* Gospels were in circulation before Luke set pen to paper? Surely the word "many" does not apply only to Matthew and Mark (John wrote much later)?

Further reflection throws a different light on this matter, however. If there already were many Gospels in circulation that were based on the

---

68. Jeremias and Schneemelcher in Schneemelcher, *New Testament Apocrypha*, 1:92–109.

direct accounts of eyewitnesses and servants of the Word (Luke 1:2), what need was there for Luke to send his book to Theophilus? The fact was that he wanted to provide a reliable *written* report of the things about which Theophilus had already been taught *orally* (Luke 1:4), so that he will know that the things he had been taught are indeed reliable. This formulation would indicate that up to that point Theophilus had no *written* account available to him of the events that had taken place around Jesus.

Yet Luke says that many had already composed narratives, and he does not suggest that their narratives were inadequate. We must think here of the many preachers who went about telling the story of Jesus, based on information gleaned from eyewitnesses and servants. Thus Philip "told [the Ethiopian government official] the good news about Jesus" (Acts 8:35). Theophilus had likewise been told what Jesus said and did. He knew the "orderly account" that many had composed to facilitate their preaching.

But this story had to be *published* as well, which meant that it had to be composed in a manner that allowed for circulation as a written historical account.[69] Luke did not limit himself to some annotations for personal use—he wrote a book. He committed the story to paper *for others,* and by dedicating it to Theophilus Luke may also have ensured its circulation: some scholars think that the man to whom a book was dedicated helped defray the cost of publication.[70] Luke's book does not differ in essence from the many other "orderly accounts" that were already circulating among preachers. What makes it new is that Luke's narrative transcends the immediate needs of the missionary enterprise and is a *published* work. The notebook for the evangelist's personal use now becomes a publication for the convert. Luke was the first among his fellow-Christians to *compose and publish* the written story. (Later we will examine why other, comparable Gospel accounts were also put into circulation; see 1.3.7.)

Thus we may conclude that there is no indication that any other Greek Gospels were *in circulation* during the period in which the four

69. For a discussion of Luke 1:1–4, see section 1.3.6 below, which deals with a point not discussed here: when Luke writes that he *also* has decided to write an orderly account, does this mean that the *many* others he is joining in this task have also provided *written* accounts?

70. T. Zahn, in *Das Evangelium des Lucas* (Leipzig: Deichert, 1913), 56, refers to Josephus (*Against Apion* 2.41 §296) and others for the idea that at that time the dedication of a book tacitly implied that the person to whom the book was dedicated would also bear the costs of further publication. Josephus dedicated both volumes to Epaphroditus, with an eye to others who, like Epaphroditus himself, were interested in the Jewish people.

familiar books were written. The introduction to Luke's Gospel rather suggests the opposite: although various preachers possessed biographies of Jesus, Luke writes his book at a time when Theophilus had only the *oral* narrative at his disposal.

1.2.3.4 THE GOSPEL OF THE HEBREWS

The situation is rather different when we turn to the non-Greek tradition. Here many early Christian writers were indeed aware of another Gospel. Some even made use of it. Many offered comments on one or more passages from this book. It is usually referred to as the Gospel of the Hebrews.

The closer we get to the Hebrew origins, the greater the possibility of encountering authentic material. It is therefore intriguing that we find in the Hebrew tradition a Gospel that was nevertheless ultimately rejected by the church and that we unfortunately know only from fragments. This Gospel must also have circulated in Greek form; otherwise it is difficult to explain how someone like Irenaeus could quote it, and how Greek papyrus fragments could have been found that also contain what might be brief passages from this Gospel.

More than one scholar has seen in these quotes from the Gospel of the Hebrews a gateway to further research. Are we here afforded a peek behind the veil? And will we find another view of Jesus there? Might this be an older, more Jewish view? We read, for example, quotes from the Gospel of the Hebrews such as this:

> At once my mother, the Holy Spirit, took me by one of my hairs and carried me off to the great Mount Tabor.[71]

The reference to the Holy Spirit in feminine terms ("my mother") is striking and is supposed to reflect early Jewish-Christian usage. Another quote has to do with Jesus' appearance to James:

> When the Lord had given the linen cloth to the priest's servant, he went to James and appeared to him. James had sworn never to eat any more bread from the hour in which the Lord had drunk from the cup until he might see him as risen from the dead. Shortly thereafter the Lord said, bring a table and bread. And it immediately stood before them. He took the bread, blessed it and gave it to James the righteous and said, My brother, eat your bread, for the Son of man is risen from the dead.[72]

---

71. Origen (*John* 2.6 [wrongly cited by Vielhauer and Klijn as 2.12] in *MPG* 14.132–33; *Jeremiah* 15.4 in *MPG* 13.433) and Jerome (*Micah* 7.6 in CCSL 76.513; *Isaiah* 40.9 in CCSL 73.459; and *Ezekiel* 16.13c in CCSL 75.178).

72. Jerome, *On Illustrious Men* 2 (*MPL* 23.641).

Other quotes contain sayings of Jesus that are not familiar to us, such as:

> I chose for myself the most worthy: they are the ones given to me by my heavenly Father.[73]

> You can never be happy if you do not look upon your brothers with love.[74]

What do we actually know about this Gospel tradition? According to modern scholars, there were two, or possibly even three, Jewish-Christian Gospel accounts:

1. The Gospel of the Hebrews
2. The Gospel of the Nazarenes (which some think is identical to 1)
3. The Gospel of the Ebionites

However, this expansion to two or three Gospels is, in my opinion, based on incorrect conclusions drawn from information found in early Christian literature[75]—information that is not always taken seriously enough. When, for instance, Jerome states in various places that he has translated the Gospel of the Hebrews into Greek and Latin, his statement is dismissed with the argument that the same Gospel must have been translated into Greek before, during the time of Irenaeus.[76] By the same logic we could also deny that Jerome translated the Bible into Latin because such a translation had already been made much earlier! Why could Jerome not have produced a new translation of the already well-known Gospel of the Hebrews, so that people who spoke Greek and Latin would be able to read this Jewish-Christian document (which—despite earlier quotes in Greek—would not have been widely known)?[77] If we take the information from Jerome and other writers seriously, we can form a clear picture of the actual situation: there were not two, let alone three, Jewish-Christian Gospels, but only one, the "Gospel of the Hebrews."

73. Eusebius, *On the Theophany* (Syriac) 4.12 (GCS, Eusebius 3.2.183).
74. Jerome, *Ephesians* 5.4 (*MPL* 26.552).
75. Vielhauer believes that there were three Jewish-Christian Gospels: the Nazarene Gospel, the Ebionite Gospel, and the Gospel of the Hebrews (P. Vielhauer, *Geschichte der urchristlichen Literatur: Einleitung in das Neue Testament, die Apokryphen und die Apostolischen Väter* [Berlin: De Gruyter, 1975], 648–61). See also A. F. J. Klijn, "Patristic Evidence for Jewish Christian and Aramaic Gospel Tradition," in *Text and Interpretation: Studies in the New Testament Presented to Matthew Black*, ed. E. Best and R. Mcl. Wilson, (Cambridge: Cambridge University Press, 1979), 169–77.
76. See the contribution of P. Vielhauer and G. Strecker on the Jewish-Christian Gospels in Schneemelcher, *New Testament Apocrypha*, vol. 1.
77. Jerome mentions this translation more than once. *On Illustrious Men* 2 (*MPL* 23.641) mentions a translation into Greek *and* Latin; *Micah* 7.6 (CCSL 76.513): "recently translated by us"; *Matthew* 12.13 (CCSL 77.90): "recently . . . translated into Greek."

The characteristics of this Gospel can be summarized as follows, based on scattered remarks by early Christian writers:

1. It is a Gospel written with Hebrew characters but in the Aramaic language. The usual term for Aramaic is "Syriac," but in order to distinguish the language of this Gospel from regular Syriac, which used its own alphabet(s), the comment was added that it was written "with Hebrew letters." These wordy explanations suggest an Aramaic text written in Hebrew characters, as is also found in parts of the Old Testament (Daniel 1–7 and other passages) and in the Jewish Targums.[78]

2. The common name for this document is "the Gospel of the Hebrews." This would not have been the title used by Jewish-Christian readers themselves. They regarded their book as the Gospel according to the twelve apostles or the authentic Gospel of Matthew. In all probability it is the Greek translation of this Gospel to which others attached the name Gospel of the Hebrews.[79]

3. This book was in use among the Ebionite Jewish Christians, a group that denied the virgin birth and had a docetic understanding of Jesus' death.[80]

78. The language is simply referred to as "Hebrew" in Jerome, *Matthew* 12.13 (CCSL 77.90); *Micah* 7.6 (CCSL 76.513); *Isaiah* 11.2 (CCSL 73.148); 40.9 (CCSL 73.459); as well as in Eusebius, *On the Theophany* (Syriac) 4.12 (GCS, Eusebius 3.2.183). Somewhat more cautious is the designation "in Hebrew letters" (Eusebius, *On the Theophany* 19 [*MPG* 24.685]; Jerome, *Letter to Hedibia* 120.8 [CSEL 55.490]). The reason for this more cautious designation becomes clear when Jerome remarks in his *Dialogue against the Pelagians* 3.2 (*MPL* 23.597ff.) that the Gospel of the Hebrews was written in Chaldee, specifically in Syriac (Aramaic), but with Hebrew letters. Eusebius also describes the Gospel of the Hebrews, used by Hegesippus, as "Syriac" (*Ecclesiastical History* 4.22.8).

79. We find the title "the Gospel of the Hebrews" in the works of several authors: Clement of Alexandria (*Stromata* [*Miscellanies*] 2.9.45 [GCS, Clement 2, p. 137]); Origen (*John* 2.6 [*MPG* 14.132–33]); Jerome ([*On Illustrious Men*] 2 [*MPL* 23.641]; *Dialogue against the Pelagians* 3.2 [*MPL* 23.597ff.], and others); Eusebius, in reference to Hegesippus (*Ecclesiastical History* 4.22.8); Epiphanius (*Panarion* 30.3 [*MPG* 41.409]). In *Dialogue against the Pelagians* 3.2, Jerome also says that this Gospel was regarded by its users as "the Gospel of (according to) the apostles." Most users saw it as the authentic Gospel of Matthew (but see point 6).

80. Eusebius, *Ecclesiastical History* 3.27.4; Jerome, *Matthew* 12.13 (CCSL 77.90). Epiphanius (*Panarion* 30.3 [*MPG* 41.409]) writes that the Ebionites (whom he had learned about firsthand from a certain Josephus) used only the Gospel of Matthew and not the other Gospels. They called this "the Gospel of the Hebrews." Later (see point 5) Epiphanius would remark that they used this Gospel of Matthew in an abridged and mutilated form. This explains why Irenaeus calls the Gospel of the Ebionites the Gospel of Matthew. This is a brief reference that does not deal with the question whether changes had been introduced; it deals exclusively with the fact that *only one Gospel* was being used and that even the letters of Paul were rejected (Irenaeus, *Against Heresies* 1.26.2 [*MPG* 7.686–87]; 3.11.7 [*MPG* 7.884]; for the deviant ideas of the Ebionites cf. 3.21.1 [*MPG*

4. This Gospel contains sayings and topics that are not found in the other four, which are precisely the parts of the Gospel of the Hebrews that are most frequently quoted by early Christian writers.[81]

5. In many respects, the Gospel of the Hebrews is in agreement with that of Matthew. This becomes clearer when the early Christian writers do not quote it for its unique elements but pay attention to the book as a whole, which they then characterize as a somewhat mutilated and altered Gospel of Matthew that can be used in the exegesis of Matthew by way of comparison.[82]

6. The Nazarenes are also mentioned as a group who used this Gospel.[83] On the other hand, Jerome says that he came across a Gospel of Matthew written "in the original language" among the Nazarenes in Berea and copied it.[84] And Epiphanius mentions

---

7.946] and 5.1.3 [*MPG* 7.1122]). For the Ebionites, see A. F. Klijn and G. J. Reinink, *Patristic Evidence for Jewish-Christian Sects* (Leiden: Brill, 1973), 19–43.

81. Clement of Alexandria quotes this Gospel for an unknown saying of Jesus (*Stromata* [*Miscellanies*] 2.9.45 [GCS, Clement 2, p. 137]); Origin quotes the striking passage in which the Holy Spirit is referred to as mother (see *John* 2.6 in *MPG* 14.132–33; *Jeremiah* 15.4 in *MPG* 13.433); Eusebius reports that Papias borrowed another story, about a woman taken in sin, from this Gospel of the Hebrews (*Ecclesiastical History* 3.39.17); Jerome notes that according to this Gospel it was not the temple curtain but a heavy temple lintel that broke during the earthquake at the time of Jesus' crucifixion (*Letter to Hedibia* 120.8 [CSEL 55.490]); Eusebius mentions another version of the parable of the talents in which the man with five talents spends them among prostitutes and flute-playing women, for which he is punished (*On the Theophany* 19 [*MPG* 24.685–88]).

82. Irenaeus believes that the Ebionites, on the basis of their own Gospel (Matthew), can be accused of deviation, just as the Marcionites could be accused on the basis of theirs (Luke). The fact that changes had been introduced is not relevant here. The point is that the passages that (still) linked their Gospel to the broader New Testament of orthodox Christianity provided quite enough evidence to refute them (*Against Heresies* 3.11.7 [*MPG* 7.884]). Epiphanius reports mutilation (for instance the removal of the birth story at the beginning) in *Panarion* 30.13 (*MPG* 41.428–29). But Jerome uses the Gospel of the Hebrews more than once for comparison with passages he is discussing in Matthew. He himself even says that he *often* makes use of it (*Matthew* 27.51 [CCSL 77.275]). Examples can be found in *Matthew* 6.11, where he refers to the Gospel of the Hebrews, which uses the word *machar* (meaning "[bread] for tomorrow"), and *Matthew* 27.16, where he notes that Barabbas "is called son of one of their Sadducees" (CCSL 77.37, 265). See also *Matthew* 23.35 (CCSL 77.270), where Zechariah is not called a "son of Barachiah" but "son of Ioioda."

83. Eusebius mentions "those Hebrews who have accepted Christ" (*Ecclesiastical History* 3.25.5). Jerome mentions the Nazarenes (*Matthew* 23.35 [CCSL 77.220]; *Dialogue against the Pelagians* 3.2 [*MPL* 23.597ff.]; *Isaiah* 11.2 and 40.9 [CCSL 73.148, 459] and *Ezekiel* 16.13c [CCSL 75.178]), in one instance together with the Ebionites (*Matthew* 12.13 [CCSL 77.90]).

84. *On Illustrious Men* 3 (*MPL* 23.644–45). What is striking is that at one point in his commentary on Matthew, Jerome makes use of the Hebrew text of Matthew. He had already made reference to it in his preface and made a notation at 2:5 that in the original language, Matthew spoke of Bethlehem as a city in *Judah* (to distinguish it from Galilee), not *Judea* (CCSL 77.2, 13).

that these Jewish Christians, who still held to the law of Moses (without Ebionite deviations in doctrine), used the "normal" Gospel of Matthew and in the original language.[85] There appears to be a contradiction here, yet that is all it is: an apparent contradiction. We also read that the Gospel of the Hebrews was regarded by *most* of the Nazarenes as an authentic Gospel of Matthew[86]— but apparently not by *all* of them. We must therefore make a distinction: the Nazarenes around Berea used Matthew's Gospel, while most Nazarenes used the Ebionite version. By way of hypothesis we suggest the possibility that the Greek-speaking Ebionites translated their Gospel of the Hebrews into Greek, whereupon the Greek-speaking Nazarenes decided to follow this Jewish-Christian Gospel and *not* the edition used by the "Christians outside the law." The Nazarenes in the region where Aramaic was spoken did not have to make special effort to distinguish themselves from the non-Jewish, Greek-speaking Christians, who did not follow the law of Moses, and from their Greek Gospel of Matthew. Thus the early Christian writers in the areas where Greek was the common language regarded the Gospel of the Hebrews as the book used by the Ebionites and the Nazarenes, while writers referring to the Nazarenes in the original Aramaic-speaking areas observe that the normal Gospel of Matthew was in circulation there, while the Ebionites used the edited version of Matthew—the Gospel of the Hebrews.

In conclusion, the following can be said on the basis of the early Christian writers:

a. Among the Nazarenes in Berea there was still a Gospel of Matthew in the original language in circulation.
b. The Gospel of the Hebrews is an Ebionite adaptation of this Gospel of Matthew. It was later regarded by most (Greek-speaking?) Nazarenes as the original Gospel of Matthew.

85. *Panarion* 29.9 (*MPG* 41.405). For the Nazarenes, see Klijn and Reinink, *Patristic Evidence*, 44–52. Klijn and Reinink erroneously attach little value to the information provided by Jerome, because in his discussion of Matt. 13:53–54 he is thought to have claimed that the Nazarenes deny the virgin birth, while elsewhere he makes the opposite assertion (Klijn and Reinink, *Patristic Evidence*, 47). However, in the Matthew 13 discussion Jerome is not referring to the *sect* of the Nazarenes but to the *inhabitants of Nazareth!*

86. The Gospel of the Hebrews with its deviations was naturally not regarded as an authentic Gospel of Matthew by most *orthodox Christians*. Jerome's designation relates to most of the *Nazarenes*. See *Matthew* 12.13 (CCSL 77.90) and *Dialogue against the Pelagians* 3.2 (*MPL* 23.597ff.).

c. The unique elements in the Gospel of the Hebrews may go back to an ancient and reliable tradition (the appearance to James, for instance), but they are suspect to the extent that they appear to reflect a connection with the deviant notions of the Ebionites (the Holy Spirit as mother, probably the mother of Christ, while Jesus is then the child of Joseph and Mary).[87]

d. There are no traces of any other or older Jewish-Christian Gospels.

1.3 The Four Evangelists

1.3.1 The Story of Jesus and Ecclesiastical Tradition

The information about Jesus' life on earth, so scarce and inconclusive outside the Bible, is abundant in the four Gospels. The question for many is, is this information not only more abundant but also less inconclusive than the extrabiblical material? While for centuries the church has relied on the accuracy of the reports the four evangelists offer us, the past century has been dominated by categorical doubt on this point. The critical approach to the Gospels which in the first centuries was found among the opponents of Christianity has now become generally accepted in modern Christian theology. The Gospels are viewed (as described in 1.1.2) as edited and theologically oriented statements of the faith of the oldest Christian communities and of the diverse legends that had formed around the historical person of Jesus. Given the scarcity of other information about Christ's life on earth, this negative view of the Gospels cannot but lead to deep uncertainty about the foundations of the Christian faith. The identity crisis of modern Christianity is a direct consequence of its increasingly vague understanding of the historical Christ. And at the foundation of that loss is the movement away from the Gospels as historically reliable sources of information about Jesus' words and deeds.

This critical attitude toward the four Gospels is a complex phenomenon. We will list a few of its components and then focus on one of them.

1. One's view of the Gospels is partly determined by one's willingness or unwillingness to accept what they contain as the substance of faith. It can hardly be otherwise. If history really happened as the evangelists tell

---

87. Origen explains the designation of the Holy Spirit as "mother" *metaphorically*: just as all who do the will of Christ can be called "brothers and sisters," so the Spirit, who does the will of Christ, can even more rightfully take the name "mother" (*John* 2.6 [*MPG* 14.133]). Jerome provides a *grammatical* explanation: in Hebrew the word for "spirit" is feminine (*rûaḥ*), in Greek it is neuter, and in Latin it is masculine. Since there is no gender distinction in the godhead, the imagery thus could change, depending on grammatical gender. Thus the feminine word *rûaḥ* in Hebrew can attract the feminine image of the "mother" (*Isaiah* 40.9 [CCSL 73.459]; *Micah* 7.6 [CCSL 76.513]).

us, then their accounts compel us to agree that all the world should kneel before Jesus Christ, God's son, who was born of the Virgin Mary, died for our sins, and will come again with his holy angels to redeem all creation. Those who are not willing to accept these realities will quickly be inclined to escape the force of the message of the Gospels by discrediting the Gospels themselves. This then becomes the starting point for a negative critical approach to the Gospels. Even if all negative literary and historical criticism of the Gospels could be refuted, it would still not be enough to counteract this movement away from the Gospels. Arguments and counterarguments are important, but experience shows that one's choice on this point is determined by something *more* than arguments.

2. The negative criticism of the Gospels in the twentieth century justifies itself mainly by means of literary criticism, which dismantles the Gospels and seeks to locate earlier, underlying sources. When it comes to the *exegesis* of the Gospels, literary criticism per se can be important: in order to do proper exegesis we must determine whether a given Gospel should be read as an integral textual unit or as a composition consisting of different layers, in which case we need to discern how older elements are provided with new commentary.

These problems must be addressed in exegesis, but the answers will have no effect on our understanding of the story of Jesus' life—because literary criticism *in and of itself* does not say anything about historical reliability. We can end up with a historically reliable report even via oral tradition, collections of sayings of Jesus, and/or primitive historical accounts, and finally the incorporation of all this material by the evangelists. It all depends on the attitude toward the historical facts on the part of the various people who transmitted and wrote down these materials. The problem, as Sevenster has pointed out, is the hybrid character of modern literary criticism of the Gospels: it illegitimately—and perhaps barely consciously—mixes literary and historical criticism.[88] So it makes little sense to examine the findings of modern literary criticism of the Gospels if we want to write a history of Christ's life on earth.

It would be more difficult to quickly dismiss all this if we had concluded that convincing proof had been forthcoming for the so-called two-document hypothesis. But this is not the case. The four-source theory should also be mentioned here in addition to the two-source hy-

---

88. J. N. Sevenster, "De vraag naar de echtheid in de synoptische evangeliën," in *Bultmanniana: Een vraag naar criteria* (Wageningen: Veenman, 1969), 24–76. For the problem of criteria, see also M. Lehmann, *Synoptische Quellenanalyse und die Frage nach dem historischen Jesus: Kriterien der Jesusforschung untersucht in Auseinandersetzung mit Emanuel Hirschs Frühgeschichte des Evangeliums* (Berlin: De Gruyter, 1970).

pothesis[89] and the many variants on the source theories.[90] The revival of the Griesbach hypothesis should also be noted, according to which Mark would have been the last Gospel.[91] Furthermore, the works of Stoldt, Riesner, and others, point out the value of oral tradition or the weakness of the two-document hypothesis.[92]

3. Historical criticism of the Gospels—often mixed with literary criticism—is based on the alleged contradictions between the Gospels themselves as well as between the Gospels and the extrabiblical sources. It is assumed that the four evangelists were in fact the ones who closed the gate on the legends about Jesus that were formed within the church. Thus they reflect the tradition of the community, not the history of Jesus Christ. The Gospels are historically reliable only insofar as this church tradition is congruent with the historical Jesus. But by now it must be obvious that every criterion for determining historicity is missing. If we cannot know anything about Jesus' life on earth from the Gospels that have been passed down to us, we certainly cannot know anything from a community tradition that is unknown to us and that we must reconstruct from these very Gospel accounts!

Historical criticism can be approached from two angles. First, we can try to determine whether the contents of the Gospels are really incompatible with the notion of a clear—if incomplete—historiography. This is the subject to which the greater part of this book, beginning with chapter 2, is devoted. But we can also enter the discussion from another angle by taking church tradition as our point of departure. Historical criticism has—rightly—a high opinion of this tradition. But it is strik-

89. B. H. Streeter, *The Four Gospels: A Study of Origins* (London, 1924). The four-source hypothesis assumes, besides Mark and Q, a written source behind Matthew and a proto-Luke.

90. For Lindsey's modified two-source hypothesis, which is followed by Flusser, see Lindsey, "Modified Two-Document Theory." See W. Schmithals, *Einleitung in die drei ersten Evangelien* (Berlin: De Gruyter, 1985), 182–233; A. J. Bellinzoni, ed., *The Two-Source Hypothesis: A Critical Appraisal* (Macon, Ga.: Mercer University Press, 1985); and M. E. Boismard, "The Two-Source Theory at an Impasse," *New Testament Studies* 26 (1979–80): 1–17.

91. The work of W. R. Farmer in particular should be mentioned. The discussions he revived for and against the Griesbach hypothesis can be found in W. R. Farmer, ed., *New Synoptic Studies: The Cambridge Gospel Conference and Beyond* (Macon, Ga.: Mercer University Press, 1983), and in C. M. Tuckett, ed., *Synoptic Studies: The Ampleforth Conferences of 1982 and 1983* (Sheffield: JSOT Press, 1984).

92. H. H. Stoldt, *History and Criticism of the Marcan Hypothesis*, trans. D. L. Niewyk (Macon, Ga.: Mercer University Press, 1980); R. Riesner, *Jesus als Lehrer: Eine Untersuchung zum Ursprung der Evangelien-Überlieferung* (Tübingen: Mohr, 1981); J. M. Rist, *On the Independence of Matthew and Mark* (Cambridge: Cambridge University Press, 1978); J. Carmignac, *La naissance des Évangiles Synoptiques*, 3d ed. avec réponse aux critiques (Paris: O.E.I.L., 1984); E. P. Sanders, *The Tendencies of the Synoptic Tradition* (Cambridge: Cambridge University Press, 1969).

ing that the *unknown* tradition, which is presupposed to lie behind the Gospels, enjoys great popularity, while the *known* tradition as related by the early Christian writers is treated with disdain. A classic case of familiarity breeding contempt! Is the much-vaunted respect for the traditions of the oldest communities then really sincere? That which is taken for tradition today is often merely a reflection of modern theology, while the familiar tradition fundamentally refutes that same modern theology. We gladly respect tradition, but we want the object of that respect to be the actual, known community tradition and not the hypothetical tradition twentieth-century scholars propose.

There is in fact no trace of a primitive, legend-creating community.[93] What we do find, right from the beginning, are communities that honored the Gospels as the memoirs of the apostles,[94] and writers who quoted from them with respect.[95] And there was still firsthand knowledge of the evangelists—these men, after all, had been in the community since its inception! It is worthwhile discussing the four evangelists from the perspective of the church tradition, as we will do below.

In the Greek manuscripts we see the Gospels since earliest times bearing the names of Matthew, Mark, Luke, and John.[96] These are men who either participated in the story of Christ on earth or had direct contact with witnesses who saw and heard Jesus. If these are indeed the people who vouch for the reliability of the contents of these Gospels, then we know for certain that we have arrived at the oldest sources, the primary witnesses of the history of Christ. But how much value can we place on this traditional ascription of authorship we find expressed in the manuscripts? We will now examine the evangelists one by one.[97]

1.3.2 Matthew

According to the unanimous early tradition, the apostle Matthew is the author of the first Gospel. This unanimity is in itself not conclusive

---

93. Legend formation actually took place at a later time, as is shown by the history of the "supplementary Gospels," which are part of the apocryphal literature of the New Testament.

94. Justin Martyr, *First Apology* 66.3; 67.3.

95. See the quotes in the Apostolic Fathers. For an appraisal, see my *Wie maakte de bijbel? Over afsluiting en gezag van het Oude en Nieuwe Testament* (Kampen: Kok, 1986), 32–44.

96. The Gospels are in complete agreement in all the manuscripts, even in the oldest papyri, about the authors' names. Without exception, the authors are always named and the names are always the same.

97. The Greek and/or Latin text of many quotes from the ancient church fathers that deal with the authors and the development of the Gospels have been collected and made accessible in appendix 2 of K. Aland's *Synopsis Quattuor Evangeliorum: Locis parallelis evangeliorum apocryphorum et patrum adhibitis edidit Kurt Aland,* 14th rev. ed. (Stuttgart: Deutsche Bibelgesellschaft, 1985).

evidence—errors can also be unanimously accepted and handed down. The question is whether this tradition is ancient as well as unanimous. By means of a quote from Eusebius we can trace the tradition to a writer from the beginning of the second century, Papias of Hierapolis, who wrote a since-lost work about the Gospels. He had had personal contact with the disciples of the apostles and may even have had direct contact with the apostle John. He states that he always inquired of them what the apostles and the Lord himself had said.[98] In Papias we have a man who can still draw on the material that was known in the circle of the apostles and their disciples, and who was also extremely interested in investigating the immediate past. According to Eusebius, this Papias says the following about Matthew:

> Matthew made a stylized report of the stories [*logia*, i.e., stories of what Jesus taught and did] in the Hebrew language; everyone passed them [the stories] down as best he could.[99]

To fully understand this passage, we should note that in writing about Mark, Papias remarks that that apostle wrote down the stories without organizing them, thereby maintaining Peter's own narrative order. Matthew thus differed from Mark in that he *organized* the story; his work is characterized by the fact that it is a literary composition (*syntaxis*). This is also reflected in the comment that each one interpreted or passed down the stories as best he could: Matthew had compositional abilities while Mark was a fastidious recorder of Peter's sermons. The heart of Papias's report is therefore related to the differences in organizational structure among the Gospels, which can be traced to the various skills of their authors and the different situations from which the Gospels arose. It is striking that the Gospels were apparently already used side by side as a matter of course so that the differences attracted attention and required a certain amount of explanation.

---

98. Eusebius, *Ecclesiastical History* 3.39.3–4. For the text of this passage, see the note in sec. 1.2.3.1.

99. Ibid., 3.39.16. Because in the nineteenth century the term *logia* was understood as referring only to the "sayings (of Jesus)," it was relatively easy to arrive at the hypothesis of a so-called Sayings or Logia Source. Initially this was called L; later the designation was changed to Q (German *Quelle* [source]). The idea of "sayings" was maintained, however, in terms of the content of Q. Papias, however, refers to reports about what Jesus taught *and did* when he uses the word *logia*. See also U. H. J. Körtner, *Papias von Hierapolis: Ein Beitrag zur Geschichte des frühen Christentums* (Göttingen: Vandenhoeck & Ruprecht, 1983), 154–59. The end of the quote is often understood as indicating *various different* translations of the Hebrew Logia Source. But the verb *hermēneuein* can also mean "to report, interpret, pass on." This meaning is more appropriate here because Papias is not dealing with translations. Rather, he is discussing how Mark organized his Gospel in comparison with Matthew. Each evangelist interpreted the stories of Jesus as best he could.

Papias remarks, more or less in passing, that Matthew wrote in Hebrew. He takes no special interest in this information and writes it down simply as a known fact. But it is precisely this kind of information, which holds no interest for the author, that gives his remark greater value.

For Papias it goes without saying that Matthew is the author of the first Gospel. He does not treat this as something he needs to belabor but simply takes it as his starting point. Apparently he does not expect any objection or contradiction. This means that even in the time before Papias it must have been generally assumed that Matthew wrote this Gospel. This pushes the unanimity of the tradition as well as the witness of the tradition to the age of the Gospel back to the second half of the first century, when many people were still alive who could refute erroneous traditions from their own knowledge of the events and who could have known Matthew and the other apostles.

Finally, it should be mentioned that it is surprising to find Matthew, rather than someone else, mentioned as the author of a Gospel in the Greek-speaking world. As far as we know, the apostle Matthew carried out his work east of Palestine. He is never mentioned as an apostle among Greek-speaking peoples. Greek-speaking Christians would have had no reason whatsoever to highlight Matthew's name, because he had no special status with them. This means that we have here a tradition that is not only old but also unexpected and therefore more plausibly authentic.

The fact that the Gospel of Matthew is written in good Greek does not argue against this last point; it is merely evidence of a skilled translator. And the Gospel would not have been translated so soon if there had been many Gospels in circulation at the time. So we must assume that it was one of the first Gospels and that it was translated quickly because of its apostolic authorship.

This Gospel is also clearly aimed at people who are familiar with the Jewish way of life. Many even believe that it was first written for Jewish Christians. There were both Hebrew- and Greek-speaking Christians among the Jews in the first community immediately following Pentecost.[100] One is further reminded of the many Greek-speaking Jews in the Diaspora—in Egypt, Syria, Asia Minor, and Rome. We need not be surprised that a Gospel aimed at Jewish Christians also began to circulate in a Greek version.

Scholars in the twentieth century are inclined to dismiss the tradition of a Hebrew original (thereby placing Matthew's authorship on

---

100. See S. Greijdanus, *De toestand der eerste christelijke gemeente in zijn betekenis voor de synoptische kwestie* (Kampen: Kok, 1973).

shaky footing), since the tradition is not in keeping with the well-known two-document hypothesis, which sees Matthew as a later reworking of Mark, made within the Greek-speaking world. Much work has been done to prove Papias wrong. Kürzinger, for instance, has put forward the idea that Papias did not mean the Hebrew *language* but a Hebrew *style* characterized by Semitisms. Apart from other problems inherent in this view,[101] we must note that it does not reflect the view of Matthew held during the first centuries A.D. Besides, there is another witness to the Hebrew version of the original, independent of Papias, to lend weight to our argument.

Jerome says that there was a Hebrew edition of Matthew in the library in Caesarea.[102] He also came across a copy among the Nazarenes in Berea, which he copied. Jerome carefully distinguishes this original version of Matthew from the (mutilated) version that was in use among the Ebionites and many other (Greek speaking?) Nazarenes: the so-called Gospel of the Hebrews.[103] In his brief commentary on Matthew we find a place where he uses the Hebrew original.[104]

In addition, Pantaenus claims to have found a copy of Matthew in Hebrew among the Christians in India,[105] left behind by Bartholomew.[106]

Why are there no extant copies of this Hebrew Gospel of Matthew?[107] The answer is certainly related to the fact that most of the Christians in

101. When the context clearly indicates that "style" is intended by the word *dialektos*, then the word should indeed be given that meaning. But in Papias the context does not imply a comparison of styles (Mark's style vs. Matthew's). In addition, there is not a single known parallel for the term "Hebrew style." The phrase *Hebraïs dialektos* is always used in reference to the Hebrew *language*. That is how it was understood by the generations immediately following Papias. For Kürzinger's view, see J. Kürzinger, *Papias von Hierapolis und die Evangelien des Neuen Testaments: Gesammelte Aufsätze, Neuausgabe und Übersetzung der Fragmente, kommentierte Bibliographie* (Regensburg: Pustet, 1983).

102. Jerome, *On Illustrious Men* 3.

103. Jerome speaks about the Gospel of the Hebrews in his *On Illustrious Men* 2, and in paragraph 3 he distinguishes it from the Hebrew copy of the Gospel of Matthew.

104. *Matthew* 2.5 (CCSL 77.2, 13).

105. Eusebius, *Ecclesiastical History* 5.10.2–3.

106. Klijn wonders what people in India were to do with a Hebrew Gospel, and suspects that it was probably a Syriac Gospel. But just as copies of the Authorized Version (King James Version) or American editions of this version, left there by missionaries, can still easily be found among Christians in African states, so it is quite possible that Bartholomew left his Hebrew edition behind. Pantaenus does not say that the Christians he met in India had no other biblical manuscript than this. He reports it more as an unusual find and as something left by his predecessors than as information about the range of liturgical texts used by Christians in India ("Patristic Evidence," 173).

107. There are no clear indications that the original Hebrew version of Matthew underlies the later Hebrew version to which the Du Tillet and Shem-Tob editions, independently from one another, go back. Cf. G. Howard, "The Textual Nature of an Old Hebrew Version of Matthew," *Journal of Biblical Literature* 105 (1986): 49–63.

Jewish-Christian sects (Cerinthians, Ebionites, Nazarenes) used the Gospel of the Hebrews. Most of them incorrectly regarded this edition as the authentic Matthew, and they pushed aside the *original* Hebrew (Aramaic) version of that Gospel. The Gospel was preserved in its Greek translation, which was almost as old as the original, as can be seen from its early distribution in the Greek-speaking churches. There it was used by Gentile Christian converts together with Jewish Christians who did not belong to the Jewish-Christian sects.

1.3.3 Mark

Just as the first Gospel is generally attributed to the apostle Matthew, so Mark, the nephew of Barnabas, is generally considered to have been the writer of the second Gospel. It is striking to find this name attached to one of the Gospels: Mark, the young man who was a bit of a disappointment on the first missionary journey (Acts 13:13; 15:37–38), the author of a biography of Christ! It is all the more striking because he was not one of Jesus' disciples. It is precisely this improbability of Mark as the author that argues in favor of the tradition's authenticity.

We have here a tradition that is demonstrably old. Even during the time of the apostles, Mark was regarded as a Gospel writer. We know with historical certainty that Mark is indeed the author, a certainty we owe to the same Papias from the early second century whose work we briefly discussed in the section on Matthew.

Papias mentions a tradition that he ascribes to the *presbyteros* John. If this is not the apostle John, son of Zebedee, it is in any case one of Jesus' disciples.[108] So the tradition reported by Papias is exceedingly old.

This tradition mentioned by Papias does not concern Mark's name as such—it is simply assumed that he is the author of the Gospel that bears his name. This is how self-evident the fact of Mark's authorship was for the presbyter John during the apostolic period.

The tradition that was handed down to Papias, and which he in turn passed on, has to do with a characteristic of this Gospel. While Matthew has given us a stylized, literary work, we find nothing of the sort in Mark. Why not? The tradition offers us an answer: the special character of this Gospel is a result of the circumstances of its origin. Mark wrote more or less as the mouthpiece of Peter, and he was determined to preserve the apostle's teaching as exactly as possible. This explains why Mark's book shows traces of a narrated report and not of a stylized composition. Papias's information thus tells us not only that Mark was known as the author right from the beginning, but also that he repro-

---

108. Eusebius, *Ecclesiastical History* 3.39.3–4.

duced the words of Peter, the first apostle, with great care. The fragment, located in Eusebius, reads as follows:

> This, too, the presbyter [John] used to say: "Mark, who had been Peter's
> interpreter,[109] wrote down carefully, but not in order, all that he remem-
> bered of the Lord's sayings and doings. For he had not heard the Lord or
> been one of his followers, but later, as I said, one of Peter's. Peter used to
> adapt his teaching to the occasion,[110] without making a systematic
> arrangement of the Lord's *logia*, so that Mark was quite justified in writ-
> ing down some *logia* just as he [Peter] remembered them.[111] For he had
> one purpose only—to leave out nothing that he had heard, and to make
> no misstatement about it [the *logia*]."

The entire fragment is permeated by a single thought: Mark is repro-
ducing Peter's preaching, and for this reason his Gospel offers us neither less nor more. Not less—it is a very carefully rendered approxima-
tion of what Peter heard and saw as a firsthand witness. And not
more—it does not rise above the limitations that oral instruction imposed on the style of the whole or of parts of the whole. Mark is truly

---

109. The word *hermēneutēs* can mean "translator," but it can also mean "interpreter,
mouthpiece." Cf. how Papias, in reference to Matthew, says that every evangelist "inter-
prets or renders" (*hermēneusen*) the stories about the Lord as best he can: see above, sec.
1.3.2 and notes. See also Kürzinger, *Papias von Hierapolis*, 46–47.

110. Kürzinger explains the expression *pros tas chreias* ("according to need") from
the standpoint of the technical terminology of rhetoric. *Chreia* is a short stylistic form
used to express the saying of a sage (sometimes accompanied by a brief historical introduction). Kürzinger translates as follows: "[Peter] taught according to the manner of the
chreiai" (*Papias von Hierapolis*, 51ff., 103). This information could be of significance in
helping to explain the Gospels' development. It is used extensively by G. W. Buchanan in
Jesus: The King and His Kingdom (Macon, Ga.: Mercer University Press, 1984). The fact
that Papias's quote contains various stylistic terms argues strongly in Kürzinger's favor.
Nevertheless, there are unavoidable difficulties: (1) The preposition *pros* does not fit this
interpretation. (2) Papias had already referred to the smaller narrative units as *logia*
(Mark did not want to introduce anything false; this *logia* refers to the stories of Peter).
(3) After intensive analysis, Buchanan arrives at only twenty-eight actual *chreiai* in the
Gospels; the form is too brief to serve as an all-embracing characterization of Mark's Gos-
pel (G. W. Buchanan, "*Chreias* in the New Testament," in *Logia*, ed. J. Delobel [Leuven:
Peeters, 1982], 501–5). For a broader discussion of *Chreiai*, see R. F. Hock and E. N.
O'Neil, *The Chreia in Ancient Rhetoric*, vol. 1 of *The Progymnasmata* (Atlanta: Scholars
Press, 1986).

111. The reference here is not to Mark's recollection of Peter's words. Nowhere does
Papias say that Mark wrote only after Peter's death. What is meant here are *Peter's* recol-
lections (*apomnēmoneumata*). The verb (*apemnēmoneusen*) refers to what was previously named (*emnēmoneusen*); the comparison is thus between Peter's recollection (of
Jesus' sayings and deeds) on the one hand and Mark's writing on the other. In neither case
is the subject "internal" memory (*mimnēskomai*) but rather the act of revealing something stored in one's memory to another ([*apo-*]*mnēmoneuein*). This results in the
apomnēmoneumata literature, to which Justin Martyr also assigns the Gospels as the
apostles' "memoirs" (*First Apology* 66.3; 67.3).

"his master's voice." If the oral catechism lacked *syntaxis* (polished style), then one should not expect *taxis* (polished structure) from Mark. On the other hand Mark, even though he was not a contemporary of Jesus, does give us direct access to what the Lord himself said and did. The resulting reports (the *logia*) are not distorted or blurred.

Peter calls Mark his "son" (1 Pet. 5:13). We might call the second Gospel "Peter's child"!

1.3.4 Luke

According to the unanimous tradition of the patristic writers, and according to the title in all the manuscripts, Luke is the author of the third Gospel. This tradition is not as old as the tradition concerning Matthew and Mark. We find Luke mentioned for the first time in Irenaeus (second half of the second century),[112] but the reference makes it clear that Luke's authorship was generally accepted and considered self-evident at that time. Irenaeus's information concerns the relationships among the Gospels and assumes that the authors of these writings are all well known. According to Irenaeus, Luke wrote after Matthew and Mark.

The fact that in the middle of the second century Marcion, a fanatical disciple of Paul, limited himself to the Gospel of Luke (from which he deleted significant portions that did not fit his theories) must be connected with Luke's having been a disciple of Marcion's beloved apostle Paul (Col. 4:14; Philem. 24; 2 Tim. 4:11). Even before Marcion it was apparently generally accepted that this coworker of the great apostle to the Gentiles was the author of the Gospel that bears his name. Otherwise it would be difficult to explain why Marcion kept this Gospel and not that of Mark, which contained far fewer of the references to the Old Testament that so disturbed him.

The second part of the historical work of which the Gospel constitutes the first part is the Book of Acts. There we find rather long passages in which the writer uses the first-person plural, thereby indicating that he was part of Paul's retinue.[113] This confirms that the writer of this two-part work was a travel companion of the apostle. When the tradition unanimously points to Luke as the author, the name is relatively unexpected. We have little additional information about him. Who would have had anything to gain by bringing this name to the fore? The tradition seems authentic here.

---

112. See in Eusebius, *Ecclesiastical History* 5.8.1–5.

113. These are the so-called we passages that are found in the narratives of the second missionary journey, the third missionary journey, and the great voyage from Caesarea to Rome (Acts 16:10–17; 20:5–15; 21:1–18; 27:1–28:16).

The author of the third Gospel had, via the apostle Paul, direct access to reports from people who had seen and heard Jesus. We know that Paul himself made use of their information and carefully passed it on as "tradition" in his letters.[114] He also sought information about the life of Jesus from Cephas.[115] So, as Paul's companion, Luke was as close to the primary witnesses as Mark, who was allowed to act as Peter's mouthpiece in his Gospel.

In this section we have limited ourselves to the information that can be deduced from tradition and from the Book of Acts. The prologue of Luke's Gospel and the conclusions that can be drawn from it will be dealt with separately and form a supplement to the matter at hand (see below, 1.3.6).

1.3.5 John

According to unanimous church tradition and the unanimous witness of the manuscripts, which all identify him as the author, the last Gospel was written by the apostle John.

The writer presents himself in the Gospel as an eyewitness (19:35). He indirectly identifies himself as the apostle, the son of Zebedee (21:24; cf. 21:20–23). The apostle who leaned on Jesus' breast at the Last Supper (13:23–26), often referred to as "the apostle whom Jesus loved," lived for a long time after Pentecost—so long that it came to be believed that he would be the only one of the apostles to remain alive until Jesus' Second Coming. The only thing we know about John is that he was still in Ephesus at a very advanced age. Both the Gospel itself and church tradition unequivocally point to this apostle as the author of the last Gospel, which was aimed at refuting the heretics who did not confess Christ as the Son of God (John 20:31).

1.3.6 Excursus: The Prologue of Luke

The four Gospel writers, according to a tradition that is unanimous and ancient, were themselves followers of Jesus from the very beginning or at least among the followers of those who had seen and heard Jesus. If we consider that Mark actually reproduced the sermons of Peter, we see that three of the four Gospels come directly from apostles: Matthew, Peter, and John. This is no unimportant fact in determining whether we can take their writings seriously as primary sources.

---

114. Cf. for instance Rom. 6:17b; 1 Cor. 11:23ff.; 15:3ff. See B. C. Lategan, *Die aardse Jesus in die prediking van Paulus volgens sy briewe* (Rotterdam: Bronder, 1967).

115. Once he visited Jerusalem to get information from Cephas (Gal. 1:18; *historēsai* is more than "to visit"; it indicates that the purpose of this visit was to obtain information). Paul no doubt asked Cephas about the events that he himself had seen as an eyewitness.

But all this is summarily brushed aside by someone like Schmith-als.[116] It is his opinion that on the basis of Luke 1:1–4 we must conclude that absolutely no *apostolic* Gospels ever existed. Indeed, Luke does write like a secondary witness. He knows of many who wrote Gospel accounts before him, but he emphatically distinguishes them from the eyewitnesses and servants of the Word. He also takes a rather detached stance vis-à-vis those Gospels, and because he is critical of them he believes that it would be good if he were to produce a better work himself. Isn't Luke's preface then proof that no respectable and primary sources had been produced by firsthand witnesses? Before concluding this chapter, we need to pause for a moment and consider this much-discussed introduction to the Gospel of Luke. In doing so we will not concern ourselves with the prologue's function in the Gospel or with its character compared to extrabiblical book introductions. These matters are best explored in a commentary on Luke's Gospel. Here we will concentrate on a few questions that are important for determining whether we can view the Gospels as apostolic sources for the story of Christ's life on earth.

We are faced with the following questions:

1. Was *Theophilus* familiar with a number of ("many") written Gospels, and is Luke now writing to correct, supplement, or confirm them?
2. What is the special circumstance that induces *Luke* to write his book?

1. When we discussed the possibility that there were more Greek Gospels in circulation during the earliest period than are now known to us, we discussed Luke 1:1–4 briefly (see section 1.2.2.3). We saw that Luke was not speaking about many who had already *written for others*, but about many who had already *put together* (*anataxasthai*) a *narrative* (*diēgēsis*) about the events that had taken place at that time. The facts had been organized into orderly accounts[117] intended for Jew and

---

116. "Because it is hardly conceivable that Luke's apostolic Gospels could have been scorned or could have escaped celebrity, we must assume without a doubt that no 'Gospel' record was made by an *apostolic* hand" (W. Schmithals, *Einleitung in die drei ersten Evangelien* [Berlin: De Gruyter, 1985], 33–34).

117. W. C. van Unnik stresses that the word *diēgēsis* is a technical term for a historian's finished product, and he points to the extensive discussions of the requirements for a *diēgēsis* in the textbooks on rhetoric (pp. 14–15). But the design and structure of none of the Gospels, not even Luke's Gospel, is governed by the technical requirements for a *diēgēsis* as formulated by the discipline of rhetoric and the historians. Furthermore, the word *diēgēsis* is not limited to the *written* products of historians and men of letters. In fact, the opposite is true: the work of the historian should have the qualities of a *story*.

Greek, to be used for evangelistic purposes. It is quite possible that these preachers of the Gospel carried their "story" with them in written form. Even so, their work consisted of preaching and instructing, not of putting written material into circulation. Theophilus's oral instruction (*katēchēthēs*) also consisted of these sayings (*logōn*, stories). Luke does not say that Theophilus had already *received* one of the orderly accounts in written form, but rather that many had indeed *"drawn up"* such stories. The facts on which the preaching was based were organized, probably in a more or less fixed form, but Theophilus only had access to the oral transmission of these stories in sermons. Theophilus had not heard fragments or bits of information about Jesus but an organized and complete story, drawn up by those who made use of the information passed down by eyewitnesses. Evidently the preachers did not leave their stories behind in written form, even though they themselves may have kept such written texts as memory aids.

What makes Luke's work so special is that he is backing up the preached story by offering it in written form. It would have made no sense to write a book for Theophilus if this man, as a catechumen, already had a great many written Gospels at his disposal,[118] all directly based on the information of eyewitnesses. It would have been useful, however, if Luke were to supplement the oral catechism by sending a written text in which everything was written down and could be consulted, and that aspired to precision (*akribōs*) and composition (*kathexēs*), the characteristics of the written word.

We conclude that Luke's writing presupposes a situation in which there were as yet no written Gospels in circulation. Although orderly accounts of the eyewitness tradition had indeed been drawn up, these served as a basis for the preachers' oral instruction and were not intended for publication. So Luke's book cannot be regarded as an indirect correction, supplement, or confirmation of *published* writings, but

---

Even if the historian writes a book, it should not read like a collection of archival material but should bear the marks of a real, lively *narrative*. So it is striking that Luke does not use the verb *syntaxasthai*, which is normally used in discussions of the *written* production of stylized historical narratives, but the less specific verb *anataxasthai*, which means "to arrange, to organize," without having any direct reference to *written* compositions ("Once More St. Luke's Prologue," *Neotestamentica* 7 [1973]: 7–26).

118. According to Van Unnik, verse 4 implies that Theophilus evidently had had no access to the written Gospels referred to in verses 1–2. After all, he still depends on oral information about Jesus' life on earth. Apparently the flow of information was not much more than a trickle. But arguing against this is verse 2, in which Luke speaks of the traditions that have reached *us*, while he also assumes that Theophilus is aware of the work of the "many" alluded to in verse 1. So the opposite conclusion is to be preferred: the traditions referred to in verses 1–2, with which Theophilus was familiar, could, according to verse 4, not have been *written* traditions but consisted of oral preaching and narratives (ibid.).

it can be seen as a confirmation of the narratives that had been drawn up by others and had been passed on orally and were known to people like Theophilus.

2. Why has Luke taken it upon himself to write this account at this particular time? This question requires that we look more closely at the composition of Luke 1:1–4.

If one assumes that there were already more written Gospels *in circulation*, then Luke places himself *beside* other authors ("It seemed good *also* to me to write") and his motivation is that he has checked everything once again ("Since I myself have carefully investigated everything from the beginning"). Schematically this can be presented as follows:

Many writers (v. 1):
    based on eyewitnesses (v. 2).
I too (v. 3b):
    based on investigation (v. 3a).

But then comes the question, Why is Luke investigating everything if the other writers were already in touch with eyewitness accounts? In that case there certainly would be little to improve. Does Luke set himself up as some kind of inspector of the traditions passed down by eyewitnesses? And what sources did he have that were superior even to the accounts of these earliest witnesses?

If we assume, however, that Theophilus knew only orally transmitted stories and that the orderly accounts about Jesus (possibly written) had not been distributed but only served as preaching aids, then we reach a different version of the structure of Luke 1:1–4. Schematically this can be designated in the following way:

Many preachers already use orderly accounts (v. 1):
    which are based on the information passed on by eyewitnesses (v. 2).
I am giving you such a written narrative (v. 3b):
    which is based on an investigation of the facts (v. 3a).

Now we have a clear justification for Luke's work: he is making sure that Theophilus *himself* also has use of such a reliable record of the facts of Jesus' life.

But why does Luke decide to write *himself*? He could just as easily have tried to convince one of the preachers to have the latter's version of the eyewitness material about Jesus copied to give to Theophilus. In that way Luke might have spared himself a great deal of work. But this is not what he chose to do. Perhaps the accounts that "many" had drawn up were not cast in a form suitable for publication. When people write something down for their own use it is not always easy for others to make use of it.

But there is another factor. Luke, on his own, goes back to the eyewitnesses and to the facts themselves. In doing so he taps the same sources from which the narrative compositions of the "many" were derived, but he does this independently of them. His book can thus be used to *confirm already existing accounts* that were distributed by means of oral preaching. Luke approaches the same basic history, but he does so *by following his own path.*

Some scholars believe that Luke was a firsthand witness to part of Jesus' life story (possibly before becoming a Christian). Thus he was not a servant of the Word from the beginning, but as an eyewitness he would have lived through these events himself. The verb *parakolouthein* can mean "to examine something," but it can also mean "to be present at and live through" certain events. Since Luke 1:1–4 concerns events, it would seem logical to assume that the meaning intended here is "to live through all those facts."[119] Luke did this as a follower from afar or as an interested physician, possibly connected to the court of Herod Antipas.

Luke 1:3 is then to be translated as follows: "Therefore, since I myself have carefully followed everything from the beginning, it seemed good also to me to write." This translation implies that Luke must have been a witness to Jesus' life on earth. Indeed, his presence cannot be limited to traveling with the apostle Paul (in that case Luke 1:3 would only relate to the "we-passages" in Acts).[120] The prologue of the Gospel introduces only the Gospel, not Acts, which was given a new preface.

An objection to viewing Luke as an eyewitness from the sidelines of Jesus' life, however, is the fact that the phrase *"carefully* followed" would not naturally be used to refer to being present at certain events. How can one be *carefully* present? "Careful" is a very suitable way to characterize the *examination and investigation* of facts, however. The same objection applies to the ancient Christian idea that from the very beginning Luke did not follow the *facts* but the *persons.* In that case he had to have been a follower of the disciples of Jesus (comparable to someone like John Mark). But it is difficult to *carefully* be a follower of

---

119. The definition "to be present at and to live through (certain events)" is one that is expressly indicated by H. J. Cadbury in his "Commentary on the Preface of Luke" in *The Beginnings of Christianity,* ed. F. J. Foakes Jackson and K. Lake, vol. 2, part 1 (London: Macmillan, 1922), 489–510.

120. A. J. B. Higgins, "The Preface to Luke and the Kerygma in Acts," in *Apostolic History and the Gospel: Biblical and Historical Essays Presented to F. F. Bruce,* ed. W. W. Gasque and R. P. Martin (Exeter: Paternoster, 1970), 78–91.

someone. Finally, it is not possible for Luke, who would not have been a servant of the Word but an eyewitness, to speak in verse 2 about that which the eyewitnesses have handed on to *us*. In verse 2 Luke counts himself among the people who are *dependent* on the eyewitnesses because they were not eyewitnesses themselves.

The verb *parakolouthein* can easily relate to an investigation of events. Like other terms in Luke 1:3, it is a common term in the work of historians. And in the manner of a historian, Luke has carried out his own investigation of what has taken place. His work is systematic ("from the beginning," "orderly account")[121] and reliable ("everything," "carefully"). Thus he becomes an *independent witness* to the truth of prior reports that had been circulated orally and had reached the ears of Theophilus.

The circumstances were favorable for Luke's project. The style and word choice in the prologue of his Gospel reveal that as a physician he had enjoyed a good education and was well aware of the historian's writing style. Details in the Book of Acts suggest that he was familiar with the world around him (he knew the differences between various Roman forms of address, geographic details, etc.). He had also for years been a traveling companion of Paul, so that he had had the chance to meet many people both within and outside Palestine. Aptitude, education, and circumstances made him suitable for the extraordinary task he had taken on.

It was also a good time for Luke to take on this project. Many of the people who had witnessed Jesus' life and ministry were still alive. Luke could do research in the mountains of Judea and in Jerusalem, where the beginnings of the gospel had attracted a great deal of attention—at the births of John the Baptist and of Jesus (Luke 1:65–66; 2:18) as well

121. Much has been written about the meaning of *kathexēs* in Luke 1:3: what is involved in the ordering that Luke engages in to achieve his *orderly account*? Is it chronological or theological? An extensive word study was carried out by M. Völkel ("Exegetische Erwägungen zum Verständnis des Begriffs *kathexēs* im lukanischen Prolog," *New Testament Studies* 20 [1973–74]: 289–99). He translates it into Latin as *continua serie:* Luke's book is related to every part of a logically coherent whole. By extension this involves a relatedness of the material compiled by Luke to the whole of salvation history (R. J. Dillon, "Previewing Luke's Project from His Prologue [Luke 1:1–4]," *Catholic Biblical Quarterly* 43 [1981]: 205–27). But when we begin with the assumption that Luke, supplementing the oral narrators and preachers, composes a narrative of the events he had investigated himself in a fixed, *written* form, we can relate *kathexēs* to the comprehensiveness that is typical of the written form. Many had already passed on the story of Jesus' ministry to the rest of the world, but now Luke gives a complete description, a well-rounded and comprehensive written composition. The *continua serie* (Völkel) is well suited to a written account of events that were already known and were being circulated, but not to the systematic presentation of a written book in which the author has the peace and quiet necessary to tell everything from start to finish.

as at the presentation in the temple (2:38). He may have met Mary and spoken with her (Luke 2:19, 51). And as a man with an intellectual background, Luke could easily have had or made contact with the court of Herod Antipas (Luke 8:3; 13:31–55; 23:8–12; Acts 13:1). Many people who with great interest had followed Jesus on his last journey to Jerusalem were still alive (Luke 12:1; 14:25), and Luke probably also spoke with the companion of Cleopas (Luke 24:18).

We conclude that Luke was in an excellent position to examine all events once again, and that such an undertaking could serve as an independent confirmation of the preached gospel, while its publication in book form made it possible for hearers of the gospel to read and preserve the complete story of Jesus.

1.3.7 Four Key Witnesses

On the basis of a clear, unanimous, and sound tradition we may regard the four Gospels as having come from the circle of those who had seen and heard Jesus. The prologue of Luke does not call this into question but rather, as the only Gospel not written by or on behalf of an apostle, confirms it. Matthew, Peter (through Mark), and John belonged to the inner circle of the Twelve. Two of them were even among the three most prominent apostles. One was called "the Rock" by Jesus, who chose him as the one upon whom he would build his community. Luke, the man who examined everything as an investigative historian, confirms the witness of the apostles. The four evangelists act as key witnesses for Jesus' life on earth. Compared to them, all other authorities are second-tier, even apart from the fact that the information about the life of Jesus from other sources is scarce indeed.

Why did these four individuals become the writers for the church of the ages? Why not fewer, or more? Such questions cannot be answered or can be answered only in part. We cannot know why there are not three or five primary documents. The fact that it did not happen this way is related to historical circumstances.

When Theophilus did not have his own copy of the Gospel narrative and Luke was able to fill this gap, Luke naturally picked up his pen and set to work. When his book was published and earned a place for itself (possibly with the help of Theophilus), and when it began to be distributed as a result of Luke's work with Paul, the need for others to put together a similar document disappeared. Luke probably was not the only outsider able to write such a report, but he was the first who had the opportunity to take on this task because of the circumstances of his life.

The Jewish Christians found themselves in the happy situation of having no fewer than twelve apostles in their midst, who immediately took up the task of preaching. In addition, all the other witnesses who had seen and heard Jesus and had also been disciples of Jesus (the "elders") belonged to this circle of Jewish Christians. Those who told the story were all members of the family! The idea of putting together a written composition may only have occurred when Matthew took leave of the brothers, so it was the apostle Matthew who wrote down the Gospel for Jewish Christians. The Greek translation of his Gospel, like the Septuagint before it, reached non-Jewish Christians as well, and as an apostolic document was honored just as highly there as it was among the Jewish Christians.

Peter never intended to write a Gospel account, but his work took him far from Palestine, into an area that stretched from Babylon to Rome. He was, after all, the Rock for the worldwide church! It is understandable that Christians longed for a written record of his oral preaching in addition to his two letters, so that after his passing they could continue to be reminded of this apostle's teachings (cf. 2 Pet. 1:12–19; 3:1). It was Mark who recorded his preaching. After a time, however, his report was somewhat overshadowed by the Gospel of Matthew, which was composed more as a *book*.

The church would not have had more than these two or three Gospels if John, faced with heresy, had not later felt compelled to produce a unique compilation of his own memoirs. John added an extra seal to the witness about the Son of God.

Because Luke's book was given rapid circulation through Paul, the world traveler, and Matthew achieved fame via Jewish Christians, who lived all over the world, there was less of a need for the Gospel of Mark. John had a specific reason for writing a "late arrival" among the Gospels. But for the other apostles, the need to worry about producing a written record declined. One Gospel would have been quite enough if books at that time had been distributed as quickly as they are today. Now there were two books from two different spheres, the Gentile Christians (Luke) and the Jewish Christians (Matthew), and a published version of Peter's preaching (probably in the period when Luke was already available but the Greek version of the apostolic record of Matthew was not).

Thus, although historical circumstances cannot prove that it could not have happened any other way, they allow us to form a clear picture of how things may have happened in this particular way.

The Christian church that received the four Gospels paid attention not only to the ways of men but also to the will of God, so that which grew out of historical circumstances was received as a nonarbitrary gift from God. The question is not only whether we *could* have gotten along with fewer Gospels, but also whether the fact that we have four must be viewed as imposing an *obligation* on us to accept and use all four Gospels. The latter was the generally held belief. And although churches in one region may have read one Gospel more often and churches in another region, another, all four Gospels were preserved as a quartet. In the second century, Tatian even combined the Gospels into a single narrative in his *Diatessaron*. And Irenaeus compares the four Gospels to the four points of the compass and to the four creatures before the throne of God (Rev. 4:7).[122] In Ezekiel 1 these four living creatures bear the throne of God, who is seated above the cherubim. In the same way the four evangelists bear the incarnate Christ and reveal his fourfold glory. John (the lion) shows how Christ, the eternal Word, has reigned since the beginning. Luke (the steer) points to the priestly sacrifice of Jesus, who like a slaughtered animal prepares for the joyful return of the prodigal son. Matthew (the man) shows how Jesus was born as a true man of the Virgin Mary. Mark (the eagle) announces the coming of Christ, who enters the world as the Son of God. In later symbolism these four creatures are related differently to the four evangelists and are viewed as characterizing the human writers rather than their views of Jesus.[123] But Irenaeus is not concerned with the evangelists and their characteristics, but rather with the way in which the multifaceted wisdom of the Christ is revealed to the churches in full splendor by means of the prism of the evangelists. The four Gospels must also be maintained in the face of heresy, because the single focus of these four key witnesses is the one Christ. He can be known from each of the Gospels, but he can be more fully known from all four. This deepening of our knowledge about Christ's life on earth is important for a church that is being built to expand into the four corners of the world.

122. *Against Heresies* 3.11.7–9.
123. Augustine prefers the following assignment of symbols to the evangelists: Matthew the lion, Mark the man, Luke the calf, and John the eagle. This, he believes, better characterizes each of the four books as a whole, rather than primarily their introductions (*On the Harmony of the Evangelists* 1.6.9).

2

Four Gospels—One History?

When in the eighteenth century Reimarus wrote his critical essays on the life of Jesus, he did not yet have modern criticism at his disposal to deal with the age and origin of the Gospels, so his historical criticism was focused directly on the apostles themselves. He claimed that they had been dishonest in their reporting of the facts. Here, at the very beginning of the modern critical approach to the Gospels, we already find that establishing the date of the Gospels on the basis of ecclesiastical tradition and the scarce data we find in the Gospels themselves—as we did in chapter 1—does not in and of itself refute the charges of modern criticism. Historical criticism is not silenced when it comes face to face with eyewitnesses. This was true in the days of the apostles and is still true today.

But the context of criticism has changed since the days of the apostles. Since the passing of the eyewitnesses we have had to rely on the written accounts of the events, but these accounts seem to arouse suspicion. After all, the four Gospels, which are supposed to date from the very early days of Christianity, are not in full agreement among themselves. While they agree in many respects, there are also discrepancies in their accounts. Are these differences actually contradictions? If so, then this may be an excuse for taking critical distance from the documents. Although the rest of this book is devoted to discussing questions related to this point, it is useful to first spend some time in this second chapter with the question of contradictions in general.

The first point that comes up for discussion is a short review of the history of this problem, since the phenomenon of the differences between the Gospels has been dealt with in a variety of ways over the centuries. Next we will turn to the character of the documents that present the gospel to us: are they perhaps in principle resistant to a particular historical approach? Third, we will discuss a number of aspects of what are called differences or contradictions. Are differences of necessity contradictions from a historical point of view?

2.1 Harmonization?

The differences among the Gospels were already observed in the first centuries by both enemies and friends of the Christian faith. When non-Christians began to explore the documents of a group of people that no longer could be silenced by slanderous allegations or torture, they were struck by the fact that the four descriptions of Jesus' life did not always agree. They used this as an argument not only for dismissing the Christian Bible as a document that lacked the necessary literary qualities to be considered reliable but also for denouncing it as historically contradictory. The Bible-reading Christians were not unaware of the fact that a comparison of the Gospels gives rise to occasional questions, and those questions were openly discussed in biblical exegesis. However, discussions of this kind became more and more necessary because of the use or misuse opponents made of these problems. Already in the work of Origen and Eusebius we find incidental comments as well as more systematic discussions of alleged discrepancies.[1] But it was Augustine who at the end of the fourth century saw the need for a full treatment of the problem. Because of his earlier contacts with the Manichaeans and the Neo-Platonists, he knew all too well the rather elaborate historical criticism of the Gospels that existed in these circles, and he saw it as his duty to refute this criticism in his book *On the Agreement of the Evangelists.*[2]

Although this work was never completed, it set the tone for many centuries. Augustine leaves room for a variation in the presentation of the same facts by each of the evangelists, and as a rule he avoids forced solutions. He also assumes that the evangelists knew each other's work and that Mark is a shortened account of Matthew. This explains the word-for-word agreement we often find among the Gospels, in addition to the differences among the four accounts.

Augustine's work was resumed and completed during the Middle Ages by Jean Carlier Gerson, the great advocate of church reform who lived at the end of the fourteenth and the beginning of the fifteenth century. In his *Monotessaron* he synthesizes the four Gospels into a single document that combines the full text of all four Gospels into a fifth, in-

---

1. See the discussion in H. Merkel, *Die Widersprüche zwischen den Evangelien: Ihre polemische und apologetische Behandlung in der Alten Kirche bis zu Augustin* (Tübingen: Mohr, 1971), 94–121 (Origen), and 130–50 (Eusebius). A textbook covering this material is H. Merkel, *Die Pluralität der Evangelien als theologisches und exegetisches Problem in der Alten Kirche* (Bern: Lang, 1978).

2. See H. J. Vogels, *St. Augustins Schrift De consensu Evangelistarum unter vornehmlicher Berücksichtigung ihrer harmonistischen Anschauungen* (Freiburg: Herder, 1980). Merkel, *Widersprüche,* 218–61.

tegrated historical narrative. Gerson's work was in fact a single-column harmony of the Gospels, based on Augustine's principles.[3]

The Lutheran scholar Andreas Osiander chose a different path. His harmony, written in the year 1537, is based on much stricter rules than those of Augustine and Gerson.[4] Osiander's highly developed doctrine of inspiration, combined with a strongly mechanistic understanding of historical writing, compelled him to develop a system in which each difference in the description of the events was in fact a difference in the events themselves. That meant an enormous proliferation of facts. In Osiander's work the reports of the evangelists are often not integrated but separated. For instance, Osiander's predecessors had always assumed that the story found in all three Synoptics about the raising of the twelve-year-old girl referred to a single event, all the more so because all three, each in his own way, combine it with the story of the healing of the woman subject to bleeding. Matthew does not mention the name Jairus, and he does not refer to the father as a leader of the synagogue but merely as a leader. For Osiander this is reason enough to assume that Matthew is talking about the healing of the little daughter of a government official, while Mark and Luke report a comparable healing in the house of Jairus, a leader of the synagogue. For Osiander this is sufficient grounds for assuming that there were two different women subject to bleeding, one in Matthew and one in Mark and Luke.

Osiander's extreme over-harmonization led to a great deal of discussion, but in the end it gained only a small following.[5] In the nineteenth century Karl Wieseler saw the need to oppose the criticism of Strauss and Bauer and became intensively occupied with the Gospels. He chose a chronological approach and tried to construct a progressively more detailed historical framework for the events.[6] The question of the historicity of the narratives then is closely related to whether or not they can

---

3. It is striking that Christoph Burger does not mention the *Monotessaron*, either in his comprehensive study of Gerson (*Aedificatio, Fructus, Utilitas: Johannes Gerson als Professor der Theologie und Kanzler der Universität Paris*, [Tübingen: Mohr, 1986]) or in his article on Gerson in *Theologische Realenzyklopädie* 12:532–38. D. Wünsch provides some information in *Evangelienharmonien im Reformationszeitalter: Ein Beitrag zur Geschichte der Leben-Jesu-Darstellungen* (Berlin: De Gruyter, 1983), 15–20.

4. Wünsch, *Evangelienharmonien*, 84–179.

5. See Wünsch, *Evangelienharmonien*, 180–256, which describes the rich literature after Osiander. More in the line of Augustine is the great harmonizing work of Martin Chemnitz, completed in 1626 by Johann Gerhard. The same is true for the first real synopsis, the *Harmonia Evangelica* (1699) of J. Clericus (see H. J. de Jonge, *De bestudering van het Nieuwe Testament aan de Noordnederlandse universiteiten en het Remonstrants Seminarie van 1575 tot 1700* [Amsterdam, 1980], 61–62).

6. K. Wieseler, *Chronologische Synopse der vier Evangelien: Ein Beitrag zur Apologie der Evangelien und der evangelischen Geschichte vom Standpuncte der Voraussetzungslosigkeit* (Hamburg: Perthes, 1843). Idem, *Beiträge zur richtigen Würdigung der*

be brought together in a coherent historical and chronological pattern. The possibility of constructing such a chronological framework is the hallmark of historical authenticity.

Since the mid–nineteenth century the word *harmonization* has acquired a highly negative connotation. It is often used to typify the approach to the Gospels that was common during the centuries before the Enlightenment. After modern biblical scholarship began to lay claim to the "correct" approach to the Bible in historical-literary criticism, everything that deviated from that approach was simply denounced as "obsolete harmonization." The idea that the Gospels cannot be harmonized and are in part at odds with each other has become a dogma for which few people still require proof—a dogma that simply condemns those who disagree as old-fashioned and unscholarly. Their lack of scholarship is reflected in their interest in the harmonization model that was categorically repudiated long ago. Thus there is hardly any incentive to improve on, or where necessary replace, the work of Augustine, Gerson, Osiander, or Wieseler. Not only is their work considered defective (which, being human work, it certainly is), but it is primarily condemned as methodologically incorrect: for eighteen centuries the Gospels were mistakenly read as history books. This failed to do justice to their special purpose. Harmonists are charged with turning the witnesses of the Christian faith into historical ventriloquists, and the twentieth century does not want to make that mistake again.

Clearly we cannot bypass the question of whether the books that contain the gospel are capable of being consulted for answers to historical questions. Should we be listening to them with a different set of ears?

2.2 The Character of the Gospels

2.2.1 Biography?

The special character of the Gospels is often expressed in negative terms: they are not biographies. This statement blends truth with untruth. If we think of a biography as a literary-historical product, it is not difficult to see that the Gospels do not deserve to be called biography. They lack the comprehensiveness of a biography as well as many things that are normally found in biographies. On the other hand, we sometimes find biographical material that is disproportionally detailed relative to the large amount of biographical material that is miss-

---

Evangelien und der evangelischen Geschichte: Eine Zugabe zu des Verfassers "Chronologische Synopse der vier Evangelien" (Gotha: Perthes, 1869).

ing. For example, place names are sometimes very carefully recorded but quite often left out. Jesus' age is mentioned a few times in Luke (the twelve-year-old Jesus in the temple; Jesus' ministry beginning when he was about thirty years old), but such information is missing in the other Gospels, and Luke leaves us in the dark when it comes to dating the rest of the events of Jesus' life. We learn so little about Jesus' life before his public ministry that no self-respecting biographer would want to have his name attached to these books. That's one side of the story.

The other side, however, is that the Gospels have a great deal in common with historical biographies. The focus is on one person. All the Gospels are devoted to a description of his sayings and his works. Other people come into the picture only insofar as their activity or words had something to do with Jesus. Jesus' life is traced from his birth or from the beginning of his ministry through his death and resurrection. The geographical and chronological framework is very clear and deliberate. Thus in a sense the Gospels *can* be called biographies. They provide us with a very special, incomplete, but structured description of Jesus' life on earth. Whenever people claim that the Gospels are not historical descriptions by saying that they are not biographies, they are doing the evangelists an injustice. Their biographies are unusual and unique because of the uniqueness of Christ. The standard biographical model used for describing the life of a person, a general or an emperor, does not work well in this case. This is God's Son who has come to earth, and his coming compels us to make a choice: reject or accept him. His life is not an object for biographical description as such. The writer must adapt to a different scale: the divine words and deeds that Jesus used to present himself to us. These words determine the pattern that the disciples use in their historical descriptions. The unique appearance of the incarnate Word results in a unique way of describing his earthly life: all emphasis falls on the words and deeds with which he astonished and instructed Israel and the apostles.

From a literary-historical perspective the Gospels cannot be readily compared with other writings, such as biographies. But from the perspective of revelation history the form of the Gospels makes sense. The evangelists write the history of Jesus with the same perspective and focus that he presented in his own deeds and words. In this way an unusual biography is born in which little is said about birth and youth—and that not even in all the Gospels—while all four evangelists focus a great deal of attention on his suffering and death. Jesus Christ taught his disciples to see that *this* was the purpose of his life on earth, and this central focus results in Gospels that are biographies, but biographies that cannot easily be compared with those of any other person.

2.2.2 The History of a Beginning

A special characteristic of the historical writing in the Gospels is that all four evangelists insist that they are only writing about a *beginning*. The events they are describing are not simply events that took place in the past—rather, they are the start of a development that has continued right up to the time of the reader. Christians reading the Gospels later have experienced how the gospel has been preached in their own context with the guiding power of the Holy Spirit. They have been converted, and now they live through faith in Christ as he was preached to them. The Gospels show how the history of the Spirit, which is the history of all Christians, began with the coming of Jesus and with his work on earth as the Christ of God.

Thus Luke sees his second book, which deals with the outpouring of the Holy Spirit and the apostles' preaching of the gospel to places as far away as Rome, as a continuation of his first book, which dealt with the life and work of Jesus on earth. There he wrote about "all that Jesus began to do and to teach until the day he was taken up to heaven" (Acts 1:1–2). In the Book of Acts, Jesus is still the subject, the one who acts, albeit now from heaven and by means of his Holy Spirit. It is Jesus who pours out the Spirit (Acts 2:33), and his name continues to heal in Jerusalem (Acts 3:16). When Stephen dies as the first martyr, he sees the heavens open and Jesus sitting on the right hand of God, involved in what is happening on earth (Acts 7:55–59). Saul sees Jesus on the road to Damascus (Acts 9:5), and years later he sees him again in prison (Acts 23:11). The Lord is truly risen: in the Book of Acts Luke writes about his continuing work, which Theophilus was also permitted to experience (Luke 1:1, 4). This means that his first book did not present the life of Jesus on earth as simply a thing that happened in the past but as the beginning of our Christian present. That present did not stop at the end of Acts either. The Book of Acts is open-ended, concluding as it does with Paul preaching freely in Rome. Perhaps Luke had intended to write a third book, about Paul's appearance before the emperor. But even a third book would not have concluded the story; it would merely have been another interim report about the continued progress of the gospel of Jesus.

The Gospel of John is no different. Even in his prologue John points to the continuing impact of the coming of Jesus, the Word, to earth: "Yet to all who received him, to those who believed in his name, he gave the right to become children of God" (John 1:12). And he ends his Gospel with an open window to the yet unwritten future. He had already ended his book in 20:30–31 ("But these are written that you may believe that Jesus is the Christ, the Son of God"). It seems like a redundancy when we find another conclusion at the end of chapter 21: "Jesus did many other things as well. If every one of them were written down, I suppose that even the whole world would not have room for the books that would be written." Usually this passage is understood to relate to the works that Jesus did during his life on earth. But what John refers to at the end of chapter 21 is what Jesus said about what he would do in the future. Peter had been urged to entrust his life to Jesus and to follow him to the death (John 21:18–23). Jesus continues to lead the way, although now from the Father's headquarters in heaven (John 20:17). At this point John says that he has reached the end of his book. One could continue to write indefinitely about all the things Jesus did thereafter and still continues to do in this world. In Acts, Luke takes the story a little farther than John. But John wrote his Gospel at the end of the first century, and by that time so much had been accomplished in Jesus' name all over the world that John simply opens the window and asks the readers to look through the window and focus their attention on all that has happened since. He decides not even to begin writing everything down—there would be no end to it!

Mark also ends his Gospel with a colon. He tells how the Gospel began with John the Baptist and the baptism of Jesus (Mark 1:1–3, a lead-in to 1:4–13). But when he reaches the end of his book, he does not reach the end of the gospel. The book stops but the gospel goes on; the Lord Jesus is taken up into heaven and the apostles scatter all over the world to preach, while the Lord helps them and confirms the word by the signs that follow (Mark 16:19–20).

Matthew also lets it be known that the Gospels describe an open-ended, continuing history. He begins with the birth of the promised Immanuel: "God with us!" (Matt. 1:23). And that is also how his book ends. Jesus' final words in Matthew are, "And surely I am with you always, to the very end of the age" (Matt. 28:20). The book of the genealogy of Jesus Christ, the son of David, the son of Abraham (Matt. 1:1) is ended, but Christ remains. That is why the Gospel is part one, as it were, of Jesus' history.

In order to be able to clearly see the Gospels as historical, it is important to understand that the writing is dominated by the reality of Easter and Pentecost. This does not mean that instead of history we are getting later-developed *convictions* projected backward on the white screen of the past. The manner in which the Gospels are written rules this out (see below, section 2.2.3). But it does mean that the history is written from the perspective of the *concerns* of later believers. Our curiosity about many historic details remains unsatisfied; this is no inventory of a dead past that must be recorded as accurately as possible to protect it from corruption. The focus of the evangelists is concentrated on Jesus' own teaching: his commandments remain significant for later believers. Attention is paid to the language spoken by his signs and wonders: their message touches coming generations as well. His suffering and death are carefully reported because by announcing his suffering Jesus himself indicated that this was the purpose of his coming, and because at the Lord's Supper believers are called to eat and to drink "in remembrance of" him—remembering above all his living to die for our sins and to rise for our salvation. The focus of attention is dominated by the awareness that what is being written is a continuing history that is still valid and active: the reality of the resurrection and ascension streamline the Gospels' description of Jesus' life on earth.

2.2.3 Looking Back with Enlightened Eyes

An idea that has been dominant in the twentieth century is that to a significant extent the Gospels present the story of Jesus' life mixed with the convictions and traditions that developed later in the Christian community. The actual portrait of the earthly Jesus—rabbi, prophet, or magician—is then painted over with colors derived from the palette of the later veneration of Christ. So the failure of his life is recast in the more positive terminology of sacrifice. His apocalyptic idealism is turned into belief in the resurrection, and the Son of man is presented as the Son of God. In short, the twentieth-century image of Jesus has more in common with the ideas of Jesus' enemies or of the disciples who left him than with the image presented by the evangelists.

It is not easy to prove the truth of the gospel, but it *is* possible to show that the modern view of the Gospels is not compatible with these writings. The surprising thing is that the Gospels clearly show a break between the period of Jesus' life on earth and the post-Easter era. The evangelists do not give the impression at all that their later belief had *always* been their belief. With great honesty they show that in the beginning even they had a different view of Jesus. Peter's objections to Jesus' plan to suffer and die indicate a clear discontinuity between his earlier convictions and his later belief (Matt. 16:22–23; Acts 3:13–26). This break is not disguised or suppressed. The apostles and evangelists owe their view of Jesus to the fact that God himself gradually opened their eyes and their hearts to the truth (Luke 24:25).

In the Gospels we are made aware of the disciples' initial lack of understanding. When Jesus warns them of the yeast of the Pharisees and Sadducees, they think he is talking about forgotten bread (Matt. 16:5–7). When he gives them the sign in the temple, they still do not understand what he means. Only after Easter do they recall his words, and then they understand that Jesus had been talking about his rising on the third day (John 2:17, 21–22).

It is the Holy Spirit who gives the disciples their understanding of history. This does not mean a later interpretation of the facts, but an opening of the eyes. The Spirit teaches, but he also causes them to recall what Jesus himself said (John 14:26). That is why the Gospels so candidly reveal how blind to the facts or to their significance the disciples often were at first. When as preachers of the gospel and as evangelists they are able to see the story of Jesus in positive terms, it is because the Holy Spirit removed their blindness and opened their hearts. The facts were not in need of a subsequent or different interpretation—the disciples were in need of conversion. The facts do not constitute a neutral history—they tell the story of the coming of the Son of God in the darkness of a rebellious world. The darkness resists and refuses to objectively acknowledge the light, which lays siege to the darkness and pushes it back. The history of this resistance and opposition is also part of the gospel, so it is not concealed but openly described, along with the victory over the forces of opposition by Christ himself.

When scholars refuse to accept the historicity of the Gospels and assume that they are dominated by later interpretations, they are obliged to overlook these frank descriptions of the disciples' early failures. Indeed, if the later communities had painted over the picture of the historical Jesus from the perspective of their own faith, what would have been the sense of coming up with, or even including, the story of the misunderstanding about the yeast of the Sadducees, for example? Why would they include a backward projection of the sacrificial view of Jesus' death and at the same time say that the apostles refused to accept it at first? Or is this a conscious lie? We could imagine that, looking back through the lens of later experiences, initial convictions and later developments could get mixed up so that it becomes unclear when one came to believe in a particular vision. But such a blurring of precise memories and an anachronistic blending of the elements from the past is quite different from constructing an initial rejection of an idea that was only to have occurred later. There are only two options: either the evangelists speak the historical truth, or they deliberately falsify it. A great deal of clarity could be gained if twentieth-century scholars would return to this inescapable dilemma, which still presented itself in stark clarity to someone like Reimarus.

2.2.4 Writing with a Special Objective

When reading historical documents, which the Gospels purport to be, it is important to take particular note of the writers' specific objective.[7] What tendency or bias does their work show? Does this tendency remain subordinate to the presentation of the facts? We can speak of tendentious history only if the tendency dominates and becomes a bias that distorts the facts. What function does the specific objective of each of the evangelists serve in their writings? The answer to that question is important in determining how we can use their books as historical sources.

John's objective is clearly personal, as he himself states at the end of his book: "Jesus did many other miraculous signs in the presence of his disciples, which are not recorded in this book. But these are written that you may believe that Jesus is the Christ, the Son of God, and that by believing you may have life in his name" (John 20:30–31). The writing is intentionally selective, and the selection is dominated by the desire to provide extra documentation of who Jesus is, which must have been a response to the misunderstandings about Jesus that were already emerging (see John's letters, e.g., 1 John 1:1–5; 2:21–25; 4:1–6). In the Gospel of John we find a surprising combination of the general (long speeches that tell how Jesus bore witness to himself) and the specific (lively details drawn from memory or taken from diary entries; see John 1:29, 35, 44; 2:1). Thus, the truth of the preaching about the incarnate Word is bound up with the reliability of the historical witness (John 19:25; 21:24); they have heard, seen, and touched the Word of Life (1 John 1:1–3).

It is much more difficult to detect a specific objective in the other three evangelists. While John wrote his book after the other evangelists and assumed that the basic story was well known, the first three evangelists write reports of Jesus' life that are independent of one another, and these reports were to be the first written reports in their respective circles—the Jewish Christians (Matthew), the followers of Peter (Mark), and the smaller circle of the convert Theophilus (Luke). The time had not yet come for a more specific focus, since the general objective still had priority: a written summary of the narratives about Jesus that were already in broad circulation by word of mouth (see section 1.3). Thus the specific objectives are only secondary; they are expressed in the accents and emphases that are introduced within the narratives or in fuller descriptions of matters that the others do not mention. The general objective that the three have in common, therefore, has priority over the subordinate specific accents.

Thus Matthew can be identified on the basis of a few special characteristics. He pays a great deal of attention to the fact that Jesus is the

---

7. See, for instance, S. Greijdanus, *Hoofddoel en Gedachtengang van Lucas' Evangelieverhaal* (Kampen: Kok, 1922). J. P. Versteeg, *Evangelie in viervoud: Een karakteristiek van de vier evangeliën* (Kampen: Kok, 1980).

fulfillment of Old Testament prophecy, the goal of Israel's history, and the central figure of the New Testament church, where Gentiles are also welcomed along with Abraham's offspring. It is no accident that at the beginning of his book, Matthew typifies Jesus Christ as the son of David, son of Abraham, and that he describes the history running from Abraham to Jesus as the prehistory of Christ (Matt. 1:1–7). He also points out at the beginning of his Gospel that in Jesus the Immanuel prophecy of Isaiah is fulfilled (Matt. 1:18–25). In addition to providing us with references to the Old Testament quoted by Jesus himself, Matthew also adds his own quotes showing fulfillment of Old Testament prophecies, perhaps also based on Jesus' teaching (Matt. 2:15, 17f., 23; 4:14f.; 8:17; 12:17ff.). Jesus' explanation that he has come to fulfill the Law and the Prophets (Matt. 5:17) is an important narrative thread for Matthew. This fulfillment leads to a new Israel founded on Cephas and the apostles (Matt. 16:18f.; 18:15ff.). But focusing on these accents in Matthew must not blind us to the fact that Mark and Luke also treat the theme of the fulfillment of the Scriptures, and that they also indicate that Christ's community consists of both Jews and Gentiles and is being created by means of the preaching of the gospel. So in Matthew the accents may well relate more to the audience for whom he is writing than to his own theological objective.

In Mark we come up against the same problem. Is his book a typical Gospel of deeds with the focus on the breaking through of the kingdom? Mark also includes speeches given by Jesus: the parables, the eschatological discourse. Overall, Mark devotes a much smaller percentage of his work to Jesus' discourses than Matthew and Luke, but it is difficult to see in this a conscious and consistently implemented objective on the part of the author. When Mark writes down Peter's sermons, it is understandable that the historical details increase and that the speeches seem somewhat abridged.

Typical for Luke, it is said, is his attention to Christ's mercy and to the importance of the period between ascension and second coming. The latter, however, is barely touched on in the Gospel itself, but rather in the continuing story in Acts. And don't we read quite a bit about Christ's mercy in Matthew and Mark, too? We run the risk of seeing a theme in anything that, statistically speaking, is mentioned with slightly more frequency.

It is not accidental that the first three evangelists, unlike John, say nothing about any specific objective in their work. The early church was already in a quandary when it came to assigning to each of the Gospels specific symbols that would reflect their individual characteristics. Some want to see Matthew as the evangelist with the human face, while Mark bears the face of an eagle and John that of a lion, but Augustine agrees with those who see it otherwise (Matthew: lion; Mark: man; Luke: ox; John: eagle).[8] The faces turn out to be interchangeable, which should not surprise us in the first three independent descriptions of *the same* preached life story or gospel to which all the apostles gave unanimous witness in the world.

The twentieth century is strongly dominated by the idea that the Gospels should be regarded as so many theological concepts disguised as history. It would be incorrect to read the Gospels as historical reports, possibly each with its own specific tendency or accents. We are only really opening up the Gospels when we peel away the outermost, historical layer in order to find the theological core that formed the editorial motive for writing the entire book. Many monographs have been written in this century about the theology of Matthew, of Mark, and of Luke; the team of three historical writers, once seen as working in tandem, is now dissolved and turned into three theologians with divergent agendas.[9]

But here we confront an unavoidable methodological problem. How can we find the hidden code for each Gospel's theological uniqueness when they have so much in common? One solution has been to look at what seems to be unique material in each Gospel. Matthew and Luke, for instance, both contain birth stories, but Mark does not. Such an observation could only serve as a foundation for further delineation of Mark's uniqueness if we were sure that the absence of a birth story in Mark is deliberate and that it could *not* have fit in his Gospel. And this cannot be proven. Peter's preaching begins with Jesus' public ministry, starting with John the Baptist. If Jesus' birth is not dealt with in that concrete preaching situation, it does not mean that Peter, if asked, could not have provided separate information so that Mark could also have included these statements in his report. In Luke we find an extensive report on the period after the departure from Galilee and before Holy Week. Luke has less to say about Galilee. Why? Was he not able to spend more time on this period? Or did he neglect it because he was able to follow the period after Galilee from close range or because he had heard about it from individual witnesses? The point of view of a disciple who underwent his most important development in Galilee can differ chronologically from that of an interested outsider whose interest

8. Augustine, *On the Harmony of the Evangelists* 1.6.9.
9. See, for instance, G. Strecker, *Der Weg der Gerechtigkeit: Untersuchung zur Theologie des Matthäus*, 2d ed. (Göttingen: Vandenhoeck & Ruprecht, 1966); M. Sabbe, ed., *L'Évangile selon Marc: Tradition et rédaction* (Gembloux: Duculot, 1974); F. Bovon, *Luke the Theologian: Thirty-Three Years of Research (1950–1983)*, trans. K. McKinney (Allison Park, Pa.: Pickwick, 1987); M. de Jonge, ed., *L'Évangile de Jean: Sources, rédaction, théologie* (Gembloux: Duculot, 1977).

is heightened by the rush of the crowds on the road through Perea. If three people were to give a report about the Kennedy era, there would be many areas of agreement if they had all experienced that era in the same way. Nonetheless, there would be differences in their choice of narrative material and in the aspects each chose to cover in detail or succinctly. But it would be illegitimate to place the reports side by side and to deduce an editorial objective from the apparent differences: connecting wires that were not meant to be connected results in a short circuit. Such a method would only be appropriate if an author expressly set out to rewrite someone else's work because he did not agree with it. But we cannot assume that this is the case with the Gospels without coming into conflict with the historical facts of the tradition and the presentation of the Gospels themselves.

We would be on firmer ground if we were to focus on the passages that the evangelists *do* have in common. Any differences between the Gospels in those parallel passages might in fact betray each Gospel's theological uniqueness. For example, in Mark 4:38 we read, "Teacher, don't you care if we drown?"—a rather brusque question in which the disciples address Jesus man to man and call him to order. It is tempting to connect this to a primitive stage in the development of Christology.[10] In Matthew and Luke, the respect for the person of Jesus in the community has increased. The doctrine of the divine sonship has been developed, so all the human expressions are rewritten as well. Thus in Matthew (8:25) we read, "Lord, save us! We're going to drown!" and in Luke (8:24), "Master, Master, we're going to drown!" But are the differences really so great? The way in which Jesus was awakened indicates that the disciples were worried about Jesus' sleeping; apparently he failed to notice that the disciples were in danger of drowning. But we also recall that Luke was the only one to report a statement that is at least as abrupt as Mark's. In Luke we read that Martha says to Jesus, "Lord, don't you care that my sister has left me to do the work by myself?" (Luke 10:40). And how do we explain the fact that Mark says nothing about Jesus' physical hunger when he was tempted in the wilderness, while both Matthew (4:2) and Luke (4:2) point it out? If we add to this that in Mark we read that Jesus was with the wild beasts and that the angels waited on him (1:13), while Luke is silent on this point, then we would be more than justified to claim that Luke's writing is based on a human Christology while in Mark the divinity of the Creator is conferred on Jesus. However, these and similar statements suffer from the error of limited selection. Only a small portion of the infor-

10. H. R. Boer, *Above the Battle? The Bible and Its Critics* (Grand Rapids: Eerdmans, 1975), 73.

mation within each Gospel is examined, not all of it, thus creating forced contrasts between the Gospels, which, when viewed as a whole, are in fact quite harmonious, certainly in their Christology. Matthew knows that God himself is among us when Jesus becomes man (Immanuel). Mark immediately calls him God's Son, the angel of the Lord, who baptizes with the Holy Spirit (Mark 1:1–11). Luke knows that Jesus has come as the Most High (Luke 1:76–78). When we notice these statements of clear agreement among the evangelists, it becomes impossible to inflate the importance of incidental differences in word choice or selection of facts to the extent that they reflect divergent theological objectives.

2.2.5 Reporting the Facts

What kind of listening attitude do the evangelists expect from us? According to many scholars today, they do not expect the attitude of people who are interested in learning a bit of history.

Source criticism sees the evangelists as people who are dealing with older sources without having any independent knowledge of the original historical events. They are more like archivists for a church library than primary witnesses. In section 2.2.2, we saw that the evangelists themselves do *not* see their own work in this way. They present themselves as people in a position to begin relating the events that took place through the Holy Spirit in the world of the first century. That is why their Gospels are open-ended books. This is not a collection of sources but a factual report about a beginning. The people who were the first eyewitnesses and servants of the Word could tell the story and write it down (or have it written by others). The intention of the evangelists is to tell a *history* that is just as real as the history of the church, in which readers see themselves included through the preaching of the gospel.

In *form criticism*, the origin of many of the sayings and deeds ascribed to Jesus in the Gospels is sought in the formative community of the earliest church. In section 2.2.3, we saw that the Gospels resist such a construction; they do not contain a blend of facts and later interpretations. The narrative makes it clear that at first the apostles had the greatest difficulty accepting the facts and opening their eyes to their significance. The reality of Christ, through the Spirit, finally convinced them and made them able to see the events according to their real meaning and to describe them. This is not a case of plain and simple history being buried under the fallout of later communal theology. The opposite is true: the reality of Christ calls the community and its theology into being. That which the evangelists, with opened eyes, are eager to describe is a history.

The approach of *redaction criticism* to the Gospels sees the evangelists as people with a desire to express their own theological position through the way they re-present traditions about Jesus. In section 2.2.4, we examined the extent to which there seem to be individual objectives and the extent to which they can be recognized in the Gospels. The results showed that only John reveals such a clear tendency. Because John's aim was to document the reality of God's Son on earth, it was doubly important for him to let the facts speak from personal memory. The other three evangelists report the story of Jesus' words and deeds, each with his own unique narrative accents to be sure, but their widespread agreement entirely rules out the idea of diverging theological models.

Our *conclusion* regarding the character of the Gospels is that they were written to be read by all believers and by others as reliable reports of the beginning period of Jesus' work as the incarnate Son of God. In reading the Gospels, a good listening attitude—one that matches the intent of the Gospels—is to try to imagine how it all happened and what exactly took place in Palestine, which is as historical as Herod and Pilate! And this *historical* character of the Gospels is absolutely essential. In his second letter, the apostle Peter puts it this way:

> And I will make every effort to see that after my departure you will always be able to remember these things. We did not follow cleverly invented stories when we told you about the power and coming of our Lord Jesus Christ, but we were eyewitnesses of his majesty. For he received honor and glory from God the Father when the voice came to him from the Majestic Glory, saying, "This is my Son, whom I love; with him I am well pleased." We ourselves heard this voice that came from heaven when we were with him on the sacred mountain.[11]

2.3 History and Its Presentation

2.3.1 Differences in Presentation

The character of the Gospels is such that they can be read as sources of historical information provided by eyewitnesses and even demand such a reading. But having reached this conclusion, we find ourselves faced once again with the phenomenon of the differences in the presentation of history among the individual Gospels. Don't these differences indicate that the history has been very inadequately told? Undeniably a comparison of the Gospels raises some questions, but before we draw any conclusions regarding the historical character of these books, we

---

11. 2 Peter 1:15–18.

ought to reduce these differences to their proper proportions. After all, these differences occur within a larger framework of agreements. From a statistical point of view, the similarities in the way the evangelists report certain events are many times greater than any differences. This means that we ought to take these similarities as our point of departure and then find out how the small differences can be explained. Even if it appears that certain stories cannot be harmonized in every detail and that the narrator may have made a mistake here or there, this is no reason for brushing aside as unhistorical the large amount of material where agreement exists.

This is all the more true when we realize that the agreement between the evangelists increases, and is in fact strongest, when statements from the Savior are reported, while the variation in writing style is greater when the narrator attempts to describe the historical context. Then the narrator's individual style and manner of description play a larger role. This statistical pattern is most likely to occur in a situation in which the life and words are described of someone who was personally known to the writer or whom the writer has learned about from firsthand witnesses. After all, a narrator has more flexibility in talking about facts and circumstances than in reporting a person's own statements.

The danger of harmonization is that the differences in writing style may be handled incorrectly by being undervalued in too-facile harmonizations, or by being overvalued in hasty decisions to separate the stories. The error into which many twentieth-century scholars have fallen is to see the differences in reporting as decisive, while failing to be aware of the limited significance of these differences when viewed in the context of the Gospels as a whole with their overwhelming agreement. The difficulty today is not that scholars pay attention to the problems that arise from these differences, but rather that they come to a *categorical* judgment with regard to the quality of the historical writing in the Gospels. If a historian were to dismiss the testimonies and diaries from World War II in the same way, he would quickly run out of source material altogether. The historian first reconstructs a historical framework based on agreements among his sources and then will attempt to fit into this framework any data that at first seem anomalous. The historian is aware that historical reality is always complex and that different reports often present different aspects of that reality.

2.3.2 An Abundance of Historical Material

To reach a sound understanding of the way Jesus' life was recorded in the Gospels, it is important to realize that the narrators had an abundance of historical material before them from which they were able to choose only a limited number of elements to use in their narratives. For three years the Lord Jesus preached and taught, first in the synagogues and later in the open fields because of the growing crowds. This was not a three-year course arranged in a series of lessons, but repeated instruction to ever-changing groups of new people. Within this repetition, the variation in word choice, examples, and narrative development as well as common material played a significant role. This means that in the Gospels virtually identical sayings of Jesus can be found in different contexts. Thus we find the Lord's Prayer (the "Our Father") in the Sermon on the Mount in Matthew, but in Luke it appears at a later time (Matt. 6:9–13; Luke 11:2–4). Apparently there was a later occasion to repeat this lesson to the disciples because they had not sufficiently grasped its significance. We find the image of the lamp not being put under a bushel in several historical connections (Luke 8:16; 11:33; Matt. 5:15), but there is absolutely no reason to assume that Jesus used a particular image only once.

The same is true for the many miraculous healings: countless blind, lame, and possessed people were treated by Jesus. So a story about the healing of a blind man does not always have to refer to the same event as a comparable healing story told by another evangelist. Because of the abundance of historical material, one evangelist will tell about one thing and another evangelist about something else, while both, each in his own way, are explaining how Jesus took on himself people's burdens and infirmities.

Other events may in a sense also have been repeated. If Luke had described only the commissioning of the seventy (or the seventy-two), while Matthew and Mark described the commissioning of the Twelve, we might be tempted to say that obviously Luke's view of the commissioning was very different from that of the other evangelists. But fortunately what we discover is that Luke also describes the sending out of the Twelve (Luke 9:1–16; cf. Matt. 10:5–15; Mark 6:7–13). The commissioning of the seventy takes place in addition to this (Luke 10:1–20). We now know that the second commissioning had the force of a repetition, expansion, and intensification. History turns out to have been broader and more complex than we would have expected on the basis of Mark or Matthew alone. This kind of verification is not always possible, but the example warns us to exercise discretion: one thing does not necessarily preclude another. The announcements of coming suffering are repeated. Because all the evangelists mention that repetition, it is easier to accept it as fact. But why should we deem such a repetition less plausible if each evangelist reports only part of the series? We must not limit the scope of the investigation at the outset by overly restricting our own imaginative powers.

2.3.3 The Narrator's Perspective

Photographers and filmmakers strive to produce images that are faithful to reality, yet they must of necessity delimit the infinite three-dimensional reality around them to fit the photographic image. In the same way, narrators must select from the continuous stream of events pieces that fit in the frame of their narrative. The selected pieces may faithfully represent reality while at the same time ignoring other pieces of the same reality. When another narrator selects a slightly different piece, the reported stories seem only partially harmonious when in fact the only difference is in the diverging *perspectives* of the narrative.

Thus Matthew reports the healing of the two demoniacs in the country of the Gadarenes (Matt. 8:28–34), while both Mark (5:1–20) and Luke (8:26–39) speak of one demoniac inhabited by Legion. Neither Mark nor Luke mentions that only one person was healed that day and not two. Their story does not unequivocally rule out the possibility that someone else was healed at the same time, another demoniac who shared the main character's wildness. Nevertheless, at first glance it appears strange and improbable that two evangelists limit themselves to a story about one of these two persons. But it becomes more understandable when we note that in Mark and Luke the story ends with the preaching about this event in the Decapolis. It is quite possible that of the two men who were healed only the main character asked Jesus if he could go with him, and that only he was told to preach the story in his own region. Matthew is silent about how the day ended. For Mark and Luke, the ending is an essential element in the narrative. Because their aim is to tell about the man who became a preacher in the Decapolis, he alone is made the focus of their story, while the other person involved in the healing receives no attention at all.

Not only does the Gospel narrator's perspective play a role, but his technique does too. He may choose to finish a topic once he has started it, as Luke does (3:1–20) when he continues the narrative of John the Baptist until he reaches the moment when John the Baptist's ministry comes to an end with his arrest by Herod Antipas. Then he goes back to pick up the chronological thread at the moment when John was still at liberty and Jesus was baptized (3:21–22). Thus events that follow one another in the Gospel may actually have occurred in a different sequence. For instance, in Matthew we see a later report of the anointing of Jesus by Mary at Bethany. This event, expressed in Jesus' own words, becomes an element in the Passion: wherever the gospel of Jesus' suffering and death is told, she will also be remembered (Matt. 26:12–13). Therefore Matthew places this account among the opening words of the Passion story (Matt. 26:1–2), consciously detaching it from the time when Jesus was in Bethany (Matt. 21:1, 17). John, on the other hand, places the anointing in its chronological place: during the stay in Bethany (John 12:1–11). In this way the narrator, by means of compositional technique, may create the impression that his account contradicts those of the other evangelists, while in reality that may not have been the case.

In reading the Gospels, it is important to be aware not only of the abundance of historical material from which the author is drawing but also of the narrator's perspective and the technique he uses. In this way the reader avoids postulating contradictions that are really only differences.

2.3.4 The Reader's Perspective

In reading the Gospels, problems can also arise due to the reader's limited perspective or misdirected interest. When the evangelists wrote their accounts, they could presuppose that their readers shared with them a body of common knowledge not only about the historical context, society, and the climate of the time, but also about the life of Jesus and his apostles. Much of this prior knowledge disappeared with the passing of the generations and was unknown to later readers who lived in countries and cultures that were very different from those in which Jesus lived out his life on earth. The task of the exegete is to bridge this growing gap with supplementary information and explanations. This includes gaining insight into what exactly took place. Sometimes that can no longer be reconstructed. It is likely that the readers of Mark's Gospel knew who Simon of Cyrene was because they knew his sons, Alexander and Rufus. Without that knowledge it would have made no sense for Mark to name the sons to further identify the father (Mark 15:21). Familiarity with Alexander and Rufus provides more background to the report about Simon of Cyrene: did his sons become Christians? Or was their father already a follower? Because Alexander and Rufus are unknown to us, this incidental supplementary information is lost on the later reader.

A similar situation arises in the case of certain Jewish customs. Did people really always wash themselves when they came home from the market (Mark 7:3–4)? And what was the background of this custom? The answer is important for gaining a clear understanding of Jesus' confrontation with the scribes. Yet we lack sufficient information on this point, so that for us the history is probably somewhat more blurred than it was for the first readers. In itself this is not a problem— seeing more faded contours in contrast to the sharper ones—but it *does* become a problem when we lose sight of the fact that a blind spot has formed in our field of vision and we begin to think that we have all the necessary information. We see this when we discover that some events suddenly become clearer or that we see them in a different light when we consult a second or third Gospel. The same would happen if we could consult eyewitnesses. They would be able to clear up any misunderstandings. But because we have no such opportunity, we must be cautious in passing judgment. The conclusion that a story conflicts here or there with the story of another evangelist can never be more than a provisional opinion, calling for further inquiry or investigation. After almost two thousand years, the reader is not always in a good position for such an investigation, so it should not perplex us if some things remain unexplained. The only possible cause for perplexity would be if such unsolved problems were the rule instead of the exception.

We should also add here that the types of questions posed by later readers are often out of step with the kind of information the evangelists intended to provide. After the passing of time, thousands of curious questions arise for which the writer had no intention of providing an answer. We are curious about the precise sequence of all the events, while the evangelists, who as a rule did take note of the order of events, did not always consider this sequence important. In his description of the healing of a blind man near Jericho, for instance, Luke never set out to clarify the question as to how his story relates to comparable stories in the other accounts. Nevertheless, that does occur to us, because we see questions arising here. In short, our range of interest and the way we ask our questions often exceeds the framework within which the evangelists wrote. When their descriptions do not offer answers to these questions, it does not mean that the actual history would not have been able to bear the weight of our inquiry.

Such precise answers to all questions, however, are not needed to sustain belief in the reported facts. Modern man accepts a great many facts and events he only learns about by hearsay (radio, the press), without knowing or being able to discover the details. The opposite is also true: there were people who could have managed to acquire firsthand knowledge of everything about Jesus' life on earth and who still refused to accept the facts. The Jewish Sanhedrin heard the eyewitness account of the guards at the tomb and discussed everything thoroughly with them. The Sanhedrin was also aware (via Judas?) of Jesus' prophecy that he would rise from the dead. They had immediate access to the predictions and to the facts. Even so, they hid the facts under a purchased lie. The Christian faith rests on the facts of the gospel, but it remains faith, and for that reason it can be kept alive by Gospel accounts that tell us much, but not everything.

2.4 Conclusion

Four Gospels—one history? That was the general question of this second chapter. Our conclusion is that while harmonization sometimes tries to reach a more precise knowledge about Jesus' history than is possible, the antiharmonization mentality today spurns the many historical facts that we do find in the Gospels. The problems are not such that they justify a categorical rejection of the Gospels as reliable sources for the history of Jesus' life.[12] Indeed, such problems are to a certain extent unavoidable in a finite description of infinite reality. But this does not detract from the Gospels' historicity, although it does detract from the possibility of always obtaining a flawless image of the events. Those who respect the Gospels as witnesses of the arrival and the work of God's Son on earth, however, will gladly go to the trouble of keeping the historical image pure and as sharply focused as possible. So we cannot leave our discussion here in this second chapter with just a few general considerations but must move on to a more detailed discussion of the various periods of Jesus' life on earth.

12. See also C. L. Blomberg, *The Historical Reliability of the Gospels* (Leicester, England: Inter-Varsity, 1987). P. W. Barnett, *Jesus and the Logic of History*, New Studies in Biblical Theology 3 (Grand Rapids: Eerdmans, 1997).

3

The Periods of Jesus' Life on Earth

3.1 The Value of Periodization

The Gospels each contain a limited selection of narrative material taken from the whole history of Jesus' life on earth. In order to make a proper comparison of these selections, we need a clear picture of the historical framework within which these events took place. Dividing history into various periods is a helpful way to create an organizational structure for the data. As it turns out, all four evangelists supply markers that can be used to identify periods. We can begin by comparing these markers and later study the content of the individual Gospels period by period. When Luke, for instance, writes about things that are similar to things the other evangelists have written about, but places them in a different period, we know that for chronological reasons we cannot assume that comparable materials actually describe the same event or discourse. By locating the narratives in certain time periods we decrease the risk of incorrectly equating stories. Because Jesus repeated many sayings and miracles in a variety of forms, such an incorrect equation is a real danger and occurs relatively frequently.

A second advantage to defining periods is that it helps us get a first impression of each Gospel's unique characteristics. Finding the answer as to why an evangelist omits or highlights a particular period can help us determine or clarify his purpose in writing his account.

Dividing the life of Jesus into periods involves one or two issues that demand separate attention and are not adequately dealt with when the Gospels are simply laid side by side, story by story. Some of the divisions are self-evident—they correspond to the fixed elements in the human life. The period of birth and youth comes first; death is at the end. Some of the divisions are also obvious from the facts: the era of John the Baptist comes first, followed by the period of Jesus' ministry; the work in Galilee precedes the Passion in Jerusalem. One would have to abandon the Gospels entirely if these major divisions were dispensed with. But a number of less distinct dividing points remain—and these are the ones that affect the comparison of the Gospels. For example, the course of the period of the transition from John to Jesus and of the years of ministry in Galilee in John's account is different from accounts of those periods in the other Gospels. There is also a difference between Luke and the other evangelists when it comes to the duration and significance of the time between the departure from Galilee and the Passion in Jerusalem. These points will be the object of primary attention in the following sections.

3.2 From Birth to Baptism

Only two of the Gospels provide narratives about Jesus' birth and the period that followed, up to the beginning of his public ministry after his baptism by John. Matthew 1–2 and Luke 1–2 are the only sources here. The events they write about will be discussed in chapter 4. Here our only concern is why this period is completely absent in Mark and John. Both of them also take as their starting point the fact of the incarnation of the Son of God (Mark 1:1), the incarnation of the Word (John 1:14), but they are silent about the special events that accompanied Jesus' arrival on earth. So is it true after all that the history told in the Gospels gradually developed as a partially invented story? Are we dealing here with a historical core (ministry, misunderstanding, crucifixion) that was later embellished with well-intended but less factual or less historically based stories about birth and resurrection in order to create points of contact with the realm of God's eternity as well as setting the stage for a later Christology? Because so many scholars follow this line of reasoning when they observe that the birth narrative appears in only two Gospels, it is important to give some thought to this phenomenon.[1]

The facts of Jesus' birth and youth have just as much significance as the other facts of his life. Each day of his stay on earth was a day lived before the face of God as our substitute. Yet this first period in revelation history served a different function than the later periods. The ministry of John the Baptist attracted public attention, as did Jesus' ministry in Israel. Peter could state that Cornelius knew about all those things (Acts 10:37). And Mark reports what Peter preached, a message that began with John the Baptist (Mark 1:1–13). At first, Jesus' preaching was about the nearness of God's kingdom and the need for repentance and faith. The earlier events, Jesus' birth and youth, were not part of what was preached to the people. This does not mean that these events were supposed to be secret or remain unknown, but rather that

1. For a broader discussion, see my article "Geboortegeschiedenis als sluitstuk?" *De Reformatie* 54 (1978–79): 741–45.

they had a different place in the revelation to Israel than the preaching of the kingdom and the commandments and promises of Jesus.

The place of the earlier events can be compared to the foundations of a building: just as solid as the walls, but not immediately visible. When Jesus in his ministry and preaching does not demand attention for the special events surrounding his birth, the reason is closely linked with his humility. He never seeks honor for himself. He has come to make the Father known. He wants people to believe in him because of his words and the signs he performs. But even when the unbelief of the people causes his suffering, he does not try to escape by making a last-minute appeal to the choir of angels which some aged shepherds would still have been able to confirm. Those who feel that it is beneath them to believe in the incarnate Son of God and who choose not to accept his suffering, need no additional information about the period prior to John the Baptist. Christ did not come to Israel to read his own biography to the people but to fulfill the promises of John: forgiveness of sins and baptism with the Holy Spirit. So the birth story has no place in the Savior's teaching, and those Gospels that take his teaching as their starting point can thus tell the whole story from John to Easter without making any separate mention of the birth. This applies to Mark, and in a somewhat different way to John. John wants to show that Jesus is the Christ, and he primarily writes from his own memories of how Jesus revealed himself. The birth story is not part of the things of which he can speak and write as an eyewitness. That is why John's testimony relates to his years as a disciple, first of the Baptist and later of Jesus himself. And because Jesus did not testify about himself during that time, the early history remains in the shadows.

The circumstances of Matthew's and Luke's writing are quite different. Matthew gives Jewish Christians Jesus' genealogy (Matt. 1:1), which is why he also goes back to Jesus' beginning (Matt. 1:18). His selection of material from Jesus' birth and early years is determined by his preference for elements that refer to the fulfillment of the Scriptures. Matthew is not putting together a complete file of Jesus' history; rather, he shows on the basis of a few stories how Scripture was also fulfilled at the beginning of Jesus' life (Matt. 1:23; 2:6, 15, 18, 23).

Luke writes for Theophilus, and his intent is also to write an account "from the beginning" (Luke 1:3). His perspective is broader than Matthew's; he includes the early history of John the Baptist, as well as events around and after the birth. Luke is especially eager to write about the moments when the outside world came in contact with the facts of Jesus' early history. While in Matthew we find the intimate history of angels who spoke to Joseph in private (Matt. 1:20; 2:12, 13, 19), in Luke we read about facts that were announced to and discussed in a

broader circle (Luke 1:58, 65; 2:10, 20, 38, 46). Just as it is understandable that Mark and John are silent about the birth narrative because
Jesus himself disregarded it in his teachings, so is it understandable
that Matthew and Luke include these events because their books have
a different purpose.

For the facts had not remained unknown. The silence of the priest
Zechariah was enough to leave a whole temple court full of people
speechless; they understood that he had seen a vision while in the sanc-
tuary (Luke 1:22). Within a year the news had spread throughout the
Judean highlands and was a topic of conversation within a broad circle:
the LORD appeared to Zechariah and is doing miraculous things in his
house. He has also made this priest a prophet about things that are
going to happen soon (Luke 1:67). Not long afterward, remarkable rumors were heard in that same Judean countryside about shepherds who
had been visited by angels (Luke 2:8, 20). In Jerusalem the voice of
prophecy rings out once again in the temple, and many hear the words
of Simeon, while Anna spreads the news of Jesus' birth, with its promise
of great things to come, to all the faithful in Jerusalem (Luke 2:28, 38).
Fascinating topics of conversation for a wide range of people! Because
Jesus grows up in Nazareth and John in the desert, and because thirty
uneventful years pass after Jesus' birth, the knowledge of the events surrounding their birth lies dormant. When Jesus' ministry begins, he is
known as the man from Nazareth in Galilee (John 7:41–42). There
seems to be no reasonable way to link him with Bethlehem, because
even if he was known to have been born there, the fact remains that
Bethlehem is not his hometown. But it should not surprise us that Luke
later apparently knows of the connection between Jesus and Bethlehem, either because Luke or his parents actually lived through the event
in Judea (where they, like so many others at the time, may have resided
as non-Jews, in Jerusalem or Caesarea) or because he heard about it
from people who were present at the time. In either case, his knowledge
was supplemented by more detailed information that must have come
from Mary, possibly through an intermediary (Luke 1:26–56).

The more private family history offered by Matthew must have become known in the community through the presence of Jesus' mother
Mary and his brother James; they were able to testify to the little-known
stories of the angelic visitations in Joseph's dream and the wise men,
and to the silent period of the flight to Egypt and the time spent outside
Palestine. They also knew why the family did not return to Bethlehem
but went to live in Nazareth. And it is not impossible that Jesus later explained the scriptural reasons behind all this to his family, so that Matthew's fulfillment quotes may have come from James's memories of
Jesus' own teaching. We know that Jesus surprised the elders with his

knowledge when he was only twelve years old (Luke 2:47), and that he increased in wisdom even during his childhood and youth (Luke 2:40, 52). Why would his mother and brothers not remember the wisdom with which he spoke to them about the family's eventful history during the time of his arrival and his early years? Even when they initially rejected this teaching in their unbelief (John 7:3–5), it still remained in their memories and could later be activated through the awakening of faith. Matthew, who is one of the apostles and has had close contact with Jesus' family members in Jerusalem, is able to begin at the beginning, with his origins of Jesus Christ, thanks to firsthand information.

From a historical-biographical standpoint, the period of Jesus' birth and youth is qualitatively similar to the periods that followed in his life. But from the standpoint of *revelation history* this first period is quite different from the later ones. Christmas sermons are only preached after Easter has taken place, not because these events did not exist or were not known earlier, but because it is the privilege of the believer to praise the beginnings of him who himself was silent about those beginnings in his preaching in order to draw all attention to his teaching and suffering for the atonement of sin. In retrospect everything appears to have been intended from the beginning, and Matthew and Luke write about that beginning to provide believers with certainty about the things they have been taught (Luke 1:4).

3.3 From Jesus' Baptism to John's Arrest

All four evangelists include the narrative of Jesus' baptism in the Jordan (Matt. 3:13–17; Mark 1:9–11; Luke 3:21–22) or a recollection of that event (John 1:32–34). And three of the evangelists closely link the baptism with the temptation in the wilderness (Matt. 4:1–11; Mark 1:12–13; Luke 4:1–13). No doubt is possible: baptism and temptation together are a historical and chronological unit.

Following this, however, the first three evangelists jump ahead in time. They describe how Jesus emerged as John's successor after the baptism and temptation. For this reason they jump ahead to the moment when John was arrested and Jesus carried on with John's preaching in Galilee (Matt. 4:12–17; Mark 1:14–15; Luke 4:14–15). Luke does not mention John's arrest in so many words, but in chapter 3 he had already stated that John's ministry led to his arrest (Luke 3:18–20). In Luke 7:18 we also see that John was already in prison when "all these things" that Luke tells about in 4:14–7:17 took place; John heard about them from his disciples. The first three Gospels indicate that there is a seam between the baptism and the ministry in Galilee, but they do not indicate whether this was a period of any importance, since it falls outside the focus of their narrative. We might even get the impression that Jesus went to preach in Galilee immediately after the temptation in the wilderness. But on closer inspection this appears to be no more than an impression, since the first three evangelists date Jesus' ministry in Galilee not from the date of the temptation, but from the date of John's arrest. Since that moment is not discussed any further, the evangelists clearly suggest that there is a period between Jesus' baptism and John's arrest about which they say nothing.

John does provide us with a description of events that belong to this period, and from his Gospel we can deduce that it was an interval of some duration. John is intent on offering us his own memories of Jesus as the Christ, the Son of God, and because of this he cannot report any material about the birth. What he can do, however, is make his own contribution to what might be called the "preliminary history" of the Galilean ministry. John spent that time as a disciple, first of John the Baptist and then as an early disciple of Jesus, and that is why it is important for people from a later period to learn how even at that time Jesus spoke about himself and performed publicly the signs and wonders that revealed who he was.

In John 3:28 John the Baptist appears to be still active. The material that precedes this point in John's book is presented in chronological order. It covers events from five consecutive days (John 1:19–28; 1:29–34; 1:35–43; 1:44–52; 2:1–11) as well as incidents that took place afterward in Capernaum (2:12) and in Jerusalem (2:13–3:21). After this comes a period in which Jesus baptized in Judea (3:22–36). Only in chapter 4 do we read about the return to Galilee after the Passover Feast (4:13; cf. 4:43–45). In the meantime winter has come (4:35). The reason for the withdrawal to Galilee is that the Pharisees have noticed that Jesus' following has become larger than John's (4:1). Evidently the evangelist sees an implicit threat in this—the Pharisees' observation is hostile. A prophet has no honor in his own country (Israel, and specifically Jerusalem), so Jesus moves to the north of Galilee, where he will be better received (4:43–45).

The observation that Jesus is gaining more followers than John can constitute a genuine threat to Jesus only if John has already been seized, arrested, or killed as a dangerous person. So the moment of the return to Galilee, about nine months after Jesus had gone to Jerusalem and Judea, must coincide with the arrest of John the Baptist, as the first three evangelists indicate. It should not surprise us, therefore, that on his next visit to Jerusalem to celebrate a feast, Jesus speaks of John's ministry in the past tense: "John *was* a lamp that burned and gave light" (5:35).

The Gospel of John suggests that the period between the baptism and the ministry in Galilee lasted about ten months. In the narrative focus of the first three evangelists these months are merely a bridge, a transition: only after John's arrest did Jesus step forward as the one to follow John and continue to preach about the kingdom that is coming soon. But John the evangelist throws light on the period when Jesus was still working more or less in the Baptist's shadow. The later image of Jesus as John's successor gains in power when we can see its contours beginning to take shape already during this early period.

3.4 The Galilean Period and the Gospel of John

The first three evangelists mark the *beginning* of the Galilean period (after John's arrest) as clearly as they mark its *end*. The moment when Jesus left for his last journey to Jerusalem is clearly defined (Matt. 19:1; Mark 10:1, cf. 9:30; Luke 9:51), which makes the Galilean period easily recognizable in the first three Gospels.

The situation is quite different in John's Gospel. At first it seems as though John knows absolutely nothing about a long and extensive ministry in Galilee. In John we encounter Jesus much more often in Jerusalem. This is not surprising for the period before the arrest of the Baptist, but it seems strange for the time thereafter. Yet John 5 and 7–10 take place almost entirely in Jerusalem. What we have here, however, is possibly an optical illusion. John's narrative is very selective; he takes drawn-out memories and strings them together. What seems like an overview of Jesus' life is in reality chronologically arranged snapshots of a much longer period. John prefers snapshots taken in Jerusalem. He sketches the meeting between Jesus and the most prominent leaders and shows how Christ bore witness to himself in the country's capital. This approach may give the impression that the Galilean period is virtually absent. On closer inspection, however, we see that although large sections of the Galilean ministry are absent from John's writing, they were not absent from his awareness. Between the lines, John lets us see that for a long time Galilee was the real setting, and that in fact Jerusalem came into the picture only now and then, during visits on the occasion of religious festivals. The fact that John highlights these particular events does not detract from the general pattern that we see more clearly in the other evangelists. For example, we read in John 7 that Jesus' brothers are irritated because he is carrying out his ministry mainly in Galilee. It is John rather than the other evangelists who notes this fact, so he appears to be well aware of the Galilean ministry (John 7:1–4). John also knows that in Jerusalem Jesus is considered a Galilean whose field of activity is the hinterland (John 7:41, 52). Thus John carefully indicates that the Jerusalem episodes that he describes in great detail occurred during feasts, when Galileans came to the capital city and

Jesus was often among them (John 5:1; 7:10). The difference between John and the other three evangelists on this point is only apparent and disappears under careful comparison.

But is the reverse also true? John may presuppose a long Galilean ministry, but are the other three aware of the festival journeys to Jerusalem? To put it another way: the festival journeys in John presume that the Galilean ministry lasted quite a long time; do the Synoptics also describe a longer period or do they see it as a much shorter time, a year at most? It is often suggested that the accounts contradict each other on this point, but that is not the case. In Luke 13:34 we read that Jesus often visited Jerusalem, although Luke says no more about those journeys or about what happened while he was on the road ("O Jerusalem, Jerusalem, . . . how often I have longed to gather your children together"). We must also consider the possibility that Mark and Matthew assumed that the journeys to Jerusalem took place, although they do not write about them. After all, there is no reason to believe that Jesus did not do what every other religious Galilean did. It would have been more worthy of mention if he had always stayed home during the feasts than if he had made the normal trips to Jerusalem.

This line of reasoning would not be appropriate if the first evangelists were clearly assuming a period of less than one year, in which case there would have been no time for more than a few festival journeys. There are indirect indications, however, that the Galilean ministry did last more than one year, even according to the first evangelists.

1. The episode concerning picking heads of grain on the Sabbath (Matt. 12:1–8; Mark 2:23–28; Luke 6:1–5) occurs shortly after a Passover Feast. Harvest time is approaching (in most manuscripts, the Sabbath in Luke 6:1 is designated as "the second first Sabbath," which may refer to the beginning of the new liturgical year during the Passover month).
2. We find a second seasonal designation in a *later* episode: the miraculous feeding of the five thousand. This took place when the grass was green (Mark 6:39), which happens on the barren steppe only in spring (Matt. 14:13; Mark 6:31–33; Luke 9:12).

These details in the first three Gospels indicate that the period of the Galilean ministry began in the winter after the journey through Samaria (John 4:35), and that two spring periods followed before the Passion journey began. So the Galilean ministry lasted at least a year and a half or two years.

The information in John forces us in the same direction. Because he reports high points from events and speeches that took place in the context of feasts in Jerusalem, his Gospel can more easily serve as a means of determining the *duration* of a period.

The Passover Feast mentioned in John 2 is not being considered here because it occurred in the period after the baptism by John but before the journey to Galilee. The Passover in John 11:55 also falls outside this discussion, since that was the Passover of Jesus' death, and the Galilean period had obviously ended by then. The same is true for the Feast of Dedication mentioned in John 10:22: prior to and following this feast Jesus was no longer staying in Galilee but in Perea. In John 10:40 we read that Jesus *again* departed for the other side of the Jordan, to the place where John had been baptizing in the early days. This is Bethany on the other side of the Jordan (John 1:28), to be distinguished from Aenon near Salim where John baptized later (John 3:23). This Bethany across the Jordan lay outside Judea (cf. John 10:40 with 11:7) and also outside Galilee (cf. John 1:28 with 1:44). Jesus' stay in Bethany on the other side of the Jordan, interrupted by a journey for the Feast of Dedication, belongs to the period after the Galilean ministry.

In the remaining part of John's Gospel (4:1–10:21), we read about a Passover in 6:4 and a Feast of Tabernacles in 7:2. In 5:1 we read about a "feast of the Jews"; this preceded the Passover mentioned in chapter 6 (cf. John 6:1–2). What sort of feast was this? It takes place after the winter of John 4 and before the Passover of chapter 6. This means that it could have been any feast of the liturgical year, and for the following reason: the first feast following the winter in chapter 4 is a Passover. Because the feast of the Jews in chapter 5 comes before the Passover of chapter 6, this last-mentioned Passover cannot have immediately followed the period of John 4. In other words, between the arrival in Galilee during the winter and the Passover of John 6, a year and a few months have elapsed. Sometime during that period the feast of the Jews mentioned in chapter 5 takes place. After the Passover of chapter 6 comes the Feast of Tabernacles (John 7), still in the Galilean period. This means that Jesus' work in the north lasted at least from the winter (John 4) to the Feast of Tabernacles in the second year thereafter—a period of about a year and nine or ten months, perhaps even longer!

So on closer inspection it appears that both John and the other three evangelists had knowledge of the Galilean ministry, which lasted at least close to two years. Although the attention they pay to this period differs, all four Gospels know of its length and its significance. The most elaborate descriptions are in Matthew and Mark, which is not surprising. The apostles Matthew and Peter (the source of Mark) received their calling and instructions in Galilee. From Galilee they were sent to preach throughout Israel and to cast out evil spirits. For them, much of what happened in the later period involved repetition and disappointment. The fresh enthusiasm with which they had begun wanes during their journey to Jerusalem; they are prepared to die with Jesus, but they no longer travel around performing healing miracles and casting out demons. A new wave of deep emotional involvement came during the Passion Week: first the inspiring sounds of the hosannas and then the disillusionment of the arrest and flight.

For someone like Luke, as for many in Israel, the situation is different because he was not one of the original servants of the Word (Luke 1:1–2). He pays proportionately less attention to the Galilean period because he is more interested in the period of travel. This time of travel was of great significance for the ever-growing crowds, and Luke the observer was perfectly willing to give this period its due. For John, the point is not the various periods of Jesus' ministry but rather the selected testimonies about Christ that can be found in every period. That is why he too pays attention to the travel period, albeit indirectly, as the following section shows.

3.5 The Journey from Galilee to Jerusalem

In one verse, Matthew and Mark take us from Galilee via Perea to the Judean landscape. In Matthew we read, "When Jesus had finished saying these things, he left Galilee and went into the region of Judea to the other side of the Jordan" (19:1). One could travel straight from Galilee through Samaria to Judea without encountering the Jordan on the way (as in John 4, for instance), but Matthew clearly says that Jesus followed another route that ran through Perea, by which one would enter Judea from the east by crossing the Jordan. Mark has a comparable statement: "Jesus then left that place and went into the region of Judea and across the Jordan" (10:1). This passage is rather puzzling; Mark probably mentions first the most distant region to which Jesus traveled and then the region he visited on the way. If so, it might have been better to mention the regions in reverse order. In many manuscripts this verse reads differently: "He went to the region of Judea through the region beyond the Jordan." Because in the rest of the story Mark mentions only Jerusalem as the destination, we may assume that in 10:1 it was his intention to refer to Jesus' entering into *Judea*. This means that both Matthew and Mark knew about a journey through Perea but decided not to discuss it further.

It is very different in Luke, who speaks of this journey in elaborate detail. It even becomes something of a theme in part of his Gospel—the journey to Jerusalem. Luke sees the final destination, Jerusalem, on the horizon from the very beginning of the journey in Galilee, and no matter how long and roundabout the journey may be, he keeps reminding

us of the goal by pointing to it repeatedly. We find these repeated re-
minders after the beginning of the journey (9:51, 57) in 10:1, 38; 13:22;
14:25; 17:11. The material between these points deviates from that in
the other Gospels and either is not found there or is quite different.
Only after 18:15 does Luke run again more or less parallel to the first
two evangelists. So his so-called travelogue takes place largely before
and simultaneous with Matthew 19:1–2 and Mark 10:1–2, where both
of these evangelists move the stage in the span of two verses from Galilee to Judea. This means that more than a third of Luke's Gospel takes
place in the transition between two verses in Matthew and Mark, a phenomenon that has attracted much attention.

It is often held that Luke here has, unhistorically and artificially, created his own block of narrative material by bringing together a lot of the
material that the others had already used in the Galilean period. This
view is based on the observation that many of Jesus' pronouncements
the first two evangelists report as having been made in Galilee are recorded in almost the same way in Luke during the travelogue. Yet there
must have been an abundance of similar healings and repeated teachings (see section 2.3.2). Therefore, if Luke's account of Jesus' activity
and teaching during the journey strongly resembles that of the Galilean
ministry in the other Gospels, it does not necessarily mean that he talks
about the same events as the other Gospels.

On the other hand, it is of course possible that an evangelist has chosen to arrange certain materials thematically rather than chronologically or topographically. So we may indeed consider the possibility that
Luke's travelogue is his own compilation of earlier historical events.

But several facts argue against this view.

1. A great many of the *pronouncements* of Jesus in this travelogue
   are unique and are not found in the other Gospels (many of the
   parables, for instance).
2. A *smaller number* of the pronouncements of Jesus are comparable
   or similar to sayings that the other evangelists report during the
   Galilean ministry. But Jesus' teachings are full of repetition, both
   when speaking to the crowds and when teaching the disciples.
   Therefore Luke could quite easily have recorded a later version of
   the same teaching because he spends less time writing about the
   Galilean period.
3. The *events* that take place during the journey are without parallel
   in the Galilean period.
4. The pronouncements of Jesus in the travelogue almost always
   form a cohesive *unit* with the narrated events (table conversation,
   discourse in response to a question, etc.).

5. In the travelogue there are *no motives* for arranging the material in any particular way (such as, for example, the question of clean and unclean, the meaning of discipleship, etc.). It is impossible to find a motive for Luke's creation of an artificial arrangement of his material. The only possible motive could have been the travel theme, but this is merely a thin historical thread that is used to connect the various events.

So our conclusion must be that Luke intended the travelogue as he presents it: a report of what took place during the journey about which the first two apostles have so little to say. In the previous section we discussed the possible causes for the difference in emphasis in the accounts of this period of travel. What the apostles experienced as a dark tunnel leading to Jerusalem, for which they could not understand the reason, was an impressive mass event for people on the outside. That is why Luke the outsider pays so much attention to this period. Another reason might be that the unremitting compassion of the Savior, despite increasing rejection, made a deep impression on him.

Although John offers no description of the journey, we can deduce from his Gospel that there was a period of some length between the departure from Galilee and the last stay in Judea. We have already seen in John 10:40–42 that both before and after his visit on the Feast of Dedication (John 10:22–39) Jesus stayed at Bethany across the Jordan, where John the Baptist performed his first baptisms (see section 3.4). Jesus does not make a definite move into Judea—where it has become very dangerous for him—until the illness and death of Lazarus make it necessary (John 11:7–8, 16). After the raising of Lazarus, the Sanhedrin begins to discuss the possibility of killing Jesus. He therefore decides to stop moving freely among the people and goes from the Bethany of Lazarus (in Judea) back to the desert, to the hamlet of Ephraim (John 11:53–54). Passover is almost at hand (John 11:55). The retreat in Ephraim must have been very brief, because Jesus is back in Bethany in Judea six days before the Passover (John 12:1). During this short retreat, the people did not know where Jesus was (John 11:57).

So we see in John the following sequence of events:

1. Stay in Bethany across the Jordan.
2. Visit to Jerusalem for the Feast of Dedication.
3. Further stay in Bethany across the Jordan.
4. Journey to Bethany in Judea; raising of Lazarus.
5. Short retreat in Ephraim.
6. Traveling through Bethany in Judea on the way to Jerusalem.

Matthew and Mark skip numbers 1–3 as well as number 5. The material they present as having taken place during the time after Jesus had arrived in Judea but had not yet begun the official final journey toward Jerusalem must be assigned to period 4 (Matt. 19:1–20:16; Mark 10:1–31). The material that follows in Matthew 20:17 and following and Mark 10:32 and following belongs to period 6 and thereafter.

Luke provides much more travel information, so this allows us to fill in more of the periods that are indirectly hinted at in John. Thus the events from Luke 9:51–10:37 can be placed in the journey through Perea that ended with the first stay in Bethany across the Jordan (period 1 in the list above). The visit with Mary and Martha (Luke 10:38–42) could have taken place during the visit to Jerusalem on the Feast of Dedication (John 10:22–39), which then coincides with period 2. Thereafter Jesus was again in Bethany on the other side of the Jordan (period 3). In an environment where everything reminded people of John the Baptist, the disciples ask Jesus to teach them to pray as John taught his disciples to pray (Luke 11:1). The crowds come and gather around Jesus (Luke 11:14–29; 12:1). From this Bethany, Jesus travels in the region across the Jordan (Luke 13:10, 22). Then comes the time for the final journey to Judea, where he will die. Luke describes that moment in 13:31–35. According to the Pharisees, Herod Antipas is threatening to deal with Jesus as he did with the earlier prophet who baptized near Bethany. Jesus indicates that he does not want to evade death but to take it upon himself in Jerusalem. For this reason Herod must simply be told that Jesus (without allowing himself to be intimidated) intends to go on with his work in Perea for a few more days. He will use those days to complete his work there and to travel to Judea. We must apparently take the days Jesus refers to in Luke 13:31–35 literally. The definitive transition from Perea to Judea comes a few days after the announcement of Herod Antipas's threat. Jesus must "keep going today and tomorrow and the next day" (Luke 13:33) in order to leave Herod's jurisdiction and enter that of Jerusalem. Jesus makes this journey during the days of Lazarus's illness and death and does not leave Perea and enter Bethany in Judea until a few days after Lazarus's death (John 11:6–7, 17; this is period 4). Because the days of travel from Perea to Bethany in Judea include a Sabbath (Luke 14:1), it took more than one or two days to cover a rather short distance. During this time Jesus is mobbed by the multitudes. Crowds of people travel with him, and another crowd comes from Jerusalem to join them, drawn by the report of the raising of Lazarus (Luke 14:25; John 11:45).

Only at the end of Luke 14:1–18:30 do we again find material that runs parallel with Matthew and Mark (Luke 18:15–30). So the announcement of the journey to Jerusalem in Luke 18:31 heralds the period *after* the retreat in Ephraim.

The parable of the rich man and the poor Lazarus has a unique characteristic: the use of a proper name. This parable has a surprising transparency if it was told just before or just after the raising of the actual Lazarus from the dead. Indeed, the return of Lazarus brought no change in the faithless attitude of many of the people, and it confirmed how true the parable really is. Those who do not listen to the *Law and the Prophets* will also not be brought into line by the return of another *Lazarus*. Perhaps now we can better understand why the wonderful raising of Lazarus, who had already been dead four days, is not even mentioned by the first three evangelists but is given such detailed attention by John. Seen from the disciples' perspective, the raising of Lazarus has not changed anything, and Jesus had already raised other dead people anyway. But for John it is new and strong evidence for what he is constantly trying to show: Jesus is the Christ, the Son of God.

The only fact that seems to be in conflict with the sketch of the traveling period presented here is found in Luke 17:11–19, the story of the healing of the ten lepers, of whom only one—a Samaritan—returns to thank Jesus. According to the above reconstruction, at the time of Luke 17 Jesus is traveling from Perea to Bethany or has already arrived there. Yet in Luke 17:11 we read, "Now on his way to Jerusalem, Jesus traveled along the border between Samaria and Galilee." This remark is very confusing. We get the impression that the story of the returning Samaritan leper took place before Jesus arrived in Perea and long before he went from Perea to Bethany. We must, however, draw a clear distinction between the period when the healing was performed and the moment of the Samaritan's return. The encounter with the ten lepers took place when Jesus, at the beginning of his journey, was traveling along the border of Galilee in the direction of Perea. He came up against the border with Samaria and probably followed a road that ran alternatingly through Galilean and Samaritan territory. The lepers were ordered to go to the priest in Jerusalem and to show themselves to him. Part of this "showing" was the ceremony of purification—a ceremony that took weeks to perform. When one then adds the journey from northern Samaria to the temple city, it is clear that in the meantime Jesus would have advanced a long way on his own journey before the healed lepers could return to him.

We also need to be aware of the fact that Jesus' words ("Where are the other nine?") assume that enough time has passed for the lepers to have made the journey to the temple and to have completed the ceremonial requirements. There had also been enough time for them to search for the Master somewhere in Palestine and to thank him. Luke tells the story not for the sake of the healing but because of Jesus' words to the one thankful Samaritan. These words are spoken long after Jesus traveled along the border between Galilee and Samaria. The story is placed in the period just before or in Bethany at the time of the raising of Lazarus, so the introductory formula refers backward in narrative time. In order to understand what is going on when Jesus is approached by a grateful Samaritan, we need to know beforehand that while Jesus was traveling on the journey just described through the borderland between Samaria and Galilee, he healed ten lepers. The conclusion of that incident (as well as the incident itself) is told when Jesus is almost at the end of the journey and he is about to go to Jerusalem. It was then, after all, that the end of the story took place, to the surprise of all the bystanders. They had probably forgotten the healing. How moving then is the Samaritan's expression of gratitude!

3.6 The Period of Jesus' Death, Resurrection, and Ascension

We can be brief about this last period. All four evangelists describe it in detail. The eyes of the apostles were later opened to Jesus' own announcement of the approaching Passion, and they came to understand that this was the purpose and high point of his life's work. In a fuller discussion of this short period (chapters 16–17), we will concern ourselves with the various problems that arise here when comparing the details of the Gospels. With the abundance of narrative material, the approach taken by all four evangelists, the briefness of the period, and the magnitude of the events, any effort to set down the details with precision runs into difficulty because the threads of the events are not always easy to untangle. But the period as such can easily be identified in all four Gospels.

3.7 Periodization and Chronology

The designation of periods involves the fixing of time spans of particular lengths within which various events took place. In addition to verifying the existence of such periods and determining their sequence, one can also attempt to establish their absolute length. This leads us to the chronology of the New Testament.

Chronology is a complex matter. On the basis of often complicated combinations of historical facts from different areas, one must try to find specific dates that correspond to the historical chronological data and allow for the necessary time between the various events. A detailed treatment of the chronology of Jesus' life would lead us into too many secondary issues. For this reason we are limiting the discussion to a summary of what has been given broader treatment elsewhere.[2]

The only date we find in the New Testament is in Luke 3:1: "In the fifteenth year of the reign of Tiberius Caesar," which is the period of August 19, A.D. 28–August 19, A.D. 29. It depends on the method of calculation whether the fifteenth year of Tiberius coincides with this period in part or entirely. Roughly speaking, we can say that the reference is to A.D. 28 or 29. During that year, as Luke says, the word of God came to John in the desert. So the ministry of John the Baptist began no earlier than A.D. 28 or 29.

Jesus did not come immediately to John for baptism. If we consider that John's preaching gradually became well known so that finally the entire populace flocked to him, and that Jesus was among them, we can state that Jesus' baptism occurred no earlier than in the middle of A.D. 28, and probably somewhat later.

At the time of his baptism, Luke says, Jesus was "about thirty years old" (3:23). This is not exact, but it characterizes Jesus as a man in his early to mid-thirties, no older. So the date of his birth must be set before the year that now (incorrectly) serves as the beginning of the Christian era.

We know that Jesus was born before the death of Herod the Great. Herod died around 1 Nisan, 4 B.C. Because Jesus came to earth during a season in which the cattle were still grazing on the summer steppes (Luke 2:8, 15), the birth can be dated no later than the summer of 5 B.C. In this case, he would have been 32 or 33 at the beginning of A.D. 29 or A.D. 30 respectively. This age corresponds with Luke's characterization of him: a man "about thirty years old."

We cannot place the date of Jesus' birth much earlier than this. For one thing, it would be less realistic to call him "about thirty years old" if he were much older than 32 or 33 at the moment of his baptism. Also, a birth in approximately 8 B.C. is out of the question, because when Jesus attends the Passover feast in Jerusalem at the age of twelve (Luke 2:40–52), the atmosphere is carefree. This would not have been the case if Archelaus had still been governor, but fear of him does not figure into the story (Matt. 2:22). This means that Jesus did not turn twelve until Archelaus had been deposed in A.D. 6. So working backward, we can calculate that he could have been born no earlier than 7 B.C., but the

2. Compare my *"Na veertien jaren": De datering van het in Galaten 2 genoemde overleg te Jeruzalem* (Kampen: Kok, 1973), 65–113, and my "The Year of the Death of Herod the Great," in *Miscellanea Neotestamentica*, ed. T. Baarda et al. (Leiden: Brill, 1978), 2:1–15. See also the discussion on Luke 2:2 in my commentary on Luke (*Lucas: Het evangelie als voorgeschiedenis*, Commentaar op het Nieuwe Testament, 3d series [Kampen: Kok, 1993]).

Chronology of the Life of Christ

6 B.C.	-*	summer–autumn	Period of preparation
5 B.C.	-	spring–summer	Birth
5 B.C.	-	summer–autumn	Flight to Egypt
4 B.C.	+		Return from Egypt, settling in Nazareth
9 A.D.	-	spring	Visit to the temple at age twelve
28	+		Beginning of John the Baptist's ministry
30	-	beginning of the year	Baptism of Jesus
30	-	shortly before Passover	Stay in Cana/Capernaum
30	-	spring until winter	Stay in Judea
31	-	early January	Journey through Samaria to Galilee
31	-	spring	Sabbath conflicts (picking heads of grain)
31	-		Healing the lame man in Jerusalem (festival visit)
32	-	Passover season	First miraculous feeding of the five thousand
32	-	autumn	Feast of the Tabernacles in Jerusalem
32		late autumn	Departure from Galilee to Perea
32		December	Feast of Dedication in Jerusalem
33		beginning	Further stay in Perea
33		February?	To Judea; raising of Lazarus
33		late March	Retreat in Ephraim
33		early April	To Jerusalem
33		April	Crucifixion and resurrection
33		late May	Ascension

*The symbol (-) means that the event may have happened one year earlier than the year indicated. The symbol (+) means the event may have happened one year later.

phrase "about thirty years old" in Luke 3:23 makes 6 or 5 B.C. more likely.

If Jesus was baptized in the year A.D. 28 (no earlier than the middle of that year) or A.D. 29, then the Passover at which he performed the sign in the temple (John 2) could have been no earlier than A.D. 29 and more likely it was in A.D. 30.

Between this Passover and that of his death at least three full years passed. In discussing the various periods (see 3.3 and 3.4), we concluded that two of the Passover Feasts occurred during the Galilean period. So the earliest possible year for the crucifixion would be A.D. 32. This year cannot be correct, however, because neither 14 nor 15 Nisan fell on a Friday that year, as we learn from astronomical data combined with calculations from the Jewish calendar. This means that Jesus' death is to be dated in the year A.D. 33. (A date of A.D. 34 is possible based on calculations from the Gospels, but it is less probable on the basis of Pauline chronology.)

Almost every element of this chronological summary could be discussed in more detail, as could objections to it. But many who approach chronology as a comprehensive *system* rather than as a collection of conclusions based on incidental bits and pieces of data by and large arrive at the same results as those offered here.[3] The list of dates in the adjacent table is an unavoidably sketchy summary.

---

3. For example, G. Ogg, *The Chronology of the Public Ministry of Jesus* (Cambridge: Cambridge University Press, 1940); H. W. Hoehner, *Chronological Aspects of the Life of Christ* (Grand Rapids: Zondervan, 1977).

4
Birth and Youth in Joseph's House

Between Jesus' birth and the beginning of his public ministry following his baptism by John is a space of more than thirty years. Compared with the few years that were to follow, we can say that almost the entire life of Jesus on earth took place before the period the Gospels describe in such detail.

Mark indirectly suggests that Jesus worked as a carpenter, and that is how he was known in Nazareth (Mark 6:3). How many years might he have spent at this trade? As the son of a carpenter (Matt. 13:55), he could have been trained at an early age by his father Joseph. He may have worked for more than twenty years as a craftsman, helping with the construction of new buildings in Galilean cities such as Sepphoris, one of Nazareth's neighboring towns. Yet what we know about these decades amounts to little more than Luke's summary statement, "And Jesus grew in wisdom and stature, and in favor with God and men" (Luke 2:52).

In the previous chapter (3.2), we discussed how the period of Jesus' birth and youth occupies a place of its own in *revelation* history. This explains why the evangelists present only a limited amount of information about the extraordinary acts of God in the birth of Jesus, and why they concentrate on the period in which Jesus revealed himself to the people as the Son of the Father. We learn enough to join with the angels in praising God's good will toward men at Jesus' birth (Luke 2:13–14), but not enough to offer any kind of biographical sketch of the first thirty years of Jesus' life.

Therefore this chapter will only be concerned with the episodes that are discussed in the Gospels. In the first two sections we will compare the material found in Matthew and Luke, and we will address a few problem areas that emerge from this comparison. The third section will deal with Jesus' genealogies: in what way does Jesus belong to the family of David? Next we will explore in some detail the composition of Joseph's family and the question as to whether Jesus' brothers and sisters were also children of Mary. This requires an in-depth study of the Gospels that will occupy a chapter by itself.

4.1 Preparation and Birth

Luke discusses the events that attracted the attention of many before and during Jesus' birth. First there is the strange incident in the temple: at the end of the midday prayer, the priest on duty, one Zechariah, was not able to bless the people. It was assumed that he had had a vision of Yahweh while in the temple. Later that year, word spread through the Judean hill country that a son had been born to this same aged priest, and that at the birth the priest's tongue was loosened in words of prophecy. Luke describes the events behind the rumors: the appearance of Gabriel to Zechariah in the temple (Luke 1:5–25) and the birth of John the Baptist, the forerunner of the Lord himself (Luke 1:57–80).

That same year a group of shepherds saw a vision of angels, who spoke about the birth of the Savior in Bethlehem. And in Jerusalem all who awaited Jerusalem's redemption heard from an old woman, Anna, about the birth. Here again Luke provides the background of the stories: the appearance of Gabriel to Mary to announce the birth of God's own Son and to prepare her for becoming Jesus' mother (Luke 1:26–38); the prophetic song Mary sang while visiting Elizabeth, and her three-month stay there (Luke 1:39–56); the journey of Joseph and Mary to Bethlehem and the birth of Jesus in the city of David (Luke 2:1–7); the announcement to the shepherds of his birth (Luke 2:8–20); and the circumcision of Jesus on the eighth day (Luke 2:21).

Matthew also tells about Jesus' birth, but he limits himself to the events that occurred within the family. It became known that Mary was pregnant by the Holy Spirit. An angel then prepared Joseph to care for his betrothed wife and the child. The child was to be the promised Immanuel of the house of David, and the angel told Joseph that at his birth the child was to be given the name Jesus (Matt. 1:18–25).

The narratives of Matthew and Luke are like two roads that cross each other but because of an overpass never touch. Yet they do seem to presuppose the same circumstances on several points. In both accounts the birth takes place in Bethlehem and the mother is the Virgin Mary. And in both accounts Joseph is the man who protects Mary and accepts the child as his own, although the child was not fathered by him but by the Holy Spirit. This information is known in the family and by Joseph. In Matthew 1:18 we read that Mary "was found to be with child through the Holy Spirit." The verb (*heurethē*) refers to an observation by others, in this case the family and Joseph. It does not say that she "was found to be with child," but that she "was found to be with child through the Holy Spirit." Matthew does not tell us how such a thing could have been known, but Luke's information does suggest an answer to this question. Mary stayed for three months in the home of Zechariah and Elizabeth,

who were "upright in the sight of the Lord." There was absolutely no
reason to suspect that Mary had committed adultery during this time.
However, she appears to have become pregnant during her stay. What
is more, Elizabeth's child miraculously leaped in her womb when Mary
entered her house, and Elizabeth, a woman of faith, respected in Israel,
was prompted by the Holy Spirit to call Mary "mother of my Lord"
(Luke 1:41–44). In addition, she appeared to know about the angel's appearance to Mary before Mary was able to tell her about it (Luke 1:45).
All this supports Mary's own story about what Gabriel had told her, so
that the only possible conclusion was that her pregnancy was "of the
Holy Spirit."

At first Joseph hesitates to take Mary as his wife because God has en-
listed her for a very special and holy purpose. But the angel convinces
him otherwise in a dream and even tells him that he has a job to do: the
promised Savior will come to the house of David, and Joseph may receive him on behalf of the house of David. Joseph will be both set aside
and involved.[1]

Mary was already pledged to be married to Joseph. That meant that
they were subject to all the obligations and responsibilities of marriage,
even though their marriage had not yet been consummated. A pledge to
be married could only be terminated by divorce. If any child was born
during this period prior to marriage, it belonged to the man to whom
the woman was pledged to be married. Joseph chooses a course of action suited to the exceptional situation: he takes Mary as his wife but
has no marital relations with her until she has given birth to the holy
child. Thus Joseph maintains his respect for the work of the Spirit and
at the same time assumes the duties that have been laid upon him
(Matt. 1:24–25).

Luke says that Joseph traveled to Bethlehem with Mary "who was
pledged to be married to him and was expecting a child." Doesn't this
contradict what we find in Matthew, who assumes that Joseph took
Mary as his wife immediately after the appearance of the angel? Although this would seem to be the case, Luke actually says exactly the
same thing as Matthew. The fact that Joseph goes to Bethlehem with
Mary proves that he has already taken Mary as his wife. But Luke does
not say with so many words that Joseph had no marital relations with
her until the child was born. So he indicates the uniqueness of the situation in his own way: Joseph took her along on the journey to Bethlehem, but she went with him as if she were still pledged to him instead of
married to him. Luke describes the situation *de facto*, Matthew, *de jure*.

---

1. See my commentary on Matt. 1:18–25 (*Matteüs: Het evangelie voor Israël*, 2d ed.,
Commentaar op het Nieuwe Testament, 3d series [Kampen: Kok, 1994]).

What is striking in both Matthew and Luke is that Jesus' birth is both brought about and announced by God himself—through Gabriel to Zechariah and Mary; through angels to the shepherds; through the prophetic inspiration of Elizabeth, Zechariah, Simeon, and Anna to many around them; through an angel in a dream to Joseph. It is this revelation of God through Jesus' birth and through the events surrounding it that determines the choice of material: later readers would find here indisputable evidence for the uniqueness of Jesus Christ. He is not a person who managed to gain influence, but he is God's Son who surrendered his influence to become a human being, a man in David's house—a house that had declined into the insignificance of Bethlehem, the family seat.

4.2 From Bethlehem to Nazareth

Both Matthew and Luke show us how, after the birth in Bethlehem, the life of Jesus and his parents continued in Nazareth. In Luke the transition to Nazareth seems unproblematic and matter-of-fact. We read: "When Joseph and Mary had done everything required by the Law of the Lord, they returned to Galilee to their own town of Nazareth" (Luke 2:39)—as if there had been no flight to Egypt and as if Joseph, on the return from Egypt, had not intended to go to Judea and went to Galilee only out of fear of Archelaus and by order of an angel (Matt. 2:13–23). How can these two evangelists write such very different reports of the journey from Bethlehem to Nazareth?

In considering this question we need to realize that Matthew and Luke may be writing about the same person but that they are doing so independently of each other, each from their own perspective. Luke has given us a detailed description of how Mary lived in Nazareth. This is the place Joseph left, with Mary, to go to Bethlehem. At the same time, the expected child is to inherit the throne of David (Luke 1:32) and is to be born in the "city of David" (Luke 2:4). Given these facts, it would not have been strange if Joseph and Mary had gone to live in Bethlehem or Jerusalem, especially after the great things Simeon and Anna had said about the child in the temple. Those would have been appropriate cities for him to live in. But instead, they return to *their* town. Nazareth is not really an appropriate town for Jesus. It is *their* town, and Jesus, God's Son and David's heir, must grow up outside Bethlehem and Jerusalem, in Nazareth, the city of his earthly parents. Luke reveals the tension more fully in the story that immediately follows, about the twelve-year-old Jesus in the temple. Jesus feels *at home* in Jerusalem. Here he is in his Father's house, among his Father's things (Luke 2:49). Yet he continues to obey his parents and follows them back to Nazareth. Although Luke is silent about the flight to Egypt and the return to the Promised

Land, his account suggests something unexpected and special about the family's settling in Nazareth. That is why we should not interpret Luke 2:39 as indicating that Joseph and Mary returned to Nazareth immediately after the presentation in the temple. Luke wants to make the point that Jesus grew up in Nazareth *despite* everything that was said about him in the temple in Jerusalem. This does not rule out the possibility that the way to Nazareth was longer and more roundabout than it appears to have been in Luke. Similarly, Luke tells us in 3:19–20 what eventually happened to John the Baptist. If he had not followed this with the story of Jesus' baptism we might think, on the basis of 3:19–20, that John's imprisonment followed right on the heels of his preaching and that the baptism of Jesus that is described by the other evangelists never took place.

In Matthew the perspective is different. He tells his readers nothing about where Joseph and Mary lived. He reports only how Jesus, born king of the Jews, came into the world in Bethlehem in complete fulfillment of prophecy (Matt. 2:5–6). In Luke Jesus' parents *return* to Nazareth, in Matthew they *withdraw* there because the narrative begins with the focus on Bethlehem. Matthew presents the negative assessment of Nazareth as the home of the newborn *king* somewhat differently than Luke, for whom the exceptional events in Judea, involving angels and prophets, *settle back down* to the level of the father and mother's hometown in Galilee. For both evangelists, Nazareth is a humiliating end to the birth story. Only Matthew explores more deeply the divine direction that led the parents to Nazareth so that the words of the prophets could be fulfilled (Matt. 2:19–23).

There are still some questions regarding the order of events, however. Matthew first reports the arrival of the wise men after Jesus' birth, then the flight to Egypt, the slaughter of the innocents in Bethlehem, and the return and settlement in Nazareth. Between the circumcision and the return to Nazareth Luke mentions only the presentation in the temple. When did this presentation take place—before the arrival of the wise men or afterward?[2] It would seem strange for Joseph and Mary to

---

2. A third possibility is that the presentation in the temple took place much later, after the return from Egypt and the settlement in Nazareth. The sacrifice of purification could not be made *before* the fortieth day, but it was not obligatory to make it *on* that day. I defended this possibility of a late date for the presentation in the temple in *De Reformatie* (46 [1970–71]: 101–3), but after a closer examination of all of Luke 2, it seems to me incorrect to interpret Luke 2:39 as an indication of a return to "their" town of Nazareth after they had already made it their home upon returning from Egypt. Such an interpretation reads too much of Matthew into Luke. If the explanation of Luke 2:39 is based on Luke's narrative alone (as we do here), any support for a much later date of the presentation in the temple evaporates and we appear to be limited to the two possibilities mentioned here: before or after the arrival of the wise men.

offer the sacrifice of the poor at the time of the presentation in the temple if the wise men had already visited them with gifts of great value (gold, frankincense, and myrrh). On the other hand, one wonders whether the wise men arrived in Jerusalem *before* the presentation in the temple, since no one knew about the newborn king when the Magi arrived in Jerusalem, while Simeon's prophecy and Anna's report must have alerted many of the capital's pious citizens to the special event that had taken place in Bethlehem. This last point would seem to carry more weight, especially because we get the impression, at least from Matthew 2, that the wise men arrived in Jerusalem and Bethlehem relatively soon after Jesus' birth. Later, when rumors about the things said by Simeon and Anna made the rounds, Herod may have been reminded of the Magi and he may suddenly have realized that they had been gone a long time, which then led to the slaughter of the innocents. Yet why did Mary and Joseph offer the sacrifice of the poor if gold, frankincense, and myrrh had already made their way into Joseph's house? Because these gifts were not meant for the parents, but for the child. The sacrifice of purification was to be made by and for the mother from the joint resources of both parents. The wealth they received from the wise men was not part of Joseph and Mary's possessions. Perhaps it was used for Jesus' needs in Egypt, but it did not stop Mary and Joseph from offering the sacrifice of the poor after the wise men had left.

There seems to be one objection to this order of events: if the Magi visited Herod during the first forty days of Jesus' life, it is curious that the king ordered the immediate execution of all children two years old and under "in accordance with the time he had learned from the Magi" (Matt. 2:16). It looks as though at least one year must have elapsed between Jesus' birth and the encounter with the wise men. Yet this is not the case. After all, Herod did not spare the lives of the newborn babies. He was taking into account the possibility that Jesus had been born shortly before the Magi came to Jerusalem! We have to assume that the hard-hearted Herod meant to take no risks. He simply had all young children killed, from toddlers on down; after all, soldiers cannot concern themselves with precise ages, so they grabbed all children who were within that range. It was a simple, low- or no-risk operation. The wide margin of error Herod applied also had to do with the information Herod received from the Magi about the time that the star appeared. The time was clear, but neither Herod nor the Magi could know for certain whether the star was supposed to coincide with the conception or the birth of the king of the Jews. If the latter were the case, then the wise men were still at home when Jesus was born, and they still had to make preparations for the journey as well as the journey itself. If, on the other hand, the appearance of the star coincided with the conception, then the chance was greater that the child had been born only shortly before their arrival. Uncertainty about the required method of calculation would result in a margin of at least close to a year, and when for the sake of safety the margins were adjusted at both ends, as an anxious and bloodthirsty king would have been likely to do, it is no wonder that Herod's soldiers took the lives of one- and two-year-old children in Bethlehem. Because Bethlehem was just a small village, the number of deaths did not make world headlines, and because the victims were powerless children, few political repercussions were to be feared at the time.

In summary, we arrive at the following order of events on the way from Bethlehem to Nazareth:

1. Arrival and departure of the Magi.
2. Presentation of Jesus in the temple on the fortieth day.
3. Flight to Egypt at the urging of an angel.
4. Slaughter of the innocents in Bethlehem.
5. Return and settlement in Nazareth after Herod's death.
6. Jesus' visit to the temple at age twelve.

4.3 In David's Family

The child Jesus was given to David's family by the grace of God. He was not begotten by man, but by the Holy Spirit. His mother Mary was pledged to be married to Joseph, one of David's descendants. Although they had not yet come together as husband and wife, Mary was legally regarded as Joseph's wife. Through his pledged wife, Joseph received the son that had been promised to the line of David. This he received not of "a husband's will" (cf. John 1:13), but through the grace of God. Through an angel he learned of his task as David's descendant: on behalf of the house of David, he would be allowed to receive the child that was to be born of the pregnant virgin (Isa. 7:14) and to name it as he would his own child. So Joseph, David's descendant, acted as the earthly father of Jesus: he gave him the name (Matt. 1:25) and he was looked upon as Jesus' father by his contemporaries (Luke 3:23). The children who *had* been fathered by Joseph were called Jesus' brothers and sisters (Mark 6:3).

How, then, can Jesus be considered a descendant of David in Joseph's family? Through his mother Mary? Often all emphasis is placed on *her* descent from David. Through Mary, Jesus would have been a true descendant of David. The fact that Joseph was also a descendant of David (Matt. 1:2–17) would have been a plus but not of critical importance for the lineage from David to Jesus. But if this were indeed true,

it is strange that we find *Joseph's* genealogy in the Gospels. This is undoubtedly the case in Matthew 1, and the genealogy in Luke 3 also runs
not from Mary but from Joseph back to David and Adam. Some hold
that Luke 3 in fact contains *Mary's* genealogy rather than Joseph's.[3]
This would immediately explain why there are so many differences between the lists of names in Matthew and Luke. The idea of two genealogies, one for Joseph and one for Mary, is in itself attractive, but we do
not think that it can be supported. In Luke 3:23 we read the following
introduction to the genealogical register: "Now Jesus himself was about
thirty years old when he began his ministry. He was the son, so it was
thought, of Joseph, the son of Heli," and so on. Some are of the opinion
that the qualifying phrase "so it was thought" indicates that Jesus was
in reality the son of Mary, whose father was Heli. But if this is what
Luke meant, he had a strange way of expressing it: why didn't he name
Mary as the person whose ancestry he is giving? We also have to keep
in mind the *function* of Luke 3:23. Luke shows here that in the eyes of
the people Jesus was not a great and imposing figure at the time of his
ministry. He did not possess the dignity of advanced age and was in the
eyes of his contemporaries still a young man, a man in his early thirties.
Furthermore, he was considered to be the son of Joseph, who may have
been a son of David but who, like everyone else, was descended from
Adam. The Son of God was only a young man when compared to the
leading elders, just a young man among other human beings. That is
how they saw him—and not without justification. He was in his thirties
and he *was* considered Joseph's son. The point Luke is trying to make,
however, is that during his ministry he was *not* seen as the Son of God,
as he was designated from heaven at the start of his ministry (see the
preceding verse, Luke 3:22!). Considering the context of Luke 3:23,
there is no reason to assume that Luke presents a genealogy *as if* it were
Joseph's while really presenting the genealogy of Mary. Luke—as well
as Matthew—gives *Joseph's* family tree. Apparently Joseph's genealogy
is essential to Jesus' link with David's family.

The same thing strikes us when we continue reading what the Gospels say on this point. Nowhere in Matthew is there mention of a Davidic descent of Mary. We read only that Joseph is from the house of
David (Matt. 1:16), and he is called "the husband of Mary, of whom was
born Jesus, who is called Christ." This designation is significant. Because Joseph, a descendant of David, had taken Mary as his betrothed
wife, Jesus, who was born of this woman, is also born into *David's*

3. See S. Greijdanus, *Heilige geschiedenis volgens de vier evangelieverhalen: Geboorte van Jezus Christus en aanvang van Zijn publieke optreden* (Goes: Oosterbaan & Le Cointre, 1951), 145–46.

house. This is why Matthew focuses on the history of Joseph: how did Joseph become willing to truly make the child of his betrothed wife a child of David's house (Matt. 1:18–25)? In Luke, on the other hand, Mary is given more prominence, yet Luke names Joseph, not Mary, as being of the family of David (Luke 1:27; 2:4). When Zechariah prophesies about the horn that has been raised up in David's house (Luke 1:69), this can in the context of Luke 1 refer only to the fact that God has performed a miracle in the betrothed wife of Joseph of the house of David. All we can deduce from Luke is that Mary had family ties with the house of Levi (Luke 1:5, 36), and no more. If she did have ties with David's family beyond Joseph, apparently they are not important enough for Luke to mention. The fact that she belonged to that family by being pledged to be married to Joseph was all that was necessary![4]

Exactly what was the family connection between David and Joseph? The lineage is shown in both Matthew 1 and in Luke 3. The first evangelist presents a historical review from Abraham to Jesus in which he traces the line of royal succession. This kind of historically important lineage through a royal house is genealogically not always the most direct. Luke presents the most direct genealogical line. He does not begin with the past and work his way up to the present, but rather moves backward, from the descendant to the forefathers, from Joseph back to David and Adam. His presentation is a significant document for Greek readers, who were enamored of family trees that connected people with heroes and demigods. Jesus is no more and no less than a human being among human beings. Since the goals of Matthew and Luke are very different—a historical survey of Israel by means of a list of names as opposed to a record of the human origins of Jesus—it is not so amazing that they travel different routes through the dense foliage of the family tree.

The differences between the lists of names in Matthew and Luke mainly fall in the long period between David and Shealtiel/Zerubbabel, and the period between Shealtiel/Zerubbabel and Joseph. It is not unusual for two separate paths through family lines, once they diverge, to remain separated for many generations. If one chooses to follow the lineage of one son, rather than of another son, of a particular father, the

4. Appealing to Acts 2:30 ("one of his descendants," lit., "the fruit of his loins") and Rom. 1:3 ("who as to his human nature was a descendant of David") as proof of *Mary's* Davidic origins is unsatisfactory. Acts 2:30 uses a phrase from 2 Sam. 7:12, where we find the promise made to David concerning the coming of his great Son. The expression "fruit of his loins" can hardly be applied literally to Jesus, since he was born without male involvement. The same is true for Rom. 1:3. The expression "descendant of David" does not apply in the biological sense. Both Rom. 1:3 and Acts 2:30 are concerned with the fact of Jesus' membership in David's family, not with how he came to be part of that family.

Family Ties between David and Joseph
(according to Matthew and Luke)

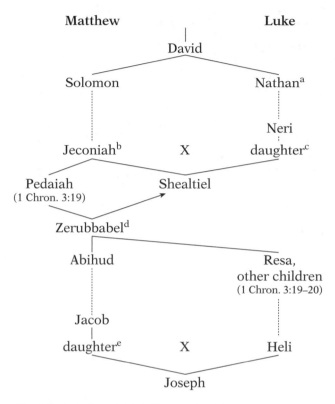

Matthew   Luke

David

Solomon   Nathan[a]

Neri

Jeconiah[b]   X   daughter[c]

Pedaiah   Shealtiel
(1 Chron. 3:19)

Zerubbabel[d]

Abihud   Resa,
                   other children
                   (1 Chron. 3:19–20)

Jacob

daughter[e]   X   Heli

Joseph

a. Son of Bathsheba: 2 Sam. 5:14; 1 Chron. 3:5; 14:4.

b. According to modern English translations of 1 Chron. 3:17, Shealtiel is the son of Jeconiah ("The descendants of Jehoiachin the captive: Shealtiel his son, . . ."). The translation "the captive" is the result of a small emendation of the Hebrew text, which literally reads, "The descendants of Jehoiachin: Assir and Shealtiel his son" (so also the KJV). If the Hebrew text is correct and there was indeed an Assir between Jeconiah and Shealtiel, the conjectural daughter of Neri must have been married to Assir, while Jeconiah was Shealtiel's grandfather rather than his father. In this chart we follow the modern English versions.

c. If Neri had only a daughter (married to Jeconiah [or Assir; see preceding note]), it is obvious that her son became the heir of his grandfather Neri. At the same time he was the son of Jeconiah (or grandson in the case of Assir being his father [see preceding note]). In this way he united the lineages of Solomon and Nathan.

d. Zerubbabel was undoubtedly regarded as the son of Shealtiel. Both Matthew and Luke agree on this point. See also Hag. 1–2. In 1 Chron. 3:19 he is named as the first son of Padaiah (the son of Jehoiachin/Jeconiah). If Shealtiel died childless, Padaiah could father a son by means of the levirate; that son would be regarded as the son of the departed Shealtiel.

e. If Jacob had only one daughter, the situation of Neri described in a preceding note would apply here as well. The fact that Jews trace their family connections through the mother as well as the father is mentioned in Josephus, *Life* 1 §§2, 4.

lineage may reconnect with that of the other son many generations later, when a distant descendant from one son marries a far descendant of the other. This is what happened, for example, in the case of two of David's sons, Solomon and Nathan. The diagram on the previous page is a *possible* reconstruction of Jesus' family tree. Owing to the absence of further data, especially from the confused time of the Babylonian captivity, it is impossible to say for sure how the lists in Matthew and Luke should be integrated. But it is useful to attempt a *possible* integration because there is a tendency to dismiss both genealogies as unhistorical. This means that too little consideration has been given to the complexity of family ties in real life and to all the different ways in which those ties can be represented. The diagram intends to do no more than underscore this by working out one *possible* solution.

5

Jesus' Brothers and Sisters

5.1 Brothers and Sisters—but How?

In Nazareth, Jesus was part of a family with parents and children. Later the inhabitants of the village would say, "Isn't this the carpenter? Isn't this Mary's son and the brother of James, Joseph, Judas and Simon? Aren't his sisters here with us?" (Mark 6:3). In Matthew's account, Jesus is called "the carpenter's *son*"; the four brothers are listed, but the names of the last two are switched, while the sisters once again remain anonymous (Matt. 13:55–56). These sisters appear infrequently in the Gospels (only in Mark 3:32, according to most manuscripts).

But Jesus' *brothers* are mentioned more than once. They are with Mary, the mother, at the wedding at Cana (John 2:12). Later, when Jesus comes home to Capernaum, they come to visit him with Mary and with Jesus' sisters (Mark 3:31–32; Matt. 12:46–47; Luke 8:19–20). Still later, when the brothers urge him to appear more publicly in Jerusalem (John 7:3–10), we learn that they do not believe in Jesus. But after Easter we see the brothers, as well as Mary, gathered with the disciples (Acts 1:14). They play an active role in later missionary work, traveling even outside Palestine (1 Cor. 9:5). So it is understandable that James, the brother of the Lord, became generally known outside Palestine (Jesus' appearance to James at Easter, 1 Cor. 15:7; Gal. 1:19; 2:9, 12). At a later stage he became the leader of the Christian community in Jerusalem (Acts 12:17; 15:13; 21:18). His letter was preserved as authoritative (James 1:1). Jude calls himself James's brother, which seems to indicate that James had gradually become so well known as "brother of the Lord" that Jude no longer had to refer to himself in the same way and could confine himself to a modest reference as the brother of James (Jude 1:1).

Are these brothers (and sisters) of Jesus also Mary's children? The standard response to this question throughout the centuries has usually been negative. Early in the history of the Christian church these brothers and sisters were regarded as the children from an earlier marriage of Joseph, so that their legal status was that of *half brothers* and *half sisters*, who in fact had no blood relationship with Jesus, Mary's son. This explanation has remained dominant in the Eastern Church.

121

In the West, the view developed by Jerome prevailed: they were *cousins* of Jesus.[1] The word "brothers" is therefore used in this broader sense to mean "next of kin." According to this view, which is usually combined with the notion that Joseph did not have marital relations with Mary even after Jesus' birth, not only does Mary remain a virgin, but Joseph continues to be a man who has never in his life had sexual intercourse with a woman—thus the holy family is held up as the model for the ascetic and monastic life!

Initially the Reformation churches also held to the tradition that did not view Jesus' brothers as full brothers. Gradually, however, the conviction gained ground in Protestant circles that they were *true* brothers and sisters. This was the general opinion during the nineteenth and twentieth centuries. Zahn's thorough study of the subject around the turn of the century seemed to bring the argument to a decisive conclusion.[2] But it also served to polarize the issue between the Roman Catholic exegetes, who almost universally clung to the Jerome tradition, and the Protestant interpreters, among whom Jerome's opponent Helvidius seemed to have scored a late triumph.

For the sake of interconfessional discussion, the Catholic exegete Blinzler reopened the issue in a 1958 article,[3] which was later expanded and published in book form.[4] He hoped to demonstrate that this was not a case of exegesis (Protestant) against dogma (Catholic), but that the question as such deserves universal attention because the biblical data as well as the oldest tradition provide ample reason to question the idea, so self-evident to Protestants, that Jesus' brothers and sisters were also Mary's children.[5]

Although the question has limited significance for exegesis, it is worthwhile for a clear view of the biographical aspects of Jesus' life story to take a few moments to briefly examine Blinzler's new plea for an ancient tradition.

5.2 How Old Is the Tradition (Hegesippus)?

Blinzler's two main arguments are based on (1) Hegesippus and (2) Mark 15:40. Hegesippus, who lived in the second century, came

---

1. Jerome opposed Helvidius, who around A.D. 380 defended the claim that Jesus' brothers were also Mary's children. See J. Blinzler, *Die Brüder und Schwestern Jesu* (Stuttgart: Verlag Katholisches Bibelwerk, 1967), 130–44.
2. T. Zahn, "Brüder und Vettern Jesu," in *Forschungen zur Geschichte des neutestamentlichen Kanons und der altkirchlichen Literatur* (Leipzig, 1900), 6:225–364.
3. J. Blinzler, "Zum Problem der Brüder des Herrn," *Trier Theologische Zeitschrift* 67 (1958): 129–45, 224–46.
4. Blinzler, *Brüder und Schwestern Jesu*.
5. Ibid., 7, 11–20.

from the East and is considered to have belonged to the generation that came immediately after the apostles. His book against the Gnostic heretics (*Hypomnēmata*) is known to us only through Eusebius's work on church history. According to Blinzler, Hegesippus tells us that Simon and Jude were sons of Clopas and cousins of Jesus. James is also said to be a cousin, but through another uncle.[6] Information like this from the second century must naturally be taken seriously. We may question, however, whether Hegesippus really made these claims.

Blinzler bases his view on a translation of the relevant passage that reads as follows: "When James the righteous had suffered martyrdom like the Lord and for the same reason, the son of his [i.e., Jesus'] uncle, Simeon the [son of] Clopas, was appointed bishop; everyone demanded that he be chosen because he was a second [i.e., another] cousin of the Lord."[7] Translated in this way, it does indeed seem that Simeon was a cousin, as was James, for that matter, although not via the same father.

This translation, however, leaves much to be desired. Many scholars rightly translate the passage approximately as follows: "When James the righteous had suffered martyrdom like the Lord and for the same reason, the son of his [i.e., James's] uncle, Simeon of Clopas, was appointed bishop. Everyone demanded that he be chosen as second [bishop] because he was a cousin of the Lord."[8]

Without going into the linguistic details,[9] this translation recommends itself as the better of the two for the following reasons:

1. In other fragments of his work that have been preserved, Hegesippus calls James simply the *brother* of the Lord and does not use the word *cousin*.[10] Now it may be that by the word *brother* he meant *cousin*, but then why doesn't he just call Simeon of Clopas a *brother* in the above quotation, analogous to the reference to James? He refers to this Simeon as a *cousin*, according to Blinzler's translation even a "second

6. Ibid., 94–110.
7. Ibid., 96–97. Eusebius, *Ecclesiastical History* 4.22.4.
8. Compare Blinzler, *Brüder und Schwestern Jesu*, 105.
9. *Palin ho ek tou theiou autou Symeōn ho tou Klōpa kathistatai episkopos, hon proethento pantes onta anepsion tou kuriou deuteron. Palin* can hardly be understood to mean another uncle's child, because James is not treated as an uncle's child but as the brother of the Lord. What must be intended here is that *once again* (or *further, next*) a bishop was appointed. *Ek tou theiou autou:* this is more likely a reference to James (the main person in the preceding part) than to Jesus; now a son of James's uncle is being appointed. *Onta anepsion tou kuriou* would be superfluous if the uncle of Jesus had already been referred to. The meaning of the sentence is that Simeon (who was a son of James's uncle) was not chosen as *James's* cousin (which he was) but as *Jesus'* cousin (which is more important). *Deuteron*, an accusative, must be connected with the relative pronoun *hon*, so that it is indirectly connected with *episkopos*. So the difference in cases between *episkopos* and *deuteron*, which Blinzler stresses, plays no role here.
10. See Eusebius, *Ecclesiastical History* 2.23.4.

cousin [of Jesus]." But Hegesippus never spoke of James as a "[first] cousin," so it seems obvious that *Simeon* is referred to as a cousin of the Lord to distinguish him from James, who was known as brother of the Lord. This Simeon, then, is not the second *cousin* but the second *bishop* after James, who was the first bishop.

2. The quotation lacks an explicit reference to James as the brother of the Lord, but when Hegesippus calls him "the righteous," it is an implicit reference to James the brother of the Lord. Elsewhere Hegesippus says in so many words that "James, the brother of the Lord" was known to everyone as "the righteous."

3. Hegesippus refers to Jude as "brother [of Jesus] in the flesh."[11] Now we know that Hegesippus has the word *cousin* in his vocabulary, as we saw in the above quote. It is striking that he does *not* speak about a "cousin in the flesh"; Simeon is simply called Jesus' cousin. If Jude had also been a cousin and not a real brother, the added phrase "in the flesh" would have been superfluous. By adding this phrase, however, Hegesippus makes it known that Jude was not only a spiritual brother of Jesus but also a brother *in the literal sense of the word*. This is not a reference to a cousin.

We conclude that Hegesippus is actually saying the opposite of what Blinzler proposes. Hegesippus makes a distinction between James and Jude on the one hand (they are real brothers) and Simeon on the other (he is a cousin). Just as Simeon was a cousin of Jesus and had Joseph and Mary as aunt and uncle, Jesus, James, and Jude were cousins of Simeon and called Clopas their uncle.

But this still does not suggest that Jesus' brothers were also Mary's children. What is lacking here is support from the tradition for the idea of *cousins*. It can even be said that the oldest tradition offers positive support for the notion that James and Jude were brothers of Jesus and *not* cousins. The cousin hypothesis, introduced by Jerome in the fourth century, has no demonstrable roots in tradition and also contradicts the oldest known information found in the tradition!

5.3 Mary, the Mother of James and Joses

Blinzler bases his second main argument on Mark 15:40. There we read, "Some women were watching from a distance. Among them were Mary Magdalene, Mary the mother of James the younger and of Joses, and Salome." It is the second of the three women named here who is of particular interest: the names of her two sons are the same as those of two of Jesus' brothers—his two oldest brothers (Mark 6:3). This is espe-

---

11. Ibid., 3.20.1.

cially noteworthy because the unusual name *Joses* (a variant of Joseph) appears nowhere else in the New Testament. In principle this could be a reference to Jesus' mother, named here between Mary Magdalene and Salome. But Mary the mother of Jesus would certainly have been named first and would not be referred to so indirectly. So this must be another Mary. But if her sons are the so-called brothers of Jesus, then this, according to Blinzler, is proof that these men were related to Jesus (cousins?) but that they were born of another mother whose name also happened to be Mary.[12] After finding another father for Simeon and Judas (Clopas) in the work of Hegesippus, Blinzler now finds another mother for James and Joses in the Gospel of Mark—another Mary. So all four are only "brothers" in a broad sense (kindred, cousins), and they were not even all born into the same family but into two families of aunts and uncles of Jesus.

This argument looks rather impressive at first glance, but on closer inspection it proves to be less than conclusive. When confronted with names in a book, it does in principle make sense to take into account the possibility that these names may refer back to people mentioned before. Thus the name Joses may very well refer to the same man as the one called the brother of Jesus in chapter 6. However, Mark, both in chapter 6 and in chapter 15, does not name Joses first, but James. In Mark 6, Jesus' brother is simply called *James* (with no qualifying addition). But in Mark 15 the reference is to a James who (unlike the reference in Mark 6) is further identified as James *the younger*. This clearly indicates some James other than the brother of Jesus mentioned in Mark 6. But if this is true, then the Joses in Mark 15 may also not be the same person as the one mentioned in Mark 6. If James the younger and his brother Joses are different from James and Joses, Jesus' brothers, then their mother Mary must be different from the mother of the Lord.

5.4 Relatives and Acquaintances at the Cross and Grave

Can anything more be said about the composition of Joseph's family and about Jesus' family relationships? If Mark 6 and 15 do indeed refer to two different Marys, what might be the relationship between two

---

12. Blinzler, *Brüder und Schwestern Jesu*, 74–93. J. J. Gunther, "The Family of Jesus," *Evangelical Quarterly* 46 (1974): 25–41, argues for the *identification* of Jesus' mother with Mary the mother of James the younger and Joses. This identification leads, in my opinion, to problems. Gunther's hypothesis that this indirect reference to Jesus' mother stems from apologetic motives, or from the fact that the relationship between Jesus and his mother had cooled, is not convincing. See also J. W. Wenham, "The Relatives of Jesus," *Evangelical Quarterly* 47 (1975): 6–15.

women whose children have almost identical names? If Jesus' "brothers" were not his cousins, then who were?

We find the largest concentration of friends and family around the cross and at the grave. In Jesus' earthly life, as for many people, family ties are most pronounced when there is a death in the family. At the cross we find the following individuals named by one or more of the evangelists:

Jesus' mother (Mary)	John 19:25
The sister of Jesus' mother	John 19:25
Mary the wife of Clopas	John 19:25
Mary Magdalene	John 19:25; Matt. 27:56; Mark 15:40
Mary the mother of James the younger and Joses	Matt. 27:56; Mark 15:40
Salome	Mark 15:40
The mother of the sons of Zebedee	Matt. 27:56

This list would be shorter if the "sister of Jesus' mother" were the same as Mary the wife of Clopas. The wording in John 19:25 leaves room for this interpretation: "Meanwhile, standing near the cross of Jesus were his mother, and his mother's sister, Mary the wife of Clopas, and Mary Magdalene." It could be argued that by dropping the "and" between "his mother's sister" and "Mary the wife of Clopas," John wants to suggest that Mary the wife of Clopas *is* the sister of Jesus' mother. Yet it is also possible that John wants to arrange the women two by two: first Mary the mother of Jesus with her sister, then two other Marys: the wife of Clopas and Mary Magdalene. Zahn opts for the latter, and rightly so:[13] it is highly unlikely that Mary's sister would also be called Mary! On the other hand, it is not unlikely that John would group the women into two groups of two: Mary the mother of Jesus and her own sister, and then two close friends, Mary the wife of Clopas, who had married into the family, and the devoted Mary Magdalene.

It is striking that Matthew and Mark make no mention of the presence of Jesus' mother at the cross. But both evangelists mention the names of a few women to illustrate their comment that many women who had followed Jesus from Galilee were also standing at the cross. Of all these women, the evangelists name only a few of the better-known ones. Mary, Jesus' mother, does not belong on this list; she is not an attendant but a mother. John on the other hand chooses to mention her

---

13. Zahn, "Brüder und Vettern Jesu," 6:338–39. The opposite view in Gunther, "Family of Jesus," 29–30, is disputed by Wenham, "Relatives of Jesus," 10.

because he wants to tell how the Savior entrusted her to the care of his apostle John.

Two of the above-mentioned women are present at the entombment:

Mary Magdalene	Matt. 27:61; Mark 15:47
Mary the mother of James and Joses	Matt. 27:61; Mark 15:47

Matthew mentions, although not in so many words, Mary the mother of James and Joses in 27:61: it is clear that "the other Mary" refers back to "Mary the mother of James and Joses" named in 27:56. Mark also abbreviates his reference somewhat ("Mary the mother of Joses"). Evidently these two women were very close, because we see them together on Easter morning as well:

Mary Magdalene	John 20:1; Matt. 28:1; Mark 16:1; Luke 24:10
Mary the mother of James and Joses	Matt. 28:1; Mark 16:1; Luke 24:10
Salome	Mark 16:1
Joanna	Luke 24:10

When Matthew mentions "the other Mary" in 28:1, he once again is referring to the Mary more fully identified in 27:56, the mother of James and Joses. Mark now refers to her simply as the mother of James, for the sake of variety.

Joanna, whom only Luke mentions, was the wife of Chuza, the manager of Herod's household (Luke 8:3). She came from the court of Herod Antipas! There is no reason to regard her as family. She belongs to the group of women who provided assistance and traveled with Jesus.

Salome, mentioned by Mark as being at the cross and at the resurrection, was probably not the sister of Jesus' mother, because she was counted among the attending women of Galilee.[14] It is possible that she is the same woman who is elsewhere called "the mother of the sons of Zebedee" (Matt. 27:56). Matthew refers to her this way in 20:20 as well. Mark does mention the sons of Zebedee in his Gospel (1:19–20; 3:17; 10:35), but never "the *mother* of the sons of Zebedee." It is quite possible that he was used to calling her by the name by which the leader Peter knew her and referred to her: Salome. There is no reason to regard Salome as family.

---

14. Zahn and others equate Salome, the mother of Zebedee's sons, with the second of the four women in John 19:25: the sister of [Jesus'] mother. In that case John and James would also have been cousins of Jesus. This seems highly improbable, however, because there is absolutely no trace of a family connection, either in or outside the Gospels.

Mary the mother of James (and Joses) has more than once been thought to have been the mother of the apostle James, the son of Alphaeus (Mark 3:18). But this is unlikely. Why would she then also be called the mother of Joses? And why does Mark refer to James *the younger*, which would seem to indicate someone other than James the apostle, who is never called "the younger"? If this Mary the mother of James is to be equated with one of the other women gathered at the cross and the grave, it could only be Mary the wife of Clopas who is mentioned by John.

Mary the wife of Clopas/Mary the mother of James and Joses. We saw in Hegesippus how Clopas later came to be known as an uncle of Jesus. Considering the frequent use of the name Miriam (Mary) at that time, it is not so strange that Clopas and Joseph both were married to women named Mary. The fact that they had the same name precludes the possibility that they were sisters. There remains the possibility that Joseph and Clopas were brothers or that one of the Marys was a sister of Joseph or of Clopas, in which case Mary, the wife of Clopas, would be a sister-in-law of Mary, the mother of Jesus. Hegesippus says that Joseph and Clopas were brothers,[15] so it would not be unusual for their children to bear the same family names (James, Joses, Simeon). While one James was later referred to as "the brother of the Lord," his cousin and namesake could have been characterized as "the younger." While one Mary was called "the mother of the Lord," her sister-in-law was referred to as "Mary the wife of Clopas" or "Mary the mother of James the younger and Joses." From Hegesippus we know that Jesus' relatives were rather well known in the oldest Christian communities, so that further identification in the case of similar names was helpful. As an aside we also note that Clopas in John 19:25 could have been the same person as the man on the road to Emmaus who is mentioned by name: Cleopas (Luke 24:18).[16]

On the basis of the information the evangelists provide in the narratives of the crucifixion, burial, and resurrection, we conclude that James the younger and Joses, as well as Simeon, who is mentioned elsewhere, were very probably cousins of Jesus. Clopas and Mary were therefore his uncle and aunt. The two related families contained at least the following persons:

Joseph and Mary: Jesus; James, Joses, Jude, Simon, daughters.
Clopas and Mary: James the younger, Joses, Simeon.

15. Eusebius, *Ecclesiastical History* 3.1
16. Zahn, "Brüder und Vettern Jesu," 6:350. Less likely is the identification with Alphaeus (by which the sons of Clopas are identified with the apostles); see Wenham, "Relatives of Jesus," 12–15.

This shows that it is indeed possible to tell the cousins from the brothers in the Gospels. The brothers of Jesus cannot simply be pushed out of Joseph and Mary's family.

5.5 Did Jesus and His Brothers and Sisters Have the Same Mother?

If Joseph had had children from an earlier marriage and married Mary as a widower, Jesus could have had "brothers and sisters" without Mary having any more children after Jesus' birth. These would be brothers and sisters legally but not genetically, because Mary's child Jesus was not fathered by Joseph but by the Holy Spirit. The normal meaning of the word "brother" is thus preserved. This is not the case with the cousin hypothesis because, as even Blinzler must admit,[17] *adelphos* is only used to indicate cousins in special cases (abbreviated references, emotional contexts). But *adelphos* is appropriate in the case of children in a single one-family unit, even when they are half brothers or genetically unrelated brothers.

It is not easy to provide categorical proof that Mary had more children after the birth of Jesus. If Joseph did not have marital relations with his wife until she had given birth to her child Jesus (Matt. 1:25), then it can be assumed that he did so afterward. But that does not necessarily mean that more children were born to them. And although Jesus is called Mary's "firstborn" son (Luke 2:7), such a qualification would continue to apply even if he were her only child. Luke is not talking about whether she had more children but whether she had had previous children.

But it is even less easy to prove conclusively that Mary did *not* have more children after Jesus, although Blinzler presents several arguments that might point in this direction. How could Mary have accompanied Joseph to the Passover Feast every year (Luke 2:41) if she had a large family with small children under twelve years of age? But this fails to consider the possibility that Mary sometimes stayed at home.[18] Every custom has its exceptions, given sufficient reason. Furthermore, this argument appears to be based on a very narrow view of the options open to someone like Mary, intent on reaching a goal. Perhaps she took the little ones with her, or perhaps there was someone at home to care for them. Because of who Jesus was and the unique events that surrounded his birth and life, we must be careful not to draw conclusions too quickly when dealing with issues that involve him or his family.

17. Blinzler, *Brüder und Schwestern Jesu,* 47–48.
18. Ibid., 65–66.

This also applies to Jesus' words to his mother from the cross. According to Blinzler,[19] he would not have entrusted her to the care of the apostle John if she had other sons of her own. But wouldn't the same argument apply if Mary, as a widow, lived with the family of her brother or sister and could count on the support of her cousins? In either case Mary would have had relatives to take care of her and Jesus' charge to John would have been superfluous. Furthermore, what Jesus was talking about from the cross was *spiritual* guidance for Mary, which the yet unbelieving brothers could not provide!

Blinzler also points out that Mary is never called "mother of James" and James is never called "son of Mary."[20] But this is not so strange. Jesus is the focus of the family, after all, and we see this reflected in the way in which names were used. Even James the younger is never called the son of Mary, though no one would deny for that reason that a certain Mary was his mother.

Blinzler's most appealing (though unconvincing) argument is that the outspokenness with which the brothers express their criticism of Jesus in John 7 suggests *older* brothers, children from an earlier marriage.[21] Yet it is not their age that gives them their outspokenness, but their unbelief!

If this question cannot be conclusively proved either way, we are still left with a dominant impression. When we read the accounts with an open mind, they give us hardly any reason to think of the brothers and sisters of Jesus as being anything other than children from the marriage of Joseph and Mary.[22] If they were older children of a former marriage, wouldn't this have left traces in the way they were referred to in the Gospels? Jesus then would intentionally have been called "son of Joseph" when beginning his ministry in Nazareth (Luke 4:22), but later, when brothers and sisters enter the picture, would have been known as "son of Mary" to distinguish him from the brothers who were *Joseph's* children. If this is a clue, it is presented so subtly (being observable only to someone comparing Luke with Mark) that we can draw no conclusions from it.

Therefore our conclusion is that *exegetically* there is no reason to wonder whether Jesus' brothers and sisters were indeed Mary's chil-

---

19. Ibid., 69–71.
20. Ibid., 67–69.
21. Ibid., 66–67.
22. See also J. Wenham, *Easter Enigma: Do the Resurrection Stories Contradict One Another?* (Exeter: Paternoster, 1984), 132–39 (appendix 3: "The Mother and Brothers of Jesus"). Wenham discusses a variant of the cousin hypothesis that is found in J. McHugh, *The Mother of Jesus in the New Testament* (London: Darton, Longman & Todd, 1975).

dren. Although we cannot be absolutely sure, on the basis of known facts we have every reason to assume a common maternity. *Dogmatically* it is significant that the possible descent from a different mother is evidently not relevant for the New Testament, so that it can also hardly be of significance for Christology or Mariology.

6

John the Baptist and Jesus

6.1 John the Baptist

From the very first, John the son of Zechariah and Elizabeth was marked as the herald of the promised Savior. After John's ministry the Messiah himself was to be expected. Thus John is part of the story of Jesus.

At the announcement of John's birth, the angel Gabriel tells the priest Zechariah that the son who will be given to him will go before the Lord "to make ready a people prepared for the Lord" (Luke 1:16–17). When John is born, Zechariah prophesies through the Holy Spirit, "And you, my child, will be called a prophet of the Most High; for you will go on before the Lord to prepare the way for him" (Luke 1:76).

John made his home in the desert, living in solitude until the day when he would be presented to Israel as a prophet (Luke 1:80). That official presentation came in the fifteenth year of the reign of Tiberius, when the word of God came to John in the desert (Luke 3:1–2). From then on, he spoke to all of Israel—a true desert prophet with the appearance and the message of a preacher of repentance: Repent, be converted! The reason for his appeal is that God's kingdom is near. The king is coming! No one can have any doubt that this soon-to-be-fulfilled expectation is focused on a *person*: John speaks of one who comes after him. The grandeur of the expectation is proportionate to the eminence of the one who is coming. John deems himself unworthy to be even the humblest servant of this person, unworthy to tie the thongs of his sandals. His stature is superhuman—he is God himself, for whereas John baptizes with water, he will baptize with the Holy Spirit. Only God himself can pour out the Spirit on his people, as was promised by the prophets when they spoke of the coming messianic age.

The tremendous surge of people to the banks of the Jordan for the baptism of repentance in anticipation of the approaching general amnesty for sinners leads to critical reactions from Jerusalem. A committee is sent to investigate. They ask John who he is, but John refuses *any* title for himself. He will not even place himself on a level with *Elijah*, although in fact he *is* the Elijah who had been promised, the forerunner of the Lord. In his testimony he points away from himself, using the words of Isaiah 40 to call himself the voice of one crying in the desert, "Make straight the way for the Lord." Once again, John announces the coming of the Lord himself (John 1:19–28). This interview takes place in Bethany across the Jordan, the first place where John baptized.

6.2 The Baptism of Jesus

This Bethany across the Jordan is where Jesus is also baptized (see John 1:28–34). Jesus left Nazareth in Galilee when everyone flocked to John (Luke 3:21–22; Mark 1:9–11). It is understandable that the prophet initially refused to baptize Jesus—he knew himself to be Jesus' inferior (Matt. 3:13–17). But when the baptism is nevertheless performed at Jesus' command and Jesus thus demonstrates his solidarity with sinful people, the heavens open. The Spirit descends in the form of a dove and a voice calls Jesus the Son in whom God is well pleased.

This is a great experience for John. Later he talks about it with his disciples, and he also adds another element to his own witness. He has already said that the person who was to come after him existed before him: God himself! But when Jesus bowed his head in the Jordan and the Spirit descended like a dove, John received a deeper understanding. He now calls Jesus the "lamb of God"—God's Son is the sacrificial lamb that God has sent for the general amnesty for all sinners who repent and believe (John 1:29–36).

After the Spirit descends on Jesus, it becomes immediately clear that his path on earth is to be marked by suffering and temptation. No sooner is the baptism finished than the Spirit leads him into the desert to be tempted by Satan like a powerless human creature (Matt. 4:1–11; Luke 4:1–13).

6.3 Jesus' First Appearance

Jesus' preaching ministry begins when John is taken prisoner and Jesus goes to Galilee. But between Jesus' baptism and John's arrest there was a period of nine months to a year in which John (with his disciples) continued his ministry while Jesus also had begun to appear in public, performing signs (see section 3.3). John the evangelist tells us a bit more about this interval.

When we read John 1–4, we notice that all events and conversations in these chapters are colored by the comparison between John and Jesus. The evangelist follows the example of John the Baptist who pointed to Jesus, calling Jesus greater than himself, thus causing a number of his disciples to follow Jesus instead. Considering the great expectations that John had evoked among the people, Jesus seems rather inadequate: a person from Nazareth. Yet those of John's disciples who choose to go with Jesus quickly discover that he is divinely omniscient; from afar he sees Nathaniel sitting under the fig tree, and he fathoms this Israelite's upright heart (John 1:44–52).

The first sign Jesus performs is the miracle at Cana in Galilee (John 2:1–11). Once again we see a connection with John. After John, the preacher of repentance, comes Jesus, the one who brings the celebration of the wedding feast. The scale of his work far surpasses the need at this village feast. The water—John's element—turns into fine wine. It is the beginning of the miracles: with Jesus, the celebration of redemption begins!

At the next feast in Jerusalem, the Passover, Jesus drives all the sacrificial animals from the temple; the zeal for God's house will consume *him!* John had come to understand that Jesus is the Lamb of God. Jesus sweeps all other sacrificial animals aside. He has come to build the heavenly temple through his own death (John 2:13–25).

The conversation with the Pharisee Nicodemus, who is amazed by Jesus' miracles, touches once again on the transition from John to Jesus. The prophet of repentance baptized with water but promised the baptism of the Spirit. Jesus affirms this promise: to enter the kingdom of God that has been proclaimed, one must be born of water *and* the Spirit (John 3:5). And it is by Jesus' being raised up that this saving gateway to the kingdom will be opened. This is the purpose for which God, in his love, sent his Son into the world, that whoever believes in him will not perish but will have eternal life (John 3:16).

John the evangelist comes full circle by ending this selective series of events with John the Baptist himself. John has been baptizing at Aenon near Salim. But Jesus' disciples are baptizing as well, and they are attracting more followers than John. Seeing this, John's disciples come and question him. Once more, John proves to be the prophet who heralds the coming of Jesus. The friend of the bridegroom rejoices at the sound of the bridegroom's voice. Jesus must increase and John decrease, for Jesus comes from heaven and has been sent by God to bring eternal life (John 3:22–36).

Little else is known about this interval between Jesus' baptism and his ministry in Galilee. He has already become widely known by this time. The crowds of people who come to see him and his disciples are growing. His miracles cause amazement and attract attention, even in Galilee. In the first three Gospels, this interval receives little attention in comparison with the next period. But John highlights it. This period, in which John the Baptist and Jesus both minister in public, allowed the people to perceive clearly that there was a close connection between these two men. It is, as it were, a handing off of the baton. Baptizing links the disciples of John with those of Jesus. The testimony of the great prophet establishes a link between his disciples and the lamb of God. Jesus' own words and miracles also show a deliberate connection with John. When after John's arrest Jesus begins his ministry as the one who was to come after John, he does not appear as a usurper but as the one John the Baptist knew and expected.

6.4 The Cleansing of the Temple

There is one episode from this period which—historically speaking—demands a bit more attention. This is the story about Jesus' appearance in the temple during a Passover Feast, when he spoke the well-known words, "Destroy this temple, and I will raise it again in three days" (John 2:13–25).

In the first three Gospels we find the cleansing of the temple at the *end* of Jesus' ministry, marking the beginning of his last stay in Jerusalem following the triumphal entry (Matt. 21:12–17; Mark 11:15–19; Luke 19:45–48). John is silent about this event—or has he moved it to the *beginning* of his Gospel to serve as a thematic introduction? Many scholars have answered this question in the affirmative. A number of them immediately seize this point to illustrate how ahistorical John's narrative is: he gives the impression that the cleansing of the temple took place at the beginning of Jesus' ministry, while it actually occurred at the end. In the same breath these scholars add that there could not have been *two* cleansings of the temple, one at the beginning and one at the end of Jesus' ministry. Anyone who accepts that there must have been two similar events, so these scholars argue, simply shows how harmonization fails to do justice to the individual nature of each of the Gospels. The Gospels are to be read as testimonies rather than as reports of events, they insist, and thus there is no problem if John decides to move the cleansing of the temple elsewhere. But those who read the Gospels as history stumble over the idea of the Gospels as mere testimony and come to the conclusion that there were two cleansings of the temple. Because this question is often treated as a typical example of the ahistorical character of the Gospels, it deserves a more careful examination.

It is, of course, quite possible that a particular writer has chosen to highlight a certain event in his narrative by treating it outside the chronological development of the narrative. But John clearly tells us that the cleansing of the temple he is describing really occurred at the beginning, when John the Baptist was still a free man. The incident in the temple is explicitly dated: *after* the wedding at Cana and the short stay in Capernaum and *before* the longer stay in Galilee (John 2:1, 12–13, 23; 4:45). John knew exactly when these events of Jesus' early ministry took place, down to the day and even the hour (John 1:29, 35; 2:1; 4:6, 52–53). He surely must have known what he was doing when he placed the cleansing of the temple at the beginning of the ministry.

The story John tells is also substantially different from the later cleansing of the temple. In fact, the later event involved a shutting down of *all* temple activities (Mark 11:16). Jesus appears as the Lord of the temple, so people ask him about the nature and origin of his authority (Mark 11:28). His appearance is a significant threat to the temple—a temple that does not recognize him as the son of David but accommodates the murderers who are waiting for an opportunity to put Jesus to death (Mark 11:9–10, 18). The den of robbers that is determined to bring about the downfall of the Messiah (Mark 11:17) is itself threatened with ruin, even as the fruitless fig tree is on the verge of ruin (Mark 11:12–14, 20–21, which constitute the framework for the narrative of the cleansing of the temple). Absent from this severe and reproachful performance at the end of Jesus' ministry are the words of promise from the beginning: "Destroy this temple, and I will raise it again in three days." These words from John 2 hardly *can* have been spoken at the cleansing of the temple at the end. Otherwise it would be incomprehensible that only the very last witnesses against Jesus finally came up with distorted versions of this statement and that they did not even agree with one another (Mark 14:55–59). If Jesus had made his temple statement only a few days earlier and for all to hear, the Sanhedrin would have known about it. But now the witnesses have to delve into their memories, searching for things he might once have said. John 2 tells us that this statement was made at the beginning, when the Sanhedrin was not yet so watchful and suspicious. John's dating, and the way in which, according to the other Gospels, the temple statement was later used by false witnesses, do fit in with one another.

The activities accompanying the temple statement in John 2 are also quite different from those that occur during the later cleansing of the temple. Jesus first drives out, not the money changers (Matt. 21:12; Mark 11:15; Luke 19:45), but the sacrificial animals that were being offered for sale (John 2:14–16). Here he does not condemn them for turning the temple into a den of robbers but for turning it into a marketplace. There is no need for this selling of animals to continue—the true Lamb has come whose zeal for God's house will consume him. Jesus makes a whip of cords (John 2:15) such as those used by cattle drivers and drives all the sheep and cattle from the temple area (John 2:15). This whip does not feature in the later cleansing aimed at the *people* in the temple. But it illustrates the unique significance of the episode that occurred at the beginning of the ministry. Later the disciples will come to understand that the cleansing was to be a sign of his own sacrificial death. He himself was the temple that would be torn down and rebuilt again in three days.

In a sense we can agree with the critics that there were not two more-or-less identical cleansings of the temple. At the beginning of the ministry a sign was given in the temple that had to do with Jesus' own significance for the people of Israel. The cleansing of the temple at the end says something about the impending closing of the temple and about Jesus' authority in this house of God. This difference makes it easy to take John's dating seriously and to connect the temple episode in John 2 with the period in which Jesus was working along with John and showed his greater power and purpose.

6.5 Josephus on John the Baptist

More or less by way of excursus, we need to look at an extrabiblical description of John's ministry. In chapter 1 (1.2.2.1), we discussed the testimony about Jesus by the first-century Jewish historian Josephus. Josephus is more expansive on the subject of John. Writing as an outsider, he fails to understand the connection between John and Jesus. Thus he tells of the popular movement that formed around John and the ripple effect of his ministry. In an unrelated passage Josephus mentions the life of the person who became known in Rome as "Christ" thanks to the rise of Christianity. Josephus's treatment of Jesus' life clearly shows that he expects his non-Jewish readers to be interested. But his approach is different when it comes to John. This is a name that is virtually unknown among the non-Christians of the Roman Empire, and Josephus introduces him in the discussion on his own initiative. He shows how the story of John is an integral part of the Jewish history he is relating.

Josephus sees this organic tie when he deals with the defeat of Herod Antipas at the hands of Aretas, king of Nabatea. Herod had been married to a daughter of Aretas, but he had sent this princess away in order to marry Herodias. Aretas's attack on Herod and his house in response to this insult ended in defeat for the Jews in the territories ruled by Herod Antipas, Galilee and Perea. How did the Jews regard this defeat? Josephus writes:

> But to some of the Jews the destruction of Herod's army seemed to be divine vengeance, and certainly a just vengeance, for his treatment of John, surnamed the Baptist.

After inserting this historical comment, Josephus goes back in time and relates the story of John the Baptist:

> For Herod had put him to death, though he was a good man and had exhorted the Jews to lead righteous lives, to practice justice towards their fellows and piety towards God, and so doing to join in baptism. In his view this was a necessary preliminary if baptism was to be acceptable to God. They must not employ it to gain pardon for whatever sins they committed, but as a consecration of the body implying that the soul was already thoroughly cleansed by right behavior. When others too joined the crowds about him, because they were aroused to the highest degree by his sermons, Herod became alarmed. Eloquence that had so great an effect on mankind might lead to some form of sedition, for it looked as if they would be guided by John in everything that they did. Herod decided therefore that it would be much better to strike first and be rid of him before his work led to an uprising, than to wait for an upheaval, get involved in a difficult situation and see his mistake. Though John, because of Herod's suspicions, was brought in chains to Machaerus, the stronghold that we have previously mentioned, and there put to death, yet the verdict of the Jews was that the destruction visited upon Herod's army was a vindication of John, since God saw fit to inflict such a blow on Herod.[1]

Josephus writes about John from a very specific angle: the connection between his death and Herod's defeat. Because of this narrow focus Josephus is silent on things that are mentioned in the Gospels. Josephus does not mention the cause of the conflict between Herod and John: Herod's taking of his brother's wife. Yet Josephus must have been aware of the connection, because he knows that the people see Herod's defeat in the battle against Aretas as a just punishment: God shows that Aretas's anger is justified. In other words, John is proven right. Herod should not have sent his wife away in order to marry his brother's wife. When John admonished the tetrarch about his action, Herod killed him. Now he himself is the victim of his own evil deeds!

Josephus also leaves out the details of John's execution: the beheading that resulted from Salome's dance and Herodias's intrigues. As a non-Christian, Josephus is also completely silent about John's reference to Jesus as he who is to come after him. In Josephus's account, the whole point of John's preaching is missing.

Even so, his report offers us a confirmation of the Gospel story from a different side. The Gospels are correct in pointing out that John's ministry led to a popular movement. Herod evidently was driven to take action against John not only by his irritation at John's rebuke but also by

1. *Antiquities* 18.5.2 §§116–19.

his fear that the people might take the side of the prophet in this matter and rise up in a religious revolt against his regime.

6.6 John Is Arrested, and Jesus Succeeds Him

The evangelists pay much more attention to the imprisonment of John. They too interpret it as a sign from God. The Gospels say that John "had been put in prison" (Matt. 4:12; Mark 1:14). No person is mentioned as having been responsible for the arrest. The use of the passive form frequently indicates that it was ultimately God who was acting. John was greatly loved, and who would want to turn him over to Herod? We find here an allusion to divine guidance: God worked it so that John would end up in Herod's prison. For Jesus this is a sign that he must begin his ministry as the one who comes after John, but also—especially—that he comes after a prophet who has been handed over to the authorities by God. In John's arrest we see a foreshadowing of Jesus' own arrest. How does John's arrest relate to the power of the one who comes after him, who is greater than John? Evidently John's arrest and martyr's death are in line with what is to come. John continues to pave the way for the Lord: first he did so by going to the people with his message, and now he paves the way with his imprisonment and death. Jesus will follow him—first by preaching to the people, and then by being arrested and executed. The signs already point in that direction: John points out in his Gospel that Jesus moved to Galilee under the threatening cloud of increasing rejection. The prophet is not honored in his own country, so he moves on to the remote district of Galilee, the homeland where for the time being his miracles are still regarded with admiration (John 4:1–33, 43–45). Matthew also uses the word "withdraw" to describe the journey to Galilee (Matt. 4:12). No matter how much attention Jesus will receive for his miracles in Galilee, and no matter how much he ministers to the people through the power of the Holy Spirit (Luke 4:14–15), from this moment on the shadow of John's arrest falls on the ministry of "the mightier one coming after John," and neither God nor Jesus removes that shadow. Apparently this is a significant part of John's task as forerunner: wherever the prophet goes, there the Messiah will follow. It is not for nothing that the prophet killed by Herod refers to Jesus as the sacrificial "lamb of God" who is offered up for the sins of the world.[2]

2. For a more detailed discussion of John the Baptist, see chapter 2 in the companion volume, *Het evangelie van Gods zoon* (Kampen: Kok, 1996; English translation forthcoming).

7

The Galilean Period in the Gospels

7.1 Historical Sequence and Narrative Perspective

During his public ministry, Jesus spent most of his time in Galilee. He went there after the arrest of John the Baptist and, except for a few journeys to attend religious feasts in Jerusalem (see section 3.4), stayed for some two years, which is why he came to be known as "the Galilean" in Jerusalem. As is to be expected, the Gospels devote a great deal of attention to his work in Galilee. John, in his selection of stories, is more interested in what happened during the festival visits, yet he too tells us something about Galilee (John 4; 6; 7:1–10). Luke divides his attention between the Galilean period and the journey through Perea. In 4:14–9:50 he describes Jesus' work in Galilee. The most detailed accounts, however, are in Matthew and Mark, who devote more than fourteen and eight chapters respectively to this period (Matt. 4:12–18:35; Mark 1:14–9:50).

A problem comes with all this information, however: the material clearly is not always in chronological order. During the last part of the Galilean period—the period of withdrawal and preparation for the Passion Week—all four Gospels run parallel and follow the historical developments. But the long section that precedes it and relates to the public ministry in the Galilean synagogues and amid the crowds that came flocking to him is not told in the order of the actual events. For instance, in Matthew we find the chapter with all the parables (chap. 13) after the story of the sending out of the Twelve (chap. 10), but in both Mark and Luke the parables come first (Mark 4; Luke 8), followed by the story of the sending out of the Twelve (Mark 6; Luke 9). Which sequence coincides with the actual events? At least one evangelist has deviated from the historical order. There are many examples such as this. They show that the evangelists have apparently arranged the material in their own way—which makes a reconstruction of the sequence of events more difficult.

Why have the evangelists chosen their own trajectories through the material from the Galilean period, while elsewhere they closely follow the chronological sequence? The question would be less intriguing if the evangelists had taken a more casual approach to the *entire* sequence of historical events, but this is certainly not the case—not in the birth narratives and not in the accounts of the Passion. So why, in this first and largest part of the Galilean period, do we find such a radical departure from their normal pattern? Several special circumstances may point toward an explanation:

1. The material covers a long period and contains a tremendous amount of *repetition*. Jesus preached everywhere, over and over again. There were so many sick people cured in so many places that the total impression tends to cloud the details. It is pointless to be overly concerned with strict chronology in describing this period; far more practical is a rough sketch that provides readers with the most prominent and typical events.
2. Not only was there much repetition, but a tumultuous *development* was also taking place. People came in droves, and Jesus' fame spread. Negative reactions were also gaining strength and came from different corners. The period is a tangle of frequently conflicting events, and the solution to unraveling this tangle is not to present a day-by-day account of events but to describe the various *elements* that are historically superimposed. While this approach enhances the clarity and conciseness of the narrative, it diminishes our ability to see the precise sequence of events.
3. The *involvement* of the disciples in the major events increased over time. They grew from admirers or followers into insiders and partners. Their observation of the events underwent a development. Compare, for instance, the very early question found in John 1:38 ("Rabbi, where are you staying?") with the quick initiative taken on the Mount of the Transfiguration ("Rabbi, it is good for us to be here. Let us put up three shelters—one for you, one for Moses and one for Elijah," Mark: 9:5). When the evangelists in the later section of the Gospels follow a more chronological narrative line, it reflects their own increasing involvement in the events—most of the apostles did not constantly accompany the Savior until after the Sermon on the Mount, when they received a call and a mission. This includes the apostle and Gospel writer Matthew.
4. After the last stay in Galilee, the Savior's *instruction* about his future suffering gave the apostles clues for understanding the events that were to follow. They had no such interpretive clues when they were experiencing the welter of events during the early and middle part of the Galilean period. This is why the evangelists

differ from each other and deviate from the chronological sequence more in describing this period than elsewhere.

We might say that the less chronological way of narrating the Galilean period is very true to life and is one of the characteristics of a historical report by contemporaries who themselves were involved in the events. This should not keep us from trying to establish the historical course of events, insofar as the Gospels allow it. The evangelists even help in this respect. Their records are not a-chronological; they regularly indicate how this or that event followed an earlier event. But they are *intermittently* rather than *consistently* chronological. Comparing the various sections of the four Gospels that are chronologically arranged can help us move toward establishing an overall sequence of events. This certainly has value—not only for exegesis (if only to keep us from drawing too many conclusions concerning the chronology) but also to afford us a clear view of the evangelists' approach as historians. This means, however, that we have to work methodically: (1) establish the chronological elements in each evangelist; (2) identify or differentiate the accounts that exhibit similarities; (3) use identical accounts to connect the chronological clusters from the various Gospels; (4) discuss remaining problems.

In this chapter we will deal with the Galilean period from the narrative perspective of the evangelists. In chapters 8–10 we will approach it from a chronological perspective, insofar as it is possible to reconstruct the chronology.

7.2 The Narrative Perspective of Each of the Evangelists

The Gospel of John relates only a few fragmentary episodes from the Galilean period. There is no evidence of a special narrative perspective in John's writing, so we will limit ourselves in this section to the first three evangelists. All three give a *general* sketch of Jesus' ministry in Galilee. Next they offer a number of what might be called dioramas, which help us form a clear picture of the many events during this turbulent period.

Matthew provides the general characterization of this period in 4:12–17. This pericope is often labeled "Move to Capernaum," but there is more to it than that. Matthew begins in verse 12 with the general statement, "When Jesus heard that John had been put in prison, he returned to Galilee." The next sentence, "Leaving Nazareth he went and lived in Capernaum" (4:13a), illustrates how far Jesus had withdrawn into Galilee. Capernaum lies "by the lake in the area of Zebulun and Naphtali" (4:13b). This added geographical designation—the remote former tribal lands of Zebulun and Naphtali—must have been chosen because the evangelist is occupied more with the region in which Jesus worked than with his place of residence. The prophet Isaiah had already foretold that a great light would appear in the dark and remote corner where the light of Israel's independent existence as a nation had first been extinguished when Zebulun and Naphtali were deported (2 Kings 15:29). The prophecy from Isaiah 8:22–9:1, which Matthew quotes in 4:15–16, is not about the Messiah's place of residence but about the territory where the light will shine. The prophet explicitly names Galilee, and thus Matthew's reference to Capernaum points beyond the city of Capernaum to *Galilee* in general. This is confirmed in 4:17: "From that time on Jesus began to preach, 'Repent, for the kingdom of heaven is near.' " What does "from that time on" refer to? Not to the move to Capernaum, which is only emblematic of the beginning of the ministry in *Galilee*, but to the moment of John's imprisonment. Jesus now takes over the preaching of John the Baptist and continues to proclaim his message (cf. Matt. 3:2 with 4:17). Thus Matthew 4:12–17 does not tell us when the move to Capernaum took place. Days and weeks are not important here; rather, Matthew briefly characterizes the beginning of a new period in the life of Jesus: John's preaching is continued by Jesus—in Galilee, the land where darkness first fell.

Matthew presents the first diorama in 4:18–8:17. The calling of the four disciples indicates that Jesus is a "fisher of men." The onrush of the multitudes proves it, as does the great speech that Jesus then delivers on the mountain. The crowds hold their breath—he teaches with authority. And it is clear that he is greater than the Law and the Prophets when, after the Sermon on the Mount, he heals a leper and extends his compassion to a Gentile in Capernaum. The prophecy of Isaiah 53 is being fulfilled!

A new diorama begins with 8:18. There is a break in the narrative at this point. Verse 18 says that "when Jesus saw the crowd around him he gave orders to cross to the other side of the lake." But the action in 8:5–17 is nowhere near the sea but at the home of Peter's mother-in-law. As far as location is concerned, there is no connection between verses 5–17 and verse 18. This is the beginning of a new diorama that ends with 9:34. The stories in 8:18–9:34 are linked by chronological notes. For a while we closely follow the sequence of events: the conversations about following Jesus, the crossing of the lake and the unexpected heavy storm, the driving out of the evil spirits in Gadara, and the return to Galilee, where in Capernaum Jesus forgives a paralytic his sins and heals him. Then we walk out of town and come to Matthew's tax collector's booth. As a result of the dinner at Matthew's house we hear conversations about fasting. And during these conversations Jairus comes to Jesus on his daughter's behalf. After the girl is healed and

Jesus leaves Jairus's home, he finds himself being followed by two blind men. No sooner are they healed than a demoniac appears. Matthew lets the rosary of memories glide through his fingers.

But this series of specific, consecutive events finally ends, and in 9:35 we lose the chronological thread once more. In 4:23 we have already heard that Jesus went to all the synagogues of Galilee. Matthew returns to this same summary statement in 9:35, but then he takes a different exit from this traffic circle. He now traces how Jesus' compassion for the multitudes *expanded* with the commissioning of the Twelve. After describing this in detail in chapter 10, Matthew once again returns to his familiar starting point in 11:1: "He went on from there to teach and preach in the towns of Galilee" (4:23; 9:23; 11:1). The diorama of the commissioning is complete.

What has happened to John the Baptist in the meantime? In 4:13–17 Matthew made the general comment that Jesus took over John's ministry after the latter's arrest. In 11:2 we return to John in prison—another exit from the traffic circle. But this time Matthew takes a long time to return. After reporting Jesus' answer to John's questions, Matthew immediately proceeds with an orderly narrative of various incidents involving opposition to Jesus. During this same period, when John is asking questions and Jesus is upbraiding the crowds for accepting neither John nor himself (Matt. 11), the Sabbath conflicts take place (12:1–14), followed by the accusation that Jesus performs miracles through the power of Beelzebub (12:22ff.). Finally Matthew shows how the increasing rejection leads to Jesus' speaking in parables. Gradually we arrive at the last period of withdrawal and the announcements of the coming Passion. There are no clear indications that Matthew once again returns to a chronologically earlier point in the Galilean period.

In summary, we find the following narrative perspective in Matthew:

> General description of the Galilean ministry: 4:13–17.
> Jesus attracts attention through his healing and teaching: 4:18–8:17.
> An illustrative series of events: 8:18–9:34.
> An expansion of Jesus' ministry through missionary work: 9:35–11:1.
> Reactions from all sides: 11:2–16:12.
> Focusing on the disciples: 16:13–18:35.

Mark, like the other evangelists, begins with a general description of Jesus' ministry in Galilee. After John's arrest, Jesus went to Galilee to announce the gospel of God's kingdom with the words, "The time has come. The kingdom of God is near. Repent and believe the good news!"

(Mark 1:14–15). Then Mark supplements this sober comment with a first diorama in which we see Jesus call four "fishers of men" and travel from Capernaum to the surrounding synagogues, attracting so much local attention that he is finally forced to go out to lonely places and receive the crowds there (1:16–45).

In Capernaum a new series of events then starts that is chronologically unrelated to this first chapter. Clearly, the beginning of this series occurs after Jesus' visit to Capernaum mentioned in chapter 1. Indeed, in 2:1 Mark says, "A few days later, when Jesus *again* entered Capernaum." But this does not tell us whether this visit occurred after everything else described in chapter 1 (the proclamation of the gospel throughout Galilee and the healing of a leper). That is possible but not necessarily so. It is clear, however, that from this point on (2:1) Mark adheres to a chronological order. After the incident with the paralytic in Capernaum comes the calling of Levi, and the discussion about fasting occurs as a result of the meal in Levi's house (2:1–22).

Another new series begins in 2:23. Mark now does not indicate a chronological connection but simply says that "one Sabbath" Jesus went through the grain fields. Then Mark presents a connected series of narratives: Sabbath conflicts, withdrawal to the sea, commissioning of the Twelve, return home, and the parables. Although he does not always clearly indicate chronological connections (there is uncertainty about 3:20), Mark's narrative rather strongly suggests a historical sequence that is no longer interrupted by a switching of gears.

This would mean that Mark for the most part stays with the order of events, and that only 2:1–22 is rather loosely embedded in the narrative. Is there an explanation for this deviation from the chronological sequence? If, on the basis of comparison with the other Gospels, it should turn out that 2:1–22 chronologically follows 1:16–45, we might formulate the question differently: is there any reason for the fact that Mark does include one point in the narrative sequence at which he goes back in time—the chronological regression between 2:22 and 2:23? The reason is easy to see. Mark first follows the progress of Jesus' impressive ministry (healing, cleansing, forgiving, the bridegroom's feast) and then goes back to a point from which he can follow the progress of reaction, hostility, and suffering. In 2:23 he has to go back in time, because it was during the Sabbath conflicts that the aggression toward John's successor began.

In summary, Mark's narrative perspective is as follows:

General characterization of the Galilean period: 1:14–15
Jesus' presentation: healing, compassionate, festive: 1:16–2:22
Reactions to Jesus' message; Jesus' program: 2:23–9:50

Luke has an elaborate general description of the Galilean period. He tells how Jesus returned to Galilee in the power of the Spirit and how news of him spread for miles around while he taught in the synagogues (Luke 4:14–15). This is followed by an illustrative and characteristic diptych composed of the preaching of Jesus in Nazareth (4:16–30) and his ministry in Capernaum (4:31–44). At the end of this diptych Luke comes back to his general description: Jesus taught in the synagogues of Galilee (a few manuscripts here read "Judea"). The events in Nazareth bring to a close the period in which Nazareth was Jesus' home base—in chapter 2 Luke devotes a great deal of attention to the fact that Nazareth is the place where Jesus grew up. The ministry in Capernaum marks the new center of Jesus' activity. The question whether the narrative about Nazareth anticipates an event that the other evangelists place later is something we will set aside for the moment (see 8.3).

Unlike Matthew and Mark, Luke has little chronological order in his narrative after chapter 4. He provides each pericope with its own setting, and each is chronologically unrelated to the previous pericopes. The miraculous catch of fish (5:1–11) took place when the crowds were pressing in on Jesus in order to hear him speak (5:1). But in the previous chapter there is no mention of an onrush of crowds near the lake. The situation is clear, but it is not anchored chronologically. The same is true of the healing of a leper that is described next (5:12–16), which took place while Jesus was "in one of the towns" (5:12). The incident occurred on a particular day, but the next pericope begins with the words, "One day as he was teaching" (5:17). Once again, the very general setting of this incident fails to tell us whether this event took place before or after that of the previous pericope. Occasionally Luke does indicate sequence; Levi's call, for example, is placed after the story of the paralytic (5:27). The introduction of the appointing of the Twelve and the Sermon on the Mount is also very general: "One of those days . . ." (6:12). At most this could mean that the Sermon on the Mount was delivered during the period of the Sabbath conflicts. After the Sermon on the Mount Luke dates the healing of the centurion's servant in Capernaum (7:1) and after that the raising of the boy in Nain (7:11). We find this kind of incidental linkage of a small number of pericopes also in 8:1, 22, 26, 40. Luke does not follow any chronological order until after Peter's confession in Caesarea Philippi (9:18ff.).

Does this lightly structured description of the Galilean period reflect the fact that Luke was not in the area at this time and had to make do with miscellaneous reports that he later complemented with other information and then strung together without any clear chronological pattern? There is little point in providing a summary here as we did for Matthew and Mark, but we can consider a few meager structural elements in the following section.

7.3 Comparing the Gospels

It is possible to draw connecting lines between the Gospels at those points where the evangelists are clearly describing the same event. Moreover, when an evangelist relates one or more other events chronologically to one of these connecting points, the chronological relationship between those events and the connecting point can be taken into account in the other evangelists as well.

A simple example is found in Matthew 11:2–16:12. Within this diorama the evangelist stays with the chronological order. We can easily place Mark 2:23–8:21 alongside this passage from Matthew. The section in Matthew contains more material than that in Mark, but the sequence of the material the two evangelists have in common does not differ. In Mark 4:35–5:43, however, there are a number of chronologically connected incidents that Matthew puts elsewhere, outside 11:2–16:12: the storm on the lake, the demoniac in Gadara, and Jairus's daughter. Because Mark follows a chronological sequence from 2:23 on, we may assume that the material Matthew had already used in an earlier diorama has to be located chronologically between the events of Matthew 13:53 and 13:54.

After this conclusion, based on Mark, it is now Matthew's turn to give an indication of sequence within that Gospel. The string of events we just mentioned (storm-Gadara-Jairus) is chronologically linked to other facts in the diorama of Matthew 8:18–9:34. Between Gadara and Jairus are the healing of the paralytic, the calling of Matthew, and the discussion of fasting (Matt. 9:1–17). This particular block of material is found in Mark before the point at which Mark takes a step back in time (Mark 2:1–22). We have already seen in our analysis of Mark that the material from 2:1–22, viewed chronologically, could have belonged to a period that occurred some time after 2:23 and following. On the basis of the comparison of Matthew and Mark, we know that in order to locate Mark 2:1–22 chronologically we would have to place it after 5:20 (Gadara) and before 5:21 (Jairus). Conversely, we now also know on the basis of the chronological order in Mark that the diorama in Matthew 8:18–9:34 should be placed after the day of the parables, since in Mark the crossing to Gadara follows that particular day (Mark 4). Thus we know that the events in Matthew 8:18–9:34 took place after the incidents related in Matthew 13:1–53 (even though they precede them in the narrative).

This comparison helps us on yet another point. In Matthew we found a separate diorama showing the expansion of Jesus' mercy through the commissioning of the Twelve (9:35–11:1). We have already raised the question whether this commissioning actually took place before the

parables. Mark has the answer: the narrative order parables-commis-
sioning (Mark 4 and Mark 6 respectively) is apparently meant to be the
chronological order as well. Matthew placed the commissioning in a
separate diorama without chronological links. Based on Mark, we now
can assume that the commissioning, told in Matthew 10, took place
after the parables related in Matthew 13. In the next chapter, this integration of Matthew 8:18 and following and the material in Mark 2:1 and
following will be worked out in more detail, and the loosely ordered
narratives of Luke can then be integrated as well.

The very first part of the Galilean period in Matthew, Mark, and Luke
requires a separate discussion, however. We are faced with the question
whether events that seem identical are in fact identical. In the preceding we simply assumed that there was only one healing of Jairus's
daughter, only one case of driving out demons in Gadara, and only one
day of parables. If we were to insist on pursuing the harmonization approach promoted by Osiander and others (see 2.1) and assume that
each evangelist *always* wrote his account in chronological order, then
the unavoidable conclusion is that several almost identical repetitions
of events took place. Our main objection to this approach, which frequently leads to absurdities, is that its basic assumption is not supported by the Gospels themselves, which show that their narrative
order does not always coincide with the chronological order. But there
are also cases of identification or differentiation that are less clear-cut,
and it is those that play a role in the early phase under discussion.

There is first of all the question as to whether the address in Luke 6
represents the same address that Matthew gives in more detail as the Sermon on the Mount in chapters 5–7. They cover many of the same topics
(the Beatitudes; love of enemies; do not judge; house built on the rock).
In fact, there is nothing in Luke 6 that does not appear in Matthew 5–7.
A possible difference in the location of the Sermon on the Mount (to be
discussed in 9.1) does not detract from the general agreement between
Matthew and Luke. This is one address that is reported in more detail by
Matthew than by Luke. Luke tells us that the appointment of the Twelve
preceded the address (Luke 6:12–16). Mark's account of the appointment
is in 3:13–19. He does not mention the Sermon on the Mount, but he
clearly indicates that the Twelve were appointed after the Sabbath conflicts occurred. All this indicates that the Sermon on the Mount should
be located after the conflicts concerning the Sabbath. Since these conflicts took place in the early spring, when there were ears of grain to pick,
the Sermon on the Mount must also have been delivered in the spring,
the most suitable season for a mass outdoor gathering. In Matthew's
structure this means that part of the diorama about John the Baptist's
question and the subsequent Sabbath conflicts (11:2ff.) goes back to the

period before the Sermon on the Mount. In other words, Matthew's first diorama (4:12–8:17) covers a considerable length of time. And that is to be expected: all those crowds did not flock to Jesus in just a few days. A partial confirmation can be found in Luke, who also presents the Sabbath conflicts before the Sermon on the Mount (6:1–11 and 6:12 respectively). And when the Twelve are chosen, he notes that the appointment occurred "one of *those* days"—the days of the Sabbath conflicts!

After the Sermon on the Mount, Luke provides one of his rare chronological connections: the healing of the centurion's servant in Capernaum takes place after this sermon (Luke 7:1–10). We get the same impression in Matthew, although he says only that the healing of the leper (Matt. 8:1–4) took place after Jesus had come down from the mountain. But when he puts the entry into Capernaum and the healing of the centurion's servant immediately after the healing of the leper (Matt. 8:5–13), it seems reasonable to assume that this incident also took place after the Sermon on the Mount.

The difficult problem that now confronts us is the following: after the account of the centurion's servant, Matthew tells the story of the healing of Peter's mother-in-law (8:14–15) and the healings that took place at the end of that day (8:16–17). Should we locate these events after the Sermon on the Mount as well? But since it seems as if Jesus' power to heal only became evident on that particular Sabbath, shouldn't we then regard this as one of the earliest incidents? This general question comes into sharper focus when we look at Mark and Luke. Luke tells the story of Peter's mother-in-law early, in chapter 4. It is, of course, possible that something that is told at the beginning may actually have occurred later, but it is not that simple in this case. Luke also talks about Jesus being driven out of Nazareth and settling in Capernaum. He gives us the impression that this was Jesus' first visit to that city. This impression is confirmed by the fact that the first thing that takes place is the confrontation with an unclean spirit in the synagogue. This spirit attempts to turn the people of Capernaum against the man "of Nazareth" (Luke 4:34). Jesus casts the demon out and astonishes the people with his authority. The healing of Peter's mother-in-law takes place upon Jesus' leaving the synagogue, and after that, in the evening, follows the healing of many others who had gathered around. The next day Jesus resumes his tour of the synagogues. When we stand back and ponder these events, they seem to be more suited to the early period when Jesus was going from synagogue to synagogue than to a later period when the crowds came flocking to him and he withdrew to lonely places, including the mountain of the famous sermon.

We get the same impression in Mark. After the call of the four disciples, we go with them straight to Capernaum (Mark 1:16–20 and 1:21ff.).

Then come the first encounter with the demoniac in the synagogue, the healing of Peter's mother-in-law, the healings during the evening, and the continuation of the synagogue visits the following day (Mark 1:21–39). Mark himself says in so many words that Jesus was only forced to stay in lonely places *after* these events (Mark 1:40–45). When we recall that Luke detaches the incident with the centurion from the incidents discussed here and puts it in a completely different place (Luke 7) and at a different time (after the Sermon on the Mount), it would seem advisable to place the first incidents in Capernaum (synagogue; mother-in-law; evening healings) quite soon after the calling of the first four disciples, and to place the healing of the centurion's servant at a later point, when Jesus returned to the city after the Sermon on the Mount.

This solution works well for Luke and Mark, but not for Matthew! Matthew also places the healing of the centurion's servant after the Sermon on the Mount, but he locates the healing of Peter's mother-in-law and the evening healings (but *not* the demoniac in the synagogue) there as well. Some harmonists now try to argue their way out of the problem by making a distinction: Peter's mother-in-law was healed of a fever both before and after the Sermon on the Mount. Although this would, of course, have been possible, it would seem to be an artificial solution. The circumstances of the healing are specifically stated (Sabbath; fever; the grasping of the hand; the mother-in-law immediately getting up to serve). We must assume that the two accounts refer to a single healing of Peter's mother-in-law. It is better to end up with an unresolved problem than to force a solution by making an implausible distinction.

Exegetically it should be possible to look even further for the inner logic of the Capernaum passage in Matthew 8:5–17. In Luke and Mark the healing of Peter's mother-in-law follows the confrontation with a demon in the synagogue (on the Sabbath). Matthew omits this important incident in the synagogue and instead talks about the centurion (a story that Luke puts elsewhere by itself). Does Matthew have an editorial reason for doing this? In Matthew, the story of the evening healings is not followed by the continuation of preaching in the synagogues (as in Mark and Luke), but by a fulfillment quote from Isaiah 53. The point of this prophetic chapter is not so much that "He took up our infirmities and carried our diseases" as that no one believes the Servant of Yahweh despite his efforts. On the contrary: Gentiles will accept what Israel refuses to acknowledge (see Isa. 52:15–53:3; cf. also Rom. 10:16; 15:21). Now Jesus, in connection with the centurion, says, "I have not found anyone in Israel with such great faith" (Matt. 8:10). Does Matthew want to support this reproof of Israel with a *reminder* of what was done by Jesus in this very city, to his own people, without them having come to the kind of faith the centurion exhibits? The fulfillment of Isaiah 53 is then related not only to the evening healings but also to the fact that Israel refuses to accept his majesty, despite the evidence that Jesus carries their diseases—so the centurion, a man from among the Gentiles, precedes them. If this is indeed the significance of the connection in Matthew 8:5–17, it must mean that in 8:14–16 the evangelist is *looking back* to what once took place in Capernaum when Jesus was visiting Peter's mother-in-law.

7.4 Narrative Sequence and the Synoptic Problem

To conclude this chapter on the Galilean period in the Gospels, we will briefly examine a very different approach to the changes in the narrative sequence in the Gospels. Since the first half of the nineteenth century, the theory that Matthew and Luke are actually redactions of the older Gospel found in Mark was based on, among other things, a comparison of the narrative sequence of the evangelists. Karl Lachmann was the first to point out that Mark ought to be seen as the source and point of departure of the other two Gospels. He based his view on the fact that the three Gospels usually follow the same sequence of events, but that on occasion their sequences differ. If we take Mark as the source narrative, we notice that Matthew and Luke sometimes deviate from Mark's order of events, but that whenever Matthew and Luke both differ from Mark, they also differ from each other. This then shows that Mark underlies the other two Synoptics.

In recent years this hypothesis has been rather heavily criticized. There are several exceptions it fails to explain—unless one assumes the existence of a primitive Gospel of Mark. But how can one reasonably build on a theory whose central argument is based on the one hand on the Gospel of Mark as we have it and on the other hand on a hypothetical primitive Mark or other unknown historical source that is posited to account for any facts that do not fit in with the canonical Mark? The unknown source may well have contained information that could have led to a very different explanation of the phenomena familiar to us.[1]

It is striking that in modern times this question of narrative order is approached exclusively from a literary perspective,[2] as if the evangelists based their work strictly on literary sources and not on actual events. If we agree that their aim was to report history, then we must first deal with the *historical* sequence. Books that are written entirely indepen-

---

1. See, for example, H. H. Stoldt, *History and Criticism of the Marcan Hypothesis*, trans. D. L. Niewyk (Macon, Ga.: Mercer University Press, 1977).

2. See also C. M. Tuckett, "Arguments from Order: Definition and Evaluation," in *Synoptic Studies: The Ampleforth Conference of 1982 and 1983*, ed. C. M. Tuckett (Sheffield: JSOT Press, 1984), 197–219.

dent of each other can still contain parallel descriptions if all are based
on a sequence of historically determined facts. Insofar as the evangelists
follow the chronological order of the events in Jesus' life, they can still
agree closely in terms of their narrative sequence without being interde-
pendent. The only grounds for considering possible dependence among
the Gospels or dependence on a common source would be a deviation
from the historical sequence *on the same points*. This might indicate a
common source, although it also depends on how frequent and how
characteristic such similar departures from the historical order are.

What conclusions can we draw on the basis of the relationship described in this chapter between historical order and narrative sequence
in the Gospels? To find an answer to this question, we will compare the
Gospels at those points where the chronological order is interrupted or
where the narrative deviates from that order (see table 11 at the end of
this book for clarification).

Matthew interrupts the chronological order by presenting the material as a series of dioramas. The first three of these, however, are in
broad chronological sequence. The historical material of the second diorama (Matt. 8:18–9:34) is taken from a period that comes after the
events of the first diorama (4:18–8:17). And the historical content of the
third diorama (9:35–11:1) in turn comes after the events of the second
diorama. We find a *regression* to an earlier time at the beginning of the
fourth diorama (11:2ff.). When we compare this with Mark and Luke,
we come to the conclusion that the boundaries of the first three dioramas do not have any kind of corresponding interruptions or boundaries
in the other Gospels. As for the regression in 11:2, we notice that Luke
also has a chronological regression at the point where John the Baptist's question occurs (Luke 7:18), but the preceding section (7:1–17)
does not correspond with Matthew. Because all the evangelists leave
John the Baptist more or less out of the picture once they begin describing Jesus' Galilean ministry, they obviously will have to come back to
John's reactions later on. When we encounter a jump here in the chronological sequence in Matthew as well as in Luke, it may be a simple
coincidence, all the more so because generally each has his own unique
way of organizing the material.

Mark has only one regression in an otherwise chronologically ordered narrative, in 2:23. This is not reflected in Matthew, but it is in
Luke—and strikingly so. At precisely the same point (after the story of
the calling of Levi and the related conversation about fasting), the chronological order in both Mark and Luke turns back to the first Sabbath
conflict (Mark 2:18–22 and 2:23–28; Luke 5:33–39 and 6:1–5). We might
wonder whether this changing of gears at exactly the same point is co-

incidental. Both evangelists could have decided independently to turn back to the Sabbath conflicts in order to introduce an explanation for the increasingly confrontational atmosphere. But how could they both have continued their narrative right up to the pericope on fasting? The similarity here between Mark and Luke may suggest a common background or mutual dependence. But is this a viable conclusion when we view it from the perspective of a comparison of Mark and Luke in their entirety?

Luke's account, as we saw, does not have a clear chronological structure. But a comparison with the other Gospels indicates that there is more historical order in the Gospel of Luke than his own indications of time (or rather, lack thereof) might suggest. In the final analysis there are only two real regressions. The relatively loosely connected events described in 4:16–5:39 do seem to have been historically consecutive. But in Luke 6:1 we find the same regression that we observed in Mark. In 6:1–7, 17, Luke relates a series of incidents that he himself connects chronologically. Afterward, however (unlike Mark but like Matthew), he turns back in time once more in 7:18 and begins again with the question of John the Baptist. Luke's choice of material in these chapters is entirely independent from Mark. There is much in Luke that is missing in Mark, and similar material is sometimes treated very differently in Luke (cf., for example, the appointment of the Twelve in Mark 3:13–19 and Luke 6:12–16). All this means that the one striking point of similarity between Luke and Mark stands isolated and solitary in the landscape of a full comparison of the two Gospels. For this reason it does not seem advisable to make this isolated point a cornerstone for the hypothesis that Luke used Mark or vice versa. What seems more likely is that this incidental point of similarity is due to influences behind both Mark and Luke—perhaps the narrative sequence that was developing in the catechesis?

It was not the intention of this section to discuss the entire Synoptic problem. We have completely bypassed any attempt at explaining the verbal similarities *and* differences between some (not all, and not even most) pericopes. The modern hypotheses concerning the literary dependence of the Gospels are based on complex argumentation. In chapter 1 we discussed the role of the tradition. In this section we have limited ourselves to checking the argument based on the sequences of pericopes. While this is not the only argument on which modern Gospel criticism is based, it does occupy a prominent place. For this reason it seemed useful in this chapter on narrative sequence to see whether narrative sequence does indeed provide arguments in favor of the hypothesis that Matthew and Luke are secondary sources, dependent at least on Mark, for the history of Jesus' life on earth.

Our conclusion is negative. Paying attention to the way the narrative sequence relates to the historical order can help us understand the unique and independent organization of each Gospel. All three evange-lists are aware that they narrate against the backdrop of a historically determined sequence, as they repeatedly indicate. At the same time they organize the abundance of material according to their own plan. There is thus every reason to regard the first three Gospels as firsthand sources for the history of Christ's work in Galilee.

8

Galilee (I)
From the Return to Galilee
to the Appointment of the Twelve

8.1 The Return to Galilee

The ministry of Jesus Christ in Galilee can be viewed as the continuation of the preaching of John the Baptist. When John was arrested, Jesus carried on with his message. Jesus of Nazareth emphatically presented himself as "he who comes after John." He is the "one more powerful" announced by the great prophet of repentance. His work in Galilee will prove this to all of Israel.

This Galilean period does not begin without preparation. Jesus has already stepped forward and attracted attention with the miracle at the wedding at Cana and the signs he performed later, during the Passover in Jerusalem. The people in Judea have already noticed that his disciples are baptizing and arousing interest as well. Jesus is no longer an unknown, and for this reason his withdrawal to Galilee does not go unnoticed. Jesus does not inconspicuously move to the north to begin preaching from a base in Capernaum. He enters Galilee as someone whose coming people look forward to. What is new is not his public ministry per se, but the fact that he now ministers in the remote region of Galilee, with the presumption that he is the long-awaited "one who is to come" announced by John.

John the evangelist tells us that Jesus returned to Galilee during the winter, traveling from Judea by way of Samaria (John 4:43–44). He also says that the people there expect something from him—the memory of the signs he performed less than a year ago during Passover is still fresh in their minds. Now they welcome him in their midst (John 4:45, cf. 2:23). Luke also notes that Jesus' return is not quiet and unobserved. He comes in the power of the Spirit, and word about him spreads through the entire region of Galilee; all praise him when he teaches in their synagogues (Mark 4:14–15). There is every reason to regard the return to Galilee as a "grand entrance."

155

So it would be incorrect, based on Matthew 4:12–17, to suppose that
Jesus first quietly settled in Capernaum and then began his ministry. In
section 7.2 we saw that this is not what Matthew wants to portray. He
tells us that it was precisely the obscure regions of Zebulun and Naphtali, the first to be depopulated by the deportation, that Jesus was looking for. The prophecy is now fulfilled: the light has come to shine in the
darkness of Galilee. This is reinforced by the fact that Jesus settles in
Capernaum during his Galilean ministry, a city located in the extreme
north in the region formerly occupied by the tribe of Naphtali. The
move from Nazareth to Capernaum is included in the Galilean ministry, but it is not the *beginning* of that ministry. Jesus' preaching had already begun with his first appearance in southern Galilee. The "one
more powerful" who would come after John and continue his preaching does not remain in the same territory as the prophet of repentance;
after John is handed over to the authorities, Jesus travels to the Galilean
hinterlands. It is the light searching for the darkness. The "one more
powerful" withdraws in humility, for which prominent individuals in
Judea and Jerusalem ridicule him when they contemptuously refer to
him as "the Galilean" and "the Nazarene."

8.2 A Miracle from Afar for Capernaum

John, the early disciple, clearly remembers Jesus' first notable miracle after his arrival in Galilee: the healing of the son of a royal official
in Capernaum. The amazing thing about this miracle is that it was performed from a distance, and the fact that it was performed from Cana
is also significant. Jesus' first miracle had been performed here in Cana:
water had been turned into wine for a wedding, in abnormally large
quantities. That event had taken place almost a year ago. Now Jesus has
returned to Cana, but he has not arrived unnoticed. This time it is not
only his mother who looks to him with expectation. People from Capernaum, where Jesus stayed after the miracle at the wedding in Cana,
travel out to meet him. The royal official has only *heard* that Jesus has
returned (John 4:47). He does not wait to see what Jesus will do next
but travels to meet him to ask for help for his sick son. Jesus heals his
son immediately—it is determined later that the son in Capernaum was
healed at the very moment that Jesus uttered his words in Cana. It is an
impressive miracle. Healers were not unknown, but who is this who
speaks and it happens, who commands and it is done at once?

This first miracle after the return to Galilee is not recorded by the
other evangelists. So many other miracles were performed that they
could easily have forgotten this first one. It is the apostle John who, at
an advanced age, digs it out of the recesses of his memory. It certainly

was a significant beginning, useful to record so that "you may believe that Jesus is the Christ, the Son of God." Wasn't John the Baptist right when he said that he was not worthy to untie the thongs of his successor's sandals?

8.3 Nazareth Cuts Itself Off

Nazareth is not far from Cana, and it is not Jesus' intention to ignore his hometown. He makes Nazareth part of his "grand entrance" into Galilee, and on the Sabbath he speaks in the synagogue there about the coming of the year of the LORD: the Spirit of the Lord is upon him to bring the Gospel to the poor, and this Spirit has sent him to proclaim freedom for prisoners, to give sight to the blind, and to release the oppressed (Isa. 61). The sermon in Nazareth is the blueprint for his work in Galilee after John the Baptist (Mark 4:16–30).

The people of Nazareth have the same expectations as the rest of the people of Galilee. They have heard of the things that happened in Capernaum. Now they expect to see him do the same things in his hometown (Mark 4:23)! The eyes of everyone in the synagogue are upon him (Mark 4:20). But they reject what Jesus gives them. He tells them, in words that are brief and to the point, that he is the promised fulfillment of Isaiah 61: the Christ, upon whom God's Spirit rests. Through him Yahweh will now redeem his people. Jesus preaches about himself. John the Baptist always referred to another, the "one who was to come." Jesus *is* this one. This is why he speaks of his own significance, even for Nazareth. Here, however, people are willing to admire the son of Joseph (Luke 4:22b) as a healer, but not to honor him as anything other than a mere human being. The people of Nazareth are willing to bask in the glory of their village's famous son, but they refuse to bow before someone from their own ranks. They understand him quite well, but his words sound like blasphemy in their ears—that is why they decide to kill him on the spot. But Jesus shows his authority by being too strong for them: he walks right through their midst and leaves (Mark 4:30). Jesus' hometown experience is emblematic of what will happen during the rest of his activity in Israel. The reaction of Nazareth is a sentiment that will continue to develop in the nation as a whole. This Anointed of God is too ordinary for them, and when he continues to claim that he is really the Lord himself, the "one more powerful" who was to come, his own people will ultimately reject him. Laden with meaning, Luke's account begins with Jesus' ministry in Nazareth—a programmatic event in more ways than one!

Luke 4:14–30 is often regarded as an account of something that took place much later. According to this interpretation, Luke is highlighting it here for thematic reasons, even though it coincided in fact with the preaching in Nazareth that is recorded in Matthew 13:53–58 and Mark 6:1–6. In the discussion above, however, we are assuming that it occurred during the first weeks of the Galilean ministry, thereby differentiating this early preaching in Nazareth from a later visit that is recorded in Matthew and Mark. We make this assumption for several reasons.

1. In Luke 4, no miracles are performed in Nazareth, whereas during the later visit astonishment is expressed over miracles that *did* take place in Nazareth (Matt. 13:54; Mark 6:2).
2. In Luke 4, Jesus is led out of the city after preaching there. During the later visit, after his erstwhile fellow citizens give evidence of their lack of faith, Jesus performs a few miracles and then departs on his own initiative.
3. In Luke 4, people explicitly refer to events that had taken place in Capernaum. Why would they dwell on the rumors that were circulating in this particular city if Jesus were already performing signs and miracles far and wide? In Mark 6:2, people talk in general about "this wisdom that has been given him." Limiting the action to Capernaum in Luke 4 is something that is more in keeping with the earliest period. The remarkable sign that Jesus performed soon after his entry into Galilee was observed in Capernaum. We often call this the second miracle of Cana, but really it was a miracle in Capernaum, since it was there that the son of the royal official was instantly healed, and there that they checked the time ("the exact time at which Jesus had said to him, 'Your son will live'"). And it was from Capernaum that the rumor spread concerning this wonderful event. The people of Nazareth have already heard about it, and with a touch of jealousy they decide that now it is *their* turn.
4. The fact that people wondered about the source of Jesus' wisdom during both visits to Nazareth might be a source of difficulty. After all, these people know his family. But this repetition should not surprise us. Considering the lack of faith in Nazareth, it would *continue* to be the typical question they would ask regarding Jesus. This is the specific form in which the general unbelief in Nazareth manifests itself. There are also other minor differences. In Luke 4:24 Jesus says that a prophet is not "accepted" in his hometown. This sort of formulation is more in keeping with the earliest phase of his return to Galilee. Matthew and Mark say that the prophet is "without honor" in his hometown. This is in keeping with the period in which Jesus already has experienced both recognition *and* rejection elsewhere in Galilee. We also

should not be surprised that Jesus visits Nazareth once again after having been expelled in Luke 4. He is just passing through, and now he has more disciples and larger crowds that follow him. Jesus also visited Jerusalem more than once, in spite of repeated attempts to kill him (John 5:18; 7:19, 30; etc.)!

Our conclusion is that Jesus was expelled from Nazareth when he made his "grand entrance" into Galilee (Mark 4) and that he later visited the village again, but once again with little result (Matt. 13; Mark 6).

8.4 The Calling of Four Disciples

Jesus already had disciples around him during the period between his baptism by John and his entrance into Galilee. The first disciples came from among the followers of John the Baptist. At John's suggestion they turned to Jesus and showed their interest in his becoming their rabbi or teacher (John 1:39). Although Jesus had not been a student of theology and was not an expert in the law, they acknowledged him and sought his instruction. This follows a pattern that was quite common in Israel: a rabbi does not recruit his own disciples, but he acquires them when they choose him as their teacher. He gets a following. The first disciples of Jesus we hear of are Andrew and Simon, then probably John and James, followed by Philip and Nathanael (John 1:35–52). Although at first the disciples came in the usual way, everyone immediately sensed that Jesus was no ordinary rabbi. John the Baptist called him "the Lamb of God, who takes away the sin of the world." It quickly becomes apparent that Jesus is more than a teacher who waits for students to come to him. He simply commands Philip to follow him. And Philip believes that this is the Promised One spoken of by Moses and the prophets. Nathanael is confronted by Jesus' omniscience ("I saw you while you were still under the fig tree before Philip called you"). He acknowledges that this rabbi is the Son of God, the King of Israel.

The first disciples are with Jesus at the wedding in Cana, and they believe in him when he performs his first sign (John 2:2, 11). They travel with him to Capernaum, Jerusalem, and Judea (John 2:12, 22; 3:22). During this period they also perform baptisms (as former disciples of John) and as Jesus' disciples they are distinct from the followers of the Baptist (John 3:26–4:3). This does not mean, however, that they have already become Jesus' permanent retinue. The Baptist was not always in the company of his disciples, and Jesus' disciples are not always with him either. After they return to Galilee, we see four of them again actively plying their trade: fishing. Fishing season has begun, and apparently

they have left the Teacher for a brief time to devote themselves to their
livelihood. This probably happened after the return to Galilee. During
the journey through Samaria the disciples are still with Jesus (John 4:8,
27ff.). We hear nothing about disciples being present at the miracle from
Cana (the healing of the official's son) and during the events in Nazareth.
It is possible that when Jesus visited his hometown of Nazareth they temporarily returned to their own homes for the time being as well.

When Jesus later travels north along the Sea of Galilee, he sees
Simon and Andrew fishing along the shore, while James and John are
a little farther down mending their nets with their father and his crew.
Jesus immediately takes them away from their work, in the same way
that Elijah took Elisha from behind his plow and recruited him into his
service. Jesus' power is great: he speaks, and things happen! Without
any hesitation, all four drop everything and follow him. This calling of
people who already were disciples has a special significance. Jesus is
gathering a permanent retinue. He is not only the rabbi who *attracts*
disciples, but, more than that, he is the king who *calls* servants for his
work and orders them to come. Galilee will soon see that Jesus is traveling with a permanent retinue. He does not bring a message without
obligations—he is beginning to organize something. The question as to
what he has in mind will gradually be answered in the coming period.

8.5 Activity in Capernaum

With his new retinue of four disciples, Jesus arrives in Capernaum
(Mark 4:31–44; Mark 1:21–39; cf. Matt. 8:14–17). This probably is his
first visit since his return from Judea, and from now on Capernaum will
be his permanent home. Jesus probably found lodgings in the spacious
home of Peter's in-laws. It is striking that this is the house he goes to as
a matter of course after leaving the synagogue, and that when people
come searching for Jesus that evening with a request for healing, this is
where they expect to find him.

The arrival in Capernaum does not go unnoticed. Once again, Jesus
makes his entrance by going to the people and addressing them in the
synagogue. He teaches with such authority that his listeners are ap-
palled: can a person really speak this way, in a tone as if he were God
himself? At that moment there is an outburst from an unclean spirit. He
tries to turn the people of Capernaum against this newcomer from Nazareth. What is Jesus doing here? Let Capernaum take care of itself! The
unclean spirit is well aware that Jesus' authoritative teaching is
grounded in his origins. He is the Holy One of God. But at the same
time, the evil spirit infects the people with the idea that this Holy One
has come to bring about their downfall. He tries to turn their dismay

into fear and loathing. But Jesus drives the spirit out in a most impressive way. The evil spirit has to clear the field, leaving behind proof of Jesus' good intentions: a fellow citizen who has been healed!

Upon his arrival at home, the victor from the synagogue would seem to be the loser on his home turf: his hostess has suddenly become seriously ill. But Jesus orders the fever to depart, and the joy of the Sabbath is restored as Peter's mother-in-law serves the Sabbath meal. His new followers have been given an encouraging sign here at home.

In the meantime, news of the incident in the synagogue has spread far and wide. Hardly has the Sabbath come to a close with the setting of the sun when all sorts of sick and possessed people are brought to Jesus. He heals them all by the light of a few Sabbath lamps, which on this particular evening burn well into the night.

The next morning, however, it becomes clear that Jesus has not come for Capernaum alone. In the early hours of the morning he leaves town to seek solitude for prayer to his Father. When the shocked disciples find their missing teacher, he tells them that he must expand his ministry to include all the towns and villages in the entire region. The incident in Capernaum must develop into ministry throughout Galilee. From this point on, Jesus' activity in Galilee that began relatively quietly is transformed into a mass movement.

8.6 Catching People

The evangelists do not provide an exact account of the preaching in the various synagogues. They do note, however, that soon the people no longer wait for the well-known teacher to come to them—they go out to him, to where he is. This means that after a while Jesus no longer travels through Galilee with only his retinue of four disciples (and perhaps also a varying number of additional followers); he is now constantly accompanied by all sorts of interested persons and is sought after to perform miracles and healings. The strikingly large number of people who are healed of their blindness, deafness, demonic possession, or paralysis helps to attract even more curious people. Now Jesus stands "with the people crowding round him and listening to the word of God" (Luke 5:1). During this period Jesus does not appear to reject the multitudes, even though he withdraws at times into solitude to pray. He lets the people come and he becomes involved with them. Thus he shows that has truly come for *all people*. The popular movement that was picking up momentum coincided with his intentions. But how?

Jesus gives his disciples a glimpse of the answer (Luke 5:1–11). At one point during this period he is with the crowds near the Sea of Galilee. Apparently the men in his chosen retinue had seized the opportu-

nity the night before to ply their old trade and try to catch some fish.
After all, they had not closed down their fishing enterprises when the
Master had first called them to follow him. And when the opportunity
presented itself, they followed the call of their fishermen's blood to go
fishing at night on the lake. In the morning, as they are putting away
their nets, Jesus asks for their help. He commandeers a boat that belongs to Simon and uses it as a floating speaker's podium to keep from
being pushed into the lake by the pressing crowd. After finishing his
teaching, Jesus performs the miracle of the miraculous catch of fish in
broad daylight for Simon and his companions. As the Lord of creation
he commands the fish. Understanding this, Simon falls to his knees:
"Go away from me, Lord; I am a sinful man!" But Jesus teaches Peter,
James, and John that his majesty is no reason for them to leave his retinue. On the contrary, it is through this majesty that Jesus will turn his
retinue into fishers of people. "From now on you will catch men," he
tells them. This is a curious statement. Jesus has already made a good
catch of people from the looks of things: a crowded beach full of men
and women. But he appears to have something else in mind. All these
people must be "caught" for Jesus. They are swimming nearby, true, but
they are still outside the net. They give no sign of submitting to the
words they are hearing. Nevertheless, Jesus is working toward the future in which many will, like Simon, bow before him and surrender
themselves to the divine authority of God's Son. Being interested in
Jesus is not the point; submission to him is what it is all about. This submission will be brought about through the ministry of his followers.
When the period of suffering and humiliation is over, Jesus will gather
these people by the thousands in Simon's net on the day of Pentecost.
The perspective that is opened up by the miraculous catch of fish goes
well beyond the interest and expectations on the part of the curious and
needy crowds of the Galilean ministry.

The story of the miraculous catch of fish in Luke 5:1–11 is often identified with the calling of the four disciples (Mark 1:16–20; Matt. 4:18–
22). This is not surprising. The setting is the same: fishing gear and the
sea. Three of the characters seem to be the same: Simon, James, and
John. And the ending is the same: leaving everything, they follow Jesus.
But the differences are greater than the similarities, and they are decisive in making a distinction between the calling of the four disciples on
the one hand and the surprising catch of fish on the other. We list here
a number of points on which Luke 5 differs from the story of the calling
of the disciples:

1. Jesus teaches the multitudes from a ship—instead of walking
   along the shore with no crowds in sight.

2. The disciples are washing the big nets they used during the night—instead of fishing from the shore by casting nets or mending nets on the beach.

3. Instead of immediately leaving the nets, they discover that the nets have been miraculously filled!

4. Andrew is not present at the miraculous catch of fish. James and John, who used to work for a competitor, Zebedee, are now called "Simon's partners" (Luke 5:10). This must refer to their partnership as Jesus' followers.

5. After the catch of fish Jesus does not give an order to follow him. On the contrary, Simon begs Jesus to leave him, a sinful man. Jesus' order is: Don't be afraid!

6. When Jesus calls the four, he takes them on as apprentices, so to speak: "I will *make* you fishers of men" (Matt. 4:19). There is a reference to this statement in Luke 5:10, but the wording refers not to a period of training but to the promised result. Those who had been called to be made fishers of men are now told, "From now on you will *catch* men." After Simon admits that he is a sinner, not worthy to be one of Jesus' followers, Jesus goes a step further in his promises to the disciples.

7. Considering their background as fishermen, it is not surprising that on more than one occasion Jesus uses images or events related to fishing when he speaks to them. This happens again after Easter: the catch of fish is again overwhelming and represents a reminder and restatement for the apostles of their continuing mission (John 21).

8. In Mark and Matthew, when the disciples are called, all four leave their boats and their nets behind. We do not read this in Luke 5:11. There they leave everything and go with Jesus. We should understand this as referring to the enormous draft of fish. They were willing to sacrifice a night's rest to attempt to catch some fish (for themselves as well as to sell). And now that they have caught far more during the day than they dared hope to catch at night, they leave the whole business behind—a major sacrifice for good fishermen and experienced businessmen! But they leave this enormous catch of fish in order to travel with Jesus toward an even greater catch of people, who will let themselves be carried off to God's kingdom through faith in Jesus.

8.7 John's Concern: The Failure to Recognize God's Son

During this stormy period of preaching, healing, and growing crowds, a question comes from John the Baptist, now in prison, reminding us that something is missing. Jesus entered Galilee as "the one who comes after John." So ultimately his ministry is not to be measured by the popularity he enjoys at the moment but by the message that John the Baptist preached about the ministry of "the one to come."

John announced the coming of the LORD himself in the form of a human being, with sandals on his feet, the thongs of which he was not worthy to undo. The one to come after him will do God's work: baptize with the Holy Spirit. He will execute God's judgment: the winnowing fork is in his hand. People will have to bow and humble themselves for the coming Angel of the LORD.

Now the forerunner is in prison, and he hears about the things the Christ is doing in Galilee. His disciples bring him news that makes him feel uneasy and concerned. Is Jesus, with this kind of ministry, the one who is to come? Or is there still someone else coming after *him*? It is a rather somber question to raise during a celebration of preaching and healing. But it is in fact a very understandable question that focuses everyone's attention on one missing element. Jesus does fulfill the prophecy: the blind are given their sight, the dead are raised, and the gospel is being preached to the poor (Matt. 11:2ff.; Mark 7:18ff.). But what is missing is an appropriate reaction on the part of the people. Admiration is not the same as worship. John the Baptist heard the voice from heaven: This is my beloved Son! But how few of the people bow down before Jesus as the Son of God. Few join Nathanael (John 1:49) in his confession that Jesus of Nazareth is the Son of God, the King of Israel. Why does Jesus not bring the prophesied judgment on these unbelieving people? John the Baptist does not doubt Jesus, but he wonders whether Jesus intends to leave part of his work for someone who will be coming after *him*.

This question gives Jesus the opportunity to take stock. John the Baptist is given a reassuring answer: yes, Jesus really is the Angel of the LORD whom he had announced. And "blessed is anyone who takes no offense at me" (Matt. 11:6 NRSV). At the same time, Jesus involves the crowds in his answer to John the Baptist. They have to take stock as well. Does their attitude toward him correspond with the reactions evoked by John's earlier preaching about the "one who is more powerful"? If not, then judgment hangs irrevocably over the towns where Jesus performed his miracles: Capernaum, Chorazin, and Bethsaida.

In his prayer of thanksgiving to God the Father, which these speeches lead up to, Jesus publicly professes that he and the Father are one, and that God the Father has given all things over to him. He is greater than the temple and the ark of the covenant. God has revealed this to the simple, to "little children," but hidden it from the wise and learned (Matt. 11:25–27).

This stock taking ends in a striking way. The crowds are standing around Jesus. They have come from far and wide. Yet Jesus now invites them to "come to me" and to "take my yoke upon you." They are present, certainly, but not in the right way. They are in the presence of the teacher and the miracle worker, but they are blind to the presence of the Son of God. John the Baptist's intuition was correct, but he has to understand that Jesus has the patience to wait for everything the Father plans to give him. His reaction to the disappointing absence of real recognition is proof of his readiness to suffer.

8.8 Conspiracy against the Lord of the Sabbath

During this time it is also becoming clear that the leaders of Israel are discussing the possibility of putting Jesus to death. His behavior is such that they are forced to react. He emphatically allows himself liberties with regard to the Sabbath that would be inappropriate for an ordinary Israelite—that would in fact make him guilty of trespassing the LORD's clear commandment concerning this day of rest and thus deserving of the death penalty. This would constitute provocative behavior on the part of a human being who in principle submitted himself to God's law. But this is more than provocation, it is revelation: Jesus shocks people with who he is—none other than the LORD himself, the Son of God, who is not subject to the law but may handle it in any way he chooses.

The confrontation occurs on the Sabbath when the Pharisees take him to task for allowing his disciples to pick heads of grain and eat them. This was considered preparing a meal on the Sabbath, which had been a sin even during the years of wandering in the wilderness. We probably should regard this intervention of the Pharisees as a formal preliminary step toward a trial. It is the mandatory warning in which the sinner is made aware of his sin, so that during the next stage he cannot plead ignorance of the law. This is why they choose an infraction of the law committed by the disciples. The views of the teacher appear to have had a negative influence on others, which is all the more reason to bring the matter to trial. Jesus does not deny that the law has been broken. But he appeals to his special authority: the Son of man is Lord, and that means that he is Lord of the Sabbath as well. To Jewish ears such a statement is blasphemy—unless one acknowledges that the speaker really is the incarnation of the Son of God (Matt. 12:1–8 and parallel passages).

The next step is to set a trap on the Sabbath. The leaders put Jesus to the test in a synagogue where a man with a shriveled hand is present. They ask him, Is it lawful to heal on the Sabbath? It is clear that they want to catch him committing an unmistakable and unnecessary viola-

tion of the law (the man's life is not in danger), in front of witnesses.
Mark says in so many words that the Pharisees were looking for a way
to bring charges against him (Mark 3:1–6). Suddenly the threat of death
is very near. But Jesus does not evade this threat. He heals the man and
thus lays himself open to the consequences. The Pharisees now deliberate with the Herodians (the supporters of Herod Antipas, who had gotten rid of John the Baptist). These initial plans to condemn and execute
Jesus as a lawbreaker are not born of misunderstanding. They are the
misplaced reaction to an incident in which Jesus confronts the leaders
with a choice. He forces them to state publicly whether they believe that
he is the Son of God and the Lord of the Sabbath. In the synagogue he
asks them whether they would not save a sheep that had fallen into a pit
on the Sabbath. Thus, Jesus saves a human being on the Sabbath. At
issue is not whether the man's life is in danger, since this is not the case
with a shriveled hand. The point is that Jesus presents himself as the
one to whom human beings belong. He stands above them just as the
shepherd stands above his sheep, and as the Master of people he is free
to care for them on the Sabbath. Did not God give us the Sabbath day
in order to bestow good gifts on *his* people? The Son of God does likewise on the Sabbath.

Jesus' remarkable presentation of himself as Lord of the Sabbath is
the focal point of the confrontation between the Messiah and the leaders. This becomes apparent during a Jewish feast in Jerusalem (John 5).
This is probably a visit that took place some time later, but we will discuss it here, since it shows that conflicts related to the Sabbath had become the central issue during these months and that the people in
Jerusalem were aware of it, while Jesus, for his part, presents himself
in the temple city too as Lord of the Sabbath. During this feast the Lord
heals a man who has been paralyzed for thirty-eight years. We might
think that this man could have waited one more day so that he could
have been healed on the day after the Sabbath. But Jesus deliberately
chooses the Sabbath to heal this man lying near the pool of Bethesda,
and even commands him to carry a burden (another unlawful activity!):
the man has to pick up his mat and walk away. This action does not go
unnoticed as a violation of the law, and after the authorities ask a few
questions, the trail leads to Jesus. John notes that the Jews were already
persecuting Jesus in order to kill him because he "was doing these
things on the Sabbath" (John 5:16). Not only does this refer to the healing of the paralyzed man, but it indicates that Jesus was a wanted man
and plans had been made to put him to death as a habitual Sabbath
breaker. Jesus uses the opportunity to clearly express again his right as
the Son of the Father to work any day of the week. His activity on the
Sabbath does not call the law into question but serves to reveal who he

really is. Thus the people, whether they are interested or skeptical, are forced to make a choice. If people fail to recognize Jesus as the one who is more powerful, the Angel of the LORD proclaimed by John, it is not his fault. In his speech the Lord also points to the testimony of John the Baptist (John 5:31–35). John testified that he was a voice in the wilderness, calling on people to prepare a way for the *Lord*. The work that Jesus does on the Sabbath also shows that he is the Son of the Father, who has not stopped working even up to the present (John 5:17ff., 36ff.).

It is important to understand that the rejection of Jesus did not begin over some minor point or as the result of a misunderstanding. It was perfectly clear that Jesus did things on the Sabbath that the people of Israel were not permitted to do. His conspicuous actions forced people to make a decision. John the Baptist had said that people would have to bow before the Lord who was coming after him. Instead, the people are very interested but keep their distance. They do not reach the point of acknowledging Jesus as God's Son. Jesus makes sure that the people cannot permanently evade the actual choice. By his actions on the Sabbath he steps outside the bounds of the ordinary and acceptable. The spiritual leaders now are forced to set an example with their reaction to Jesus. They reject him and choose to take the path that will lead to the death penalty for Jesus. Now the people find themselves caught between demons who cry out that Jesus is the holy Son of God, leaders who brand him as a Sabbath breaker, and Jesus himself, who speaks out against the religious leaders and refuses to accept the endorsement of the evil spirits. The crowds must choose for themselves: it is *their* faith that Jesus is concerned with. This is evident from the way in which his dealings with the crowds change during this period.

8.9 The Twelve: A Restored Foundation

At the time of the first conspiracy against him (Luke 6:12), Jesus goes to a mountain to pray. Apparently there was a particular mountain to which Jesus often retreated, most likely on the northeastern shore of the Sea of Galilee. Traveling from Capernaum along the sea to the northeast, one quickly arrives in Bethsaida, just east of the point where the Jordan empties into the northern end of the sea. The mountain is a short distance away to the southeast. It could easily be reached by crossing the sea from Capernaum. What makes this retreat special is that Jesus spends an entire night in prayer (Luke 6:12). This is the only time we read about an entire night of prayerful vigil on Jesus' part. We seem to be on the verge of an important event. The following day Jesus calls his disciples together and chooses twelve of them, whom he calls "apostles": they are to stay with him at all times. They are the ones he will send out to preach, and they will be given the power to cast out evil spirits (Luke 6:13; Mark 3:14–15, cf. Matt. 10:1). The impressive tour of the Twelve throughout Israel does not come until later, after they have been commissioned by Jesus (Matt. 10; Mark 6; Luke 9). What is special on this morning is their appointment and their number. The first permanent retinue of four is now expanded to twelve. In Israel the number twelve connotes foundations. Israel is built on the foundation of twelve patriarchs and is therefore composed of twelve tribes. The choice of *twelve* apostles shows enormous presumption.[1]

The appointment of this group of twelve coincides with a special moment in Jesus' dealings with the crowds. Until now, the crowds came to him; they sought him out and pressed against him. During the period of increasing hostility from the leaders, however, the time comes when Jesus takes the crowds with him and goes before them as their leader. He shows them the way to the mountain and appears to have a special plan in mind (see section 9.1 for a further discussion). Josephus gives us several examples of popular leaders who take the people with them into the desert, usually to prepare for some sort of action. The government is suspicious of such mass retreats, as when Claudius Lysias says to Paul, "Aren't you the Egyptian who started a revolt and led four thousand terrorists out into the desert some time ago?" (Acts 21:38). When Jesus takes the crowds with him to the solitude of the mountain, he provides himself with an extended official retinue. His choice of *twelve* apostles reflects a programmatic intent. He is laying a new foundation, or is restoring the old one. The descendants of the twelve tribes were prepared by John the Baptist for the arrival of the Lord himself. Now that he has come with his signs and his Good News, many still choose to remain aloof, and the leaders have already decided to reject him by setting in motion a process to bring the Lord of the Sabbath to trial.

Now Jesus gathers the people together and presents himself to them, along with his permanent staff of twelve. That is programmatic also: the descendants of the twelve tribes are invited to come to the Lord together with these twelve whom he himself has chosen. Jesus has become the center of a core group, and now he wants to become the center of the twelve tribes. A regrouping is taking place. It is no longer necessary to orient oneself toward Mount Zion and the high priest—from now on one must orient oneself toward this mountain of the great King. The Twelve must serve as the vanguard of converted Israel. Those who

---

1. For a more detailed discussion of the Twelve, see my *Ambten in de apostolische kerk: Een exegetisch mozaïek* (Kampen: Kok, 1984), 12–15.

reject Jesus place themselves outside God's people. The lineage of the twelve patriarchs now continues via the twelve apostles. This is a call for everyone to step forward. It is also a threatening omen for the leaders who want to take God's people away from Jesus: it is they who will lose the sons of Jacob and Jesus who will win them.

We find the *names* of the Twelve in lists in Matthew 10:1–4; Mark 3:16–19; Luke 6:14–16; and Acts 1:13 (in Acts 1 the name of Judas Iscariot is missing). These lists are not entirely parallel, and all do not contain the same names. Apparently some of the men had more than one name. Yet a certain structure is evident in these lists: they all contain three groups of four that are never mixed.

The first group of four always begins with Simon (or Simon Peter, or Peter). Next we find the names of James and John (always in this order; James was probably the older of the two brothers). Finally there is Andrew, the brother of Simon. He is sometimes listed before and sometimes after the sons of Zebedee. These four persons—two sets of two brothers—were the disciples who were called at an early stage to form the first retinue of four.

The second group of four always begins with Philip. The others follow in no fixed order: Bartholomew, Thomas, and Matthew. Some scholars think that Nathanael (John 1:46–52; 21:2), who is mentioned in close connection with Philip in John 1, is the same as Bartholomew who in three of the four lists is named after Philip. It is not certain, however, that this Nathanael was one of the Twelve. If he was, then we have just as much (or just as little) right to equate him with Simon of Cana (see below), because we know that Nathanael came from that town. (Whether Matthew is the same as Levi the tax collector whom Jesus called will be discussed in section 9.7.)

The third group of four always begins with James the son of Alphaeus and always ends with Judas Iscariot. There is some lack of clarity about the names of the tenth and eleventh apostles. In both his Gospel and Acts, Luke names Simon the Zealot and Judas the son of James. The former would have been the same as Simon of Cana, who is put in the eleventh place in Matthew and Mark. They name Thaddaeus as the tenth (according to most manuscripts, Matthew here lists Lebbaeus, whose surname was Thaddaeus). Is this Thaddaeus (alias Lebbaeus) the same as Jude the son of James? This seems to be an unavoidable conclusion.

The fact that the Twelve were sent out throughout Israel in pairs created special relationships among them. It is not unlikely that these pairs are combined here into the groups of four.

We need to pay special attention to one apostle who is not very well known: Simon, who is distinguished from Simon Peter by the addition of "the Zealot" or "of Cana." He is often seen as a (former) Zealot, and the fact that Jesus recruited one of his followers from that particular circle has led to speculation. There are, after all, no former Pharisees among the apostles. Did Jesus have a special affinity with the patriotic liberation movement known as the Zealots? In two of the Gospels, this Simon is known as Simon of Cana. This must mean "with origins in Cana." Some manuscripts read *Kananaios,* which could also be understood as "coming from Cana" (cf. *Nazarēnos* and *Nazaraios,* meaning "from Nazareth"). Some scholars believe that both *Kananaios* and *Zelōtēs* refer to a Zealot. But historical research shows that the title "Zealot" was not used to refer to the radical liberation party until after the time of Jesus' ministry. Regarding this term, the following points should be made:

1. The rabbinical *Qannaim* cannot be identified with the name of the party of the Zealots and thus does not provide a basis for interpreting *Kananaios* in the New Testament as "Zealot" via the rabbinical *Qannaim.*[2]
2. *Zealots* as the name of a party did not appear until *after* the time of Jesus.[3]
3. The *party* of the Zealots did not yet exist during the first half of the first century.[4]

We must therefore interpret the title *Zelōtēs* as a nickname for this apostle: "Simon the Striver" (cf. the name *Boanergēs,* "Sons of Thunder," for the sons of Zebedee). And we can dismiss the interpretation of *Kananaios* as something other than a man from Cana. This Simon thus was distinguished from Simon Peter by the addition of his place of origin ("of Cana"), or by the use of a nickname that probably referred to his characteristic enthusiasm.

There is no reason for reaching any special conclusions regarding the environment from which the apostles came. Jesus called those whom he wanted to call, and he made a free choice. If there is anything

2. B. Salomonsen, "Some Remarks on the Zealots with Special Regard to the Term Qannaim in Rabbinic Literature," *New Testament Studies* 12 (1965–66): 164–76.

3. M. Borg, "The Currency of the Term *Zealot,*" *Journal of Theological Studies* 22 (1971): 504–12.

4. M. J. J. Menken, "De 'zealoten': Een overzicht," *Vox Theologica* 45 (1975): 30–47; cf. R. A. Horsley, "Josephus and the Bandits," *Journal for the Study of Judaism* 10 (1979): 37–47; H. Guevara, *La resistencia judia contra Roma en la epoca de Jesus* (Meitingen: Meitingen, 1981); R. A. Horsley, "The Zealots: Their Origin, Relationships and Importance in the Jewish Revolt," *Novum Testamentum* 28 (1986): 159–92. For more about the Zealots, see also my companion volume, *Het evangelie van Gods zoon* (Kampen: Kok, 1996; English translation forthcoming), sec. 1.2.3.

particularly notable, it is the total absence of references to high positions or wealthy backgrounds, such as those we find in connection with others: Jairus, the leader of the synagogue; Nicodemus, expert in the law; Joseph of Arimathea, a member of the council, and so on. The only indication of social position tells us a great deal about Jesus' mercy: Matthew, in one list, is called "the tax collector" (Matt. 10:3).

9

Galilee (II)
From the Sermon on the Mount to the Commissioning of the Twelve

9.1 The Sermon on the Mount: A New Constitution for Israel

After providing himself with a new retinue, *the Twelve*—a number with significant connotations—Jesus goes up to a mountain and speaks to the crowds in a lengthy discourse, which we know as the Sermon on the Mount (Matt. 5–7; Luke 6:20–49). Jesus later repeats the teachings it contains many times in longer or shorter units, as the Gospels show. And there is no reason to doubt that elements of the Sermon on the Mount had already been part of Jesus' teaching in the synagogues. Even at the time of his first appearance in the synagogue in Capernaum, those who heard him were startled by his new teaching, presented with authority. What made the Sermon on the Mount so special was probably not its content per se, but rather the emphasis with which Jesus summarized his whole body of instruction, as well as the location and the form of the presentation.

Jesus is not teaching in the synagogues, surrounded by the local elders. Here he has his own "elders" gathered round him, and he chooses a special place: a mountain. This event has often been compared to the giving of the law on Mount Sinai. And there are indeed significant parallels. Jesus takes the multitudes with him and leads them to the mountain; he utters his commandments with such authority that the people tremble with amazement at his teaching. Christ presents himself as the lawgiver and judge: "Not everyone who says to me, 'Lord, Lord,' will enter the kingdom of heaven, but only he who does the will of my Father who is in heaven. Many will say to me on that day, 'Lord, Lord, did we not prophesy in your name, and in your name drive out demons and perform many miracles?' Then I will tell them plainly, 'I never knew you. Away from me, you evildoers!' " (Matt. 7:21–23). John the Baptist had already said that the winnowing fork would be in the hand of him who was to come after him: now Jesus has proved to be the Judge of the world, of Israel, and of his own disciples. His commandments must be heard *and* obeyed (Matt. 7:24). He has the right to pronounce blessings and to proclaim woes (Luke 6:20–26). The crowds, who still come to him for healing (Luke 6:18–19), must now learn that it is the Lord himself who is standing before them. In the words *"I* tell you the truth" they feel the breath of Yahweh and they shudder in awe. But that is as far as their response goes, and Jesus must still endure their failure to understand and acknowledge him. So he teaches his disciples that they will be persecuted because of him (Matt. 5:11), and he explains that it is precisely this path along which they will follow him to their heavenly reward.

Is there a contradiction between Matthew and Luke regarding the *place* of this discourse? It is often suggested that Matthew reports a Sermon on the Mount and Luke a Sermon in the Plain. This would coincide with the evangelists' differing editorial points of view: while Matthew supposedly draws parallels with Sinai, Luke pays more attention to Jesus' descent to the level of ordinary people. According to this viewpoint, the historicity of the Sermon on the Mount quickly fades and all that remains are redactions of scattered traditions reported by Matthew and Luke. It is therefore important to focus on the *historical* location of this talk.

Luke writes that after the appointment of the Twelve, Jesus "went down with them and stood on a level place" (Luke 6:17). The wording here allows us to imagine a mountain plateau, although it may also refer to the foot of the mountain. Jesus spent the previous night in prayer in a lonely place, so he had to descend from the mountain, since higher up on the mountainside there would not be enough room for all the crowds to gather. In addition, a speaker who wants to address a large group in mountainous country must stand below them. When the audience sits on the slope and the speaker addresses them from a lower point, the human voice carries far and can be heard by a large audience. At Sinai this was the other way around, but there the divine voice spoke with great and awesome power. When Jesus delivers God's word with his human voice, he must go down to a lower place in order to speak audibly to the people gathered there.

Matthew seems to be presenting the situation in reverse. In the New International Version, Matthew 5:1 reads as follows: "Now when he saw the crowds, he went up on a mountainside." But the Greek literally says, "he went up to the mountain." At the end of chapter 4, Matthew describes how Jesus traveled around Galilee and how the crowds came to him from all sides. When Jesus sees this, he senses that the moment has come to address the multitudes. Just as people "go up to Jerusalem" for great feasts, so we now see Jesus "go up to the mountain." Matthew does not intend to say that Jesus *climbed* the mountain, but that he *went up to* the mountain. This does not describe the precise location of the speaker but rather the environment that was chosen for the talk.

In short, Jesus deliberately chose "the mountain" as the place to gather his disciples and the crowds when he decided it was time to promulgate his new constitution for Israel. The discourse itself is not given *on* the mountain, but at the foot of the mountain or somewhere on the lower slopes.

9.2 Lepers, Gentiles, and the Dead Are Included

After Jesus "comes down" from the mountain to the lower-lying Galilean countryside, he continues his work. The Gospels describe a few characteristic miracles from this period. To begin with, Jesus cleanses a leper who had entered the city and the synagogue—which was against the law—but he does not send him away before touching the man and thus taking on the man's uncleanness by becoming unclean himself. Then he sends the healed leper to the priest (Matt. 8:1–4; Mark 1:40–45; Luke 5:12–16). The law required that anyone suffering from leprosy had to be expelled from the community. The law could not save them from this fate—all they could do was wait for God to remove the disease. Only then could the priest take the legal steps of confirming that the leper had been cleansed and of bringing the necessary sacrifices. By cleansing a leper so soon after the Sermon on the Mount, Jesus is validating what he said about coming to fulfill the Law and the Prophets. Now he has taken our infirmities upon himself (Isa. 53)!

It is not only the ostracized lepers who are reintroduced in the community, but the Gentiles as well. After the Sermon on the Mount, Jesus enters Capernaum and is approached with a request to heal the servant of a centurion. On the way to the centurion's house, Jesus sees the man coming out to meet him. His words reveal deep faith. Jesus need not trouble himself with coming under the roof of his house. "Just say the word, and my servant will be healed." The centurion recognizes Jesus as the Stronger One, the one who speaks, and it is! Jesus marvels at the centurion's faith and observes that he has yet to find such faith in all of Israel. He links this with the promise that "many will come from east and west and will take their places at the feast with Abraham, Isaac and Jacob in the kingdom of heaven. But the subjects of the kingdom will be thrown outside, into the darkness." The healing of the centurion's servant thus becomes a sign pregnant with meaning for the future: Jesus brings not only unclean lepers but also Gentiles into the kingdom. The law excluded certain groups of people, but Jesus is greater than the law, and by his acts of cleansing and mercy he opens for all believers the door to the coming heavenly kingdom (Matt. 8:5–13; Luke 7:1–10).

The end of the law is death, and no temple sacrifice has yet been able to remove death from God's people. That will require a different sacrifice. Jesus shows that he has come to bring back those who have been excluded from God's people by death and to call them to new life. Luke tells us how, shortly after the Sermon on the Mount, Jesus raises the only son of a widow from Nain from the bier on which he was being carried to the grave (Luke 7:11–17). The people are seized with awe, and they praise God who "has come to help his people." The news of Jesus' raising of this young man spreads throughout Judea and the entire region of Palestine.

Obviously Jesus did not call the Twelve together in order to withdraw. And he did not take the crowds to the mountain to cut himself off from others. His miracles continue. And while Jesus now presents himself more openly as Israel's new center, he shows at the same time that he is doing this to welcome into his kingdom *all* those who believe. Lepers, Gentiles, and the dead: this king has come to bring *life* to Israel and the nations!

9.3 Insinuation from Jerusalem: Beware Beelzebub!

In chapter 8 we discussed how the hostility against Jesus from the Pharisees and the legal experts quickly found expression in protests against his activity as Lord of the Sabbath. Attempts are made to charge him with breaking the law and to sentence him to death. In the meantime, the crowds keep growing. After the Sermon on the Mount things reach such a pitch that Jesus can no longer appear openly in any city and is forced to seek out solitary places. And even then, many people manage to find him (Mark 1:45). His reputation continues to grow when he raises the boy in Nain from the dead. It becomes difficult to keep people away from him. Charging Jesus with not respecting the Sabbath is no longer an adequate weapon. The crowds have such awe for his works that they probably accept without much difficulty the fact that the Master does things on the Sabbath that they themselves are not permitted to do. People keep asking themselves during this period whether he may not be the Messiah, the son of David (Matt. 12:23). If he is the Messiah, he would be entitled to the liberties he takes with the law of Moses.

A second weapon is aimed at Jesus during this period, forged among Jerusalem's legal experts (Mark 3:22). They use Jesus' actions, which cannot be denied, as a lever against him by means of a theological explanation. As an alternative to the hesitant question whether this man might perhaps be the Messiah, they offer their firm conviction that Jesus' incomparable power over the demons comes from the fact that he has entered into a pact with the devil. In other words, he performs his deeds through Beelzebub, the chief of the unclean spirits. Such a monstrous alliance between a man from Nazareth and the master of all demons would adequately explain his dazzling miracles. The people are thus warned: what Jesus does may be astonishing, but it comes from the great enemy himself!

Jesus takes this insinuation, which was spread throughout Galilee by the theologians from Jerusalem and readily adopted by the Pharisees, and at the right moment puts it center stage. He is back home in Capernaum (Mark 3:20). Once again, the crowds come pouring in, and Jesus heals a man who is possessed, blind, and dumb—the height of inaccessibility! The people who see this are beside themselves: could this be the son of David (Matt. 12:22–23)? The legal experts from Jerusalem and the Pharisees, however, ascribe the miracle to Beelzebub (Matt. 12:24; Mark 3:22). So Jesus calls them together and discusses their insinuation (Mark 3:23ff.). Their accusation betrays their evil intentions: why aren't they pleased to see Satan driving out Satan? With such internal conflict, Satan's kingdom would quickly be demolished! They don't want to save Satan's kingdom from destruction by attacking Jesus, do they? The true picture is quite different: Jesus is a liberator. He rescues Satan's victims from Satan's house and shows Israel the spoils. The Stronger One plunders the kingdom of the demons, and the demons are defenseless before him. The spoils consist of people made whole—for example, the man once possessed who is now able to see and speak again.

By openly discussing the insinuation made against him, Jesus indicates his awareness of the growing hostility. Yet he endures it. Demons are driven out, yet the hostile legal experts are welcome to stay and receive instruction and admonition. Such is the care that the son of David has for those who surround and threaten him with their slander.

9.4 The Parables: Hearing and Not Hearing

What is so striking about this period is that Jesus does not withdraw into a circle of supporters. He does not allow hostility to drive him into a resistance movement. His words and deeds continue to be directed toward disciples, interested spectators, and opponents. The entire populace remains the object of his concern. The dividing line is not between Jesus and his opponents; rather, it results from the decisive choice with which Jesus continues to confront the people. Jesus himself takes and keeps control. We see this after the discussion of the Beelzebub attack, when Jesus takes the crowds with him to the Sea of Galilee and speaks to them in parables (Matt. 13:1–53; Mark 4:1–34; Luke 8:4–18). In this way he creates a division between those who do not want to listen and those who take his words to heart. Those who already have understanding will receive more through these evocative stories. The others can only stare at the incomprehensible parables and see nothing. These parables as such do not conceal the truth. Rather, they are pedagogically speaking a test for those who listen to them. The disciples have been given the knowledge of the kingdom's secrets, and now they are expected to go even further. The many interested spectators who admire Jesus' deeds but do not accept his authority see that the door of his teaching, which at first stood wide open, is now barely ajar. Anyone who wants to enter through that door must become seriously involved!

The circle is closing around those who hear the word of God (as Jesus now presents it) *and do it*. This becomes clear when Jesus' mother, brothers, and sisters come looking for him in Capernaum. They announce their arrival at the house where Jesus is living, which once again is crowded with people. We would expect him to give priority to his family, but Jesus points to his disciples and says that the most important group is the one gathered here around him. This is quite a statement, coming as it does from someone who honors his mother, brothers, and sisters! Jesus does not suggest indifference toward family. Rather, he is making a remarkable statement about the close ties being created between all who desire to come to God through him. The body of Christ, the congregation of believers that Paul will write about, is beginning to emerge here.

Luke places the arrival of the family after the parables (Luke 8:19–21), probably as a thematic conclusion to the parable about true hearing (cf. Luke 8:18 and 8:21b). Both Matthew and Mark are more precise than Luke in describing how Jesus crossed to the other side of the sea at the end of the day of parables. So the arrival of the family must have taken place during the morning of that day or during the previous evening. Matthew and Mark place the story before the parables (Matt. 12:46–50; Mark 3:31–35).[1]

9.5 Missionary Work in the Decapolis

At the end of the long day in which Jesus limits himself to speaking in parables, he tells his disciples to cross to the other side of the lake.

---

1. For the question as to whether it really was Jesus' family who came to get him because it was said that he had lost his mind, see my commentary on Mark 3:22 (*Marcus: Het evangelie volgens Petrus*, 2d ed., Commentaar op het Nieuwe Testament, 3d series [Kampen: Kok, 1992]).

There is something symbolic in this crossing. The crowds are insistent, but only those who are willing to go aboard with Jesus can follow him. One of the legal experts asks for permission to go wherever the Master goes. But Jesus points out to him that the Son of man is like a hunted deer, without a place to lay his head. Another disciple, who wants to bury his father before going, comes up against the absolute choice involved in following Jesus (Matt. 8:18–22). In the end the crowds see the little boat sailing away with only Jesus and his disciples on board. What is their destination?

The disciples may be asking themselves the same question that night, when a storm overtakes them and the Master lies sleeping. Have they put out to sea only to perish there? But Jesus, awakened by them, silences the waves and shows that they have nothing to fear. Jesus is not the pawn of the elements. He reaches the goal to which they are willing to follow him (Matt. 8:23–27; Mark 4:35–41; Luke 8:22–25).

This goal appears to be the shore of gentile territory: the land of the Gerasenes in the Decapolis. This region, consisting of a federation of ten cities, was formerly known as Gilead and was at one time occupied by part of the twelve tribes of Israel. But now it was home to a large herd of pigs, unclean animals. The superior power of the demons made itself felt at that time through the presence of a man possessed of many demons. This demoniac cannot be restrained by anyone and makes the roads unsafe for passersby. But when Jesus appears, the evil spirit recognizes Jesus' superiority and pleads to be allowed to enter the pigs. Jesus forces him to tell him his name, and he answers that he is a thousand demons at once (Legion). When the demoniac has been set free, the people stream into the area. They are impressed by Jesus' unique power, but they do not appreciate his presence. He endures the suffering involved in this rejection by allowing himself to be expelled from the region. He has just driven out a thousand demons and he could easily have chased away the people gathered there. But Jesus shows that he has come to save the lives of all people, even those in the Decapolis.

The healed man wants to go with him, but he is told to go back and tell everyone in the Decapolis about his healing as a sign of what the Lord has done. Thus Jesus sends out a missionary through this area that was lost to Israel, a foreshadowing of the missionary work among the Gentiles that would later take place beyond the borders of the Promised Land.

In Mark (5:1–20) and Luke (8:26–39), the story of Jesus' ministry in the land of the Gerasenes ends with the work of the man who had been possessed by the legion of demons. In these two Gospels, the focus is on this remarkable missionary who is prepared here and sent forth. In Matthew's version of the story (8:28–34), we read about *two* demoniacs.

But Matthew does not include the part about the legion of demons, nor is there any information about the healed man preaching throughout the same region that he once terrorized. Matthew tells the story as proof of Jesus' power over demoniacs, even in gentile territory, and he ends his story with Jesus' patient endurance in being rejected by the people. For this reason we may assume that there was another demoniac in the same region besides the man with the legion of demons, and that this man was also healed. The main character in the story, however, was the demoniac who became a preacher. In Mark and Luke the focus is entirely on this one man, and because of this they see no reason to report a companion who was healed at the same time. Matthew, on the other hand, reinforces his story by mentioning both the demoniac and his cohort: two men healed at once! The difference in narrative presentation is explained by the difference in narrative intent.

It is now clear why Jesus wanted to cross the lake after delivering the parables. Israel is being presented with a choice: now is the time to listen! In a related incident, the people from a nearby gentile region also find out what God is doing here on earth in the person of Jesus. The bearer of God's word returns once again to Israel, but now the people in the Decapolis know that in his own time he plans to bestow his blessing on the gentile regions as well. When Israel decides to turn a deaf ear to Christ, he will respond by spreading his mercy to the lands across the border. The inhabitants there are Gentiles living on formerly Jewish territory, but *Gentiles* nonetheless, who for a moment come into view. The centurion does not remain an exception!

9.6 The First Public Forgiveness of Sins

It is striking that during the Galilean period we do not hear the crowds ask for forgiveness of sins. If they had really accepted Jesus as the Lord whose arrival had been announced by John the Baptist, they would have come to him to beg for the grace of forgiveness. After all, John baptized the people "for the forgiveness of sins." The great messianic gift that people had come to expect was baptism with the Holy Spirit. Through his miracles and his authoritative teaching, Jesus has clearly shown that he really is the fulfillment of John's promise, the *Stronger One.* After the miraculous catch of fish, Simon Peter declared himself a sinner and threw himself at Jesus' feet, but we do not read about the crowds doing the same. No one comes to Jesus to ask for forgiveness, the great blessing that was promised to the people for the time after John the Baptist.

We know of only one exception. Jesus is staying as a guest in the house of a Pharisee, and a woman of sin comes to anoint his feet. The woman wets his feet with her tears and dries them with her hair. Luke tells us that this action astonishes the host. He thinks that Jesus does not know what sort of woman this is (Luke 7:36–50). She is a sinner, and as a sinner she honors Jesus with repentance and love. Her expectation is not disappointed: Jesus forgives her sins. The other guests are amazed and ask themselves who this is who even forgives sins! It is difficult to determine when this event took place, perhaps between the Sermon on the Mount and the parables. It is a solitary incident. Although the requests for healing continue, we hear of no requests for the forgiveness that John had promised.

Jesus himself very emphatically, without being asked, gives this gift publicly to the paralyzed man in Capernaum who is lowered through the roof of the house and laid before his feet (Matt. 9:1–8; Mark 2:1–12; Luke 5:17–26). The legal experts present are horrified. Is this not blasphemy, pure and simple? Who, other than God alone, is able to forgive sins? They are right. But their prejudice against accepting Jesus as the Lord himself keeps them from receiving a blessing. As a sign of his power to forgive sins, however, Jesus has the paralyzed man stand up and go home. This healing is special: it is a sign. From now on, the man will walk through Capernaum as living proof that Jesus forgives sins. Through him, Jesus now reminds the entire city daily that he has really come to keep the promise John made when he baptized. This event is also clearly one of the many aspects of Jesus' humiliation and suffering: he himself was forced to direct people's attention to this promise, and even then no one came to ask for it. Afraid that Jesus was committing blasphemy, they merely considered it with a doubtful expression on their faces.

9.7 A New Era for Sinners

Directly related to this first public forgiveness is Jesus' more frequent presentation of himself as the bringer of *mercy*. All the Gospels note that fairly soon after leaving the city with the crowds he ate with tax collectors and sinners in the home of Levi. He called this tax collector to be his follower and Levi obeyed, to the astonishment of the crowds. Surely there were plenty of people already interested in Jesus? But what Jesus wants to show is that he is not dependent on the favorable reactions of the crowds. He calls all those whom he wants to call, and they come. He commands, and it is. Thus a tax collector suddenly appears and invites Jesus to dine with him. Prudent Jews did not eat with tax collectors and sinners because the food might not be prepared in accordance with the law and thus might be unclean. On top of all that, this is a fasting period for the pious in Israel. So there are questions not only about Jesus' eating with tax collectors and sinners but also about his eating and drinking instead of fasting, as the disciples of the Pharisees and of John the Baptist are doing (Matt. 9:9–17; Mark 2:13–22; Luke 5:27–39). During the fast, people prayed for the salvation of Israel and the coming of the Messiah.

But as he explained afterward, Jesus, by joining in a festive meal with others, teaches the people that he himself is the fulfillment of their prayer and fasting. The bridegroom is here, the age of grace has come. Why fast, when the promised feast has arrived? Fasting and praying will once again be appropriate when the bridegroom has been taken away, for then people will long for his return. But now that Jesus is here, it is a time of answered prayer. That does not mean fasting and looking expectantly to the future, but looking up in faith. Tax collectors and sinners who come to Jesus have a share in his grace, a sign of the age that now has dawned. John's baptism of forgiveness is being fulfilled.

Levi, the tax collector whom Jesus called to follow him, is often equated with the apostle Matthew. In Matthew 10:3, Matthew is called "the tax collector," and in Matthew 9:9 Levi is referred to as Matthew and *not* as Levi. Yet this identification is not without its weak points:

1. Mark speaks of "Levi son of Alphaeus" at the tax collector's booth (2:14). This name does not appear in his list of twelve apostles, and who would connect the Matthew in 3:18 with the Levi of 2:14? Besides, this list of apostles includes a "James son of Alphaeus" (3:18), suggesting that this James is a brother of Levi son of Alphaeus, the man working at the tax collector's booth. Because Mark does make this connection, it would be strange if he failed to mention that this second son of Alphaeus was also part of the inner circle.
2. Luke speaks of Jesus' talking to a "tax collector by the name of Levi" (5:27). The rest is the same as in Mark. Luke's list of apostles includes Matthew and James son of Alphaeus (6:15; cf. Acts 1:13), without suggesting any connection with Levi.
3. Matthew calls the apostle Matthew a "tax collector," but in describing the Matthew who was called, he says only that he was "sitting at the tax collector's booth." The difference in wording between 9:9 and 10:3 is slight, but from a reading of Matthew alone we are inclined to wonder whether the same person is being referred to—all the more so when we note that even in 5:1 Matthew treats the disciples as an existing group. It is true that he does not name all twelve until he describes the commissioning in chapter 10, but it is obvious that these twelve had been together for a while and were also the ones referred to at the beginning of the

Sermon on the Mount. In 8:18 and 8:23, Matthew speaks of "the disciples" as an existing group (cf. 9:11, 14, 37). The reader of Matthew 5–9 would find it difficult to conclude from these chapters that the circle of "the disciples" (whose names are listed in chapter 10) is still open and unformed. So we must assume from the start that the Matthew at the tax collector's booth was not called to join this circle of disciples. In Matthew, as in Mark and Luke, the calling of Levi/Matthew is reported because of the banquet that follows and the discussions about fasting and the joy of the Messiah that take place on that occasion. There is absolutely no indication that he was admitted into the circle of disciples. A parallel incident occurred later with the tax collector Zacchaeus, who was also called by Jesus.

We may conclude that the Levi who was called was a brother of the apostle James, the son of Alphaeus, and must be distinguished from the apostle Matthew, even though in the first Gospel both men share the same name. Apparently Levi had two names, as did so many in the New Testament, and the name *Mattania* ("Gift of God"; *Matthaios* in Greek), was common among the people of Israel. Levi/Matthew at the tax collector's booth is not mentioned in the Gospels as a future apostle but as proof of Christ's mercy for tax collectors and sinners, a sign of the presence of the bridegroom.

9.8 Just Believe!

During this period we see Jesus putting more emphasis on the need for faith when he heals people. The most striking example is the healing of Jairus's little daughter, which is interwoven with the healing of the woman with the issue of blood (Matt. 9:18–26; Mark 5:21–43; Luke 8:40–56). The last is a great example of faith in Jesus: the woman wanted only to touch the hem of his garment so that she might be healed. But she is denied the opportunity to leave unobserved. Jesus calls her and commends her for her faith. It was her faith alone that saved her—a lesson for the surrounding multitudes. When Jairus then receives word that his child has died while Jesus was speaking with this woman, Jesus applies the same words to him: "Don't be afraid; just believe!" Apparently this message is what the people need to hear. After Jesus brings the little girl back to life, he forbids the parents to tell anyone else about it. This is a strange command. Everyone who sees the child walking around will know what has happened. The miracle speaks for itself. By forbidding the parents to talk about the incident, Jesus is indicating that he is not out to recruit propagandists. On the contrary, the healed woman and the revived girl must serve as silent witnesses to the truth of Jesus' words, "Don't be afraid; just believe!"[2]

Faith, the focal point of the interwoven incidents of healing and raising from the dead, is now explicitly demanded of two blind men, who follow Jesus when he leaves Jairus's house. They call out, "Have mercy on us, Son of David!" (Matt. 9:27–31). After he reaches his home they come to him, and he asks them, "Do you believe that I am able to do this?" Their faith is decisive for the healing that follows.

This does not mean that faith is the power by which everything is accomplished. Immediately after the healing of the two blind men, a deaf-mute possessed by demons is brought to Jesus (Matt. 9:32–34). Contact with this man is impossible. Faith cannot be demanded of him, nor can he express it. Yet the Lord heals this man, to the amazement of the people, who say that such a thing had never happened there before. In fact, Jesus at that moment is appealing to the faith of everyone present.

The Pharisees discourage this faith, however, by again sowing seeds of doubt. "It is by the prince of demons that he drives out demons." Clearly the people are without good shepherds, but the Good Shepherd, the Messiah, stands before them.

During this period, Jesus visits Nazareth once again (Matt. 13:54–58; Mark 6:1–6), but he is not able to perform many signs there because of the people's lack of faith. Once again the significance of faith is shown, though now through its absence. It is only by faith that the gates to the blessings of the Messiah are opened, but without faith people cut themselves off from life. In Nazareth it becomes clear why so many people lack this faith: they know Jesus as the carpenter's son from Nazareth, and it is simply incomprehensible to them that the Lord would come to them in this form.

9.9 The Commissioning of the Twelve

Moved by compassion for a people without good leaders to point them to Jesus the Messiah, Jesus sends out his twelve apostles to all of Israel. Traveling two by two, they pass through cities and villages with the power to heal and to cast out evil spirits. Unlike Jesus, they do not do this on their own authority, but only "in Jesus' name." Their ministry shows that Jesus can give the power of the Spirit to others. The sending out of the Twelve is an expansion of Jesus' ministry in Israel. But first the apostles are warned about the resistance of unbelief, which they are

2. For a discussion of whether the Gospels contradict each other as to the time at which Jairus's daughter died, see my commentary on Matt. 9:18–26 (*Matteüs: Het evangelie voor Israël*, Commentaar op het Nieuwe Testament, 3d series [Kampen: Kok, 1994]).

bound to encounter and which will result in persecution and discrimination for them as well (Matt. 10; Mark 6:7–13; Luke 9:1–6).

The commissioning of the Twelve shows how Jesus will gather a renewed Israel around himself. By sending them out, Jesus indicates that he is not cutting himself off from the people or withdrawing into a small circle of followers. On the contrary, he hopes to include the entire nation in this circle of followers. Twelve gates stand open for everyone seeking the kingdom of God through Jesus. The apostles travel from city to city, from village to village, visiting homes. Even people who never travel to Galilee now hear the gospel and are given proof of Jesus' divine majesty. No one can remain undecided and stand on the sidelines. He who comes after John is now knocking on all doors. His appeal to the whole nation is evidence of his claim. This is not just a rabbi gathering a following or a healer attracting interest. He is the son of David who is calling on the people to believe in him and to serve in God's kingdom. Father or mother, son or daughter, all are subordinate to the claim of the Messiah: "Anyone who loves his family members more than Jesus is not worthy of him." And the same applies to the apostles: anyone who accepts them accepts Jesus himself. The reward for this faith is sure. This is a large-scale invitation to believe. Here we see as nowhere else that when Jesus withdrew to the mountain, he never intended to turn his back on the people. The renewed constitution and the Sermon on the Mount are now being taken to everyone. And the Twelve—reminiscent of the twelve tribes of God—fulfill the claim implicit in their number by going out to the lost sheep of the house of Israel. The Good Shepherd, promised in Isaiah 40 and heralded by the voice of one crying in the wilderness, is caring for his scattered flock! While John the Baptist led the way in preparing the people, the Twelve come with the message of joy: "Say to the towns of Judah, 'Here is your God!' See, the Sovereign LORD comes with power, and his arm rules for him. See, his reward is with him, and his recompense accompanies him. He tends his flock like a shepherd: He gathers the lambs in his arms and carries them close to his heart; he gently leads those that have young" (Isa. 40:10–11).

10
Galilee (III)
Preparation for the Passion

10.1 The Shadow of John's Murderer

As the apostles begin walking two by two across the length and breadth of the country, spreading Jesus' name to an ever-increasing public, the shadow of John's murderer falls across Jesus' path. It had already been some time since Herod Antipas had the prophet of repentance killed during a banquet, yet the evangelists do not report the story until now, when they connect it with the commissioning of the Twelve. They do this for a special reason: Herod Antipas is beginning to take an interest in Jesus' ministry. His curiosity is piqued. Anything that is discussed by the entire population is of interest to a king. But Herod's opinion of Jesus, which he expresses to his courtiers, springs entirely from his own bad conscience. He keeps wondering whether John the Baptist has risen from the dead (Luke 9:7–9), and this becomes almost a certainty in his mind: John has returned, and that is why the "powers" are at work in Jesus (Mark 6:14–16; Matt. 14:1–2). Because he is the reincarnation of the murdered John, Jesus has contact with the supernatural powers beyond the grave. On the basis of what he has heard about Jesus, Herod recognizes that some aspects of his ministry are more than merely human in origin. Yet Herod's reaction is threatening. At this point it is important to know how Herod dealt with John the Baptist. Two of the evangelists choose this moment to go back in time and report the story of John's death in order to explain the implications of Herod's making a connection between Jesus and John the Baptist (Matt. 14:3–12; Mark 6:17–29; cf. Luke 3:19–20). Yesterday's murderer is once again searching for his victim! The Pharisees have already been trying to make contact with the Herodians to plan Jesus' death in connection with his claim that he is Lord of the Sabbath (Mark 3:6; cf. section 8.8), so when Herod himself becomes suspicious, it constitutes a very real death threat. His father had killed the infants of Bethlehem to avoid any confrontation with God's king.

He, the son, put to death the herald of this king. And suspicion against Jesus is now brewing in his mind.

The negative role played by Herod Antipas at this point in Jesus' life is often underestimated. Yet, not long thereafter, the Pharisees try to get Jesus out of Perea by warning him of Herod's plans to kill him (Luke 13:31). And Herod will play a decisive role in Jesus' trial. Pilate will send Jesus to Herod, giving him the opportunity to take the case and release the prisoner. But Herod will let the opportunity pass and will deliver Jesus once again into the hands of those who are determined to put him to death (Luke 23:5–12). There is a direct line from Herod's pondering the possibility that John the Baptist has returned in the person of Jesus to the execution in Jerusalem. The Pharisees and the leaders in Jerusalem have already spent much time planning Jesus' death. But now the secular authority enters the picture and the threat intensifies. The outline of Jesus' Passion begins to take shape.

Thus, after the Twelve return, we see Jesus withdraw with them. This must have amounted to an anticlimax for the disciples. They are full of joy because of the powerful miracles they were able to perform in Jesus' name, but when Jesus takes them to a solitary place (Matt. 14:13; Luke 9:10; Mark 6:30–32), he presents himself as a threatened man. He retreats to get some rest, but it is also clearly a withdrawal to safety.[1]

When the crowds insist on following him, however, Jesus does not withhold mercy. It is getting too late to buy food for the thousands gathered there, so he feeds them with five loaves and two fish. When Jesus performs this greatest of miracles, which is reminiscent of the manna in the desert, the people do not understand it correctly. They want to make Jesus king—but Jesus did not perform the miracle of the loaves and fish as a demonstration of his power in response to Herod. He distances himself from the multitudes by sending them home and devoting himself to prayer on the mountainside (Mark 6:33–46; John 6:1–15; Matt. 14:13–23; Luke 9:11–17).

---

1. The words "When Jesus heard this" (Matt. 14:13 NRSV) seem to refer to the account of the death of John the Baptist immediately preceding it (14:10–12). The NIV unfortunately makes this connection explicit in its paraphrastic rendering, "When Jesus heard what had happened." Yet this cannot be what is intended here. After all, when Jesus "withdrew from there" (NRSV), the scene of John's death is not what comes to mind. Jesus was not even present at John's death. By saying that "he withdrew from there," Matthew takes us back to the point when Herod openly shows his belief that Jesus is a reincarnation of John (14:1–2). The passage in Matthew 14:3–12 is a flashback, a review of John's death, which had taken place at an earlier time but constitutes the background for Herod's later understanding of who Jesus is. Thus, the words "when Jesus heard this" in 14:13 do not refer to John's death but to Herod Antipas's notion that the John he had killed had returned in the person of Jesus.

That night, Jesus follows, walking on the water, the small boat in which his disciples find themselves in the middle of a storm. His coming to them across the water increases their awe for the Savior: they kneel before him in the ship and confess that he is indeed the Son of God (Matt. 14:24–33; Mark 6:47–52; John 6:16–21). The insight that escaped them during the feeding of the five thousand now hits them with great force.

The apostle John relates that shortly thereafter Jesus delivers the so-called Bread of Life sermon in the synagogue at Capernaum, in which he clearly reveals the meaning of the bread that came from his hands. He gave the bread, and he is the bread. He is the bread of life that is meant to be eaten. Others will live because he allows himself to be ground like flour. He will give his flesh for the survival of the world. In fact, this sermon is one great Passion sermon. Now we see that Herod's threats and the hostility of the Jewish leaders are not disruptive elements that must be eliminated. They fit right into Jesus' plans. When Herod casts his shadow over him, Jesus turns to the crowds and announces that this is exactly why he has come: to be killed. The purpose of his life is not to rule but to serve as food for the world, to be digested by the world in order to give it life. That is the will of the Father in heaven (John 6:26–59).

10.2. Withdrawal

The third and final period of Jesus' work in Galilee is characterized by interruptions and withdrawals. In the first period we saw continuous preaching in every synagogue, and in the second period, continuous teaching to crowds who came from all sides. In the third period we still see Jesus preaching and teaching, but it seems as if on the one hand the lamp is shining brighter while on the other hand it is flickering. Whenever Jesus is present, his actions are even more impressive than those anyone had seen before. But he is increasingly absent and even abroad. He is clearly not pursuing the triumphal climax of being crowned king, but more and more he conceals himself as a sign of his approaching departure to suffer and to go to the Father. The apostles learn to understand the significance of Jesus' actions, because during this period he often meets with them privately to teach them. Finally, during and after the Feast of Tabernacles in Jerusalem, Jesus publicly reveals what will happen to him.

This period is not without *impressive deeds*. It gets to the point that people in the crowd beg to be allowed to touch the hem of his garment (the woman with the issue of blood has many imitators!). The healings in Gennesaret take place not only at Jesus' hands but also behind his back (Matt. 14:34–36; Mark 6:53–56).

The *confrontation with the opposition* from the leaders continues during this period as well. Pharisees and legal experts come from Jerusalem to entrap him. Their attempts against the Lord of the Sabbath (during the first period) no longer resonate with the crowds because of the deep impression Jesus makes on them. The slanderous accusation that he is working through Beelzebub (during the second period) has not had the desired results—in fact, the people are praising God for everything Jesus is doing. Now, in this third period, still another tactic is used against Jesus. He is accused of being un-Jewish. His disciples do not practice the customary hand-washing, which suggests that Jesus and his followers are not *pure* but ceremonially unclean. Such an accusation would drive a wedge between him and the pious Israelites, for who would want to break with their Jewish identity for the sake of this miracle worker? In the conversation that takes place, Jesus appears to talk about purity and impurity in ways that the people are not used to. His attention to inner purity is in line with Old Testament teaching, but his statement that whatever goes into the mouth does not make a person unclean implies in fact a complete dismantling of the dietary laws. Here Jesus acts as the Lawgiver who is adapting the law of Moses to the messianic age. When the issue was the Sabbath, one specific law was called into question, but now the entire tradition of the elders and a major portion of the Mosaic laws are called into question. In this new offensive the leaders from Jerusalem are partly right: the Jewish lifestyle *is* at stake! But Jesus declares that he is authorized to teach God's people a new way of life. His answer is acceptable only to those who recognize that he is truly the Son of God, the great prophet promised by Moses, to whom the people will have to listen (Matt. 15:1–20; Mark 7:1–23).

At the same time, however, we also see Jesus *withdrawing*. After confronting the delegation from Jerusalem over the laws of ceremonial cleanness and uncleanness, Jesus withdraws to the region of Tyre and Sidon. A gentile woman with a demon-possessed daughter benefits from his presence. She realizes that the people of Israel are thoughtlessly crumbling away the Bread of Life, and that this is why Jesus has left the country. Her gathering of these crumbs in faith results in the healing of her child and is a sign for all of Israel: *this* is how the Bread of Life should be received! (Matt. 15:21–28; Mark 7:24–30).

Then, when Jesus goes again toward Galilee, he makes a detour via a roundabout route. He ends up in the Decapolis, on the eastern shore of the Sea of Galilee, and heals a deaf-mute in this non-Jewish region (Mark 7:31–37). Even this healing takes place in a withdrawn way: in the background, and with the command to remain silent about it. The healing does not remain unnoticed, of course, but Jesus' attempt to keep it hidden throws a mantle of mystery over the scene. What does he really want? Does he want at the same time to be great and become small?

Coming from the coastal region of the Decapolis, Jesus arrives back in Jewish territory, but he stays by the back door, so to speak, at the mountain along the border. This is not a decision made out of power-lessness. When the crowds search for him and find him, he heals so many that they begin praising the God of Israel. And once again he mul-tiplies bread and fish for the thousands who have come to see him (four thousand this time, not counting women and children). There is no in-dication that his power has weakened or the people's interest has waned (Matt. 15:29–39; Mark 8:1–10). Yet once again there is a depar-ture from the direction in which the crowds want to move: after the meal Jesus sends the people away and travels to another region. Mark mentions the region of Dalmanutha, Matthew the region of Magadan (a number of manuscripts read Magdala or Magdalan). This was probably a region on the western shore of the sea.

Jesus keeps in the background. His opponents must come to him and find him. This time the opponents are not only the Pharisees but also the Sadducees (Matt. 16:1–4; Mark 8:11–12). Apparently the circle of hostile leaders is expanding. People are reacting with shock at Jesus' outspoken annulment of the laws of ceremonial cleanness and the di-etary regulations. No human being may do this—unless he is able to show authorization from above. That is why he is now being asked to produce a sign from heaven—not a sign performed by Jesus, but a sign from above that does not directly involve him but serves to prove that he is who he claims to be. Regardless of the exact meaning of Jesus' ref-erence to the sign of Jonah (which is an exegetical issue), Jesus ends his statement with yet another withdrawal. Leaving the leaders with an enigmatic answer, he disappears. Once again he embarks with the dis-ciples, this time crossing over to Bethsaida, where he heals a blind man—again in the background, and with the command to keep silent (Mark 8:13–26; Matt. 16:5–12). On the way, the Lord warns his disciples about the teachings of the hostile Pharisees and the Sadducees, and he reminds them of the miraculous feeding of the crowds in order to strengthen their faith in him: his teaching was confirmed by these acts and therefore they can fully trust him. Jesus leads the people beyond the law—he is Moses' replacement. The disciples must not stay behind with the Pharisees and Sadducees and their teachings!

No sooner does Jesus arrive in Galilee than he moves again to another spot: the region of Caesarea Philippi. This territory, which formerly be-longed to Israel and was known as Bashan, never again came under Jew-ish control. It is ruled by Philip, a son of Herod the Great. Here the dis-

ciples receive their first teaching about Jesus' coming Passion, which
also explains the reason behind the recent, repeated withdrawals.

10.3 Teaching the Disciples about the Passion

At Caesarea Philippi, Jesus pauses with his disciples to take stock.
How do people regard him? They agree he is impressive (John, a
prophet, Elijah, Jeremiah), but they do not see him as he wants to be
seen. They do not regard Jesus of Nazareth, the Son of man, as the one
announced by John, the Stronger One, the Lord himself. This, in spite
of the respect they may have for his ministry, in fact amounts to a fatal
misunderstanding. But Simon Peter summarizes the disciples' faith.
They recognize—having been taught by God—that Jesus is the Messiah,
the Son of the living God.

Nevertheless, from now on the disciples are no longer allowed to say
this openly. First they need further training. They need a new and expanded vision of the *work* of this Messiah. Otherwise, though they
might correctly explain to people that Jesus is the Son of God, they will
give a totally incorrect impression of his future in Israel. For this reason
their knowledge is temporarily put on inactive status, as it were, in
order to allow for further instruction first (Matt. 16:13–20; Mark 8:27–
30; Luke 9:18–21).

Jesus now begins to show the disciples from the Scriptures that "he
must go to Jerusalem and suffer many things at the hands of the elders,
chief priests and teachers of the law, and that he must be killed and on
the third day be raised to life" (Matt. 16:21). They greet this teaching
with incomprehension and resistance, and only after Easter does the
Lord open their hearts so that they become completely open to the
things which, when they first heard them, they had stored in memory
without accepting them (see Luke 24:44–47). The recent withdrawal
turns out to have been the introduction to the great withdrawal from
this life which now awaits him, according to the Scriptures. The disciples must also be prepared to follow Jesus and take up their cross. His
Passion demands that they, as believers, seek to imitate him (Matt.
16:21–28; Mark 8:31–9:1; Luke 9:22–27).

Shortly thereafter, the three most prominent disciples (Peter, James,
and John) are given a confirmation from above of Jesus' Passion. On
the Mount of Transfiguration they see Moses and Elijah (the Law and
the Prophets) speaking with Jesus about his departure in Jerusalem.
For the moment they must keep silent about this event; later they may
bear witness to it, in support of faith in the majesty of the Crucified (see
2 Pet. 1:12–21). The voice from heaven ("This is my Son, whom I love")
reveals that at this very moment, when Jesus has chosen the Passion

and is teaching it to his disciples, God loves his Son. Jesus' readiness to die in Jerusalem is the will of the Father and is in conformity with the Law and the Prophets, as Moses and Elijah personally demonstrate (Matt. 17:1–13; Mark 9:2–13; Luke 9:28–36). (Matthew and Mark date the Transfiguration six days before the first announcement of the Passion; Luke, approximately eight days. The difference in reckoning may have to do with whether or not the day or days of the first Passion instruction are included in the total.)

When the disciples return from the Mount of Transfiguration to join the rest of the Twelve, it almost seems as if the announcement of the coming Passion has caused their healing power to wane. The disciples are not able to heal a boy who suffers from seizures. But Jesus shows that suffering does not reduce his majesty: he heals the boy. The problem is not Christ's suffering but lack of faith on the disciples' part. He who is about to die is still the Lord of life, and the disciples must continue their struggle against the demons of this earth with prayer and fasting (Matt. 17:14–21; Mark 9:14–29; Luke 9:37–42).

After all these events, Jesus passes through Galilee once again and goes to Capernaum. He appears to be returning to his old familiar territory, but everything has changed. Jesus travels in silence and does not want anyone to know his whereabouts. This attempt to travel inconspicuously through a region where only recently people crowded around him by the thousands is explained in the second announcement of the Passion. The Son of man will be handed over! This is a new element. In the first announcement, the accent was on the necessity to go to Jerusalem and to suffer and be rejected by the leaders. Now something new has been added: Jesus will be delivered into the hands of his enemies. This time the enemies are not specified (elders, priests, teachers of the law) but characterized (men), placing the accent entirely on the announcement of the betrayal and handing over of Jesus. In time the disciples' attention will be focused on this point: "Who is going to betray you?" And later they will know that it was "Judas Iscariot, who betrayed him." But from the beginning, Jesus makes the betrayal mentioned in the *second* announcement subordinate to the need for suffering which he stressed in the *first* announcement. The betrayal *must* take place! Now we see why Jesus, traveling through Galilee with his disciples, is less free of concern than he was before, and not without reason (Matt. 17:22–23; Mark 9:30–32; Luke 9:43–45).

Arriving in Capernaum, Jesus takes the time to instruct his disciples about the question as to who is the greatest in the kingdom of heaven. Their aspirations and expectations must be completely readjusted and brought in line with the Savior's Passion. Ambitious trendsetters on the way to the kingdom of God must learn to be like children and to follow the path of service and suffering if they want to enter God's kingdom (Matt. 18; Mark 9:33–50; Luke 9:46–50). It is during this last stay in Capernaum that the incident of the temple tax takes place, in which Jesus shows himself to be Lord of the animal world when he has Peter take a coin out of a fish's mouth. With a sovereign gesture, the Son of God subjects himself to those who collect the temple tax—as if the Son were subject to taxation! Yet Jesus humbly goes along with the demand, a sign that illustrates his teaching about serving others (Matt. 17:24–27).

10.4 Announcing the Passion to Jerusalem

In chapters 7–10, John provides a broad description of Jesus' ministry in Jerusalem during a Feast of the Tabernacles and in response to the healing of a man born blind. The events to which this account refers must have taken place at the end of the Galilean period.

This is already apparent from the beginning of the narrative. In Galilee, Jesus' brothers reproach him: he may be doing great things, but he is also failing to seek any publicity in Judea and Jerusalem. At first Jesus refuses to attend the Feast of the Tabernacles. He stays in Galilee when others leave to go to the feast, which fits in with the period of withdrawal and evasion. Jesus knows that the leaders are looking for him to kill him. He accepts death, but his time has not yet come (John 7:1–9). Later, when he decides to go to Jerusalem after all, he goes quietly—not openly, but as if in secret. He does not go to the temple until halfway through the feast, when he begins to teach those who had watched for him in anticipation (John 7:10–14).

Then Jesus himself raises the question why it is that people want to kill him. Although the crowd attending the festival thinks it a crazy notion that anyone would want to do him harm, it soon becomes apparent that the citizens of Jerusalem have a good sense of what is going on. But since Jesus is speaking openly, they begin to wonder whether their leaders have come to the conclusion that he is the Messiah. When Jesus confronts the doubts of some of the people by announcing again that he has come directly from God, an attempt to arrest him shows that Jesus was right: they do want to kill him. But his time has not yet come. Many from the crowd of pilgrims come to believe in him, and this induces the Pharisees to send men to seize him. But the men return empty-handed to the chief priests and Pharisees (John 7:15–52). Everything indicates that Jerusalem has become a hostile city for Jesus, even though many people from outside the city do believe that he is the Messiah.

At this point many manuscripts include the story of the woman caught in adultery (7:53–8:11). The teachers of the law and the Pharisees turn this into a test case for Jesus, which also fits into this later period. The same kinds of attempts are being made in Jerusalem that were made earlier in Galilee, where questions regarding ceremonial purity and impurity were used to show that Jesus was un-Jewish. Jesus' attitude toward tax collectors and sinners is common knowledge. On the other hand, it is well known how strict he is on the question of divorce, which the law does permit. We have the impression that by asking Jesus whether the adulteress should be killed, as the law requires, the teachers of the law and the Pharisees have caught him in a trap. But Jesus turns their weapon back on his accusers: let him who is without sin cast the first stone.

In the following discourses (John 8:12–59), the focus is again on Jesus' departure. When people wonder once again where it is he is going, it turns out that Jesus is referring to his return to the Father by way of suffering and death. Finally the Jews pick up stones to stone him, but he leaves the temple.

The confrontation intensifies in the days when Jesus heals a man born blind (John 9). When in the end the man openly confesses that the one who healed him came from God, he is thrown out of the synagogue. A regulation that had been announced earlier now goes into effect: "Anyone who acknowledged that Jesus was the Christ would be put out of the synagogue" (John 9:22b). This excommunication of the man born blind, who was healed by Jesus and then confessed that he was the Christ of God, is an important sign of the leaders' readiness to suppress the gospel.

This incident gives Jesus the occasion to preach about himself in Jerusalem as the Good Shepherd who gives his life for his sheep (John 10:1–21). Such an explanation eliminates any misunderstanding that may have existed in Jerusalem: when plans are made to kill Jesus and are later carried out, it is entirely in line with his own calling to die on behalf of Israel. The Messiah announces beforehand in the temple that the suffering that is coming is actually part of his plan of action. He also shows that he himself determines the time, according to the will of God. Jesus' death is not something unexpected, nor is it something of which only the disciples were informed in confidence. Later, when the trial takes place, the people of Jerusalem will be able to recognize that Jesus is the Messiah precisely because of his death. When they fail to recognize him, the fault will not lie in his preaching.

After this preparation for the Passion in the temple city, Jesus most likely returns once again to Galilee. He spends a brief period in Capernaum and then gives his disciples their final teaching, as discussed in the previous section.

This brings the Galilean ministry to an end. Preparations for the Passion have now been completed through the withdrawal in Galilee, the teaching of the disciples, and the public appearances in the temple city.

11

Through Perea and Judea

11.1 Leaving Galilee

It is Luke who provides an extensive report of the period of travel between the departure from Galilee and the arrival in Jerusalem (for this period as a whole, see section 3.5). Jesus tended increasingly to keep a low profile and to withdraw entirely on several occasions toward the end of his stay in Galilee, but this changes completely when he sets out for the temple city to meet his death. He does not travel surreptitiously, as he did when he went to the Feast of the Tabernacles. Now he makes his way quite openly and allows more and more people to gather around him. In the end the crowd numbers in the thousands (Luke 12:1; 14:25). This is no accident. Jesus had widely publicized his journey from Galilee to Jerusalem in advance. He had sent out seventy disciples (probably a rounding off of seventy-two), two by two, to announce his approach in every city and village he would travel through (Luke 10:1–24). This sending out reminds us of an earlier time, when the Twelve traveled two by two throughout Israel. But now there are many more apostles. Jesus intensifies his call to the people, and he focuses on the places along the route he intends to travel to Jerusalem. The Redeemer insists that everyone be aware of his coming. He raises the question in the people's minds, What will Jesus do at the end of this journey?

More than once it appears that the disciples, in spite of the fact that Jesus had told them about his Passion, still secretly hope for a majestic denouement in Jerusalem. The emphasis that Jesus places on his journey is construed by them as an portent of the impending coming of the kingdom. But Jesus himself lets it be known again and again that, although he has great plans for bringing salvation, those plans include grace and forgiveness for Samaritans, sinners, the women who listen to him, the humble, and the despised. Thus the bystanders begin to sense a permanent tension between the emphasis Jesus is placing on his journey and the things to which he turns his attention in Perea and Judea.

We see this right from the start. The messengers who go to a Samaritan village to make sleeping arrangements meet with locked doors because their Master's final destination is Jerusalem (Luke 9:51–53). When James and John become aware of this, they want to reveal the dignity and importance of the journey by having fire from heaven descend on the village. But Jesus reveals the spirit of his journey by sparing the place and seeking shelter elsewhere (Luke 9:54–56). Apparently this part of the story does not refer to a journey through Samaria but rather through the border region between Samaria and Judea, where one might as easily find a Samaritan as a Jewish village. They are just leaving Galilee and are traveling along the border between Samaria and Galilee on the way to Perea.

Great is the goal that lies ahead them. Someone expresses the desire to travel with Jesus, but first he wants to say goodbye to his family. Jesus tells him that this is not the time for looking back. One should commit oneself unconditionally to the kingdom of God (Luke 9:61–62). Luke probably emphasizes the special character of following Jesus on this journey by linking this disciple's question with two other, earlier, and similar questions about following Jesus (Luke 9:57–60). Matthew 8:18–22 suggests that these two questions about following Jesus were asked before the storm on the Sea of Galilee. Luke provides no precise date, but he combines several similar stories as thematic for following Jesus on this great journey.

The special character of Jesus' journey does not escape anyone's notice. A legal expert responds by asking what he must do to inherit eternal life (Luke 10:25–37). In other words, how can I share in the great future that you seem to be ushering in? The answer is given in the form of the parable of the Good Samaritan. Generally speaking, this story shows Jesus' emphasis on mercy, but it is also a severe lesson for the legal expert, whose intentions toward Jesus are not positive. Jesus is about to fall into the hands of robbers. All those who love him are his neighbors. But when the legal expert sees that the man in the story is Jesus, he passes on the other side!

This incident contrasts sharply with the attentive attitude of Mary in the home of Martha (Luke 10:38–42). While Mary's sister believes that what Jesus needs to reach his great goal is primarily much help and service, Jesus lets them know that only one thing is needed: to let *him* accomplish the great work, and to listen to him with reverence. It is a very special journey, one that draws everyone's attention. Followers must be willing to be radically committed. But in the end Jesus needs no one for what is coming—he only asks that people pay attention to his teaching and his deeds.

11.2 Intermezzo in Jerusalem

During his gradual journey to Jerusalem, Jesus spends a great deal of time in Perea, especially in Bethany across the Jordan, where John had baptized. This is a place with special meaning. It symbolizes the connection between the great events that will soon unfold and the beginning of the ministry of John the Baptist, prophet and martyr! From this area, Jesus makes a brief visit to Jerusalem for the Feast of Dedication (John 10:22–42).

It is difficult to say just when this intermezzo took place. The visit might have occurred at the same time as the visit to the home of Martha and Mary in Luke 10:38–42 (see section 3.5), but this is by no means certain. If both of them lived in Bethany in Judea, near Jerusalem, it would be easy to combine a visit to their house with the journey to the Feast of the Dedication. But it is also possible that Martha lived somewhere else (in Perea, for instance), while her sister Mary and her brother Lazarus stayed in the tribal village of Bethany. Indeed, it is striking that Luke specifically states that Jesus was received by Martha (10:38; according to many manuscripts the words are "*her* home"). This suggests that Martha lived separately in an otherwise unnamed place, and that she was probably married. Since many women followed Jesus, supporting him with their own possessions (Luke 8:1–4), it would not be unusual for Mary from Bethany in Judea to be among them. On the other hand, in John 11:45 we are told specifically that many Jews went to see Mary when her brother died, suggesting that it was Mary, not Martha, whose permanent address was Bethany. Because Luke does not provide a place name, we cannot settle this question definitively, so linking Jesus' visit to Martha's house and his visit to Jerusalem for the Feast of the Dedication remains guesswork.

What is clear, however, is that as Jesus walks around Solomon's Colonnade we see that Jerusalem is also in the grip of tension regarding his move from Galilee. People ask him, "How long will you keep us in suspense?" (John 10:24). Is he really the Messiah, or not? If he is, let him tell us. Jesus reminds them of the deeds that bear witness to him, and he alludes to the threat that dominates the city. The man born blind has been expelled from the synagogue, and Jesus responds by saying that he is the Good Shepherd who searches for his lost sheep and accepts them back into the fold. He also presents himself again as the Son of God, while at the same time indicating that this is why the leaders want to kill him. This turns out to be the truth: new attempts are made to arrest him, but he escapes. The tension remains. Will he finally overpower those who threaten him, or will his enemies actually stone him or kill him in some other way? Nothing new happens. This visit is an intermezzo that confronts the people unambiguously with the situation. Even the temple city is thus being prepared for the approach of a great climax. Because Jesus decides first to retreat to Bethany across the Jordan, the city waits, unsure and hostile.

But the thousands of people on the other side of the river come to faith in him. At one time John baptized here, and everything he said about the one who is to come and about his power has come true in the person of Jesus (John 10:40–42)! The disciples of the Master now find themselves torn by two opposing forces. On the one hand, the spirit of John the Baptist still seems to be present and is driving them, and many others, toward the city, while on the other hand the threats of the leaders in Jerusalem increasingly make them less eager to continue in that direction. Only later will the disciples come to understand that these opposing forces together form the pattern of the way of the cross, and that the grand journey from Galilee had to be understood in the light of the announcements of the Passion, which the disciples had repressed.

11.3 Teaching in Perea

The stay in Perea is marked by a great deal of teaching of the crowds and of the disciples. There is much repetition in Jesus' words. Many statements that were made back in Galilee in Matthew and Mark are made here again, albeit in a different context. Yet we learn from Luke's account that this teaching is not meant as an aimless way to pass the time. It has a clear purpose. Jesus drew people's attention toward himself by sending out the seventy (or seventy-two) apostles, and now the people have gathered around him once again. His intention is not to organize them for a mass action against Jerusalem or the Romans, but to let them know that only his *teachings* hold the key to understanding his work.

At the place where John once taught his disciples to pray for the coming of the Stronger One who would baptize with the Holy Spirit, Jesus, when asked, also teaches his disciples to pray. It is a remarkable lesson, a partial repetition of the Sermon on the Mount (the Lord's Prayer) with a strong emphasis on childlike trust. The promised Holy Spirit will surely be given when they ask the Father for it in prayer (Luke 11:13).

The legal experts had already tried to drive a wedge between Jesus and the people back in Galilee. The respect and awe that Jesus commanded was spurious, they said: he must have entered into a monstrous alliance with Beelzebub (see section 9.3). Some of the people accepted this teaching of the legal experts and the Pharisees, and now people in the crowd call out that Jesus is in fact a possessed man (Luke 11:14–36). Others ask for a sign from heaven, which shows that Jesus is still a controversial figure. In response he warns them once again of the judgment that will result from this unbelief, but he also gives promises to those who accept and keep the word of God.

Indeed, this announcement of judgment is quite appropriate for John the Baptist's successor: the winnowing fork is in his hand! In the same way Jesus addresses the legal experts and Pharisees while staying in the home of a Pharisee (Luke 11:37–54). His words are not appreciated. On the contrary, from now on the legal experts and Pharisees turn fiercely against him and try to entrap him in his own words (Luke 11:53–54). The threat in Jerusalem is now an immediate threat in Perea as well.

Jesus addresses his disciples against this threatening background, within earshot of the crowds, and talks about the persecutions that await them and the perseverance that is expected of them (Luke 12:1–13:9). It seems strange: Jesus' position is stronger than ever—the multitudes want to accompany him to a great future in Jerusalem—yet he chooses this moment to talk about suffering and humiliation. Through this teaching aimed at the disciples, Christ lets the multitudes see how different his plan and program are from what they think. Disciples must hold themselves in preparedness for persecution, and those who have not turned to Jesus must be prepared to face judgment (Luke 12:1–48; 12:49–13:9). The march from Galilee becomes a journey toward the cross and final judgment.

The healing on the Sabbath of a woman who was completely crippled and bent over (Luke 13:10–17) renews the discussion of Jesus' authority. The ruler of the synagogue resents this healing on the Sabbath, since the woman's case clearly was not an emergency. But in his explanation Jesus makes it clear that he is the owner of Israel, who cares for his property on the Sabbath just as a farmer waters his cattle on the Sabbath.

While the crowds are making their way to Jerusalem, someone asks Jesus whether the road he is taking will ultimately lead to salvation (Luke 13:22–30): will only a few be saved, since Jesus speaks so insistently about judgment and suffering? In reply to this question, Jesus once again points to himself: he is the one who will say to many that there is no place for them in the kingdom because he does not know them. The Gentiles will enter ahead of Israel. Numbers are not important—faith in Jesus is decisive.

This is the last straw for the Pharisees. They come and threaten Jesus with the report that Herod wants to kill him. But the threat does not seem to frighten him. He tells them that he will die in *Jerusalem,* and that he intends to leave for Judea. Within a few days Jesus will leave the region of Perea, not to flee, but to die in the proper place (Luke 13:31–35).

It was during these last days in Perea that the incident we read about in Luke 14 must have occurred: another healing on the Sabbath, now in the home of a Pharisee. At the dinner to which he has been invited, Jesus speaks about humility and the readiness to listen to God's call. This same theme dominates the discussions during the next day of travel. For the crowds there is no other choice: take up the cross and follow Jesus. The journey to Jerusalem is impressive and emphatic, but to those who listened only superficially to Jesus' words in Perea it seems like a perilous undertaking.

11.4 In Judea

Jesus then crosses the Jordan, with the threat of John's murderer behind him and a recently deceased Lazarus awaiting him. Because of Lazarus's illness, Mary and Martha had decided to call the Master. But he delayed coming until he received word that Lazarus had died. The disciples felt that, since Lazarus was already dead, going to Judea meant taking an unnecessary risk: the leaders there wanted to kill him. Thomas views the situation grimly, and when Jesus tells them that Lazarus has died he says, "Let us also go, that we may die with him" (John 11:1–16). But Jesus' intention is quite the opposite. He wants Lazarus to live—with *them!* Raising him from the tomb (on the fourth day) is a sign to surpass all signs: Jesus is victorious not only over death but also over material decay and the corruption of the body. It is no wonder that many people in hostile Judea are now won over to faith. Lazarus's resurrection causes many people to change their opinion about Jesus (John 11:45; 12:9).

The Sanhedrin now holds an official meeting. This is the first time that we hear about a formal agreement at this high a level to put Jesus to death (John 11:47–53). In the past there have been many plans and attempts to take his life, but now these have culminated in a high-level, official decision of the supreme court. There has even been talk of destroying the recent evidence of Jesus' power that has made such an impression on many people: they consider killing Lazarus (John 12:10–11).

Because the opinion of many in Judea has changed in Jesus' favor, we see that even here Jesus finds the opportunity to minister to them and to teach. People seek him out, probably in Bethany (John 11:45). Although this period does not last long, there is a brief interval during which he receives people in one place and carries on conversations with friends as well as enemies. It looks as if the rather somber journey may turn into a triumphal procession after all. It is during this brief period that Jesus probably tells the parables of the lost sheep, lost coin, and lost son (Luke 15), in order to explain to the complaining legal experts and Pharisees why he is allowing tax collectors and sinners to come to him and why he agrees to speak with them. The parable of the rich man and the poor Lazarus (Luke 16:19–31) shows that even sending Lazarus back from the dead (the name is no accident!) is of no avail if Israel refuses to take the Law and Prophets to heart.

Luke has preserved other discourses and parables from this period (Luke 16–18; for the single returning Samaritan, see section 3.5). We find a small portion of this material in Matthew and Mark (the blessing of the children, the rich young man, and the reward for following Jesus). These evangelists also include the discussion of divorce, and Matthew adds the parable of the laborers in the vineyard (Matt. 19:2–20:16; Mark 10:2–31).

When the Sanhedrin has decided to kill Jesus by whatever means necessary because the people of Jerusalem and Judea are now also coming to him in droves, he withdraws to an unknown place. The crowds do not know that he is hiding out in Ephraim, a small town on the edge of the desert (John 11:54). Among the people who in the meantime are entering Jerusalem in great numbers to prepare for the Passover there is an exceptional tension (John 11:55–57). Jesus' emphatic journey toward Jerusalem, his raising of Lazarus from the dead, and his sudden disappearance to an unknown place increase expectations as well as hostility. Now everyone is looking for him! How will he make his entrance? And where? They know that he is on the move, but they have lost track of him. And they fail to understand what he has said again and again to explain both his goal and the way to reach that goal, because in their focusing on his arrival in Jerusalem they fail to grasp his claim that he is God's Son and Israel's redeemer.

12

The Ascent to Jerusalem

12.1 The Passion Week: Ascending to Submission

By the time he began his actual journey from Galilee, the Lord Christ had already chosen Jerusalem as his destination (Luke 9:51), but much time passed before he embarked on the last portion that would finally bring him into the temple city, without any new detours or delays. The last leg of the journey from Galilee through Perea to Jerusalem is characterized by the fact that the evangelists now explicitly refer to it as Jesus' *going up* to the city. The road through the Judean highlands leads up to Zion, and *ascent* or *going up* has become a common expression for the journey that one makes to the temple in Jerusalem. For Jesus, the moment of the actual *going up* arrives when he leaves his retreat in Ephraim and joins all those who are crossing the Jordan to go through the Judean mountains up to the holy city to celebrate the feast there (Matt. 20:17–19; Mark 10:32–34; Luke 18:31–34; cf. John 11:54–55).

Jesus links the so-called third Passion announcement with this ascent. Meeting alone with the Twelve, he tells them in confidence that this ascent will end in his death and resurrection. Here in this closed circle he also explains the *way* in which he is to die: the Jews will condemn him and hand him over to the Gentiles, who will be the ones to kill him. Apparently there are others who also realize that this ascent will be of decisive significance. The mother of the sons of Zebedee, for example, asks during this time whether her sons may receive places of honor in Jesus' kingdom (Matt. 20:20–28; Mark 10:35–45).

For his ascent to the temple city, Jesus connects up with the main route followed by most of the Passover celebrants from Galilee and Perea, the road from Jericho to Jerusalem. Evidently he goes from Ephraim to Jericho, where he joins the crowds who are also on their way to the temple (cf. Matt. 20:29; Mark 10:46; Luke 18:35–36).

The period from Jericho to Jesus' Passion and death lasts seven days. The evangelists have a great deal to say about this short week, because the climax of Jesus' life on earth has now been reached.

The duration of this period can be deduced from several details mentioned in the Gospels. We read that Jesus arrived in Bethany six days before Passover (John 12:1). He had come directly from Jericho (Luke 19:28–29). If Jesus had arrived in Bethany on Friday (for the Sabbath), the period between his arrival and Passover would have been more than six days—seven or eight, depending on how the days from Friday to Friday are counted. The journey from Jericho to Bethany would not have been made on the Sabbath (Saturday). This means that Jesus arrived in Bethany on the first day of the week (Sunday), six days before the first day of Passover Week (Friday); the first day (Sunday) and the last day (Friday) are both counted, in the same way that the three days between death and resurrection are calculated. See chapter 13 for questions regarding the date of the Passover.

12.2 Sabbath in Jericho

If Jesus traveled from Jericho to Bethany on Sunday, he must have spent the last Sabbath before his death in Jericho. This throws light on the story of Zacchaeus. What Jesus says to this tax collector is, "I must stay at your house today." The verb "stay" (Luke 19:5) and the phrase "He has gone to be the guest of a 'sinner' " (Luke 19:7) imply that Jesus *stayed overnight* with Zacchaeus. Jesus spent the last Sabbath in humiliation in order to bring salvation and joy to the home of a tax collector. This reinforces the program for ascending to Jerusalem: "For the Son of Man came to seek and to save what was lost" (Luke 19:10).

The Lord also frames his stay in Jericho with the healing of blind men. When he enters the town he restores the sight of a blind man sitting along the road, and when he leaves after the Sabbath he heals two blind men, one of whom is called Bartimaeus. Because these healings are rather controversial, we will spend the rest of this section looking at the details.

Three evangelists report a healing of the blind in Jericho. Their stories are very similar, but they also show a few clear discrepancies. Many scholars are of the opinion that these reports refer to the same blind man and the same healing. The points on which the evangelists differ then are said to demonstrate how the Gospels often are at odds with the facts. Matthew mentions *two* blind men *after* Jesus' stay in Jericho, Mark writes of *one* blind man (called Bartimaeus), and Luke also reports *one* blind man, but the story of this healing takes place *before* the entry into the city of Jericho. One healing or two; before or after the stay in Jericho? Then there are those who go a step further and wonder whether any blind man was healed at all, whether these reports are all redactions of a strictly symbolic story. This last critique is not entirely convincing. When Mark mentions the name Bartimaeus, would not his readers recognize the man? Why else would Mark mention the name of the person who had been healed, which is not usually done? If Bartimaeus were still alive, he would be able to clear everything up. After all, he knows all too well how blind he was and how well he now can see his fellow Christians! And Mark's readers knew it, too. Our problem, however, is that in addition to Mark we also have Matthew and Luke. And it does indeed seem that one evangelist must have the story wrong. But is it implausible to suggest that there was more than one healing of blind men on the Jericho road?

1. In Matthew 21:14 we read that the lame and the blind come to Jesus in the temple and he heals them. Here we would certainly be able to find blind people who were healed before Jesus' discourse and others who were healed afterward. Just as the Lord did not limit himself to one or two blind men in Jerusalem, so it certainly seems possible that he could have opened the eyes of more than one blind beggar in Jericho.

2. We should not be surprised to read about the presence of various blind men on the roads around Jericho. When people begin traveling to Jerusalem for a feast, it is the perfect time for blind poor persons to hold out their hands and beg. They have every right to expect compassion from the believers who pass by in droves and are wealthy enough to afford the trip. And Jericho is more or less the gateway to Judea for all pilgrims coming from Galilee and Perea—a good place for beggars to reserve a spot along the roadside.

3. The fact that these blind men around Jericho expected a great deal from Jesus is understandable. His last great miracle in Jerusalem, now about six months ago, was the healing of a *man born blind* (John 9:1–7). This miracle was talked about far and wide and played a major role in the discussions for and against Jesus (John 9:21). In Jerusalem and vicinity he is best known as the healer of a lame man (John 5) and of a man born blind (John 9), so it is the lame and the blind who come to him in the temple (Matt. 21:14)! The news of the healing of the man born blind will have drawn attention in Jericho as well, certainly among the blind. Information flowed rapidly from Jerusalem to Jericho.

4. It is not contradictory for Matthew to speak of *two* blind men and Mark of *one* (i.e., Bartimaeus). In several instances Matthew presents an overall summary while Mark chooses to concentrate on one person to make his story lively and concrete. Bartimaeus must have been well known to Peter and his listeners; otherwise

his name would not have been mentioned (healings in the Gospels are anonymous as a rule). So there was good reason to tell *his* story to listeners and readers. Nothing is said of the fact that a second blind man was also healed at the same time. Matthew, however, writes without any special concern for Bartimaeus. His report is more impersonal, but it is also more inclusive. He tells of *two* blind men who had their sight restored by Jesus. A similar comparison can be made between Matthew 8:28 (two demoniacs in the land of the Gadarenes) and Mark 5:1–20 (one demoniac who became a preacher in the Decapolis).

5. Luke tells of yet another healing that took place before Jesus entered the city. The strong similarity between his story and that of the healing (or healings) after Jericho in Matthew and Mark is at first glance striking, down to the choice of words. But on closer inspection we see differences as well, while the similarities are not very specific.

The differences have to do with the details of the events.

a. When Jesus, being pushed on all sides by the crowds, approaches Jericho, the blind man first asks what is going on. He is told that Jesus the Nazarene is passing by (Luke 18:36–37). There is no mention of such preliminary information when Jesus leaves the city. The blind people can hear for themselves that it is Jesus who is passing by: apparently they already know that he is in the area. Related to this is the fact that the blind man in Luke (before entering Jericho) is urged to be silent by "those who led the way." The man asks what sort of crowd is coming, and he begins to call out even before Jesus has reached the place where he sits. In Mark and Matthew the situation is somewhat different. The blind men hear from the voices of the passing crowds that Jesus is now passing by and they call out to him.

b. Mark includes a few details that are not found elsewhere: when Jesus calls the blind man, the people around him urge him on, and he leaves his cloak behind before jumping up to go to Jesus (Mark 10:49–50).

The similarities, on the other hand, are less specific than they seem at first glance.

a. In the vast majority of the healing stories we find the request for help or mercy (cf. Matt. 9:27; 15:22; 17:15; Luke 17:13). What would a blind man answer when asked what he wants, other than "Rabbi, I want to see"? Jesus' statement that the faith of the healed person has saved him is also found frequently in similar situations (Matt. 9:22; Luke 7:50; 17:19).

b. The most specific similarity is the title "son of David." But we have already heard it used by two other blind men (Matt. 9:27) and the Canaanite woman (Matt. 15:22). The designation "son of David" implies the recognition of Jesus as the promised Messiah (Luke 20:41). The people tend to use this designation whenever they are impressed by Jesus' healing miracles (Matt. 12:22–23). After the healing of the man born blind and the raising of Lazarus, a heated discussion begins in Judea between those who are ready to recognize Jesus as the Messiah and others who all the more strongly deny it (John 7:31, 41; 9:22; 11:27; 12:34). The debate ultimately leads to the question of the high priest before the Sanhedrin, "Tell us if you are the Christ, the Son of God" (Matt. 26:63). During this period, when many recognize Jesus as the Messiah, the son of David (Matt. 21:9, 15), Jesus himself asks how the son of David can also be David's Lord (Matt. 22:43–45). Taking all this into account, it can hardly be assumed that *during these last weeks* the use of "son of David" on the part of blind men, who believe that Jesus is the Messiah, is unique and can be a decisive reason to identify Luke's story with that of Mark and Matthew. Thousands of voices cry out "son of David" a few days later during his entry into Jerusalem—why couldn't more than one blind man have addressed Jesus as "son of David" in Jericho?

12.3 Sunday: Anointing

Most of the evangelists pay little attention to Jesus' overnight stay in Bethany, but John goes into more detail. After his arrival, Jesus is served a meal at which Mary anoints him, clearly having his burial in mind (John 12:1–8). The next day is the entry into Jerusalem (John 12:12), six days before the Passover (John 12:1)

The other evangelists also report the anointing. They tell us that the meal given in Jesus' honor (John 12:2) was held in the home of Simon the Leper (Matt. 26:6; Mark 14:3). John's comment that Lazarus was among those reclining at the table also indicates that the meal did not take place in Lazarus's house, even though Martha helped with the serving: apparently Lazarus was not the host but one of the invited guests (John 12:2).

At first glance, it seems that Matthew and Mark place this meal and the anointing not six but only *two* days before the Passover (cf. Matt.

26:2; Mark 14:1). This is, however, only an *apparent* difference in dating. Matthew and Mark want to place the story of this meal near the introduction to the story of the final days of Jesus' Passion. Between the Sanhedrin's scheming (Matt. 26:1–5; Mark 14:1–2) and the defection of one of the Twelve (Matt. 26:14–16; Mark 14:10–11), the evangelists award a place of honor to the woman who constitutes a solitary exception and who—criticized by all—accepts Jesus' burial in advance and assesses its true value. Doesn't the Savior himself say that what this woman has done will be told in memory of her wherever this gospel of his death and burial is preached throughout the world (Matt. 26:13; Mark 14:9)? The place of honor for this act of Mary explains the chronological dislocation in the narrative and its location in the opening lines of the gospel of Jesus' death and burial.[1]

The above comment can be further substantiated by noting that Matthew and Mark themselves indicate that the story of the anointing actually took place earlier than the point at which it is mentioned in their Gospels. This is evident in the words used to introduce their stories: "While Jesus was in Bethany" (Matt. 26:6) and "While he was in Bethany" (Mark 14:3). Jesus' visit to Bethany was already over and behind him at that time, two days before the Passover. Matthew and Mark are not saying that Jesus "went back to Bethany," but they refer to the time when he (recently) "was in Bethany." That was at the beginning of the week, when he arrived from Jericho (Matt. 21:1; Mark 11:1), during the night following the triumphal entry (Mark 11:11–12) and the cleansing of the temple (Matt. 21:17; also Mark 11:19, cf. Mark 11:12–13, 20–21). Although both evangelists indicate that several days then pass during which Jesus teaches in the temple (Matt. 26:55; Mark 14:49), they do not mention a return to the village of Bethany. This is why the remark that the anointing took place "while Jesus was in Bethany" refers back to the beginning of the week (specified in John as the sixth day before the Passover). Jesus spent his last nights outdoors, on the Mount of Olives (Luke 21:37). Because of this (Luke 22:39), Judas was able to find Jesus on the night of his betrayal (John 18:2). It was on this mountain that Jesus withdrew with his disciples for the great discourse about the end of the age (Matt. 24:3; Mark 13:3), and this is where he went after the Last Supper (Matt. 26:30; Mark 14:26). Because Jesus spent his last days and nights in and around Jerusalem, the "Bethany event" was apparently intended as an account of something that had taken place earlier in the week but that now assumes its true significance at the beginning of the narrative of Jesus' arrest, suffering, and death.

---

1. See also my commentary on Mark 14:3–9 (*Marcus: Het evangelie volgens Petrus*, 2d ed., Commentaar op het Nieuwe Testament, 3d series [Kampen: Kok, 1992]).

12.4 Monday: Triumphal Entry

The evangelists who follow the main sequence of events seem to place the triumphal entry immediately after the arrival in Bethany. But we know from John 12:12 that there is an interruption when Jesus spends the evening and night at Bethany.

John's narrative is a bit abbreviated concerning the donkey that played a role in the triumphal entry. He notes in few words that Jesus *found* a donkey and sat on it (John 12:14). The other evangelists tell us *how* he found it: by sending out his disciples to get it at a specified address (Matt. 21:2; Mark 11:2; Luke 19:30). It is curious that some see a discrepancy between the brief statement in John and the more detailed story in the other accounts.

The same is true for the alleged difference between the Gospels that describe a donkey "which no one has ever ridden" (Mark 11:2; Luke 19:30) and Matthew, who writes about a donkey and her colt, both of which are taken. Anyone who knows how impossible it is to remove a colt that is still with its mother and to attempt to ride it will understand why Mark and Luke tell us that the mother was taken as well in order to be able to bring the inexperienced colt. Even stranger, there are biblical critics who have indulged in jokes about Matthew 21:7, as if for the sake of fulfilling the prophecy of Zechariah, Matthew is suggesting that Jesus sat on both the donkey and her colt. The verse reads, "They brought the donkey and the colt, placed their cloaks on them, and Jesus sat on them." By suggesting that Jesus rode on two animals at the same time, Matthew is supposedly making a desperate attempt to give expression to his version of Zechariah 9:9: "See, your king comes to you, righteous and having salvation, gentle and riding on a donkey, and [!] on a colt, the foal of a donkey." In reality, however, Matthew simply means that the disciples placed their cloaks on the young, inexperienced (and unsaddled) colt, and that Jesus sat *on the cloaks*. The Greek literally says "on top of these." This cannot refer to animals used for riding. One does not sit "on top of" (*epanō*), but "on" (*epi*) an animal (cf. Matt. 21:5; Mark 11:7; John 12:14–15). By contrast, one can sit "on top of" a number of cloaks that serve as a saddle.

Biblical critics have also asserted that there are discrepancies with regard to the crowds that accompanied Jesus during the triumphal entry. According to the first three evangelists, the crowds begin crying hosanna when Jesus starts riding toward Jerusalem on the colt. They spread their cloaks on the road he is traveling, cut branches from the trees to lay on the road, and run ahead of him and behind him, crying hosanna with one voice (Matt. 21:8–9; Mark 11:8–10). According to Luke, this blessing of "the king who comes in the name of the Lord" began with the descent from the Mount of Olives, as soon as Jerusalem came in sight (Luke 19:36–38). In John, things are supposedly quite different. There the crowds appear first, crying hosanna, and only then does Jesus mount the colt to begin the short journey into the city (John 12:12–13 and 12:14–16 respectively). But what is being overlooked here (perhaps as a result of working from a synopsis of the Gospels) is that John speaks in part about things *other* than those treated by the Synoptic evangelists and that for this reason he presents more material. While the others limit their accounts to the crowds that traveled with Jesus *from Bethany* toward Jerusalem, John speaks of quite a different crowd. This is the crowd that comes *from Jerusalem* to bring Jesus and his companions back to Jerusalem (John 12:12–13). These people bring palm branches with them from the city. They could not have pulled them from the trees while walking along the road, because there were no palm trees around Jerusalem. Their palm branches must have come from shops in the city, or they may have found them in places where supplies for the Feast of Tabernacles were stored. When the people take such branches along in their attempt to catch up with Jesus, it means that they are going out to greet a *victor* (compare this with the palm branches that were waved when Judas Maccabeus recaptured the city and the temple, 2 Macc. 10:7). After John describes the crowd leaving Jerusalem to go and meet Jesus (12:12–13), he begins in 12:14 to tell what is happening from the other side—how Jesus finds the colt of a donkey and rides on it. John knows that there is another crowd riding with Jesus in the direction of Jerusalem. This is the crowd that *witnessed* the raising of Lazarus (12:17), the very event that serves as the inspiration for the other crowd, which is coming out to meet them (12:18). It is understandable that with both these crowds now moving toward each other, the Pharisees can only sigh, "Look how the whole world has gone after him!" (12:19). It may have been that the cries of hosanna being uttered by those who went out to meet Jesus inspired the crowds traveling with Jesus from the Mount of Olives, who then began shouting the same thing—a kind of antiphonal singing between those climbing up to Jesus and those traveling down with him (Luke 19:37–38).

In Matthew 21:1–17 and Luke 19:28–48 the triumphal entry seems to have been followed immediately by the cleansing of the temple, on the same day. This narrative style is not unusual, since the cleansing of the temple is the first great act performed by Jesus in the city after his entry. In Mark 11:11–19, however, we see that these two events, the entry and the cleansing of the temple, were interrupted by a night in Bethany. On the day of the triumphal entry Jesus inspected the temple and took stock of the situation in order to follow it up with action the next day.

12.5 Tuesday: Cleansing of the Temple

The difference between the cleansing of the temple at the beginning of Jesus' ministry (John 2:13–25) and the cleansing of the temple during the final week (Matt. 21:12–16; Mark 11:15–18; Luke 19:45–48) has already been extensively discussed (see section 6.4).

This cleansing of the temple does not take all day. What may have taken some time was the blocking of all traffic across the temple courts. Everything came to a standstill (Mark 11:16). Now all attention is focused on Jesus' activity in the temple. He heals many lame and blind people (Matt. 21:14), teaches the crowds (Mark 11:17), and receives praise from the mouths of children when they cry out hosanna, having heard it from the adults the day before (Matt. 21:15–16).

One incident that relates both to this day and the next is the cursing of the fig tree on the way from Bethany to Jerusalem. Because Matthew and Luke join the story of the entrance with the cleansing of the temple, they have no opportunity to tell this story, which is found in Mark 11:12–14: on this Tuesday morning, before the cleansing of the temple takes place, Jesus curses a fig tree because there is no sign of fruit. The cursing seems unfair to us, since, as Mark notes, it was not the season for figs. But this comment is intended to explain that Jesus *walked up to* the tree to see if there was any sign that the tree would bear fruit, to see if fructification had begun. Because it was not yet the season for figs, it was not possible to see this from a distance. Jesus does not expect ripe figs, but he goes "to find out if it had any fruit." When the tree shows no indication that fructification has begun (little buttons that can be eaten), Jesus turns it into a sign to show that Jerusalem will also remain unfruitful for the world now that it has shown itself unfruitful for Jesus. When the disciples walk past the next morning (the day after the cleansing of the temple), they see that the fig tree is completely withered, much to Peter's horror, who remembered what Jesus had said the day before (Mark 11:21–22). Luke skips this incident entirely. Matthew, as usual, summarizes it briefly, without any historical details (Matt. 21:18–22). When he notes that "immediately the tree withered" and that the disciples were amazed, it does not rule out the possibility that a day passed between Jesus' curse and the amazement of the disciples. When a tree is fully in leaf one day and completely withered the next, we can definitely say that something very abnormal is going on. The tree does not die off over a period of time, but shrivels up suddenly.

12.6 Wednesday: The Last Discourses

Monday's triumphal entry and Tuesday's sovereign cleansing of the temple, as well as the accompanying attention of so many to Jesus' teaching and miracles, greatly increased the irritation of his opponents. The Sanhedrin had been planning to put him to death since the day Lazarus was raised (John 11:47–53). But by going on retreat in Ephraim, Jesus had briefly evaded the observation of his enemies (John 11:54). And when he appeared among them once again, his opponents were hindered by the great numbers of sympathizers who were always around him. Wednesday then becomes the day on which the unbelieving leaders attempt to force a breakthrough and to drive a wedge between Jesus and his admirers among the pilgrims. It is a day of confrontations and questions designed to catch him in his own words, a day in which Jesus once again openly addresses in his teaching the rejection and hatred directed against him.

It begins immediately in the morning, when Jesus' authority is called into question. The Lord responds to this challenge with two parables that clearly relate to his being rejected by the Pharisees and the leaders of the people (Matt. 21:23–46). This so irritates them that they try to arrest him, but they finally desist out of fear for the reaction of the crowd (Matt. 21:46; Mark 12:12; in Luke 20:19 the teachers of the law and the chief priests are specifically mentioned).

A second round of confrontations begins when the Lord tells a parable in which he emphasizes the fact that God's wrath will descend on the obstinate city, and that people from all over the world will be invited to the wedding feast in God's kingdom (Matt. 22:1–14). The Pharisees and the other leaders then launch a campaign to catch Jesus by asking him questions designed to catch him in his own words. The key question is whether it is permitted to pay taxes to Caesar. Then comes a question from the Sadducees about the resurrection of the dead, and finally a teacher of the law asks a question about the great commandment. All three questions are intended to drive him into a corner and to arouse suspicion among the crowds (cf. Matt. 22:15–40). When his questioners finally fall silent in shame, Jesus asks them the great counterquestion: how can David's son also be called David's Lord? This question brings an end to the interrogation. From that moment on, "no one dared to ask him any more questions" (Matt. 22:46; cf. Mark 12:34; Luke 20:40).

The third phase of Jesus' work on this Wednesday consists of addressing concluding words to the people and their leaders, and to his disciples. Apart from the comment about the widow's offering (in Mark and Luke), the material amounts to two long discourses. In the first, Jesus addresses the crowds and the disciples together. His topic is the unbelief of Jerusalem, with the Pharisees and the teachers of the law leading the way (Matt. 23). This is Jesus' farewell discourse in the temple. After these hard words he leaves the temple, never to return again, and he withdraws from the eyes of the people as well (Matt. 23:39–24:1). His second long discourse is for the disciples only. He delivers this discourse on the Mount of Olives, the place where the Lord had been coming with his disciples the last few nights. It concerns the future of the gospel and the future of the Jewish people (Matt. 24; Mark 13; Luke 21:5–38). This is followed by a few parables related to the period in which the Lord must be expected (Matt. 25).

After the account of the triumphal entry, John records a series of comments Jesus makes in response to some Greeks who asked to meet him (John 12:20–36). These comments imply that Jesus' *hour* has come (12:23, 27). After these comments, Jesus leaves and conceals himself from the people (John 12:36). This gives John occasion to look back on the lack of faith of the people (John 12:37–41) and the fearfulness of many of his followers (John 12:42–50; the words of Jesus found in 12:44–50 were uttered earlier, perhaps on that same day). Taking everything into consideration, 12:20–50 should be regarded as a series of statements made on the last Wednesday immediately before Jesus left the temple to withdraw into the circle of his disciples.

A fourth phase of this Wednesday, brief but important, is Jesus' repeated and now *dated* announcement of his Passion and dying. When Jesus had finished his discourses, he said to his disciples, "As you know, the Passover is two days away—and the Son of Man will be handed over to be crucified" (Matt. 26:1–2). This is often called the *fourth* Passion announcement. It is striking, however, that Mark and Luke—who, like Matthew, carefully record the first three announcements—do not mention this fourth one. So it is preferable not to speak of a *fourth* Passion *announcement.* In fact, the statement made in Matthew 26:2 is simply a repetition of the third Passion announcement. It contains nothing new (death by crucifixion is also found in the third) and it is incomplete (it fails to mention the resurrection). Why this repetition? Jesus now reveals that the *third* Passion announcement will be accomplished in *two* days. Wednesday has come to an end; tomorrow is the first day of the Feast of Unleavened Bread (Matt. 26:17), and the day after tomorrow is Passover. On that Friday Jesus will die. Wednesday ends with the disclosure of the *date* of his death!

13

The Last Passover Meal

13.1 Maundy Thursday

After the Wednesday of the final discourses comes the first day of the Feast of Unleavened Bread (Matt. 26:17). This is when the Passover lamb is sacrificed (Mark 14:2; Luke 22:7). The days of Unleavened Bread are counted from 15 to 21 Nisan (cf. Josephus, *Antiquities* 3.10.5 §249), the seven days during which the Passover offerings are sacrificed in the temple (Num. 28:16–25). Sometimes, however, 14 Nisan is also included. This is a day of preparation during which people remove all leavened bread from their homes and serve the lamb at the evening meal. In that case there are *eight* days of Unleavened Bread (cf. Josephus, *Antiquities* 2.15.1 §317). The first three evangelists clearly follow the latter approach when they write about the dawn of the Thursday on which the Passover lamb must be slaughtered (Matt. 26:17; Mark 14:12; Luke 22:7). In other words, they consider this Thursday the fourteenth day of Nisan.

The terminology used in connection with the Passover and the Feast of Unleavened Bread is complicated. The fourteenth day of Nisan is the day of preparation: all leavened bread is removed from the houses, the lambs are slaughtered, and during the evening the Passover meal is eaten. Because of this evening meal, 14 Nisan is sometimes called the Passover Feast (Lev. 23:5; Josephus, *Jewish War* 6.9.3 §423; *Antiquities* 2.14.6 §313).

The fifteenth of Nisan is the beginning of the Feast of Unleavened Bread. This feast lasts seven days, during which large sacrifices are brought into the temple (Lev. 23:6; Num. 28:17–25; cf. Josephus, *Antiquities* 3.10.5 §249; 9.13.3 §271; 11.4.8 §110). The fifteenth of Nisan is then counted as the first day (16 Nisan is the second day, see Josephus, *Antiquities* 3.10.5 §250). The fifteenth of Nisan is actually the day of Israel's liberation (Josephus, *Antiquities* 2.15.2 §318). The Jews also refer to the Feast of Unleavened Bread (15–21 Nisan) as Passover (cf. Luke 22:1; Josephus, *Jewish War* 2.1.3 §10; *Antiquities* 10.4.5 §70; 14.2.1 §21; 17.9.3 §213; 18.2.2 §29; 20.5.3 §106).

Because the leavened bread is removed on 14 Nisan, this day is referred to as "the Day of Unleavened Bread" (Josephus, *Jewish War* 5.3.1 §99). If this day (14 Nisan) is counted with the feast (15–21 Nisan), then one can also speak of a "period of unleavened bread" of eight days (Josephus, *Antiquities* 2.15.1 §317; cf. Mark 14:21; Luke 22:7).

When Matthew 26:2 states that the Passover is two days away (*ginetai*), we must think of 15–21 Nisan: there is no mention of the slaughtering of a Passover lamb. Rather, Matthew uses "Passover" as a set term for the feast that is approaching (*ginetai*): the Feast of Unleavened Bread.

The same is true for Mark 14:1. The passage "the Passover and the Feast of Unleavened Bread were only two days away" also implies that 15 Nisan is the first day of a feast that was called both Passover (among the Jews) and the Feast of Unleavened Bread (primarily among the Greeks?). Taken together, all this means that the Thursday of Passion Week, one day after the Wednesday of Mark 14:1 and preceding the Passover (which on that Wednesday was "two days away"), was 14 Nisan.

During the evening of this fourteenth day of Nisan, the inhabitants of Jerusalem and the many thousands of pilgrims partook of the Passover lamb.

Understandably there is no mention of Jesus appearing in the temple on this day. He had given his farewell discourse there on Wednesday, but beyond that, this Thursday is a special day. During the morning everyone is busy cleaning house and removing all leavened dough, food remnants, and mold from every nook and cranny. During the afternoon the ingredients for the Passover meal must be prepared. A central aspect of this meal is the slaughtering of countless lambs in the temple, starting at three o'clock in the afternoon. With all the people busy cleaning and then standing in line to await their turn with the priest to have their lamb slaughtered, there is no time for any teaching in the temple.

Now there are other matters to attend to. The disciples ask the Master where they should prepare the Passover meal (Matt. 26:17; Mark 14:12). Jesus responds by giving Peter and John the task of going into the city and getting everything ready for the evening. At this point the Lord is staying outside the city on the Mount of Olives, and the disciples he sends enter Jerusalem from outside the city (Matt. 26:18). There they find an upper room in which everything has been put in order. It has been cleaned of all its leavened bread and is waiting in purified readiness to be used by a group of men who want to celebrate the supper of the lamb. The owner knows of Jesus' plans. Perhaps the Master had quietly made prior arrangements for this room so that its whereabouts would not be known to Judas. He wanted to eat this Passover meal with his disciples before giving the traitor the opportunity to do his work.

Peter and John get everything ready. They buy the lamb and have it slaughtered that afternoon in the temple court. Then they prepare it, along with the herbs, bread, wine, and possibly meat from a thanksgiving offering. Jesus himself does not enter the city until evening, when it is time for the Passover meal (Luke 22:14), which he comes to eat with his disciples. He has "eagerly desired" to eat this Passover meal with them before his death (Luke 22:15). At the end of the Passover meal, the Lord's Supper is instituted to commemorate his approaching death for the atonement of sins. Long farewell speeches are made, and prayers are offered. Finally Jesus goes to Gethsemane to be arrested in the dark of night. All four evangelists describe this series of events, which conclude Maundy Thursday and are the introduction to the trial and crucifixion on Good Friday.

13.2 John and the Dating of the Passover Meal

Thursday evening, according to the first three evangelists, is the evening of 14 Nisan, and therefore time for the eating of the Passover lamb. Does this apply to John's Gospel as well? Many scholars claim that John considers Thursday to be 13 Nisan and that in his account 14 Nisan does not come until Friday, so that the Passover lamb was eaten on the evening of the day in which Jesus was crucified. That would mean that the last meal that Jesus ate with his disciples, when he instituted the Lord's Supper, was not a Passover meal. The implications of a different dating are important. Furthermore, if there are contradictions in the date of such a decisive moment, the reliability of the Gospels is called into question. If the writers themselves were present, as the Gospels suggest, then surely they would know whether Jesus' death coincided with the sacrifice of the Passover lambs in the temple or whether they had partaken of the supper of the lamb the evening before. Many critics regard John's different dating of Good Friday as proof of the proposition that the Gospels provide a theological interpretation in which actual events play a subordinate role: John's purpose behind the different dating of the Last Supper is an attempt to make Jesus' death coincide approximately with the slaughtering of the Passover lambs. In doing so his interpretation of Jesus' death is based on the significance of this particular Lamb for Israel.

We first should note how strange it would be if John, who places great importance on the correct reporting of verifiable facts (John 19:35; 21:24), were to move the crucifixion by one day when everyone knew, or could easily find out, when it had taken place. Things that happen just before or on a feast day are the very things we are least likely to get wrong when we try to remember them. In addition, John's Gospel does not explicitly equate Jesus with the Passover lamb, and we would not be likely to arrive at this equation by merely reading John's Gospel. The connection is postulated by scholars wishing to account for the curious fact that John seems to use different dates. But why would this evangelist conceal his true intentions? Why would he suggest that Jesus is to be identified with the Passover lamb only by shifting the date in the narrative?

Nevertheless, John's text does raise a number of questions about his dating of the days during Passion Week. A detailed study of all the explanations that have been offered is beyond the scope of this book. We must also pass over the recent theory that Jesus and his disciples celebrated the Passover meal according to a different liturgical calendar (possibly that of the Essene community) rather than the official Jewish calendar. (In that case John would have followed the calendar of the leaders and the temple, and the other evangelists would have based their accounts on the calendar used by Jesus and his disciples.) There is no trace of support within the Gospels for such a hypothesis, nor are we commenting here on whether the use of two calendars within one temple city during this period can be demonstrated on the basis of extrabiblical sources. The Gospels unanimously support the view that Jesus was completely in line with the teachers of the law and the priests with regard to the *times* of the feasts.

We are limiting this discussion to the main facts of the Gospels themselves, taking issue with the essay on this subject by P. Billerbeck, which is still a classic.[1] We cannot avoid going into more detail here; the reader who is not interested in this issue can skip this excursus and go on to the next chapter.

It is Billerbeck's opinion that John undeniably presents a dating of the days in question that is different from that found in the other evangelists. We, on the other hand, claim that on closer inspection John also dates Thursday as 14 Nisan (not 13 Nisan) and the Friday as 15 Nisan (not 14 Nisan). The following points must be considered in this discussion.

1. The story of the foot washing and the meal begins in John 13. This passage opens with a statement of time: "It was just before the Passover feast." What does the writer mean? Surely the feast days that begin with 15 Nisan. He does not speak of the evening when the Passover lamb is to be eaten, but of the *feast*, which runs from 15 to 21 Nisan. If John re-

---

1. "Die Angaben der vier Evangelien über den Todestag Jesu unter Berücksichtigung ihres Verhältnis zur Halakha," in H. L. Strack and P. Billerbeck, *Das Evangelium nach Markus, Lukas und Johannes und die Apostelgeschichte*, vol. 2 of *Kommentar zum Neuen Testament aus Talmud und Midrasch* (Munich: Beck, 1924), 812–53.

ferred to the festivities that take place at the end of 14 Nisan, he could hardly describe the evening of the thirteenth as "before the Passover feast." The day following the thirteenth cannot be described in its entirety as "Passover feast." The foot washing and the last meal with the disciples therefore take place on the evening before 15 Nisan, which is the end of the fourteenth day of Nisan. Even in John, the Last Supper is also a Passover supper!

2. Several details in John 13 support this. The dipping of a piece of bread (13:26) suggests the presence of a sort of sauce: the bitter-herb sauce is part of the Passover meal! When Judas leaves and goes into the night, the disciples think that he may be going to buy "what was needed for the feast" (13:29). This can hardly refer to the buying that Judas would have done in the night from 13 to 14 Nisan in preparation for the Passover meal that would be served the following evening: Judas could not have done that until half a day later, on the fourteenth, after all the leavened bread had been removed from the houses and rooms. The passage also states that Judas may have gone to buy what was needed for the *Feast*. Once again, the idea here is the actual Passover feast that begins on 15 Nisan, after the supper of the lamb. This first day of Passover week is a day of festive gathering, as is the twenty-first, and the only work permitted on those days is that which is strictly essential (no regular work: Num. 28:16–25). The disciples' surmises about Judas' departure relate to a date on the calendar that is already moving from 14 to 15 Nisan!

3. In John 19:14, at the moment when Pilate introduces Jesus to the people as their king, we read: "It was the day of Preparation of Passover Week." The Greek text reads, *ēn de paraskeuē tou pascha* ("It was now the Preparation of Passover"). This phrase could also be translated as "Preparation *for* Passover," but the translation "of Passover" is literal and gives a clear sense. It is the day of Preparation that falls *during* Passover. If the phrase were translated as "Preparation *for* Passover," it could refer to the preparations undertaken on 14 Nisan for the supper of the lamb served during the evening. Billerbeck's opinion is that this interpretation is the only one possible, because what we supposedly have here is a translation of the technical rabbinic term ʿereb pesaḥ (the preparation for the Passover meal). Although this idea is argued forcefully, the evidence is lacking. It is also very unlikely that the Greek phrase *paraskeuē tou pascha* would amount to an equivalent of ʿereb pesaḥ. The word ʿereb means "evening." Just as the German expression *Heiligabend* refers to the evening before a church feast, and the English word "eve" is used to designate evenings before certain holidays, as in Christmas Eve and New Year's Eve, so the expression ʿereb pesaḥ ("Passover evening") refers to the afternoon and evening of 14 Nisan,

when people are preparing and eating the Passover meal! It is the evening that precedes the Passover Feast that begins on 15 Nisan, and because it is a very important evening that serves as an introduction to the feast, special names for it have developed over time.

The Greek word *paraskeuē* has no association at all with "evening." It means "preparation." As such it has taken on special technical significance, namely "Friday." It is the day of preparation for the Sabbath! Meals for the day of rest are prepared on this day of preparation, this Friday. In Mark 15:42, the word is interpreted as "the day before the Sabbath." We see the same interpretation in Matthew 27:62, where the day after Jesus' death is referred to as the day after Preparation day— the Sabbath after the Friday. In Luke 23:54, *paraskeuē* is also used to refer to the day before the Sabbath. John makes no change in the way the word is used. In 19:31, *paraskeuē* is the day before the Sabbath (see also 19:42). Because the word does not mean "evening" (*ʿereb*), and because it cannot be demonstrated that the expression *paraskeuē tou pascha* is used anywhere as the equivalent of "Passover Eve" (*sēder happesaḥ*), and because the word *paraskeuē* appears in all four Gospels and always means "preparation day for the Sabbath" (i.e., Friday), the obvious translation of John 19:14 is "It was Passover Friday."

This brief sentence says two things: (a) It was Friday, Sabbath was approaching, the hour was pressing, and for this reason Pilate had to make a decision without any further delay. (b) It was the Day of Passover (15 Nisan), the *liberation day* of the people of Israel. Pilate thought it would be a nice gesture to offer the people a *king* on this particular day! Thus we discover the role this sentence plays in the context of John 19:11–16. Pilate wants to release Jesus (19:12). The Jews are radically opposed to this plan (19:12). So Pilate must render a verdict on this day before the Sabbath (postponement until the next day is not possible) (19:13). Because it is liberation day, Pilate appoints Jesus king (19:14), but the people demand immediate crucifixion for this "king" (19:15). So the governor hands him over to be crucified (19:16). Billerbeck overlooks this reasonable interpretation because he disagrees with the translation "Preparation of the Passover Sabbath"—and indeed, this formulation has little meaning. But Billerbeck is too limited in the translation options he offers, and it is regrettable that he did not consider .ne option "Passover Friday."

4. Finally, we need to look at John 18:28: "and to avoid ceremonial uncleanness the Jews did not enter the palace; they wanted to be able to eat the Passover." Doesn't this verse make it abundantly clear that the Jewish leaders had not yet eaten the Passover meal, meaning that it is still 14 Nisan? This would certainly be true if the expression "eat the Passover meal" was used only to refer to the supper of the lamb. Biller-

beck also recognizes that this is not the case. On the basis of Deuteronomy 16:2–3 and 2 Chronicles 35:7–9, this passage might be understood to mean the Passover sacrifices that were offered during the seven days of the feast. Thus the context, according to Billerbeck, makes it clear that "Passover" does not refer to the Passover lamb but to the Passover offerings (Num. 28:16–25). Therefore, if John 13 tells us that the Passover lamb had already been eaten on the preceding Thursday evening, as we have argued under points 1 and 2, then it is obvious that 18:28 must refer to the eating of the Passover *sacrifices* and the unleavened bread.

Even more can be said to support and clarify the assertion that 18:28 *cannot* refer to the Passover lamb. After all, the events in 18:28 take place early in the morning. If the leaders had become defiled by entering the governor's headquarters, they could easily have purified themselves before evening in order to partake of the Passover lamb. Fear of defilement must have had to do with the meal or meals to be eaten on the same day, which could only have been the meals of the sacrifices that were brought on the fifteenth day of Nisan. This reasoning would be wrong if Billerbeck's assertion were correct that this situation involved entering the house of a Gentile, which led to seven days of ceremonial uncleanness. In my opinion, the governor's headquarters *inside* Jerusalem, specifically the Antonia fortress, which architecturally and structurally was part of the temple complex and was also the place where the high-priestly vestments were stored, was not subject to the same laws that applied to houses that were *owned* by Gentiles. This place is a *part* of the great temple complex that was being *used* by Gentiles. That means that it had not been cleansed of leavened bread. Because it is already Passover and the leaders have already purified themselves of leavened bread, they do not want to run the risk of becoming "defiled" once again, and they want to avoid being prevented from joining in the eating of the Passover sacrifice and the unleavened bread on this particular day by having been exposed to this risk. If entering the governor's palace resulted in seven days of impurity, no one would ever enter such a building at any time, not only during special occasions. But this is not the case. The text in 18:28 deals with an exceptional occurrence arising from the exceptional character of the day. The same would apply if it were suggested that the governor was receiving people in Herod's palace rather than in the Antonia fortress. This palace was not a Roman government building either, but a palace that belonged to the Herodian family and could on special occasions serve as residence of the Roman governor.

The fact that the expression "eat the Passover" as used in John has a somewhat broader meaning than it does for the other evangelists should not surprise us. John never uses the word *pascha* to mean "Passover lamb" or "Passover meal" (unlike passages such as Matt. 26:17–19; Mark 14:12–16; and Luke 22:7–15). For John the meaning is always "the period of the Passover Feast" (2:13, 23; 6:4; 11:55; 12:1; 13:1; 18:39). "To eat the Passover" can simply be defined as "eating the sacrificial meals that were part of the Passover Feast."

5. Finally there is John 18:39. There Pilate reminds the people of the custom of releasing a prisoner "at the time of the Passover." This year he proposes that Jesus be released. Pilate's words presuppose that the time for the annual release is *now*. This means that this Friday can be regarded as "the time of the Passover," a day that is part of the Passover week (15–21 Nisan). The fourteenth of Nisan—especially the early morning of that day—could never be included as a "Passover feast day." Thus John 18:39 clearly affirms that for John, this Friday is not the fourteenth but the fifteenth of Nisan!

In summary, we can say that also according to John the Passover meal took place on Thursday evening. The Friday of the trial is the first day of Passover week (15 Nisan), liberation day for the people of Israel. There is thus no discrepancy between John and the other three evangelists with regard to the calendar days of Jesus' Passion.

14

Was the Sanhedrin Allowed to Carry Out a Death Sentence?

To get a clear understanding of the complicated events that took place on the Friday of the trial and the crucifixion, it is first necessary to understand the background. Two matters in particular must be addressed separately: First, the question as to whether the Sanhedrin at that time had the right to carry out a death sentence and therefore could have put Jesus to death—without Pilate's help. Second, what was the strategy the Sanhedrin had agreed upon by Wednesday evening, and to what extent does this strategy provide an explanation for the events of that Friday?

The first question will be discussed in this chapter, the second question in the next. Answering the first question especially requires a great deal of detail, more detail than is customary elsewhere in this book. The reader who prefers to follow the overall picture of Jesus' life may want to skip the next two chapters and move on to chapter 16, which deals with the events of Good Friday. The background information and more detailed argumentation in chapters 14 and 15 can then be referred to later if necessary.

14.1 A Question Charged with Tension

Did the Jews have the right to impose the death sentence and to carry it out during the reign of the Roman governor Pontius Pilate? This question has strong emotional dimensions. It is one that is increasingly raised in discussions between non-Christian Jews and Christians. Who is really responsible for Jesus' death? Christians can easily point the finger at the Jews, but if the Jews did have the right to carry out the death sentence themselves, it is significant that it was not they but the Romans who carried it out! Are the Jews free of blame and was Jesus a politically dangerous figure, as his crucifixion by the *Roman* officials shows? Or did the Jews *not* have the right to carry out the death penalty, and did they vent *their* rage by enlisting the Romans to do it for them? And was Jesus then a rejected Messiah after all?

These questions are not always made explicit. Many people have been made very much aware of them, however, through a book by Jewish author Paul Winter (1961).[1] Not only was this book dedicated to the victims of Auschwitz, Izbica, Majdanek, and Treblinka, among whom were the author's dearest relatives (his mother and his sister), but it was also written by a man who seemed to be driven to this study. He worked on it for many years, living like a hermit in London while earning his meager livelihood at night in the underground or as a night watchman for epileptics. Paul Winter sought, so to speak, to exorcise the doom that he felt rested on the Jews by writing a scholarly study that demonstrated that Jesus (who was not a revolutionary) was nevertheless arrested on the initiative of the *Roman* government and put to death by the Romans because Jesus' royal ambitions created too much tension among the people. Winter's book rekindled an old discussion with new intensity. It gave rise to a stream of responses. A decade later, Catchpole wrote a good overview of the Jewish historiography since 1770 dealing with Jesus' trial.[2] The tone is detached: the book presents the arguments but does not get involved in the emotional context.

Yet anyone who takes up the question of the rights of the Sanhedrin must be aware of its emotional aspects—especially in order to determine that the question itself can be addressed apart from these emotions. The question of the guilt of the Jews of that time is not dependent on the question of the authority of the Sanhedrin. And what is more important, if the Savior prayed on the cross for forgiveness for those who crucified him, why should anyone undertake, with the intent of assessing blame, studies to determine what part the Sanhedrin played or could have played in his death? We do not address the question of the Sanhedrin's authority in order to define a position toward non-Christian Jews, but rather to reach, in our exegesis of the Gospels, an understanding of how the data should be interpreted and what the historical background of these data is.

Those who search for authorities in defense of the position that the Sanhedrin at the time of Jesus had absolutely no right to carry out the death penalty need go no further than the work of such scholars as Jeremias, Blinzler, Sherwin-White, or Catchpole.[3] But those who are inter-

---

1. P. Winter, *On the Trial of Jesus*, 2d ed., rev. and ed. T. A. Burkill and G. Vermes, Studia Judaica 1 (Berlin: De Gruyter, 1974).

2. D. R. Catchpole, *The Trial of Jesus: A Study in the Gospels and Jewish Historiography from 1770 to the Present Day*, Studia Post-biblica 18 (Leiden: Brill, 1971).

3. J. Jeremias, "Zur Geschichtlichkeit des Verhörs Jesu vor dem Hohen Rat," *Zeitschrift für die neutestamentliche Wissenschaft* 43 (1950–51): 145–50; J. Blinzler, *Der Prozess Jesu: Das jüdische und das römische Gerichtsverfahren gegen Jesus Christus auf Grund der ältesten Zeugnisse dargestellt und beurteilt*, 3d ed. (Regensburg: Pustet, 1960; English translation: *The Trial of Jesus: The Jewish and Roman Proceedings against Jesus Christ Described and Assessed from the Oldest Accounts*, trans. Isabel and Florence McHugh [Westminster, Md.: Newman; Cork: Mercier, 1959]); A. N. Sherwin-White, *Roman Society and Roman Law in the New Testament* (Oxford: Clarendon, 1963); Catchpole, *Trial of Jesus.*

ested in making the opposite claim and are looking for experts to back them up can equally easily range themselves behind Juster, Lietzmann, Winter, or Cohn.[4] Interestingly enough, there are comparatively more Jewish authors who come out in favor of the right of the Sanhedrin to carry out the death penalty, and comparatively more Christian authors who argue against this right. The latter is understandable when we read John 18:31, where the Jewish leaders say to Pilate, "But we have no right to execute anyone." As a Christian source, this Gospel may carry less weight for Jewish researchers, who apparently have so much other evidence that they necessarily come to the conclusion that John 18:31 requires a different interpretation or must simply be considered in error. When Christian authors, on the other hand, believe that they can demonstrate by using rabbinic material that the Sanhedrin had no right to carry out executions under the Romans, it is clear from the start that a great deal of information is involved and that the evaluation of these materials may lead to different solutions without involving prejudice or partiality among certain *groups* of researchers. Without trying to be exhaustive, we will discuss the main data one by one.

14.2 John 18:31

The Jewish leaders say to Pilate, "We have no right to execute anyone" (John 18:31). But is it unquestionably clear that they refer to execution based on a Jewish trial and a Jewish death sentence? This is the clear opinion of Blinzler.[5] From John 18:32 ("so that the words Jesus had spoken indicating the kind of death he was going to die would be fulfilled") many want to deduce that at that time the death penalty was not always necessarily *crucifixion* and that the Jewish *right of stoning* was also an option. But Blinzler notes that John 18:32 is not formulated in response to stoning as the alternative but in response to *illegal murder* as the alternative. Attempts to simply kill Jesus, without due process, are mentioned in John 8:59 and 10:31, according to Blinzler. So John 18:32 would mean that Jesus' prophecy of a death by means of the death *penalty* and not by means of *murder* was fulfilled when the Jews brought him to the one person who at that time had the right to carry out the death *penalty*.

Against Blinzler's interpretation, however, is in the first place the moment John chooses to announce the fulfillment of Jesus' prophecy:

4. J. Juster, *Les Juifs dans l'Empire Romain* (Paris: Geuther, 1914); H. Lietzmann, "Der Prozess Jesu" and "Bemerkungen zum Prozess Jesu," in *Kleine Schriften*, vol. 2, *Studien zum Neuen Testament* (Berlin, 1958–62), 251ff.; Winter, *On the Trial of Jesus*; H. Cohn, *The Trial and Death of Jesus* (New York: Harper & Row, 1971).

5. Blinzler, *Prozess Jesu*, 165.

Why not announce it earlier, when the Sanhedrin had him arrested or when it decided to take him before Pilate? That is when the decision was made against murder in favor of a trial. Why is Jesus' prophecy recorded at the moment that the Jews, within the trial procedure, remark that they have no right to execute anyone? At the very least this suggests that the prophecy is being fulfilled by this *comment* that points to an alternative to stoning, which the Jews have no recourse to *on this day* based on their *own* religious law.

This idea is reinforced by a second point. It is striking that Blinzler cites only John 8:59 and 10:31. He ignores 11:53, where the Sanhedrin begins deliberations for taking Jesus' life after the raising of Lazarus. Apparently such deliberations are within the Sanhedrin's purview. They do not debate whether they will have him killed (*phoneusai*) but whether they themselves (!) will put him to death (*apokteinai*). Not a word is said about handing him over to the governor, which would be an obvious step if they had no right to pronounce and execute death sentences. Why all the questions intended to trip Jesus up that were asked during the previous Wednesday, if the Sanhedrin could not bring Jesus to trial? The passage in John 18:31 does not stand in contrast to the attempts at murder in 8:59 and 10:31, but it does stand in contrast to the initial deliberation of the Sanhedrin to put Jesus to death on its own (11:53). As Jewish leaders the choice up to this point was still in their hands, but now (in 18:31) they switch the trial to Pilate, and at that moment the prophecy is fulfilled that says that Jesus will die by being raised on the *cross* (the Roman death penalty).

We believe that the phrase from John 18:31 ("But we have no right to execute anyone") does not settle the matter out of hand nor does it render further research superfluous. Should it turn out that the Jews *did* have the right of execution, John 18:31 may well make good sense in the context of that historical reality.

14.3 The Claim to Jewish Jurisdiction

If under Roman rule the Jews had no right to carry out the death penalty (not even with Roman authorization),[6] then we must determine whether they had the right to administer their own justice. Under the Jewish notion of justice, the right to carry out the death penalty (in the case of a false prophet, for example) would make no sense if the sentence could not be implemented. We do know that under the Romans the Jews had the right to administer their own justice. Limits were placed on the extent of that right (see section 14.4), but the right

6. Cf. P. J. Verdam, *Sanhedrin èn Gabbatha* (Kampen: Kok, 1959), 32–33.

as such was unaffected. Jewish legal authority had continued to exist under Herod, and if it had been revoked, then it was only withdrawn in Judea (after A.D. 6 under the Roman governors) and not in Galilee (under Herod Antipas). The Sanhedrin, however, was not a Judean court. It constituted the supreme court for all of Palestine and for all Jews. We know that the Sanhedrin continued to have jurisdiction, whatever its limitations, as evidenced by the fact that the Romans reserved the right to appoint or dismiss the high priest, who was the chairman of the Sanhedrin. This put the Jewish council under Roman control, because the council's chairman would lose his job in an instant if his actions, or those of the council, were not to the occupying power's satisfaction. But such interference in the Jewish system of justice (under which the high priest held his office for life) would have made no sense at all if the council were nothing but a discussion group without any authority. Blinzler acknowledges without question that the Sanhedrin maintained the right to try criminal cases.[7] Cohn points out that in fact the entire internal Jewish judicial system was maintained under the Romans. The Sanhedrin dealt only with special cases; most cases were heard by the so-called small Sanhedrins, which consisted of twenty-three judges. Josephus reports how the Roman governor himself, Gabinius, established five regional small Sanhedrins around 60 B.C. (*Antiquities* 14.5.4 §91), and Cohn is of the opinion that these courts existed in all the larger towns in Judea and Galilee at the time of Jesus' trial.[8]

An indisputable proof of the Sanhedrin's right to administer justice is found in the story of Paul's trial. There we see ample evidence that the Jews were able to ask the Romans to send Paul to them so that they could obtain "more accurate information about his case" (Acts 23:15) and so that they could judge him by their own law (Acts 24:6 KJV).[9] When Paul makes his appeal to the emperor, it is to avoid a Jewish trial. Festus wanted him to go to Jerusalem (in his presence) to be tried by the Sanhedrin. Paul does not want to evade a death sentence if he deserves it, but he realizes that Festus already knows that he has done nothing deserving of punishment, and he refuses to be turned over to the Jews as a favor to them (Acts 25:9–11). The favor Festus wants to do the Jews presupposes that the Sanhedrin *was permitted* to try a criminal case. But as a Roman citizen, Paul cannot be handed over to the Jewish court without grounds.

---

7. Blinzler, *Prozess Jesu*, 166–67.
8. Cohn, *Trial and Death of Jesus*, 32.
9. Both the NIV and NRSV omit Acts 24:6b-8a but include it in a note. The NASB places these verses in brackets.

Winter has dealt with the implications of Paul's trial in great detail.[10] Catchpole casts doubt on the cogency of his argument, although he recognizes that the Sanhedrin did in any case have the freedom to administer its own justice. He disagrees with Winter. According to Catchpole, the Jews were permitted to *pronounce* a death sentence but they could *not carry it out.*[11] In Paul's case these two matters must be distinguished, even though it is clear that the Sanhedrin regards Paul's case as a capital offense. Catchpole's interpretation of Acts 25:9 is that Festus proposes to the Jews only that the location of the *Roman* trial be shifted to Jerusalem. But this is contrary to what we read in 25:11. Paul does not appeal to Caesar to avoid Festus's trial. He wants to avoid a *Jewish* trial by appealing to the emperor. In 25:9, the words *ep' emou* then must mean that Festus will *attend* the Sanhedrin trial in order to guarantee a fair trial and to prevent a lynching party.[12] Catchpole considers such a presence of Roman authority in the background of a session of the Sanhedrin unlikely, but we do see an example of precisely such a presence in Acts 22:30–23:10, when Lysias keeps an eye on Paul's interrogation by the Sanhedrin and is able to help him escape just in time with the help of his own soldiers! Perhaps this was an exception, but we are not discussing run-of-the-mill trials.

10. Winter, *On the Trial of Jesus*, 112–27.
11. Catchpole, *Trial of Jesus*, 250–54.
12. A. Schalit ("Zu AG 25,9 [On Acts 25:9]," *Annual of the Swedish Theological Institute* 6 [1968]: 106–13) emphatically argues, against Winter, that Festus meant only to move the *Roman* trial to Jerusalem. He proves this by showing that the Greek phrase *krithēnai ep' emou*, used in a trial situation, can only mean "stand trial *before* me." Schalit's examples clearly demonstrate (once again) that *epi* with the genitive in trial situations refers to the authority (the court) by which one is sentenced. He fails to take into account, however, that there is more in Acts 25:9. We do not read, "Are you willing to go up to Jerusalem to be tried in my presence?" Rather, what we read is, "Are you willing to go up to Jerusalem and stand trial *ep' emou* on these charges *there*?" The word *there* implies the court before which Paul will stand. This we see in Acts 25:10: "Paul answered: 'I am now standing before Caesar's court, where I ought to be tried. I have not done any wrong to the Jews, as you yourself know very well.'" Paul is not yet appealing to the emperor in Rome with this statement (he does not do this until 25:11b–12). He only states that now he is standing before the imperial court (the governor enforces the law on behalf of the emperor in this imperial province). This is also the place where he ought to be tried. Over against this court (in Caesarea) are the Jews (in Jerusalem, *there*). A trial before their bar instead of before the bar of the imperial governor would amount to handing over a man (whose innocence has been proved) to judges who will sentence him anyway. The phrase "no one has the right to hand me over to them" (25:11) can only refer to handing him over to a Jewish court of law, because there is still no indication that Festus does not want to protect the apostle (indeed, the contrary is true). In 25:9 we do not have an example of the verb "stand trial" in combination with the preposition *epi* (with the genitive). The connection lies elsewhere. Paul does not want to "stand trial *there*" (i.e., before the Jerusalem court), not even if Festus travels with him so that the *Jewish* trial takes place "in his presence."

14.4 Capital Punishment and Roman Law

The right of the Sanhedrin to carry out a death sentence is dismissed as an impossibility by those who base their argument on Roman law. Sherwin-White states that the right to carry out the death penalty belonged exclusively to Roman judicial institutions,[13] and that the governors jealously guarded this right and never entrusted its application to subordinates or to indigenous judicial bodies. The only exception was the free city-states, but Jerusalem was not one of them.

The correctness of this view cannot be denied, but the question is whether it really touches the core of our problem. The Roman right to perform executions functions within *Roman* law. The Sanhedrin would certainly not be called in to help carry it out. The question is, however, what happened in practice in situations where Roman law was not involved, for example, when a group such as the Jews still had its own legal system with laws and punishments for matters not covered in Roman law? A Roman judge would stay strictly within the parameters of Roman law and would never allow any alien elements to enter into his judicial decisions. One telling example is Gallio's action in Corinth. As soon as he discovers that the charges against Paul have to do with internal Jewish matters and with issues that touch on Jewish religious writings, he refuses to act as judge (Acts 18:15). Yet he does not forbid them to institute legal proceedings. "Settle the matter yourselves," he says. This statement does not tell us how much freedom the Jews had in their own legal inquiries, but it does appear that the only thing we can know for certain when discussing the Roman right to perform executions is that no person or institution except the Roman judge was authorized to enforce and implement *Roman* law and its punishments.

So it is quite possible that the situation in Palestine was as Cohn[14] describes it: The Jews enforced their *own* religious justice (including the punishments involved) through the smaller Sanhedrins as well as through the great Sanhedrin in Jerusalem. The Romans were the guardians of *Roman* law in Palestine. This coexistence of judicial bodies would have given the governor the right to have any crimes that were punishable under Roman as well as under Jewish law tried by a Roman court. Thus there was a limit to the number of cases over which the Jews retained jurisdiction. In addition, the governor's influence on the appointment of the high priest provided a measure of control over the functioning of the highest Jewish judicial institution.

---

13. Sherwin-White, *Roman Society and Roman Law*, 36. Cf. Blinzler, *Prozess Jesu*, 168–69.
14. Cohn, *Trial and Death of Jesus*, 33–34.

Precisely because the Roman governor never delegated his right to carry out the death penalty, we must assume, based on several statements made by Pilate, that the Sanhedrin maintained a (limited) right to carry out executions. In the first place we can point to John 18:29–31:

> So Pilate came out to them and asked, "What charges are you bringing against this man?" "If he were not a criminal," they replied, "we would not have handed him over to you." Pilate said, "Take him yourselves and judge him by your own law."

Pilate asks the Jews to formulate their charge, but they want Pilate himself to initiate an inquiry—if there were no evidence of criminal activity, they would not have handed him over to Pilate. The Jews see the Jesus affair as a matter that the Roman judge himself must take on, solve, and bring to a conclusion. The nature of the offense demands it— Jesus is a criminal. By handing Jesus over they can show Pilate that he is dealing with a man guilty before *Roman* law. If this were not true, then they would not have handed Jesus over and the internal Jewish dispute would have been settled internally. But Pilate does not fall for their performance—he sees right through it. He knows full well that this is an internal Jewish problem. He therefore declines to investigate, allowing the Jews enough room *not* to hand Jesus over and to judge him according to their own Jewish law instead. How would a Roman governor ever have been able to say such a thing unless the Jews had the right to take on cases that were not considered "criminal" or "illegal" under Roman law and to try them according to their own religious law? The Jews are not saying that they may not administer justice, but that they are not permitted to put anyone to death (i.e., on this day of the Passover).[15]

A second statement can be found in John 19:6:

> But Pilate answered, "You take him and crucify him. As for me, I find no basis for a charge against him."

If the Sanhedrin had no authority to carry out executions, it would have been inconceivable for Pilate to encourage them to try the case themselves and even to carry out the death penalty. He as governor would be sanctioning and even provoking an illegal execution. It is also strange that the Jews do not immediately make use of the right that they were

---

15. See the second section in this chapter (14.2) for a discussion of whether the Jews are reminding Pilate here of the Sanhedrin's lack of authority to execute the death penalty or whether they are informing him that today they themselves are not in the position to try a case or carry out an execution on this day.

supposedly given by special dispensation. Pilate's words, and the Jews' attitude, prove that the Sanhedrin did have limited authority to carry out executions in non-Roman criminal cases. The Jews' response to Pilate's offer (John 19:7) is

> We have a law, and according to that law he must die, because he claimed to be the Son of God.

The Jews present the matter as a Jewish criminal case, plain and simple. If the Romans were the only ones allowed to carry out the death penalty in Palestine, Jesus' acquittal would now have been a fact. But Pilate takes seriously the Jews' internal charge (which had been suppressed at first; John 18:28–32) as a charge deserving of the death penalty. This shows once again that in addition to Roman law (with the death penalty) there functioned another law (with sanctions).

Finally, we should consider the remarkable outcome of the trial. Pilate is judging the case. He declares Jesus innocent before Roman law, yet he gives the order to crucify him. This order is characterized as delivering Jesus into the hands of the Jews (John 19:16) and surrendering to their will (Luke 23:25). Pilate would have been violating Roman law if he had released an innocent man into the hands of a mob for a lynching under the guise of an execution. But he does something quite different. He does not say that he is administering Roman law, only that he is lending his cooperation to the administering of Jewish law. The entire course of the trial indicates that this is not normal. The governor is not an administrator of Jewish death sentences. Yet on this particular day this is just what Pilate does. But he never could have done so if the Jews did not have the right to administer their own criminal justice. Pilate would have been permitting an illegal act (the death penalty on the basis of Jewish law, in a case that was not a capital offense under Roman law) and would have made himself vulnerable to the displeasure of the emperor, who kept a sharp eye on the proper implementation of the death penalty.

Only one conclusion is possible: Pilate's complicity on this special day, when the Jews were not permitted to put anyone to death, presupposes that their right to punish and execute was recognized by the Romans.[16]

---

16. Winter, *On the Trial of Jesus*, 97–109, has tried to derive separate proof for this from the various kinds of capital punishment administered by the Jews. He claims that strangling was not used until the year 70, because executions were forbidden at that time and there was need for a less noisy punishment that could be carried out in secret. The vulnerability of this argument is demonstrated by Blinzler, *Prozess Jesu*, 167–68, and Catchpole, *Trial of Jesus*, 245–47.

14.5 Execution by Stoning

Various examples show that stoning as a Jewish punishment—in the context of the administration of justice—was used in New Testament times.

The apostle Paul more than once physically experienced Jewish punishments, including stoning. He writes in 2 Corinthians 11:24–25,

> Five times I received from the Jews the forty lashes minus one. Three times I was beaten with rods, once I was stoned.

This mention of the measured and restrained forty lashes minus one clearly shows that what is involved here is legal, rabbinic criminal justice and not a spontaneous outburst of rage. If the internal Jewish rabbinic criminal justice system was not allowed to function alongside the Roman system of capital punishment, it is odd that Paul was so often confronted by it!

When the apostles stood before the Sanhedrin and that body's members became enraged over the persistence of Peter and the others, they "took counsel to put them to death" (Acts 5:33 KJV). Even when we accept the reading found in a minority of manuscripts, that the Sanhedrin *"wanted* to put them to death" (NIV, NRSV [italics added]), we see the Sanhedrin *wanting* to perform this act, as is suggested in the further deliberation in which Gamaliel advises them to go no further than flogging and not to reach decisions that demand death as a penalty (Acts 5:35–40). How can the Sanhedrin discuss killing the apostles if the council had no authority to do so?

In the case of Stephen we see the same council pursue a charge that could result in the death penalty (Acts 6:12–14). It *seems* as though the stoning occurred in haste under the influence of general excitement, so that the rule of "one night between sentencing and execution" was disregarded (Acts 7:57–58). Yet this stoning occurs within the framework of the administration of justice. We see this from the fact that the *witnesses* carry out the execution (Acts 7:58). So the Stephen affair cannot be dismissed as an explosion of popular hatred resulting in a lynching party tolerated by the Romans.[17]

We find illustrations of the Jewish court wielding the right to punish capital offenses on a grand scale when we study Paul's persecution of Christians among the Jews. Saul breathes "murderous threats" against the disciples of Jesus (Acts 9:1). And his murderous threats are real. In Acts 26:10 we read his confession:

17. See Blinzler, *Prozess Jesu*, 173, and many other writers.

I put many of the saints in prison, and when they were put to death, I cast my vote against them.

There are some striking elements in this passage. (1) Paul could be authorized by the Sanhedrin to persecute and arrest Jews. (2) Death sentences could be pronounced, and Saul was one of the voting judges. (3) Paul can admit this unhesitatingly to Festus, the Roman governor, without fear of revealing something that is highly incriminating to himself and to the Sanhedrin, namely, that they had assumed illegal authority!

On the basis of this information our only conclusion can be that at the time of Jesus' trial and Paul's persecution of the church, the Jews were allowed to deal with non-Roman criminal cases according to their own internal system of justice and administer the punishments it required, including the death penalty.

14.6 Counterarguments

But is there not a great deal of information that would at least serve to neutralize the above conclusion or even put the greater weight of evidence on the opposite side? We want to discuss the most important counterarguments to test the soundness of our conclusion.

14.6.1 The Stoning of James according to Josephus

In his *Antiquities* (20.9.1 §§200–203), Josephus reports how the high priest Ananus, shortly after his appointment by Agrippa II, called the Sanhedrin together and tried and stoned James, the brother of the Savior, along with a number of his fellow Christians. At first this appears to be strong evidence in support of the Sanhedrin's right to carry out executions.

But many believe that the story takes on an entirely different slant when we take into account what happened after the incident. The sequel supposedly shows that the Sanhedrin's acts were in fact *illegal*. Josephus tells us that Governor Festus had died and that the new governor, Albinus, was still on his way to Jerusalem. Ananus saw this as the perfect moment to deal with James and his fellow Christians. But Jews who were disturbed with the way the affair had been handled took their complaints to Albinus, who became angry with the high priest. Agrippa II then hurried to mediate the dispute, and within three months after his appointment Ananus was replaced by another high priest. Does this not indicate that the stoning was illegal and was pushed through in an interim period between governors? And is this not watertight evidence that proves that the Sanhedrin did *not* have the right to put people to death?

The final word comes from the text of Josephus himself. We will let him speak here, with explanations in the adjacent column, from *Antiquities* 20.9.1 §§199–203:

(§199) The younger Ananus, who, as we have said, had been appointed to the high priesthood, was rash in his temper and unusually daring. He followed the school of the Sadducees, who are indeed more heartless than any of the other Jews, as I have already explained, when they sit in judgment.

"Heartless" (lit., "rude") means that the punishment was faster and stricter because insufficient care was taken regarding the burden of proof and the circumstances. The goal was more important than the procedure.

(§200) Possessed of such a character, Ananus thought that he had a favourable opportunity [to exercise his authority] because Festus was dead and Albinus was still on the way. And so he convened the judges of the Sanhedrin and brought before them a man named James, the brother of Jesus who was called the Christ, and certain others [or, some of his companions]. He accused them of having transgressed the law and delivered them up to be stoned.

Josephus's wording clearly suggests that the charge was not adequately supported by evidence.

(§201) Those of the inhabitants of the city who were considered the most fair-minded and who were strict in observance of the law were offended at this. They therefore secretly sent to King Agrippa urging him, for Ananus had not even been correct in his first step, to order him to desist from any further such actions.

The disturbed citizens think that the procedure of the Sadducees has been "heartless" or "rude" and that a trumped-up charge is not acceptable. Because their objections are Jewish-religious in nature, they turn to their friend Agrippa. It is noted in passing that Ananus did not handle "the first step" properly either. The first step is reported in §200, where he *assembled* the Sanhedrin. This surely is what is meant, as is suggested in §202. It is only told to Agrippa to illustrate Ananus' rude action. For the aggrieved citizenry this complaint in and of itself is no matter to write to Agrippa about.

(§202) Certain of them even went to meet Albinus, who was on his way from Alexandria, and informed him that Ananus had no authority to convene the Sanhedrin without his consent.

A few spirited citizens are not satisfied with writing a letter to Agrippa. They also bring the Roman governor into the debate, on a point that was of marginal interest to Agrippa but of central importance to the governor: the new high priest did not wait for permission to call together a gathering of the Sanhedrin! This does not necessarily mean that the governor had to grant permission for *every* sitting of the council. Ananus was a *new* chairman. The Romans had the right to appoint the chairman. At this time it was Agrippa II, the Jewish king on friendly terms with the Romans, who exercised that right. This makes things easier for the Jews. But it is quite possible that the new man appointed by Agrippa still had to wait for the governor's formal ratification before beginning his new function and chairing a meeting of the Sanhedrin. In this matter Ananus is thus formally careless ("rude").

(§203) Convinced by these words, Albinus angrily wrote to Ananus threatening to take vengeance upon him. King Agrippa, because of Ananus' action, deposed him from the high priesthood which he had held for three months and replaced him with Jesus the son of Damnaeus.

It was not the Sanhedrin that was blamed, but only Ananus. It was *his* behavior as a newly appointed official that was criticized, not the fact that the Sanhedrin had pronounced death sentences and carried them out.

When we study the passage from Josephus in its entirety, we discover that it was not the way the Sanhedrin conducted the trial that was challenged, but the way the new chairman acted. This is the only way to understand why Josephus first elaborates on the subject of the heartlessness (rudeness) of the Sadducees, to which Ananus belonged, and why he makes remarks about his character. Now it is also clear why citizens who are so strict about the *Jewish* law become troubled. It would also have been unnecessary to explain to the new governor that Ananus was wrong if Ananus had broken a general prohibition against the Sanhedrin's carrying out of death sentences. In that case the ire of the governor would have been against the entire Sanhedrin! And when

Agrippa is asked to avoid a repetition, it can hardly be in reference to illegal executions: they would have been impossible after Albinus's arrival. The issue here is carelessness in the enforcement of the legal procedures specified in the religious laws. Albinus does not think the matter important, so Agrippa, who had appointed Ananus, is called in to help.

If Josephus's text is allowed its say, this passage stands in the final analysis as strong evidence for the view that the Sanhedrin did have the right to carry out death sentences in the administration of Jewish justice.

14.6.2 The Action against Jesus Ben Ananaios

Josephus in his *Jewish War* (6.5.3 §§300–309) describes an ominous sign on the eve of the fall of Jerusalem in the year A.D. 70. During a Feast of Tabernacles, a simple man from the countryside entered the city and suddenly began to cry out, "A voice from the east, a voice from the west, a voice from the four winds, a voice against Jerusalem and the holy house, a voice against the bridegroom and the bride, and a voice against this whole people!" He did not stop his crying from that moment on but kept it up day and night for the four years before the war broke out and the three years that the war continued. And as he saw his prediction come true during the siege of Jerusalem, he was killed by a stone from a Roman catapult. His last words were, "And woe is me!"

Understandably, the people of Jerusalem did not need seven years of unceasing, threatening cries to reach the end of their tether. Severe chastisement by Jewish leaders had no effect. Because it was believed that supernatural powers were at work in this case, the man was brought before the governor. The governor had him flogged without mercy, but after each blow he heard nothing from the man but "Woe unto Jerusalem!" Albinus came to the conclusion that he was dealing with a possessed man and let him go. Thus the man was released to go about the city and to keep up his shouting for the next several years.

His crying has an unexpected aftermath. Catchpole is of the opinion that this is a religious matter (words spoken out against the temple),[18] yet the Sanhedrin hands the man over to the governor and makes it clear that as a body it is not authorized to carry out an execution.

This incident, however, does not justify Catchpole's conclusion. The Jews did arrest the man and punish him, but we read nothing about his being brought to trial. And why is he brought before the governor? The people suspect that an evil spirit is at work here, and Josephus com-

18. Catchpole, *Trial of Jesus*, 245.

ments that they were right (*Jewish War* 6.5.3 §303). The governor's inquiry does not lead to a trial either. In short, we are dealing here with a man who could not be silenced by police action (Jewish and Roman), but whom neither the Jews nor the Romans took to court because he was not deemed accountable—or because they were afraid of the evil spirit possessing the man.

Nothing can be deduced from the action against Jesus ben Ananaios regarding the powers of the Sanhedrin during that period.

14.6.3 The Stoning of the Adulterous Woman

Jeremias believes that strong evidence against the right of the Sanhedrin to carry out the death penalty can be found in John 7:53–8:11.[19] There we read the story of the woman caught in adultery who was brought to Jesus by the teachers of the law and the Pharisees, who asked him how he would judge a case in which stoning was demanded under the law of Moses. According to Jeremias, the trial before the Sanhedrin has already taken place, but the people are not able to carry out the sentence because of the Romans. So the question to Jesus is a "trap, in order to have a basis for accusing him" (John 8:6). If he says the stoning should be carried out, they can bring charges against him before the occupying power on the basis of inflammatory language. If he forbids it, he deviates from the law of Moses!

Against Jeremias's interpretation stands the fact that there is no evidence that charges in this case would be brought before the *Romans*. The question is aimed at testing to see if Jesus is breaking the *Jewish* law. Indeed, the questioners *themselves* say that their law demands stoning, and if Jesus agrees with this, then nothing unusual happens. He is not being asked whether the stoning must really be *carried out*, which is how the question should have been formulated if Jeremias's view is correct. Jesus, however, who has demonstrated his love for tax collectors and sinners and who has made remarkable statements about the law of Moses, is being forced to make a choice on a very clear and sensitive issue. It is a choice between his love for sinners and his faithfulness to the law, two things that are assumed to be incompatible. Jesus refuses to acknowledge the dilemma, however, and he simply writes in the sand. Finally he cuts through the dilemma with his counterquestion: who among those who are bringing this case before him is without sin? This is not a rhetorical question; it forces those who witnessed the adultery (and who must throw the first stone) to examine their own consciences in terms of their attitude regarding this woman

---

19. Jeremias, "Zur Geschichtlichkeit des Verhörs Jesu vor dem Hohen Rat," 148–49.

and her situation, as well as their attitude toward Jesus (to whom they have presented their question with dishonest intent). Because the issue involves an internal Jewish matter, it does not prove whether the Sanhedrin had the right to perform executions or not.[20]

14.6.4 Death Penalty for Non-Jews in the Inner Temple Courts

It is a known fact that non-Jews were allowed to enter only the court of the Gentiles on the temple grounds and were prohibited from entering the inner courts on pain of death. During the New Testament period, this stipulation could be clearly read at the entrance of the inner courts, both in Greek and in Latin. During the siege of Jerusalem, when Titus was forced by the Jews themselves to continue the battle in the innermost court, he tried to bring them to their senses. Did they want to turn this holy place into a site of murder? It was none other than the Romans who had given them permission to put to death anyone breaking the entrance prohibition, "[even] though he were a Roman." These last words (Josephus, *Jewish War* 6.2.4 §126) have led to a lively discussion.

On the one hand, Lietzmann claims that putting Jews to death was apparently normally permitted, because now separate mention is made of the right to put even a Roman to death.[21] If even Romans could be killed under special circumstances, then certainly Jews could be killed under ordinary circumstances. Blinzler, on the other hand, has noted that the privilege *as a whole* is exceptional.[22] Normally Jews could not carry out any death penalty, but in the exceptional case of the inner Temple courts *even* a Roman could be put to death! Catchpole argues that the wording "though he were a Roman" is decisive in the question we are addressing here.[23] Apparently the Sanhedrin had no right as a general rule to carry out the death penalty!

But the conclusion drawn by Catchpole, Blinzler, and others bypasses an important point: there were more people in the world at that time than Jews and Romans! In other words, when Titus declares that the Romans were so careful to protect the Jewish temple that they per-

---

20. J. D. M. Derrett, *Law in the New Testament* (London: Darton, Longman & Todd, 1970). Derrett believes that the Jews were preparing for a lynching party in order to satisfy the spirit of the law, now that the execution of the letter of the law was forbidden by the Romans (166ff.). Sherwin-White, *Roman Society and Roman Law*, 42, points out that this case of adultery could also be seen as falling under Roman law (*Lex Iulia de adulteriis*).

21. Lietzmann, "Prozess Jesu" and "Bemerkungen zum Prozess Jesu," 272–73.

22. Blinzler, *Prozess Jesu*, 170–71.

23. Catchpole, *Trial of Jesus*, 240–41.

mitted the Jews to put to death *anyone* who entered the inner courts, the stress is not on *granting* the right of execution but on *extending* it to be applied to non-Jews who, normally speaking, could never fall under Jewish jurisdiction. The law prohibiting certain people from entering the inner courts did not apply to the Jews themselves. A *Jew* would never have been put to death for entering the inner courts. But other nationalities do fall under this proscription—*even* the Romans. Catchpole is quite right when he says that Titus's wording includes at least two exceptional items, but he identifies these incorrectly as (1) the right to carry out the death penalty, (2) even on Roman citizens. The two exceptional privileges actually were (1) the right to put *non-Jews* to death, (2) even if they were Roman citizens.

The temple edict has nothing to do with the right of the Jews to put their *own* citizens to death. But it would be strange if the Jews were on the one hand not allowed to have their own internal judicial system while on the other hand being permitted to put Romans to death under special circumstances. It is more likely that the permission to kill non-Jews who are found in the inner temple courts is an exceptional extension of the normal right to punish capital offenses committed by their own countrymen (insofar as they concerned matters that fell outside the purview of Roman law).

More or less as an aside we mention here Philo's *Embassy to Gaius* (39 §307), in which he quotes Agrippa I speaking about the Holy of Holies in the temple building. The Jews themselves were not allowed to enter this part of the temple, not even priests, and the high priest himself could only go in once a year. Any infringement of these prohibitions was punished by death. Agrippa (in about A.D. 40) is assuming the existence of the Jews' own internal criminal justice system (including the right to try capital offenses). The Jewish reverence for their temple (and the sanctions imposed as punishment), lead him to comment that the Jews would rather die than allow a heathen statue to be placed in the temple. It is not impossible that Agrippa made this statement with reference to the generally known restriction preventing non-Jews from entering the inner courts, which indicated how holy the temple was. Less well known was the regulation imposed *within* the Jewish community that strictly forbade anyone from entering the Holy of Holies. *Titus* makes no mention of the right to impose the death penalty in a case where the offender is a Jew. This is, after all, an internal issue that is supposed to be self-evident; it does not result from a special favor granted by the Romans. Philo's account of Agrippa's words from around the year A.D. 40 confirms the conclusion regarding the temple edict: it was an exceptional extension of the right, normally restricted to Jews, to try legal cases and to carry out executions.

14.6.5 A Return to the Killing of Evildoers on 22 Elul

For Jeremias, the most important proof for the absence of the right to punish capital offenses under the Romans can be found in the Jewish manuscript *Mĕgîllat Taᶜănît*.[24] This is a kind of list or calendar of national or religious commemorative days—days on which there was to be no fasting. In this so-called Fasting Scroll we find the following: "On the 17th of [this month of Elul] the Romans left Jerusalem. On the 22nd of that month the evildoers began to be killed once again."[25] Jeremias's conclusion is: five days after the Roman troops were forced to leave Jerusalem (in September of A.D. 66), the Jews once again began to execute criminals. In other words, up until that moment they did not have the right to punish capital offenses!

Jeremias's conclusion is less compelling than it looks. The presence of the Romans, with their own Roman law *and* the power to enforce it, resulted in civil cases often being taken away from the Jews. The "thieves" crucified with Jesus were tried by the Romans. When this occupying power leaves, the Jews will be able to prosecute criminals once again. This return to a legal system functioning not only as a religious tribunal but also as a national-civil legal system (to deal with both Jews and foreigners in the city!) is in itself a momentous fact.

More far-reaching, however, is whether Jeremias is correct in finding a connection between what is stated about the seventeenth of Elul (departure of the Romans) and about the twenty-second of Elul. He states that the relationship between both memorable facts "is hardly open to doubt."[26] How strange it is then that in later rabbinic commentaries on the Fasting Scroll such a relationship is not even acknowledged![27] Actually, it should be described the other way around: a relationship between the various data in the Fasting Scroll is doubtful from the very start because the data are arranged according to the calendar (by month and day) and not chronologically, by year.[28] At the very least, the Fasting Scroll is not a decisive argument against the Jewish right to carry out the death penalty during the first century because the comments about the twenty-second of Elul are open to a variety of interpretations.

---

24. Jeremias, "Zur Geschichtlichkeit des Verhörs Jesu vor dem Hohen Rat," 148.

25. Text with translation in J. A. Fitzmyer and D. J. Harrington, *A Manual of Palestinian Aramaic Texts*, Biblica et Orientalia 34 (Rome: Biblical Institute Press, 1978), 184ff., 248ff.

26. Jeremias, "Zur Geschichtlichkeit des Verhörs Jesu vor dem Hohen Rat," 150.

27. See H. Lichtenstein, "Die Fastenrolle: Eine Untersuchung zur Jüdisch-Hellenistischen Geschichte," in *Hebrew Union College Annual* 8–9 (1931–32): 257–351, esp. 306.

28. See articles under *Mĕgîllat Taᶜănît* by J. Z. Lauterbach (*Jewish Encyclopedia* [New York: Funk & Wagnalls, 1925], 8:427–28) and N. N. Glatzer (*Encyclopaedia Judaica* [New York: Macmillan, 1971], 11:1230–31).

By way of hypothesis we add to the existing interpretations the following. The Fasting Scroll, when it speaks of "returning to killing the evildoers," does not indicate whether this refers to the carrying out of juridical death sentences or to killing in a war situation. The impression one gets is that it means killing criminals who up until then had not been killed but had remained alive—but many criminals *were* executed by the Roman judges. There is a historical situation that does justice to both aspects of the statement from the Fasting Scroll: beginning with the twenty-second of Elul (1) evildoers no longer remained alive, and (2) there was a *return* to killing. This historical situation is the moment when the priest Mattathias kills a fellow Jew who wants to obey the order of the Syrian soldiers and make a sacrifice on the altar in Modein (1 Macc. 2:24). This moment signaled the beginning of the Maccabean struggle for freedom. The writer of 1 Maccabees draws a parallel with the zeal of Phinehas (Num. 25:6–15). We have to realize that for more than four centuries after the fall of Jerusalem to the Babylonians, the Jews had engaged only in passive resistance. Mattathias's deed is a *return to killing* the evildoers, whether they are Jews or not.

Mattathias's act may well have taken place in Elul (September), as the following shows. Antiochus IV Epiphanes desecrates the altar in the temple during the month of Chislev (approximately December), after which follows a period of *several months* in which the Syrian soldiers try to hellenize the countryside by force (1 Macc. 1:54–58). Then Mattathias appears. His appearance sometime around September would leave a period of several months between Chislev and Elul without a whole *year* elapsing before any action was taken (in which case we might have expected "for more than a year" or "year after year" in 1 Macc. 1:58 instead of "month after month" [NRSV]). We can be more certain of the information provided by Josephus. He also speaks of the desecration of the temple during Chislev (December) and the terror inflicted on the people afterward. He then describes how the Samaritans, witnessing all this, wrote to the Syrian king to declare that their temple, religion, and culture had much in common with that of the Jews but could be considered Hellenistic; they request in advance that they may be spared the actions the king has to undertake against the stubborn Jews, their Sabbath, their circumcision, and so on. This document receives a favorable reply from the king (Josephus, *Antiquities* 12.5.5 §§257–64). The king's answer is dated in the 146th year (by Seleucid reckoning) and corresponds to 166 B.C. The specific date is the eighteenth day of the month of Hekatombaion Hyrkanios. The meaning of *Hyrkanios* is unclear, but the month Hekatombaion corresponds to our July/August. Josephus continues his story with these words: "At this same time there was a man living in the village of

Modai in Judaea, named Mattathias" (*Antiquities* 12.6.1 §265). So Josephus brings Mattathias on the scene around the time of the answer that Antiochus gave to the Samaritans, specifically shortly thereafter (the letter makes no mention of a Jewish uprising, but it does refer to attempts to hellenize them). In other words, Mattathias makes his appearance shortly after July/August. Therefore, the twenty-second of Elul (September) may well have been the day on which violence was used for the first time against evildoers in Israel. In fact, Mattathias had taken the first step toward the Jewish War, which would break out two centuries later.

This explanation of the comment in the Fasting Scroll for 22 Elul is no more than a hypothesis. It is, however, just as reasonable an explanation as (and perhaps even more plausible than) the hypothesis that suggests the taking back of a lost right to carry out executions by the Sanhedrin in the year A.D. 66.

Our conclusion is that Jeremias is incorrect in claiming that a comment from the *Mĕgîllat Taʿănît* is decisive in the question about the authority of the Sanhedrin under Roman rule.

14.6.6 Rabbinic Information

Finally, we should look at counterarguments based on various rabbinic sources.

First is the witness of Rabbi Eleazar ben Zadok, who lived during the first century of the present era. He declares that a priest's daughter was once burned at a sort of stake because she had committed adultery.[29] His statement is found in the context of a discussion about the correct way to carry out the death penalty, specifically by burning. The response Eleazar receives to the example he offers is, "At that time the Sanhedrin did not have a good grasp of the situation." This may be an allusion to the fact that during the century before the Jewish War the Sadducees still had considerable influence on the legal system via the Sanhedrin.

The passage quoted here suggests that during the first century the Sanhedrin had the *right* to carry out the death penalty. Jeremias tries to avoid this conclusion by appealing to Eleazar's age at the time of this burning of a priest's daughter. Eleazar observed the spectacle while sitting atop his father's shoulders,[30] and since as a young person he studied with another rabbi (around A.D. 47 to 49), his childhood would have coincided with the period of Agrippa I, when Jerusalem was temporarily free of Roman governors (A.D. 41–44). This calculation is very hy-

29. Mishnah, *Sanhedrin* 7.2.
30. Tosefta, *Sanhedrin* 9.11.

pothetical, however.[31] More significant is the fact that we know of no real changes in the governmental structure and the administration of justice during the short period of Agrippa's rule in Jerusalem. Agrippa functioned like a Roman governor. It was advantageous for the Jews to have one of their friends occupying this post, but there is no evidence for the assumption that the rights of the Sanhedrin changed during the few years that a Jewish king ruled in place of a Roman governor.

Even if Jeremias were correct and the burning of the priest's daughter did take place in A.D. 41 to 44, other rabbinic information still presents a problem.

In the Jerusalem Talmud we read a passage that is often used to support the claim that the Sanhedrin did not have the right to punish capital offenses in the decades before the Jewish War.

> Forty years before the house was destroyed all capital offenses were dissolved. And in the days of Simeon ben Shetach, the jurisdiction of the law of property was dissolved.[32]

The "forty years" in this quote is hardly taken seriously. Jeremias sees it as a round number for an entire period and believes that it refers to A.D. 6, when the Roman governors began to rule in Judea.[33] Starting that year, the Sanhedrin was supposedly denied the right to punish capital offenses.

Here we run into a problem. We cannot simultaneously accept that the right to execute criminals was dissolved in A.D. 6 for an uninterrupted period ("forty years") and that it was functioning in the period A.D. 41–44.

A further treatment of the reference to the forty years is not possible here. We direct interested readers to a detailed discussion by Cohn.[34] He demonstrates that the quote from the Jerusalem Talmud and the related passages from the Babylonian Talmud cannot be interpreted as indications of the discontinuation of the rights of the Sanhedrin. Why, for example, should a distinction be made between capital offenses and cases involving property rights, and why were the latter taken away 150 years earlier, in the time of Simeon ben Shetach, and by whom? Cohn's hypothesis is that the rabbis, in an attempt to defend themselves against the Christians, claimed that by about A.D. 30 (shortly before

---

31. Eleazar must at least have been a *bar mitzvah* (thirteen years old) when he began his studies. So he was born no later than A.D. 34. Would he have sat on his father's shoulders as a boy of seven to ten during the period of Agrippa's reign in Jerusalem (A.D. 41–44)?

32. Jerusalem Talmud, *Sanhedrin* 18a.42–44.

33. Jeremias, "Zur Geschichtlichkeit des Verhörs Jesu vor dem Hohen Rat," 148.

34. Cohn, *Trial and Death of Jesus*, 346–50.

Jesus' death) they no longer had the right to carry out the death penalty, so that they could not be considered culpable. This hypothesis is open to dispute. For our purposes it is enough to state that the rabbinic data[35] contradict each other, and the older Mishnaic quote concerning the execution of the priest's daughter should carry more weight than the Talmudic comment about the forty years, which did not emerge until centuries later and cannot be integrated with what we know from Josephus about the first century.

14.7 Conclusions

On the basis of what has been discussed so far, we reach the following conclusions:

1. There is no decisive evidence to uphold the claim that the Sanhedrin lost all right to carry out the death penalty under the Romans.
2. There are decisive data that suggest that the Sanhedrin retained the freedom to administer justice and to carry out sentences, including the death penalty, albeit within the limitations imposed by the presence of the Roman judicial system.
3. In part because of this historic situation, the exegesis is to be preferred that reads John 18:31 as referring to the religious unacceptability of Jewish executions on *the day of the Passover Feast.*

---

35. Mishnah, *Sanhedrin* 7.2; Jerusalem Talmud, *Sanhedrin* 18a.42–44.

15

The Plan to Kill Jesus by Cunning

In the previous chapter we discussed whether the Sanhedrin had the right to pronounce and carry out the death penalty. In concluding that this certainly was the case, we are faced with a new question: why didn't this Jewish judicial body then put Jesus to death itself by stoning, as happened later with Stephen? We must consider this question before moving on to a discussion of the actual course of events on Good Friday, because the answer is to be found at the end of Wednesday. That was when the decision was made to kill Jesus *by cunning*. The events of Good Friday follow a script that was written on Wednesday evening. For this reason we devote this chapter to a rather detailed examination of the background of the Sanhedrin's actions before tracing these actions in the next chapter.

As in the previous chapter, we cannot avoid a detailed discussion here. Readers who prefer to follow the broad sweep of events can read the next section and then skip the rest of this chapter and go to chapter 16, which deals with Good Friday.

15.1 Not During the Feast!

The Wednesday of the final discourses ends with a prediction of Jesus' death that included the date when he would die. This is closely linked with a further consultation held by the Sanhedrin at the end of that same Wednesday. Matthew mentions both in one breath (26:1–5):

> When Jesus had finished saying all these things, he said to his disciples, "As you know, the Passover is two days away—and the Son of Man will be handed over to be crucified."
> Then the chief priests and the elders of the people assembled in the palace of the high priest, whose name was Caiaphas, and they plotted to arrest Jesus in some sly way and kill him. "But not during the Feast," they said, "or there may be a riot among the people."

We also read a somewhat shorter version of this discussion in Mark

14:1–2. Mark does not report Jesus' prediction of the crucifixion, but he does mention the Sanhedrin's deliberation on the same day:

> Now the Passover and the Feast of Unleavened Bread were only two days away, and the chief priests and the teachers of the law were looking for some sly way to arrest Jesus and kill him. "But not during the Feast," they said, "or the people may riot."

At first glance one might be inclined to think only of the plot to have Jesus arrested by means of a traitor (Judas). But this does not do justice to the facts or to the text.

The fact is that Judas had already made contact with the leaders after the anointing in Bethany, which took place on Sunday. The negotiations with Judas may well have been part of the plot, but they certainly were not the basis for it. The evangelists present the agreement with Judas as being unconnected with the meeting on Wednesday evening (Matt. 26:14–16; Mark 14:10–11).

In addition, the text about the Sanhedrin's meeting reveals something else. In both Matthew and Mark, it is striking how *comprehensive* the decision is to seize and kill Jesus by cunning and how it specifies the *date* when he is to be killed. It is comprehensive because the plot involves not only the "seizing" but also the "killing." This is apparent in the Greek text, but it is also confirmed by the reason provided for this change of course. The Sanhedrin is being forced into this particular decision by the calendar. Both evangelists indicate that it is now exactly two days before Passover and the Feast of Unleavened Bread. How does this affect the attempts of the Sanhedrin to have Jesus brought before a judge, to have him tried, and to kill him? During the previous day the leaders devoted all their energy to catching Jesus by means of trick questions. But they reached the end of the day without any success. And now they are running out of time. The feast is about to begin. If Jesus is to be killed, it will have to be done by cunning, otherwise the trial will end up taking place during the feast. There is a close link between "with cunning" and "not during the feast."

This means that a plot is devised to make sure that Jesus is not killed via the normal legal process, since it would irrevocably force the trial to be held during the feast because it is already Wednesday. In Luke 22:1–2 we read that the leaders now must of necessity consider the *manner* of Jesus' death:

> Now the Feast of Unleavened Bread, called the Passover, was approaching, and the chief priests and the teachers of the law were looking for *some way* to get rid of Jesus, for they were afraid of the people.

Luke never mentions Jesus' *arrest*—the main thing is the *killing*. The problem, according to Luke, is that the feast is approaching. And the solution they look for lies in the *manner* of execution.

To better understand the actions of the Sanhedrin, we should remember that an official death sentence could never be carried out on the same day it was pronounced. After the Sanhedrin sentenced someone to death, one night of reflection had to intervene before the sentence could be carried out. If the chief priests and elders had been successful with their all-out effort to arrest Jesus that Wednesday and to have him tried, they could have had him killed on Thursday morning. But now Wednesday has passed, since it is evening. This means that the Sanhedrin has reached an impasse. Their current policy in the pursuit of Jesus must be revised. If Jesus were arrested on Thursday, he could not be brought to trial until after the Sabbath since only one night could intervene between trial and execution. Executions were not permissible on 15 Nisan, which was a feast day, or on the following Sabbath. Nothing could be done on Thursday at all. They could put Jesus in prison, but the trial would have to wait for a few days—and the execution yet another day. Now Wednesday—the last day on which it was possible to settle the Jesus affair by legal means—had passed, and the leaders must hold a meeting to discuss strategy. They decide on a policy change and come up with a plan to kill Jesus by cunning. This would avoid a legal trial after the Sabbath and perhaps enable them to avoid conflict with the many pilgrims who admired Jesus.

The course of events on Good Friday reveals that the strategy has changed from a trial by the Sanhedrin to a conviction by the Roman governor. The governor is free to do things that the Jewish leaders are prevented from doing by their laws and traditions. This change to a different type of trial has implications for the way in which Jesus will be killed. It will not be by stoning, but by crucifixion. Because the Sanhedrin cannot tolerate postponement—fearing a popular uprising in support of Jesus—Jesus' improbable prediction that he will be *crucified* is fulfilled.

Now we see the connection between the two items that Matthew tells us in one breath: Jesus' prediction of the approaching *crucifixion* and its date (Matt. 26:1–2), and the simultaneous plotting by the Sanhedrin to arrest and kill him *by cunning* (Matt. 26:3–5). At the end of Wednesday, the cross has replaced stoning. Jesus willed it, and he had already announced this course of events. The Sanhedrin is forced to make this choice now that the feast is about to begin.

15.2 Feast Days and the Death Penalty in Rabbinic Law

What was discussed briefly in the previous section must now be further substantiated by exploring the rabbinic rules for conducting a trial and administering the death penalty in relation to feast days and the Sabbath. We will do so in this section—an excursus—before examining in the next chapter how the plan to kill Jesus by cunning was implemented in the course of events on Good Friday.

15.2.1 No Administration of Justice on Feast Days

In his essay on the day of Jesus' death, Billerbeck also discusses whether convicting Jesus and carrying out the death sentence were possible and permissible on a feast day such as the fifteenth of Nisan according to the rabbinic law then in force.[1] He demonstrates that it was not permissible to administer justice on a Sabbath or a feast day, mainly because of the *work* of *writing* that was part of such activity. This means that capital offenses were not even tried on the day preceding a Sabbath or a feast day, because such an offense *might* result in a death sentence, which could not be carried out until the day following. This would lead to an impasse if the next day were a Sabbath or feast day. Thus, to safeguard the Sabbath rest and the rest on feast days, no crimes were tried on the day preceding a Sabbath or feast day. But how then can Jesus have been tried *and* killed on the fifteenth of Nisan, a feast day?

Is it possible that the Pharisaic law as codified in the Mishnah was not always followed in Jesus' day because of the Sadducees' great influence at that time? Billerbeck is of the opinion that this is not an issue in this specific case, because the Sadducees themselves were very strict when it came to the Sabbath and would also have considered it unlawful to administer justice on this particular day. Billerbeck also refers to the evidence of the Jewish writer Philo from the beginning of the first century, who includes bringing charges and administering justice as activities that were forbidden on the Sabbath.

Although it has no bearing on the conclusion he draws on this particular point, Billerbeck discusses in passing a few other points that might reveal a discrepancy between Jesus' trial and rabbinic law. We will list these briefly, with some critical comments.

1. *The Sanhedrin was not permitted to deal with capital crimes during a night session.* But this is the very reason why the Jewish council holds a brief formal morning session after the unofficial night session (see chapter 16).

---

1. P. Billerbeck, "Die Angaben der vier Evangelien über den Todestag Jesu unter Berücksichtigung ihres Verhältnis zur Halakha," in H. L. Strack and P. Billerbeck, *Das Evangelium nach Markus, Lukas und Johannes und die Apostelgeschichte*, vol. 2 of *Kommentar zum Neuen Testament aus Talmud und Midrasch* (Munich: Beck, 1924), 812–53, esp. 815ff.

2. *The Sanhedrin was not permitted to deal with a capital offense in a single session and on one single day.* But this did not occur either, because the case was cunningly shifted to the court of the Roman governor so that the Sanhedrin could wash its hands of all guilt on this point.
3. *The Sanhedrin was not permitted to meet outside the temple complex.* But this only happened with the unofficial night session and not with the formal meeting in the early morning (see chapter 16).

Because there is clear compatibility on these three points between Jesus' trial and the rabbinic law, we can be all the more confident that this law was indeed in force at that time insofar as the prohibition on the administration of justice on the Sabbath and feast days was concerned. The Sanhedrin may have taken this into account in its discussions when the feast day of 15 Nisan approached.

Billerbeck discusses yet another solution that some have used to try to escape the implications of rabbinic law in discussions of Jesus' trial. It is pointed out that this law had special provisions that were intended for exceptional situations. Thus, the argument goes, administering justice was permitted on the Sabbath if no writing was involved. But as Billerbeck rightly points out, this applied only to activities that did not really fall under "the administration of justice," such as discussions with the Herodians (Mark 3:6) or the interrogation on the Sabbath of the man born blind (John 9:13ff.).

For his part, however, Billerbeck refers to a regulation in the Tosefta (*Yom Tob* 4.4): "If nevertheless someone carries out one of these activities on a Sabbath or feast day, whether by force or through forgetfulness, intentionally or not, then what he has done is considered done." Billerbeck then wonders whether the Sanhedrin, in dealing with the extremely important Jesus affair, might not have considered that in this case an (unlawful) action could have the force of law and that the deciding factor must be the interest of the people. There is no support for Billerbeck on this point, however. The quote from the Tosefta follows the emphatic stipulation that such actions as the administration of justice are forbidden on the Sabbath or on feast days. *That* is the rule! The final provision does not undermine the rule, but deals only with a special case. The provision does not go so far as to say that juridical acts can be declared *null and void* in retrospect because they ("by force or through forgetfulness") took place on a Sabbath. It stipulates that the accomplished fact is indeed accepted, and the violation of the Sabbath (no matter how serious) is not grounds for undoing what has been done. But this stipulation, which governs the *retrospective* judgment of the validity of judicial decisions that were reached in a formally incorrect manner, can never be used *ahead of time* to decide to trespass the Sabbath by making use of the stipulation!

When Billerbeck makes further appeals to the rule that extraordinary circumstances demand extraordinary measures, and claims that as early as John 11:49 and following the Sanhedrin had decided on a sort of emergency law with respect to the Jesus affair, he arrives at a hypothesis that does not square with the Gospel accounts. What we see in the Gospels is a struggle by the Sanhedrin to maintain the law even in this special case. Great efforts are made to engage false witnesses in order to obtain a sound indictment—two witnesses as required by law—and this while the decision had already been made to put Jesus to death! A formal morning session is held to ratify the results of the night session. It certainly would have been easier to have Jesus killed in Gethsemane by servants hired to do the job. But the leaders felt compelled to act in a way that was "correct" in every detail, because the people sympathized with Jesus and kept a careful watch on the leaders' behavior. Although their hearts and minds were extremely biased, the leaders had to be very cautious to keep up legal appearances during the trial.

Billerbeck wants to hold on to the historicity of the first three Gospels by demonstrating that the trial *could* have been conducted on 15 Nisan. We believe, however, that a simpler argument to support this point is found by paying more attention to the special plan, conceived on Wednesday evening, to kill Jesus by cunning. With this plan, the leaders slip through the net of rabbinic law and still manage to put Jesus to death on time. Billerbeck has convincingly shown that crimes were not tried on the Sabbath or on feast days, and not even on a day preceding one of these special days. This does not imply, however, that the Sanhedrin was playing fast and loose with this law. On the contrary, it is the regulations of the law that compelled the council members to change their course of action in the face of the approaching feast day and Sabbath. They had to come up with a trick so as not to come in conflict with the law, which would have been unavoidable if the criminal case against Jesus had been brought on Thursday or Friday or on the Sabbath that followed. The door for a *Jewish* trial closes for the time being on Wednesday evening.

15.2.2 No Executions on Feast Days

Closely connected with the previous matter is the prohibition on carrying out the death penalty on a feast day or on the Sabbath. Billerbeck shows that according to rabbinic law, the death penalty does not "supplant the Sabbath." Sabbath rest and Sabbath joy take precedence!

There is no major difference between a Sabbath and a feast day (although meals may be prepared on a feast day), which is why the death penalty is not carried out on feast days either. When we read in Luke 4:29 and John 10:22 and following about attempts to kill Jesus on a Sabbath or a feast day, it concerns spontaneous actions, not official death sentences.

There is a series of rabbinic pronouncements that has to do with the killing of certain persons *on a feast day*. These concern special cases, such as a rebellious son, a false prophet, a man who revolts against the pronouncements of the Sanhedrin, and so on. In these special cases, the execution is not carried out in a randomly chosen location. Rather, such a person is brought to one of the feasts. By carrying out the execution during a feast, the stipulation is fulfilled that "all the people will hear and be afraid, and will not be contemptuous again" (Deut. 17:13). An execution "during the feast" is one way Jesus could have been dealt with, but this option is one the Sanhedrin wants to avoid at all costs. They would rather devise a scheme (Mark 14:2).

We seem to have become entangled in the data. On the one hand there is the rule that no one could be put to death by order of the court on the Sabbath or a feast day, and on the other hand stands the tradition of executing people for certain crimes specifically on a feast day. Do the two cancel each other out? It would seem so, but appearances are deceiving. We must distinguish clearly between a special feast *day* and a feast *period*. Both Passover and the Feast of Tabernacles last a week. The first and the last days are special feast days. The days in between belong to the week of the Feast, but they have no special character and there are no special rules for them as there are for the Sabbath and for feast days. The carrying out of certain death sentences that are supposed to act as deterrents for the whole people took place when the whole nation gathered for the great feasts. The point is that these executions were to take place, *not* outside Jerusalem and not at an arbitrarily chosen time, but *inside* Jerusalem and in the presence of the many people who have come to celebrate the feast. The exact *day* on which this can happen is not at issue, since that is covered in the laws on the Sabbath and the feast days. Thus the natural corollary is that an execution that had to be carried out during the week of a feast could *not* occur on a Sabbath or on the first or last day of a feast because these are holy days.

Billerbeck hopes to avoid this interpretation with the remark that the Feast of Tabernacles was short and did not have any "in between days" for such executions. We can assume, however, that the early morning of the second day after the feast, before the pilgrims left for home, would have been used to carry out the death penalty.

But Billerbeck definitely goes beyond the data when he assumes that because of the executions "during the feast," death sentences were apparently carried out in special cases "on a Sabbath or feast day." Supposedly such an exception was made in Jesus' case as well. *If* it were true that such exceptions existed, they would have involved only exceptional cases, among which the Jesus affair cannot be counted because his trial took place within Jerusalem. There is no reason to imagine, however, that there were exceptions to the rule: executions were never carried out on the Sabbath or on a feast day, not even if the execution had to take place "during the feast" (during the feast period).

On that basis it is possible to read the Jewish statement in John 18:31 ("But we have no right to execute anyone") as referring to the special nature of this day. The fifteenth of Nisan is the first day of the Passover Feast, and thus a holy day. Pilate is free to do what he wants, but the Jews are not permitted to kill anyone on this day. When the Jewish leaders say that *they* have no right to execute anyone, they are right—not because the Romans have taken that right from them, but because the Lord has forbidden them to disturb the rest and joy of the Sabbath or of feast days by carrying out executions. On this feast day, the first day of Passover, they are uttering the complete truth: they have no right to execute anyone.

15.2.3 Was Jesus' Trial on 15 Nisan?

At first glance, there is an unusual tension between the Sanhedrin's trick and the resulting effect. The leaders all support the idea of crucifying Jesus on 15 Nisan, and through Pilate they get what *they* want. On Wednesday evening they had said, "Not during the feast!" But 15 Nisan *is* part of the feast! It is also during this *feast* that Pilate customarily releases one prisoner (Matt. 27:15; Mark 15:6). How does what the leaders finally do relate to what they had planned two days earlier?

It does not become clear until we realize that the expression "not during the feast" was used in the context of the trial by the Sanhedrin. The council had its back against the wall. Now the Sanhedrin had to postpone its action until some time during the week of the feast. This means that both during the trial and on the day of the execution they would be standing face to face with the pilgrims who had come to Jerusalem to follow everything in the temple city with the most acute interest. And this crowd that has come to Jerusalem is, to a significant extent, filled with admiration for Jesus. This is something the Sanhedrin dares not face, so a plan is devised to kill Jesus by cunning, and not by means of the Sanhedrin's judicial process. The trick consists in handing the case over to Pilate. He can absorb the agitation of the people better than they can. And with the involvement of the Roman governor, Jesus can be gotten rid of in a few short strokes. The crowds will not have time to realize what is happening and to react. Jesus is thus, in fact, killed on a holy day—with the consent and even the urging of the Sanhedrin. But in this way they cunningly avoid a Jewish trial during the week of the feast. "Not during the feast!"—and therefore he is crucified by a *Roman* on the day of the Passover feast. Everything has to be taken care of before the "in-between" days of the feast, when the Sanhedrin could have dealt with the Jesus affair according to Jewish law.

16

The Good Friday of Suffering and Death

A great deal has been written about the course of events on the day of Jesus' death, particularly his trial. All the evangelists provide detailed accounts of this most important day of Christ's earthly work in the depths of his humiliation. But it is sometimes difficult to combine all the details into a single story. This is not surprising. The events of some days follow each other in calm sequence, while those of other days are more like a swirling, splashing stream. Good Friday, with its tremendous tension, is such a day. Many things happen at the same time—and the Sanhedrin acts with cunning. This means that we are dealing with two levels: that which actually happens and the intention behind the action. There are also divergent interests at work: the interests of Judas, the Sanhedrin, Pilate, the people, the disciples. Sometimes these coincide, sometimes they become entangled. So for the sake of organizational convenience, and after the digressions of the last three chapters, we will not interact with the literature dealing with Good Friday but instead focus on presenting a reconstruction of the day's sequence of events.

16.1 As Prisoner before Annas

When the Sanhedrin's armed soldiers lay hands on Jesus in Gethsemane, they naturally take him to the authority that ordered them to make the arrest. Most of the evangelists then tell how the Lord was brought before the Jewish leaders in the home of Caiaphas. There is still one other small link in the chain of events, however, and though it is not essential for the narrative, John does include it: Jesus' initial brief interrogation before Annas (John 18:13–24). This interrogation takes place inside the building where Caiaphas will later conduct the questioning in the presence of the Sanhedrin (cf. the order in John 18:13, 15). We know that the disciple John was the only one to enter the palace of the high priest with Jesus, because he was known to the high priest (John 18:15). So John is the only evangelist who can tell us more about what happened immediately after entering this building. From a distance he saw how Jesus was taken straight to Annas, while in the meantime the members of the Sanhedrin were arriving (Mark 14:53). As someone known to the high priest, John was also more familiar than the other evangelists with the relationships inside the palace. At the moment Caiaphas is formally the high priest, appointed and recognized by the Romans. But according to Jewish law, Annas, his predecessor, outranks him: a high priest served for life. Even though the Jews had to accept and adapt to the reality of an occupying power, among themselves they continued to accord Annas a place of honor. He is one of the chief priests, and a former high priest at that, which is why he is the first to have a brief meeting with Jesus in order to formulate his advice.

Annas sees no reason to release Jesus and sends him to the courtroom as a man who in his opinion deserves to be tried. He makes his opinion in the Jesus affair clear to the Sanhedrin by sending Jesus to the council still in chains (John 18:24).

In the meantime, John has managed to get Simon Peter into the building (John 18:16), and thus Peter was primarily a witness to what took place during the night—the interrogation by Caiaphas and the mocking. Mark, the man who records Peter's preaching, describes these events, as do Matthew and, in part, Luke. John, however, skips the rest of that night's events. Those events were handled in sufficient detail by the other evangelists whose books were written before his. So John, after this detail about Annas, moves on directly to the Pilate story.

16.2 Preliminary Trial at Night

The entire Sanhedrin—the elders, chief priests, and teachers of the law—meets during the night under the leadership of Caiaphas, the high priest (Mark 14:57, 59). They base their proceedings on the earlier advice of Caiaphas: Jesus must die. Better that Jesus die than that the whole nation perish (John 11:47–53)! Since then, in part because of the deep impression made by the raising of Lazarus, it has taken much effort to arrest Jesus. They did not succeed in driving a wedge between Jesus and the crowds. They were not able to catch him with their trick questions. Finally, on Wednesday evening, a decision had to be made to switch over to arresting and killing Jesus *by cunning*. The first part of the plan has now been carried out. With the assistance of the defector Judas they were able to have Jesus arrested by night without being observed. Now they must get ready for the second part of the plan, so the members of the Sanhedrin gather for a night session.

It is a plenary session, but it is not official. Although everyone is present, no legal action can be taken at such a meeting. According to Jewish law, the court can only meet during the daytime. After all, the law must be able to withstand the light of day! In addition, the Sanhedrin is supposed to meet in the temple complex. But tonight, instead of gathering in the official location, they meet in the home of the chairman. This nocturnal gathering is abnormal and unofficial. It is more or less a preparatory plenary consultation in anticipation of the official session to be held in the morning (see section 16.5).

Part of the plan to proceed by cunning is the involvement of false witnesses. But this step leads nowhere. The leaders are unable to fabricate a charge that satisfies all the legal requirements for statements of evidence. The high priest is forced to have Jesus himself speak about his claims. Jesus is questioned, not to find out more about him but to get incriminating material that is solid enough for a death sentence. Then, before the highest ruling body of his people, Jesus reveals who he is: the Christ, the Son of the living God. He also tells them what his future will be: he will sit on the right hand of God, according to the promise in Daniel 7. For the high priest this statement is reason enough to dispense with any further witnesses. The evidence for the charge of blasphemy has been adequately provided by Jesus himself. The punishment for blasphemy in Israel is death. And that was the whole point of the proceedings: to find grounds for the death penalty (Mark 14:55).

The conclusion of the unofficial night meeting is brief and to the point: it is legally sound to put Jesus to death. The Sanhedrin now can pursue its plan to kill Jesus by cunning with a calm heart and a clear conscience!

16.3 Mocked by the Guards

After the full session of the Sanhedrin has determined that they are obligated by both the law and their own consciences to put Jesus to death, they must wait the rest of the night. The first act in the morning will be another meeting of the Sanhedrin, this time an official session in the temple. Until then Jesus is kept under guard in the palace of Caiaphas.

The guards mock him, spit on him, and beat him, challenging him, blindfolded, to prophesy who it was that mocked and hit him. Because these events are reported immediately after the (provisional) judgment of the Sanhedrin, it appears as if they also took place during the nightly meeting. But on closer inspection we see that the incident here is the mocking in the inner court by the servants and guards. Even Mark, who provides us with a fairly seamless account (Mark 14:65), gives us this impression. We left "the guards" in 14:54, gathered around the fire in the courtyard. These were the same men who had arrested Jesus in Gethsemane. When we read in passing in 14:65 that "the guards" struck Jesus in the face, this reference to the guards refocuses our attention from the meeting room (Mark 14:55–64) to the outside courtyard (Matt. 26:69). The men charged with guarding Jesus during the next few hours are the ones who toy with him now (Luke 22:63–65). The notion that the Sanhedrin stooped to such behavior, even during an unofficial session, is incorrect.

16.4 Simon Peter's Denial

It is difficult to weave the thread of Simon's threefold denial of the Savior into the pattern of that night's events. The *beginning* of the denial must have occurred after the interrogation by Annas, because Peter was only afterward brought into the palace by John (John 18:15–16). The *end* of the denial must have coincided with the beginning of the mocking of Jesus by the courtyard guards. Indeed, we read that Jesus, in the courtyard, was able to turn to see Peter, who was standing in the gatehouse. Peter himself had left the inner court some time before, because things there were getting too hot for him (Luke 22:61). This means that Peter's weakness was exposed while Jesus was standing before the Sanhedrin and shortly thereafter.

Most of the evangelists tell us that Jesus had given his disciple Simon early warning about a threefold denial "before the rooster crows" (before morning!). Mark's version is more literal and precise: "before the rooster crows twice" (Mark 14:30). Once again we sense in Mark the direct and personal recollection of Peter himself. That night Simon remembered the Savior's words too late—only after the rooster crowed a second time! Then Jesus looked at him (Luke 22:61) and the memory came rushing back, and Peter was forced to recall the prediction that at first he had rejected and repressed. And he also remembered that he had already heard the rooster crow once, after the first denial (Mark 14:68). At that moment, however, his heart was not yet prepared to ponder the words of the Savior and to take them to heart. It took a second crowing, and the Master's gaze, to break Peter's resistance to a prediction that he had indignantly rejected only a few hours before.

It seems strange that three of the evangelists speak briefly about the crowing of the rooster, while in Mark we read about a first and a second crowing. We must not forget, however, that at that time many people rose at the second crowing of the rooster. The first time the roosters crow in any case, it is still deep in the night. When they crow together a second time, morning light is not far behind. This is the "normal" rooster crow that people depended on and paid attention to: it functioned as an alarm clock (cf. Mark 13:35). The third usual crowing announced the breaking of day and was of less social significance. Three of the evangelists briefly mention the crowing that people depended on to awaken them in the morning. Only Mark is more precise. Jesus had specifically spoken of three denials before the rooster would crow a *second* time. Mark even tells us the hour and implicitly also the fact that the first crowing of the rooster failed to jog Peter's memory.

In order to gain a clear picture of what took place, we must keep three things in mind.

1. Driven through the night by fear and cowardice, Simon Peter experienced being cornered by questions from one person after another. John, on the other hand, who was also on the scene, stood more on the sidelines and watched as people again and again spoke to his fellow disciple, who made desperate attempts to shake them off. John knew some of the questioners personally (John 18:26), and he was in a familiar environment (John 18:15–16). Peter, on the other hand, did not know anyone in a strange and therefore more threatening environment. The differences in their experience and personal relationship to their surroundings can throw light on some of the nuances in Mark's (Peter's) account and John's.

2. Simon Peter's denial was not a matter of three pointed questions and three outright denials. He is the target of all the questions from the circle of bystanders who also get involved. Various individuals notice him simultaneously and several of them join in asking the same question. It is not an interrogation but an informal conversation among a group of servants! So if one evangelist speaks of a servant girl asking something, and another mentions a male questioner, it need not be a contradiction. Rather, the two accounts complement each other. When several people are speaking all at once, similar things can be heard at the same time from different directions. They agree with each other, support each other, echo each other's words. From this hubbub of voices, one evangelist chooses one voice, the next evangelist, another.

3. It is more difficult to establish the number of denials. Does each *statement* of denial Peter makes count as a separate denial, or should we count the various *conversations* within which he expresses denial toward those participating in the discussion? It is quite possible that John (who entered with Peter) remembered three denying *statements* and wrote them down, considering it sufficient, while the other evangelists note the three brief *periods* when Simon felt himself cornered and had a hard time of it. This provides a natural explanation for the differences in detail between John and the other three evangelists. John remembers the three persons, all known to him, who asked questions, while

Peter recalls being in a group and being pinned down three times.

We can elaborate on the preceding and come to some possible conclusions.

1. When John brings his fellow disciple Simon Peter inside via the gatehouse, the female gatekeeper asks them as they walk past, "You are not one of his disciples, are you?" Peter answers this question in the negative. It is an incident that happens in passing, almost casually. But John later remembers that Peter said this, and he realizes that at this point the denial had already begun (John 18:16–17).

2. After going inside, Peter joins the servants who have started a fire in the courtyard. They stand around the fire, warming themselves (John 18:18, 25), and from time to time they also sit around it (Matt. 26:58; Mark 14:54; Luke 22:55). If you want to warm yourself by a fire on a cold night, you do not remain in one position! One of the high priest's servant girls recognizes something about Peter (Matt. 26:69; Mark 14:66–67; Luke 22:56 [!]). The others in the group get involved as well (John 18:25), but in the presence of everyone Peter denies the servant girl's charge (Matt 26:70). Things really get too hot for him, and he retreats to the front gate (Matt. 26:71; Mark 14:68). At that moment the first rooster crows. Unfortunately, some modern translations have dropped this comment from Mark 14:68, choosing to follow a few manuscripts that may have had some difficulty with this apparently premature crowing of the rooster in Mark. A vast majority of the manuscripts, however, read in Mark 14:68b: "and went out into the entryway and the rooster crowed" (cf. NIV note). At that moment the first crowing of the rooster passes unnoticed; only later does Peter remember this detail.

3. But at the front gate Jesus' disciple soon comes under fire again. The servant girl on duty there turns to those standing around and says, "This fellow is one of them." This is a different servant girl from the one who questioned Peter at the fire in the courtyard (Matt. 26:71; Mark 14:69). It could be the same female gatekeeper who questioned Peter as he walked past while coming in (John 18:17). She still has her doubts, so when Peter approaches again she addresses the bystanders. Because the others present in the gatehouse are now being addressed and have become interested, we see why Luke writes about a *male person* who "a little later" asks Peter directly about his relationship with Jesus (Luke 22:58).

The exchange in the courtyard had recently taken place. And shortly thereafter this conversation is repeated at the front gate. The female gatekeeper talks about Peter with the people there, and one of the men then turns directly to Peter. This time he denies every connection, swearing an oath as he says so (Matt. 26:72; Mark 14:70a; Luke 22:58).

4. Now there is a brief period of rest. Two evangelists call it a "little while" (Matthew and Mark). Luke is more precise: "about an hour later" (the time between the first and second crowing of the rooster!). In the meantime new people have probably come in, and now Peter tries to appear less conspicuous by actively engaging in conversation. But for him conversation is poor camouflage. His Galilean accent betrays him and feeds the doubts of those standing around. Now they attack him as a group: "Surely you are one of them, for you are a Galilean" (Matt. 26:73; Mark 14:70; Luke 22:59). From John we learn that the attack is reinforced by a relative of Malchus, who says he recognizes Peter because he saw him in the garden where the arrest took place (John 18:26). Peter is being cornered. Finally he denies his Master with an oath and curses. At that moment the rooster crows, and Jesus looks at Peter from the courtyard where he has been brought. Peter goes outside and weeps bitterly (Matt. 26:74–75; Mark 14:71–72; Luke 22:60–62; John 18:27).

16.5 Jesus Convicted and Handed Over

Since the Sanhedrin can make legal decisions only during the daytime and in the temple complex, this highest judicial body meets in session during the early morning (Matt. 27:1–2; Mark 15:1), when it is daylight (Luke 22:66), in a room near the temple. When Judas comes to the Sanhedrin to return his blood money, he throws it "into the temple" (Matt. 27:5), which indicates that this is where the Jewish council met that morning. Now, after a brief confirmation of the final result of the preliminary trial of the preceding night, the formal decision is made to put Jesus to death. The expression *symboulion lambanein* or *symboulion poiein* (Matt. 27:1; Mark 15:1) means "to come to a *decision*."

Next Jesus is sent to Pilate, which was part of the scheme (Matt. 27:2; Mark 15:1; Luke 23:1; John 18:28). On a feast day such as this (and with the Sabbath coming), the Jews themselves cannot formally administer justice because it involves the work of writing, nor can they carry out a death sentence (see chapter 15). So the meeting of the Sanhedrin is not a first step in a procedure to judge and sentence Jesus according to *Jewish* law. It is an official meeting intended to serve as basis for handing

Jesus over to the governor. The Sanhedrin knows that it is morally and religiously justified when a blasphemer is killed. Because they themselves cannot administer justice on this particular day, they decide to hand the suspect over, primarily so that they themselves do not have to have any further involvement in the case during the week of the feast. Their *internal* ground for handing Jesus over is that he called himself the Son of God. Later that morning it will be shown that in presenting their case to Pilate they try to give grounds for condemning Jesus that would be more compelling to him as a Roman government official and would convince him to settle the case (see section 16.6).

Matthew and Mark have little to say about this morning session. They had already given a detailed account of the unofficial night meeting at which the rest of the plan had been decided on. But it is quite different in Luke. He only reports one session of the Sanhedrin (Luke 22:66–71). Because this account is somewhat fuller, many are inclined to equate Luke's session with the night session in the first two Gospels, all the more so because the reports have much in common. Nevertheless, this is incorrect. Luke's narrative of the official morning session is more exhaustive, while the other two are quite brief. But it is not surprising to find that Luke's report shows similarities with that of the night session. The two meetings relate to each other as a general rehearsal relates to a performance. The morning session is an *official* repetition of what was unofficially discussed during the night session. This repetition is needed to give the handing over to Pilate the seal of approval as an official act of the Sanhedrin. The heart of the session is the confirmation of the final judgment reached during the night session: "Jesus' own words make it apparent that he is a blasphemer." This is why, during the morning session, the high priest repeats the final question from the night before: "Are you the Christ?" And Jesus once again confirms what he has already said. Even in an official session inside the temple, he reveals that he is the Son of God who will take his place at the right hand of the heavenly king and will come to be judge. This makes the account in Luke so closely resemble the reports of the night session in Matthew and Mark that we can understand why many try to relate Luke's account to the night session. But it becomes apparent that he is really giving us a more detailed report of the *morning session* when we note the differences.

1. During the night session Caiaphas leads the interrogation of Jesus (Matt. 26:62–65; Mark 14:60–63), but in the morning he presides over the court whose judges interrogate Jesus (Luke 22:66–67). In Matthew 26:64, Jesus immediately answers the high priest in whose house the interrogation is being held, "Yes, it is as you [singular] say." But in Luke 22:67, he answers *them.*

2. The methods of questioning are different. In the morning session there are at least two questions: "Are you the Christ?" and "Are you the Son of God?" (Luke 22:67, 70). Even after what was said during the night session, the council probes further. With that in mind, we can understand Jesus' response in Luke, "If I tell you, you will not believe me, and if I asked you, you would not answer" (Luke 22:67–68). How does the Lord know this? Because during the night session he already told them who he is. The fact that they are now repeating their questions proves that they have not gathered to believe in him or to enter into a discussion with him.

3. In Luke's report there are no false witnesses. And at the end of the session the Sanhedrin does not say, as it did during the night session, that it needs no more false *witnesses* (Matt. 26:65; Mark 14:63), but that it has no need of further *testimony* (Luke 22:71). Jesus' own statement is sufficient and enables the council to come to a quick decision. In Luke, therefore, Jesus is led to Pilate immediately after the session of the Sanhedrin.

4. Both Matthew and Mark report Peter's denial and the mocking of Jesus by the guards after their accounts of the council's night session. Luke, however, first tells us about Peter and about the mocking of Jesus, and only then about the Sanhedrin. He does this not because he changes the sequence of events, but because he has decided not to write about the night session and only notes that Jesus was led to the house of the high priest (Luke 22:54). After the story of Peter's denial and the mocking of Jesus, Luke has reached the morning hour: the day breaks shortly after the second rooster crows. And the session described by Luke takes place after daybreak (Luke 22:66).

16.6 Before Pilate

Only Matthew tells us how Judas returned to the Sanhedrin on Friday morning to throw his thirty pieces of silver into the temple in remorse before hanging himself (Matt. 27:3–10). It is not impossible that this incident took place as the Sanhedrin was winding up its discussion about Jesus, and that Jesus was in the vicinity when his disciple Judas realized that he had betrayed innocent blood. If Judas had come any later, he would not have found the leaders, who were together on their way to Pilate.

All the evangelists provide accounts of the handing over of Jesus to the governor, and their reports complement each other. Thus only Luke tells us about the interrogation by Herod Antipas (Luke 23:6–12), while only Matthew tells of the dream of Pilate's wife (Matt. 27:19). John offers us a more detailed account of the conversation between Pilate and Jesus. If we use the reports of the four evangelists to sketch an overview of the course of events before the governor, we discern four different stages.

1. The Jewish leaders first attempt to introduce Jesus as a popular agitator who has come to stir up the people in all of Palestine (Luke 23:5). They accuse him of opposing the payment of taxes and of claiming to be king (Christ) (Luke 23:2). Jesus himself answers the governor's questions regarding the nature of his kingdom (John 18:33–37), but for the rest he refuses to answer any unsubstantiated accusations (Matt. 27:12–14; Mark 15:3–5).

When Pilate notices that Jesus comes from Galilee, he involves Herod Antipas, but this does not change the situation at all (Luke 23:6–12). Pilate now feels compelled to make the tentative decision to *release* Jesus (Luke 23:13–16; John 18:38). Curiously, Pilate does not simply go ahead and release him. He wants to do so in the context of the annual release of a prisoner on this particular feast day. He may have been under pressure from the Jewish leaders and wanted to render them powerless by inducing their own people to demand that Jesus be released. Pilate knows that the leaders have handed Jesus over to him because they are jealous of the popularity Jesus enjoys among the people (Matt. 27:18; Mark 15:10). The governor was simply applying the tried and true Roman adage, "Divide and conquer!"

So when on this liberation day of 15 Nisan the people gather en masse before the governor's palace to demand the annual release of a prisoner (Mark 15:8; Matt. 27:17), Pilate suggests that this year he let *Jesus* go (after having him flogged: Luke 23:16). It is a tense moment, but Pilate has underestimated the solidarity of a people in the face of an occupying power. Internally the leaders and the crowds are divided in their opinion of Jesus, but when these crowds stand before Pilate they close ranks with their chief priests and elders. At that point the people do not equate their leaders' advice to choose Barabbas with a popular vote against Jesus. They are not at this point concerned with what is to happen with Jesus—the only issue is, who must be released now? When it comes to endorsing a candidate for release, the crowds simply follow the recommendation of the Sanhedrin. Pilate suggests a name (Jesus), the Sanhedrin counters with requesting a robber (Barabbas). Pilate puts Jesus forward a second time, hoping the crowds will see the contrast between the two and opt for Jesus. But they stubbornly stick by the recommendation of their leaders: Barabbas (Mark 15:11; Luke 23:18; Matt. 27:20–21; John 18:39–40). Pilate's attempt to evade the pressure from the leaders has reached a dead end.

2. But Pilate ventures a second attempt at capitalizing on Jesus' popularity with the people. The choice has been to release Barabbas. But what

should be done with Jesus? This is not the sort of question that ought to be asked publicly in front of the courthouse. The Sanhedrin had turned Jesus over to the governor to be tried. After the case is turned over to Pilate, it becomes his responsibility as an official of the Roman government. Since when does Rome consult the masses on legal matters? When Pilate asks the people what they want him to do with Jesus, it shows what kind of quandary the whole situation has put him in (Luke 23:20; John 19:1–11). The crowds now cry out for crucifixion. Jesus is then flogged, dressed in a crown of thorns and a purple robe, and made to stand before the people while the soldiers strike him in the face. Though Pilate humiliates him, he finds no guilt in him (John 19:1–5). It seems strange that the crowd now insists that Jesus be crucified. Such a response reveals not only the fickleness of the popular will, but it also shows that instead of being softened by the sight of a humiliated Jesus the people become upset. Pilate does take Jesus as a king seriously. If this is a king, the Jews can have him. But such a king is an affront to their national pride. The people turn their backs on any Christ who would allow the enemy to humiliate him this way. They do not realize what Jesus' purpose is in allowing himself to be humiliated, for the good of both Jews and Romans. When the people continue to cry out for Jesus' crucifixion, with increasing force, Pilate sees that he has reached a second dead end.

At this point the governor decides against any further legal action. He decides to return the man to the Sanhedrin and refuses to have the Romans finish the case. As far as he is concerned, the Jews can crucify Jesus themselves.

3. This course of events forces the Jewish leaders to be more candid in their accusations. Now that the governor has found no grounds for their first charge (rebellion and insurrection) and is therefore considering releasing Jesus or returning him to the Sanhedrin, they must come up with different grounds for indictment. It would be preposterous for the Jews to kill one of their own on charges of sedition against the enemy and incitement to nonpayment of taxes to the emperor, while the occupying power itself has declared him to be innocent of these charges! For this reason the leaders feel compelled to reveal their own internal and religious grievances against Jesus: "He claimed to be the Son of God!" (John 19:6–7). Now Pilate sees how sensitive the Jesus affair is for the Jews. The leaders are suggesting that if Pilate can find no grounds for crucifixion under Roman law, he should carry out the execution anyway on the basis of the Jews' religious charges.

The governor is impressed by this new accusation, and he discusses it with Jesus himself (John 19:8–11). This conversation reinforces his conviction that it is better to let Jesus go and withdraw from the case altogether (John 19:12; Luke 23:20).

4. Pilate's last attempt to release Jesus consists of a renewed effort to consult the people. This time he appeals to the crowd's sense of fairness. On what *grounds* do they base their demand for Jesus' crucifixion (Matt. 27:23; Mark 15:14; Luke 23:22)? He is given no answer to his question. Instead, the people insist once again that Jesus be crucified. It threatens to turn into a riot, and Pilate feels compelled to take some action against Jesus simply to maintain law and order. He sees no way out other than to turn Jesus over to the will of the Jews, in spite of his personal feelings in the case. It is *their* responsibility. Pilate pronounces judgment, but he does what *they* want. On this occasion the governor is prepared to serve as the Sanhedrin's puppet in order to safeguard his own position.

In order to understand the entire course of events, we must remember that the Jews had decided not to put Jesus to death by means of a *Jewish* trial during the week of the feast because the leaders feared the reaction of the crowds. Instead, they devised a scheme by which Jesus would be quickly and surreptitiously turned over to the governor, whom they would force to carry out the execution on the same day (see chapter 15). A clear grasp of this strategy is often obliterated by the assumption that the Jews of that period were not permitted to pronounce or carry out any executions, making it *always* necessary to involve Pilate. But this assumption is incorrect. During Jesus' lifetime, the Sanhedrin did have the right to try their own religious cases, including the right to apply penalties prescribed in the law (see chapter 14). So when Pilate begins by saying, "Take him yourselves and judge him by your own law" (John 18:31), it is not a sarcastic comment. Judgment based on the law necessitates punishment demanded by the law (including stoning). If this were not so, the leaders would have been able to say, "We judged him according to our own law and we find him guilty of a capital offense." What they did say, however, is, "But we have no right to execute anyone" (John 18:31). This cannot mean that they had no right in the absolute sense to carry out the death penalty. If that were true, Pilate would not have been able to propose that they give Jesus a Jewish trial, and in any case the Jews would not have had to tell him that they were not permitted to do what he himself would have forbidden them to do. They could simply have said, "What we have here is a capital offense." Pilate then would have known that no more was expected of him than the ratification of a Jewish verdict and the execution of a *Sanhedrin* sentence. And that would have been permission for a *stoning!* Now, however, the Jews announce that they are not permitted to execute "anyone." The strong emphasis on the prohibition to execute anyone, "no matter who," indicates that the Jews already know that they themselves cannot try this capital offense on this particular day. That is why they do not begin any legal procedure, as Pilate suggests, but bring the man (who indeed *must* be killed) to Pilate. He can do what is categorically impossible for them on this particular day.

The fact that there really were two possible ways to put Jesus to death—Jewish stoning or Roman crucifixion—is apparent from the continuation in John 18:32. The answer given by the Jewish leaders is a fulfillment of Jesus' prophecy that he would die on a *cross*. That strange prophecy presupposed a *Roman* trial, the consequence of the Sanhedrin turning the Son of man over to the Gentiles (Luke 18:32). Such a death would not have been so exceptional if the Romans had had to carry out *all* Jewish executions. But now it is exceptional, because the Sanhedrin's verdict made stoning also an option.

All the twists and turns of that Friday morning take place against this background. What we have described up to now can be summarized as follows. Initially the Jewish leaders conceal their real reason for wanting Jesus dead, and they present the case as a matter that falls under the jurisdiction of the Roman governor. Pilate realizes that he is being used for Jewish purposes, and after a brief investigation of the charges he refuses to play along. Let the Jews judge him by their own religious laws! At this point the leaders have to admit openly that they are not permitted to put anyone to death on this day, yet they still want Jesus to be killed—today! Let Pilate do their work for them on this Jewish day of rest. They also have to admit openly their real reason for wanting Jesus dead: Jesus says he is the Son of God. The result is that Pilate declares that Jesus is *not* guilty, but he is prepared—out of sheer necessity—to carry out what the Jews want done but cannot do themselves on this particular day. He decides to *hand Jesus over* to the people and their leaders (John 19:16; Mark 15:15; Luke 23:25). In this way the leaders succeed in implementing a scheme to put Jesus to death and to avoid a Sanhedrin trial "during the feast" (during the week of the feast). And Christ's prediction is fulfilled that his death, willed by the Jews, will be by crucifixion at the hands of the Romans.

16.7 Cross and Grave

Matthew and Mark provide a brief summary of Jesus' being mocked by the soldiers, after the account of the trial and at the point when the crown of thorns and robe are taken from him and he is given back his own clothing, which he will wear as he is being led away.

From here on, the sequence of events is well known and presents no special problems. For this reason we will forgo a broad description of the journey to Golgotha and the crucifixion (Matt. 27:32–56; Mark

15:21–41; Luke 23:26–49; John 19:17–37).[1] But we must look in more detail at the problem of the hours of this day.

Mark says that the crucifixion took place at the *third* hour (Mark 15:25), so it is strange to read in John that when Pilate made his definitive decision it was already the *sixth* hour (John 19:14). Is Mark's clock fast or is John's slow? The difference is about four hours! Given the intensity with which everyone would have been following the day's events, we cannot simply assume that the reason for this discrepancy is a blurred sense of time. But how can two documents both claim to be historically reliable when at the very climax of their narratives their times are so different?

The answer lies in the fact that Mark and John use different systems for numbering the hours. Even today we have different ways for indicating hours. In continental Europe, the train that leaves "at nine o'clock" may well be listed in the train schedule as departing at 21.00. Mark follows a daytime system, in which the day runs from sunrise to sunset and is divided into twelve hours (cf. Matt. 20:1–12; John 11:9). The sixth hour is the hour at which the sun has reached its height. There are several time designations in Mark that are obviously based on this system. Thus he places the three hours of darkness between the sixth and the ninth hours (Mark 15:33), and it is clear that after this ninth hour there is still quite a bit of time remaining for the descent from the cross and the burial before the arrival of the Sabbath. Friday is not over until the twelfth hour has passed and the Sabbath has begun. According to Mark's Gospel, then, the crucifixion took place halfway between daybreak and noon (i.e., "the third hour"), while the period of darkness lasted from noon to halfway between noon and the end of the day (i.e., "from the sixth hour to the ninth hour").

Naturally, this method of telling time is flexible. The actual length of an hour would depend on whether the day was shorter or longer. During the winter, not only were the days shorter, the hours were, too. Passover falls after the spring equinox, and that means that the days were already longer than the nights. In our system of telling time, we would say that the sun had already risen before six o'clock in the morning. How much before six o'clock is difficult to say. It depends on whether Passover in the year A.D. 33 was celebrated at the beginning of April or May. Passover fell earlier or later in the solar year, depending on the

---

1. For other details concerning the road to Golgotha and the order of the words from the cross, see the commentaries in Commentaar op het Nieuwe Testament, 3d series: Jakob van Bruggen, *Matteüs: Het evangelie voor Israël*, 2d ed. (Kampen: Kok, 1994); idem, *Marcus: Het evangelie volgens Petrus*, 2d ed. (Kampen: Kok, 1992); idem, *Lucas: Het evangelie als voorgeschiedenis*, (Kampen: Kok, 1993); P. H. R. van Houwelingen, *Johannes: Het evangelie van het Woord* (Kampen: Kok, 1997).

placement of the leap year, which added one entire month to the year. If Passover was late, then the sun must have risen well before 6:00 A.M. There remains a margin of uncertainty, but we can say with confidence that Mark's "third hour," understood in terms of our time system, can be indicated as a period between 8:00 A.M. and 10:00 A.M. So the crucifixion took place at a rather early hour.

When we turn to examine the "sixth hour" mentioned in John 19:14, which was when Pilate delivered his verdict, it is immediately clear that this evangelist must have used a different method for telling time. He himself tells us that the arrival at Pilate's palace occurred "early in the morning" (John 18:28), and it is difficult to imagine that the deliberation with the governor took six hours. We have to assume that John used the *Roman* system for telling time. This system began at midnight and counted twelve hours up to noon (the height of the sun at midday), then counted another twelve hours from noon to midnight. The basis of the system was therefore not a *twelve-hour day* but a *complete twenty-four hour day*. The sixth hour, understood according to our own method, is the same as the period from 6:00 A.M. to 7:00 A.M. It is not John's intention, however, to be very *precise* about the time. He tells us that it was *"about* the sixth hour," so it could have been earlier, but it could also have been later. When we compare this verse with John 4:52, we see that the word *about* is meant as a qualifier. There the official asks for the *precise* time, and the word *about* is not used. All this tells us that Pilate's verdict was handed down between 5:30 A.M. and 7:30 A.M.

Even if Passover were early that year, the sun would have risen before 6:00 A.M. So the Sanhedrin could have completed its emergency session (which had to be official, i.e., during the daytime and in the temple) around or shortly after 6:00 A.M. The meeting room was only a short distance from the Antonia fortress, which was part of the temple complex. The walk to Herod's palace, where Antipas briefly interrogated Jesus, would not have taken very much time either. So Jesus could have stood before Pilate in the period from shortly after 6:00 A.M. to about 7:30 A.M. All this is based on the assumption that it was an *early* Passover. If it was a *late* Passover, however, then the Sanhedrin could have been ready by about 5:00 A.M. or 5:30 A.M. In that case the Lord would have stood before Pilate in the period between about 5:30 A.M. and about 7:30 A.M. These times conform to the Roman habit of taking care of administrative duties in the early morning.

John the evangelist combines two characteristics. On the one hand he possesses a strikingly detailed knowledge of Jewish life and of Jesus' own history (he was an eyewitness from a Palestinian milieu, with access to the circles of the high priest!). On the other hand, his way of describing things puts him outside the circle of normal Jewish life (his

Gospel was written at a late date and for Christians outside Palestine). Thus he presents a great deal of information about Jesus' trial that is uniquely his, but he uses a non-Palestinian system for telling time. But if we make this assumption in our reading of John 19:14, we must make it for his entire Gospel. And this indeed proves to have been the case. In 1:39 the *tenth* hour is sometime in the morning; the disciples spent *that day* with Jesus. In 4:6 we must understand the hour as being the sixth hour of the *evening*. Jesus is tired from the journey, and it is time for the evening meal and for fetching water from the well (4:6–8). In 4:52, the son of the royal official from Capernaum recovers at the seventh hour. Considering that his father has to travel from Capernaum to Cana through mountainous country, a journey of about 18.5 miles, and that he has to return home immediately the next day, we should understand this to refer to the seventh hour in the evening. The royal official arrives at the end of the afternoon just as evening is coming to Cana (the days are still shorter than the nights, because it is winter). He is able to speak with Jesus between 7:00 P.M. and 8:00 P.M. As soon as the night is over he travels back, and on the way he hears from his servants that his son recovered the previous evening at exactly that time.

17

Burial, Resurrection, and Ascension

17.1 Variations in the Narratives

Jesus' burial on the Friday of his death by crucifixion, his resurrection from the tomb on the first day of the week, and his ascension forty days after the resurrection, all occur within a span of six weeks. Most of the narrative material covering this period in the Gospels is devoted to the great turning point: Jesus' resurrection from the dead—the dawn of new life! This means that most of this narrative is related to a period of just a few days, or even one day. Thus we know, relatively speaking, quite a bit about the day of the resurrection, especially about the morning hours.

But in this case more information does not mean that we can quickly come to a clear and detailed picture of the events. Quite the opposite. Many believe that the sheer abundance of contradictions forces us to relegate the resurrection stories to the realm of legend. These discrepant attempts to construct a story around a nonverifiable faith experience leave us at best with the bare fact of "the empty grave." Whether this fact has been correctly interpreted in terms of a belief in the resurrection remains a matter of discussion for twentieth-century theologians. The (apparent?) contradictions in the Gospels here have immense consequences. Didn't the apostle Paul say that if Jesus was not raised, our faith is useless? But like Paul, we derive our assurance of his resurrection from the witnesses who saw him alive (1 Cor. 15:1–11). Our *expectation* of his resurrection may rest on the Scriptures that foretold it, but how would we know that this prophecy has been fulfilled without the testimony of those who *witnessed* the resurrection? Our faith does not depend on the harmonization of these statements of witnesses—but it would raise questions if these statements flatly contradicted each other.

So it is understandable that attempts are made time and again to compare the Gospel narratives in order to arrive at an integrated narrative. Greijdanus has devoted an entire work to the resurrection of Christ,[1] and John Wenham's more recent publication bears the reveal-

---

1. S. Greijdanus, *De opwekking van Christus* (Kampen: Kok, 1947).

ing title *Easter Enigma: Do the Resurrection Stories Contradict One Another?*[2] When these and other studies are held up for comparison, two things quickly become apparent: (1) the allegedly obvious contradictions between the Gospels are not as serious as they have been made out to be; and (2) it is not a simple matter to reconstruct the exact course of events.

We will pursue this second point in greater depth. Does the difficulty encountered here mean that we ought to approach the resurrection stories with a certain reserve? Or should we not be surprised at encountering special problems here? For a number of reasons the differences between the resurrection stories should not be regarded as particularly unusual but rather as arguing in favor of the authenticity and credibility of the accounts. At first glance we are inclined to think that a number of fresh eyewitness reports of that morning's events cannot help but produce a flawless picture—but when we give it more thought we realize that *in this particular case* total agreement would actually be grounds for suspicion! There are general and particular factors that of necessity lead to a more complex picture when a large number of eyewitnesses reports are involved—not because the fact of the resurrection is in question but because the women and men involved were in an extremely confused state that day.

17.1.1 General Complicating Factors

Three factors that frequently play a role in the Gospels are also present here in the resurrection stories.

1. There is a difference between reading a report of a cross-examination and a spontaneous account. The spontaneous witness can concentrate his or her attention on what for him or her were the most salient facts, such as the sudden arrival of one woman who has experienced something and comes to tell about it. Under cross-examination further questions can be asked, such as, Were you alone or were others with you? The answer might reveal that, indeed, there were others with this woman who for the narrator was the main character (either because she was the spokesperson or because he knew her best). But we do not have the opportunity to question the evangelists and their sources directly. This means that we must not ask more of the accounts than they can deliver by reading them as if they were final reports produced after an interrogation. John 20:1–2 tells us that Mary Magdalene went to the tomb early in the morning and then went to Peter and John in a panic. But it would be improper to conclude from John 20:1–2 that Mary

2. J. Wenham, *Easter Enigma: Do the Resurrection Stories Contradict One Another?* (Exeter: Paternoster, 1984).

Magdalene was *alone* because she is the only person mentioned. John wants to include another meeting between Jesus and this woman (John 20:11–18), which may be the reason why he places her in the spotlight from the beginning. And when Mark does not speak of *two* angels in the tomb (as Luke does in 24:4) but of only *one* (16:5), we might learn upon inquiry that Mark relates the report of a woman who noticed only one angel, the one who spoke, and neglected to mention that there was another shining figure there. When reading the Gospels, we must always take into account the characteristics of *spontaneous narrative*, especially in the resurrection stories, because the heightened emotional state of those directly involved increases the possibility of more vivid and more narrowly focused narratives.

2. The evangelists did not have the same sources for their reports. Mark offers us Peter's story, and we know that Peter was the first to be confronted by Mary Magdalene that morning. Luke's special witness may have been Joanna, the wife of a senior official at the court of Herod Antipas. Luke is the only one to mention her; as a physician he may have moved in higher social circles and have been in contact with Herod Antipas's court circles. The situation is different in Matthew. As far as we know, he was not with Peter and John that Easter morning and his initial impressions thus came from sources other than theirs. In addition, Matthew apparently was able to get more information from those close to the Sanhedrin in Jerusalem (concerning the guarding of the tomb). We know that the Gospel writers in general approach their material from more or less different perspectives, but this is especially true in the case of the resurrection accounts. Thus the story of the appearance of the angels in the tomb when told by women who have just seen Jesus himself (Matt. 28:1–10) is quite different from that same story told earlier in the morning by a few witnesses who had come straight from the tomb in a state of great upset.

3. Each evangelist has his own narrative approach. Thus each one makes selections that are consistent with his approach, ignoring some details and emphasizing others. Matthew focuses on the tomb (the tomb guards and the lie about the grave robbery) and on Galilee. Mark, on the other hand, concentrates on how the Good News penetrates first the unbelief of the disciples and then the unbelief of the world. Luke stresses the fulfillment of the Scriptures and even includes a whole section of material dealing with this theme: the men on the road to Emmaus. John shows the reality of the raising of Christ. And Paul, in 1 Corinthians 15, focuses on the verifiability of the resurrection. So it is no wonder that the choice of narrative material differs enormously, and that even when the evangelists tell the same story, they do so very differently. This phenomenon occurs regularly in the Gospels, but we see it even more

clearly in the resurrection accounts. Here four or five narrators, each with his own purpose, cover a very brief period of time, so the reader is more apt to compare the narratives than if the chosen stories had covered a longer time span.

17.1.2 Special Complicating Factors

In addition to the factors that always play a role in the reading of the Gospels, there are also a few that are unique to the resurrection stories.

1. The nature of the events and the emotional state of the disciples who observed them are incompatible. On this first day of the week, the women and the disciples must see, hear, believe, and pass on something that is totally beyond their comprehension. Their very thoughts and emotions make them unable to grasp the truth of Easter. If this truth is ever to get through to them, a very rapid process of inner change will have to take place. But no matter how rapid the process, it will be jolting and produce moments of apparently contradictory feelings.

Thus we see colliding emotions of fear and joy (Matt. 28:8). In such an atmosphere it should not surprise us to see Mark at one point accentuate the *fear* of the women (Mark 16:8), while at another point Luke describes in one breath their shock as well as their readiness to serve as messengers (Luke 24:5, 9).

Too often we imagine that there was an instantaneous change from unbelief to faith. But we need only to look at Thomas to realize how mixed and divided the feelings were. Mary Magdalene is another striking example. She experienced many miraculous events (the empty tomb, the speaking angel), yet she is blind when Jesus *himself* appears and takes him for the gardener (John 20:11–15). Later, in Galilee, even the disciples begin to have their doubts (Matt. 28:17).

The result of these special circumstances is that the initial acceptance of the experienced facts was often incomplete, so that the early reports are also in many cases incomplete. A cool-headed Christian observer would have noticed that not only was the tomb empty, but there was also an angel there to explain the situation. But for the passionate, distressed women who had laid the precious body of their Master here, everything comes to a standstill when they cannot find him and instead see only the empty tomb and the apparent disturbance of what they had prepared with reverence. Shining angels pale in comparison to the fact that *he* is not there. This may seem strange to us, so many centuries later. But is it any stranger than the fact that Mary Magdalene fails to see even the physical presence of Jesus in the garden because she is lost in the mists of thought because "they have taken my Lord away"? When this Mary comes to Peter in the early morning in a state of collapse, unable to utter anything about the empty tomb she saw and the angel's words she heard except "they have taken the Lord out of the tomb" (John 20:2), it does not mean that the angel said nothing else or that she did not see an angel at all. It only proves that it will take more than this to draw her out of the mist of grief and unbelief and awaken her to the truth of Easter. Only the voice of Jesus himself ("Mary!") makes her hear and see what was there all along ("Rabboni!"; John 20:16).

So when we read the resurrection stories, we must keep in mind the difference between what actually *happened* and what was *communicated* in the first emotional accounts told by people who were completely unprepared for these events.

2. In addition, there was also an abnormally large number of people on this Easter morning who were directly involved in the events but who had lost any sense of cohesion as a group. They find themselves thrown together in a narrow sphere of action, yet on this morning they wander about, confused, disordered, and past one another.

The eleven remaining disciples have lost touch with one another. Peter and John stay together (John 18:16; 20:2), but the others have fled. Wenham is of the opinion that they went to Bethany, but it is also possible that they hid on the Mount of Olives or with acquaintances in the city. Even at the end of the resurrection day not all have found their way back: Thomas is missing. So when the women want to tell something "to the disciples," we must not think it a simple matter. These women, as a group, had to begin a long hunt through the city, wandering about in search of addresses, stopping off to deliver their message. Or they went out in small groups so that each could track down a few people.

Furthermore, the group of women is hardly homogeneous. There are members of Jesus' family, as well as others who followed Jesus from Galilee, and finally there are some who probably came from Bethany or Jerusalem (Luke 24:10). They did not all stay at the same address, and nowhere are we told that they all did the same things and set out for the tomb or arrived there at exactly the same time.

In addition, the family ties of some of the women and disciples may have influenced their behavior on this particular day. Wouldn't one first search for one's own son or husband to tell him what has happened? There are also many different roads along which one could leave the city to reach the garden of Joseph of Arimathea. It is possible that some, coming from the tomb, entered the city through one gate while those traveling to the tomb at the same time left the city through another.

Taking all this into account, we realize that the complexity of the lodgings, walking routes, and relationships could easily have given rise to a number of reports that, without further information, we cannot always reduce to a single story that fits all the details.

But what if, in fact, all four resurrection narratives were identical? Their credibility would be attacked, not because of discrepancies, but because of the *lack* of discrepancies—the critics would charge that it is simply not possible to come up with four identical reports of a morning so emotionally charged and with so many persons all acting at once. By reflecting on the unique character of that first day of the week, we begin to understand that Easter reports that cannot easily be integrated into a seamless whole are the very ones that can make an authentic and credible impression. This is no patchwork compiled after the fact, but firsthand testimony from people who were caught off guard by the immensity of the events.

17.2 Burial

After Jesus' unexpectedly quick death, Joseph of Arimathea asks Pilate for the body. In his administrative function as a member of the council, and as a man of wealth, he has easy access to the governor. Secretly he was a follower of Jesus, so he did not agree with the plans of the Jewish Sanhedrin to put the Master to death (Luke 23:51). Now it is he who openly takes the body from the cross (John 19:38).

Nicodemus, an expert in the law, chooses his side and brings a great gift for the burial: seventy-five pounds of myrrh and aloes (John 19:39). This is used to bury Jesus according to the Jewish custom (John 19:40), which involved leaving the body untouched and committing it to the grave whole, as opposed to the Roman custom of cremation and the Egyptian practice of mummification, which involved the removal of many of the organs.

Jesus' body is wrapped completely in a linen shroud (*sindōn*, Mark 15:46; Luke 23:53; Matt. 27:59). John tells us the same thing when he says that the body was bound in cloths (*othonia*), along with the fragrant herbs and ointments, and a sweat cloth was wrapped around the head (John 19:40; 20:6–7). Considering the large quantity of ointment, we have to imagine that the entire body and head were covered, with the cloths and the surrounding shroud drenched in ointment and formed, as it were, into a fragrant, protective second skin.

Wenham refers to Lazarus (John 11:44), at whose burial only the hands and feet were bound while a sweat cloth was wrapped around his head. But there is some objection to the idea that Jesus' body was treated in the same limited way. (1) Binding the *body* (John 19:40) is more than binding the hands and the feet (John 11:44). (2) The word used in the Lazarus story (*keiriai*) is not the same as that used at Jesus' burial (*othonia*). (3) Seventy-five pounds of salve require more than a few strips of cloth. Lazarus's burial was simple, but Jesus' burial is lavish. (4) The first three evangelists clearly describe the "wrapping" of the body. The difference between Lazarus's burial and that of Jesus is an important factor in the resurrection (see section 17.8).

Joseph had a grave carved out of the rock close to the site of the crucifixion (Matt. 27:59–60). The grave is as yet unused, and the body of the Master is laid in it because of the approaching Sabbath (John 19:41–42). A temporary grave, chosen out of necessity! Joseph's plan may have been to eventually build a prophet's grave in commemoration of Jesus, marked by a monument, similar to those that had been erected for other prophets in Jerusalem (Matt. 23:29).

17.3 The Women Guard the Tomb

After Joseph shuts the innermost chamber of the tomb by rolling a large stone in front of it and Joseph and Nicodemus leave, several women remain sitting across from the tomb as a kind of honor guard. Matthew mentions Mary Magdalene and the other Mary (Matt. 27:61). This "other Mary" is the mother of James and Joses (cf. Matt. 27:56), one of Jesus' aunts (see section 5.4). Matthew does not mention Salome, the mother of the sons of Zebedee. She was at the crucifixion (Matt. 27:56) but may already have gone home with her son John when he took Jesus' mother to his residence in Jerusalem (John 19:27). These women had come with Jesus from Galilee, and now they are keeping watch at the tomb (Mark 15:47). Joanna may also have been part of the guard. In Luke 23:55–56 we read that a number of unnamed women from Galilee attended the burial and then went to prepare spices and myrrh. Luke then tells us in 24:1 that early on the first day of the week they, "together with several others" (as the end of 24:1 reads in most manuscripts), brought all this to the tomb. Then Luke provides us with a number of names in 24:10: "Mary Magdalene, Joanna, Mary the mother of James, and the others with them." The "others" are the women who gathered in 24:1. We may assume that the other three were present not only on that Easter morning but also at the burial. In that case Joanna would have been the third woman at the tomb.

Mark 16:1 seems to suggest that Mary Magdalene and Mary the mother of James, together with Salome, did not go to buy spices until the Sabbath had passed. Luke, on the other hand, gives us the impression that the women *first* prepared the spices and myrrh and then observed the Sabbath (23:56). Is this a contradiction? Not necessarily, if we take into account the varying circumstances of the women and the fact that the evangelists provide brief summaries of the events. Mark says in so many words that the spices were *bought* after the Sabbath, but in Luke there is only mention of the spices and myrrh being *prepared* at home. It is quite possible that Mary Magdalene and the other Mary, who both were *visiting* Jerusalem, first had to go to the shops to buy spices and therefore had to wait until after the Sabbath. Joanna, on the other hand, was the wife of Chuza, the manager of Herod's household, and as such she may well have had access to these luxury items, so that she could make the necessary preparations as soon as she got home. Luke's detail of the preparations may be based on Joanna's account, and Mark's on that of Mary Magdalene, so that each gives us a different aspect of the actual situation which involved several "story lines" simultaneously, which means that it is not accidental that Mark speaks of *buying*. The evangelists' accounts here are not very extensive and differentiated, because ultimately these women returned from the tomb together, with the same intention, and they also go back together with their prepared spices after the Sabbath.

Mark speaks of the plan to "anoint" Jesus' body in the tomb. This suggests fragrant herbs and oils that were set out around the wrapped body and poured over the shroud to prevent the odor of death for a longer time. The "honor guard" at the tomb on Good Friday, consisting of the two Marys and Joanna, resumes its task after the Sabbath, as these same women, accompanied by others (one of whom at least was Salome), come to care for the body.

17.4 A Roman Guard under Jewish Auspices

Matthew focuses his attention on the Jewish leaders and therefore on the tomb, which was of special interest to them. So he is the only evangelist to report the precautionary measures they took. On the Sabbath they go to Pilate to ask that the tomb be guarded. Jesus had said something about a resurrection on the third day, and they remember these words better than his disciples do. Now they are afraid that his disciples will come and steal the body in order fabricate a fulfillment of Jesus' words. Pilate has no objection to providing a guard, but it is up to the Jewish leaders to take any further measures. So the *Jewish leaders*, on the authority of the governor, place a guard at the stone and put a seal on it (Matt. 27:62–66). This guard is temporarily under their control (cf. Matt. 28:11–15). While the women who guarded the tomb observe the Sabbath in accordance with the regulations of the chief priests and Pharisees, the latter are busy putting soldiers to work to guard the tomb on behalf of the unbelieving Jews. The women and the disciples are ignorant of these measures, so they do not expect to find any strangers at the tomb when they go there after the Sabbath. We can see why this

Jewish-Roman guard plays no role in three of the accounts and why only Matthew chooses to highlight it to explain the origin of the ancient Jewish lie about the resurrection as "grave robbery" (Matt. 28:11–15).

17.5 The Earthquake

Matthew tells us that very early in the morning of the first day of the week there is an earthquake when an angel appears, who opens the tomb and sits down on the stone. His appearance is like lightning, and his clothes are white as snow (Matt. 28:2–3). The guards who were on duty during the fourth watch (from 3:00 A.M. to 6:00 A.M.) are seized with fear and become like dead men (Matt. 28:4). We do not know how long the guards remained in this condition. The earthquake seems to have taken place when the women were on their way to the garden (Matt. 28:1–2), but before they arrived: the stone had already been rolled away by the time they arrived at the tomb. Did the guards regain consciousness in the brief period between the coming of the angel and the arrival of the women, and did they run away? We know that they reported to the chief priests at the same time that the women hastily returned to the disciples (Matt. 28:8, 11). The guards were probably slightly ahead of the women in reaching their goal. Matthew must have derived his knowledge of the guards at the tomb and the earthquake from reports given by people who knew what had been told to the chief priests that morning. Thus the evidence of the soldiers is suppressed for the sake of a lie, yet despite everything it still succeeds in serving the truth.

17.6 The Women and the Empty Tomb

As noted, Mary Magdalene, Mary the mother of James, Joanna, and several other women (one of whom was Salome) go to the tomb early in the morning. They set out at dawn (Matt. 28:1) and arrive in the garden at sunrise (Mark 16:2). Their concern about who will roll away the stone is related to their reason for coming: they have brought spices with them with which they hope to care for the body of Jesus. They were not aware of any Jewish guard at the tomb or of a seal on the stone. They may have counted on the presence of a man—the gardener, for instance (John 20:15)—but on the way to the tomb they realize that it is still very early and there may be no one there yet at such an early hour to roll the stone away.

But as they approach the tomb they discover that the stone has *already* been rolled away. Who could have done this, this early in the morning? The women become rather uneasy when they realize that the tomb has been opened before they got up that morning.

The evangelists would appear to give different reports of what happened next, which leads to the following questions:

1. Do the women immediately see an angel sitting on the rolled-away stone (Matthew), or is it not until they enter the tomb that they see an angel sitting on the right (Mark), or are they filled with dismay when they find that Jesus is gone and then see two men standing there (Luke)?
2. Is there one angel (Matthew/Mark) or are there two (Luke)?
3. Where is the angel, and in what position: sitting (Matthew/Mark) on the stone (Matthew) or to the right (Mark), or standing near the women (Luke—two angels)?

To gain a clear understanding of the course of events, we have to take into account the narrative perspective of each evangelist. The best point of departure for reconstructing the sequence of events is the summary given by the men on the road of Emmaus (Luke 24:22–23):

> In addition, some of our women amazed us. They went to the tomb early this morning but didn't find his body. They came and told us that they had seen a vision of angels, who said he was alive.

We find here the following *pattern*:

1. The arrival at the tomb.
2. The entrance into the tomb.
3. The search for Jesus' body.
4. The appearance of angel(s).

When we look at the individual reports given by each evangelist, we discover that all of them fit within this pattern.

In *Matthew*'s account of the events, the focus is on the descending angel, who acts and speaks (Matt. 28:2–7). We read how the angel deals with the guards and what he says to the women. Matthew does not provide a historical perspective. In reality, the angel's statement to the women occurs some time after the guards fall "like dead men." Matthew does tell us that the angel says, "Do not be afraid," but he omits any mention of the *fact* that the women were afraid, or *why* they were afraid. We learn little from Matthew about the *course* of events.

Nevertheless it is striking that his account does fall within the above pattern. On a superficial reading, the women seem to notice the angel as they are approaching the tomb, but reading between the lines we see that this is not the case. Matthew tells us that they first *entered* the tomb.

This is apparent from the fact that in Matthew 28:8 we read, "So they left the tomb quickly" (NRSV).[3]

Matthew uses the word *mnēmeion* when the women leave. This is not a general designation for the burial place in the garden of Joseph of Arimathea, for which Matthew uses the word *taphos* (Matt. 27:61; 28:1). The *mnēmeion* is the actual burial *chamber* that lies behind the stone that is rolled in front of it. Joseph of Arimathea lays the body *in* this burial chamber and then rolls the stone in front of "the entrance to the tomb [*mnēmeiou*]" (Matt. 27:60). The women who went to Jesus' tomb (Matt. 28:1) also went inside, into the actual burial chamber behind the stone!

Once inside, they search for Jesus' body. Matthew does not record this, but it is suggested in his account. For the angel says, "I know that you are looking for Jesus" (Matt. 28:5). The women had not set out to *look for* Jesus. They knew exactly where he was, and they have come to take care of the tomb with the body. When the angel says that they are *looking for* Jesus, the women must already have lost their certainty, discovering that the body was not lying where it was supposed to be, and looking around or groping in the semidarkness of the burial chamber for that which they suddenly had to search for.

Thus the account that Matthew offers us (with a foreshortened perspective because he focuses on the activity of the angel) can still be placed within the general pattern. The women arrive, they enter the tomb, they look around, and then they are confronted by the person and voice of the angel.

Mark explicitly mentions *entering* the tomb (Mark 16:5). We have the impression that as soon as the women enter they see a young man sitting on the right. Yet Mark also suggests that the women first looked around for the body. Indeed, the young man says, "You are looking for Jesus the Nazarene, who was crucified" (Mark 16:6). The perspective in Mark is less foreshortened than it is in Matthew, and Mark's slightly abridged account also appears to have been based on the pattern mentioned above.

The angel sitting on the stone in Matthew could be the same as the young man sitting on the *right* in Mark. This rather vague expression must mean "to the *right* of the actual burial chamber." In Jerusalem today there are two examples of round tomb stones from the time of the

---

3. The majority text reads *exelthousai,* "going out of [the tomb]." Most English versions follow the critical text, which reads *apelthousai,* "going away from [the tomb]." The stylistic change from *exelthousai* to *apelthousai* can be explained by the fact that Matthew does not say that the women *entered* the tomb. Because it is the less obvious reading, *exelthousai* deserves serious consideration, especially since there is other support in the passage as well for the women entering the tomb, as discussed below.

New Testament, and in both cases these round stones were placed *at the end of the anteroom,* cutting off access to the actual burial chamber or chambers. So this stone does not lie outside in front of the first entrance to the tomb, but inside and in front of the opening to the actual burial chamber. This stone can be rolled away *into a niche.* If the stone were rolled to the right, the young man would be sitting on the stone to the right of the burial chamber in a niche that people pass when they have entered the dim front anteroom and want to continue on to the innermost chamber where the bodies are laid out.

Luke does not offer us a foreshortened perspective. He explicitly reports the arrival (Luke 24:2), the entry, the search (Luke 24:3), and the appearance of the angel who tells them that it is senseless to look for the living in a tomb (Luke 24:4–5).

It is striking, however, that Luke speaks of *two* men (in "clothes that gleamed like lightning"). Furthermore, he does not say that they were sitting, but that they were *standing.* Here Luke is more comprehensive in his narrative than Matthew and Mark. Standing or sitting is not a major conflict. Couldn't the angel have revealed himself, gleaming like lightning and sitting on a stone (in the right-hand niche), and then standing up to speak with the women, so that it could be said that an angel *came to stand* next to the women and spoke to them? Luke uses this verb frequently, and always to indicate that someone comes over to stand next to someone else (Luke 2:9, 38; 4:39; 10:40; 20:1). Apparently the seated angel came over to join the women and addressed them from a standing position.

Luke speaks of *two* men. The other evangelists do not tell us that there was *only* one and no more; rather, they concentrate on the person who is speaking. But apparently there were two angels. The question, however, is whether in retrospect even the women themselves were fully aware of what took place. They knew what they had heard and seen, but did everyone see and discern *everything* in that astonishing moment? There were at least six or seven women more or less squeezed together in a confined space. They were shattered because they had seen the door of the burial chamber standing open at such an early hour, and because the body was not lying where it should have been. Since the grave cloths were there, it must have been a scary discovery for the women! All the groping and searching in this place was done in semidarkness, for the front opening allowed little light to enter through the door to the burial chamber. And then suddenly, within this underground cave, there's a blinding flash. Someone moves and speaks; the figure is coming from the right-hand niche, where the stone has been rolled. The bright light from the niche shines into the tomb and illuminates everything with penetrating brilliance. The women did not observe this calmly. Crowded together in that small space, they stumble on top of each other with their faces toward the floor. They have to protect their eyes from the light, and they are cowering in terror (Luke 24:5). At a moment such as this, who can make a detailed observation of the number of beings? It is possible that the women lying prostrate on the floor of the burial chamber were not able to see that there were *two* figures, while Joanna may have been closer to the front and noticed that at least two figures could be distinguished. And who knows whether all the women saw everything? Perhaps there was a third figure that they all failed to see. At issue is the *accuracy* of the recollection, not its completeness! In this extraordinarily startling event, which takes place in a space a few yards square, carved into the face of a cliff, completeness of observation is not to be expected. Nor is it necessary. The accounts are true-to-life reflections of the reality with which the women are the first to come in contact.

17.7 Fleeing and Reporting

The angels have appeared and disappeared. The women are still lying face down on the ground. Suddenly it is dark around them again. After the intensely bright light, this darkness is very dark indeed! The impressions left by the tomb's open door, the bright light, and the unexpected words are all jumbled together in the women's minds. No wonder that their return to the city cannot be described in a calm, detached statement.

Mark says that they *fled* from the tomb, trembling all over and completely confused (Mark 16:8). To this the evangelist adds, "They said nothing to anyone, because they were afraid." Some commentators interpret this as meaning that the women also said nothing to the disciples, but this cannot be correct. Why would they be afraid to tell something to their own families or friends? They did fear others, those who had crucified Jesus. At the end of the resurrection day, the disciples meet behind closed doors "for fear of the Jews" (John 20:19). This fear has seized the women, too, so they hurry down the street without greeting a single person and without uttering a single word about the tremendous news. They pass through the city not as heralds but as frightened refugees. Mark 16:8 first mentions the emotions the women were experiencing (they are shaken and beside themselves) and then their fear of the outside world (they do not dare discuss even an appearance of angels with other Jews on the street). Because the women at first refuse to talk about their experiences out of fear, the hostile Jews have the opportunity to spread their lie of the grave robbery throughout Jerusalem before the good news is made public (Matt. 28:11–15).

Mark does not say anything about the women's arrival among the disciples and their own families. His focus is on the breaking through of the gospel: how did it enter the world? It was not through the women (Mark 16:8), nor through the disciples (Mark 16:11, 13–14), but only through the Lord himself, when he spurs them to action and continues to work with them (Mark 16:15–20).[4] Mark's specific purpose in chapter 16 explains why he mentions the women's public silence but does not say anything about their return to the others.

Matthew tells us how the women leave the tomb with conflicting feelings of fear and great joy and go to bring a report to the disciples (Matt. 28:8). Luke also relates how they go to tell the Eleven and the other disciples (Luke 24:9). John even gives an example of one of the encounters (John 20:2). Mary Magdalene comes with a message that is saturated with fear: "They [the others!] have taken the Lord out of the tomb, and we don't know where they have put him!" Although John mentions only Mary Magdalene, she is not the only one who returns from the tomb to tell Simon and John. She speaks together with the others ("*we* don't know"). The response of Mary Magdalene (at least as we read it in John's perhaps fragmentary account) is dominated by the emotions generated by their *searching* for the Lord. The encouraging words of the angel were not clear to them or were nor clearly heard by them. Yet some of this must have been reported, either by Mary Magdalene herself or by the other women whose stories complemented Mary Magdalene's. Later that morning we see how little the appearance and words of the angels had done to alleviate Mary's grief and fear (John 20:11–13). Her conviction that they have taken away the Lord is shaken neither by the appearance of angels nor by the appearance of the Lord himself! But even when she or the other women have told of the appearance of the angels, their report at first bypasses the apostles. They hardly take any notice—it seems like frivolous chatter (Luke 24:11)! During those first morning hours, the reports of the women have little impact as a result of the disciples' unbelief.

17.8 The Empty Shroud

At Mary Magdalene's first alarming report, Peter goes straight to the tomb, sees only the strips of linen, and goes away, full of wonder at what might have happened (Luke 24:12). John's account is more detailed. He goes with Peter and is even the first to arrive at the tomb. He

---

4. The question of whether Mark 16:9–20 belongs to the original Gospel of Mark is discussed in my commentary *Marcus: Het evangelie volgens Petrus*, 2d ed., Commentaar op het Nieuwe Testament, 3d series (Kampen: Kok, 1992).

bends down to look through the doorway of the front part of the burial area into the actual tomb, and he sees there, lying in the half-light, the strips of linen. This is enough to convince him not to go any further. With appropriate diffidence toward the dead, John stays at the front entrance. But when Peter arrives he walks right past John and goes into the burial chamber. He also sees the winding sheets, but to his horror he discovers the sweat cloth lying somewhere else. When John comes closer to see this shocking scene, he believes. Even so, Peter and John do not yet arrive at the insight that Jesus *had to* rise from the dead according to the Scriptures. Together they go back to their homes, with no words of joy for the others (John 20:3–10).

What did these two disciples see? Certainly something quite extraordinary! They conclude that the body is no longer there; the women were right on this point (Luke 24:24). But they do not panic about any possible grave robbery. John is even led to faith, and Peter is full of amazement about what may have happened. So what did they see? Folded-up strips of cloth that remind them of the Master's tidy habits? That's not what the account says. Luke tells us that Peter saw the strips of linen (*othonia*) lying *by themselves*. A mystery! John tells us more. After first arriving at the tomb and taking a quick look into the burial chamber, this apostle sees the strips of linen (*othonia*) lying there. At that point he is reassured and goes no further. And why should he? What else is there to see in the burial chamber other than the *othonia* in which the body was wrapped? The shroud is there, so the body must be there too! But then on further inspection Peter makes a discovery: the shroud is lying where one would expect to find it, but the sweat cloth that had been wrapped around his head was "separate from the *othonia*." Yet both cloths should have been found together. The strips of cloth in which the body was wrapped and the cloth for the head formed a unit. But now the sweat cloth has been pushed aside and is "rolled up [*entetyligmenon*]" (John 20:7 NRSV). This does not mean that the cloth was folded up flat, as the NIV seems to indicate. Indeed, how could it be folded after having been so heavily treated with ointment? What is meant is that the sweat cloth is still in the shape it was in when wrapped around the head on Friday evening. We find the same verb in Luke 23:53: Joseph wrapped (*enetulixen*) him in linen. We have to realize how bewildering this scene must have been. It is almost as though nothing had happened. The shroud is lying intact; the sweat cloth is still in its former shape. But the entire thing has been pushed apart. The wrapper is empty! There's nothing left but a shattered cocoon. Now we understand what Luke meant with the brief note that Peter was moved to deep contemplation because he saw the *othonia* lying "by themselves" (that is, empty, no longer connected to the sweat cloth). Grave robbery is out of the question. No one can remove a body from its shroud and sweat cloth without tearing or damaging them. But then what did happen? Belief begins to dawn in John's heart. Peter ponders the situation. But neither man is outspoken enough to mention the resurrection, because they did not yet know the Scriptures that taught that he *had to* rise from the dead. That is why the inspection of the tomb that morning did not have immediate consequences. But in retrospect the witness of these two disciples constitutes strong evidence for Jesus' actual, physical resurrection. There was more than an empty tomb. There was an empty shroud as well!

17.9 Jesus' Appearances

17.9.1 General

The day of the resurrection did not begin with Jesus' appearance. An appearance was not really necessary. He had already shown his disciples from the Scriptures that the Christ would die and rise again after three days. And just before his arrest he had privately told his disciples where they would meet him after his resurrection: "But after I have risen, I will go ahead of you into Galilee" (Matt. 26:32). After the Sabbath or at the end of the week of the feast the disciples could have returned to their homes, fully confident that they would meet the Master, alive, there in Galilee.

But after Jesus' death not one of his disciples remembers these words. All their concentration is focused on the cross, and all they can think about is Jesus who is dead. So the women return to the tomb as if this were the end of Jesus' life on earth. And when the apostles are confronted by reports of an empty tomb and the appearance of angels, they are not filled with hope, nor do they remember. Even the sign of the empty shroud fails to set them on the road to Galilee, however much it gives Peter and John food for thought.

Stronger measures were needed to break open hearts that had been blocked by unbelief. This is why Jesus finally had to appear in person before the disciples decided to make the agreed-upon journey to Galilee. The Easter story makes it clear that more than one appearance was necessary to return the disciples to a state of preparedness. Simon Peter, their leader, had to be mobilized, but this did not happen as a result of *others* having seen the Master alive. In the end Jesus had to appear personally to Peter before this disciple would take the lead. The same was true of the other apostles. They were not completely convinced either until the Savior met each of them personally, down to the last one (Thomas). Only then are they mobilized to leave the city of Jesus' death and to meet the living Jesus at the agreed-upon place in Galilee.

Matthew speaks of the stay in Galilee in so many words and describes an appearance on the mountain (Matt. 28:16–20). In Mark, it is as though everything was concluded in Jerusalem by the evening of the resurrection day. But this is an example of foreshortened perspective. If Mark tells us nothing more, it is not because he knew nothing of an agreement to meet in Galilee after the resurrection. He specifically mentions this agreement in 14:28. He also tells us how the young man in the tomb tells the women to remind the disciples of this agreement (Mark 16:7). Mark knows about it, but he does not discuss it further.

The same is true of Luke. We know from the Book of Acts that he was aware of a longer period of appearances. He even tells us how long those appearances lasted: forty days (Acts 1:3; 13:31). In Luke 24, however, the narrative is so abridged that the ascension seems to take place at the end of the resurrection day. But Luke 24 suggests that this cannot be correct. The ascension took place during the daytime and could hardly have been the finale to the encounter on the evening of the first day (cf. Luke 24:50–53 with 24:29, 33, 36).

In John, as in Matthew, we find an explicit description of events in Galilee after the resurrection (John 21). Mark's and Luke's silence about what took place in Galilee should not come as a surprise. Jesus instructed his disciples to return to Jerusalem, and from this city they were to go out into the world in the power of the Holy Spirit (Acts 1:4–5). Since the dominant focus in Mark and Luke is the spreading of the gospel to all the nations of the world, it is understandable that they would end their accounts with an abridged version of Jesus' appearance and commission in Jerusalem.

Matthew, however, has paid a great deal of attention to Jesus' teaching on the mountain (Matt. 5–7). He shows how the risen Christ took his disciples with him to the mountain once again before sending them out. Israel's new constitution is the basis of the work that the living Savior will now continue through the work of his disciples (Matt. 28:16–20).

For John it is important to go into some detail about the last great sign in Galilee. John goes back further than any of the others in the prehistory of Jesus' ministry, and he has also included an account of the *first* sign in Cana of Galilee: water turned to wine (John 2:11). He now also describes the *last* sign in Galilee: the miraculous catch of fish in the early morning (John 21:1–14). This increases to three the number of resurrection stories involving Jesus' appearance to the apostles (John 21:14), which emphasizes as strongly as possible that Jesus truly revealed himself as the Christ, the Son of God (John 20:31; 21:24). Since Matthew and John place more emphasis on the Christ and less on the spreading of the gospel as such (a more common theme in Mark and

Luke), we can understand why they did not see as great a need to follow the crucial conversations in Galilee with a report of the known fact of the farewell in Jerusalem, the ascension.

In his list of witnesses to the resurrection, the apostle Paul reports only appearances to *men* (1 Cor. 15:5–8). It is doubtful, however, that his reason behind this was a belief that the testimony of women was inadmissible as evidence. It seems more plausible that he wanted his list to contain the names of persons who would qualify as witnesses in the city of *Corinth*. All the persons he lists belong to a group of people who traveled throughout the world with the gospel (the apostles) or who had teaching authority that was respected even outside Palestine (the elders under the leadership of James). Persons such as Cephas and James were known in Corinth. Paul's list is not complete, but it is limited by his purpose: to convince the people of Corinth. His comment that most of the five hundred brothers to whom Jesus appeared are still alive also points in this direction: Paul appeals to verifiable witnesses who have visited Corinth, are known there, or can easily be located and questioned.

17.9.2 Appearances in Response to Unbelief

The *first* appearance of Jesus was to *Mary Magdalene* (Mark 16:9). She was accompanied by Mary the mother of James, one of Jesus' aunts (Matt. 28:8–10). In Matthew's account we have the impression that this appearance took place before any of the disciples had been told about the empty tomb and the appearance of an angel. Matthew 28:9 reads, according to the majority of manuscripts, "And as they went to tell his disciples, behold, Jesus met them" (KJV). This says no more, however, than that they were still busy trying to contact the disciples. We have to remember that the disciples were spread out over several locations, so the women had to make the rounds. Jesus met them while they were doing that. There is nothing in Matthew to indicate how far they had gotten with their visits to the disciples. The other Gospels tell us that Mary Magdalene had at least been to see Peter (and John) before meeting Jesus (John 20:1–2). At first she follows Peter and John back to the garden and lingers there after both apostles have left. And as she searches the area of the tomb once again for traces of the body, she sees two angels who speak to her. When she then turns from the tomb, the Savior meets her. He calls her to repentance and faith (John 20:11–18). Then, with Mary the mother of James, who was with her, she goes immediately to the disciples with the news that now includes her most recent experiences. The Savior refers to the disciples directly and in a special way: "Go instead to my brothers and tell them . . ." (Matt. 28:10 and John 20:17). In the meantime Peter and John have returned from their inspection of the grave site, and the travelers to Emmaus have already left the city (Luke 24:22–24).

The *second* appearance is to *two men walking in the country* (Mark 16:12–13). They had walked through the open country on their way to a field. Jesus appears to them "in a different form." But their report is met with incredulity, like that of the women.

These two unknown disciples are often incorrectly equated with the travelers to Emmaus. The latter travel purposefully toward a village, not a field, and it cannot be described as a walk "in the country." In addition, the travelers to Emmaus find quite a different situation when they return to Jerusalem—the Lord had already appeared to Simon (Luke 24:34)—whereas the two unknown disciples return with their report earlier in the day and are met with unbelief (Mark 16:13).

The *third* appearance involves the leader of the Eleven, *Simon Peter.* He related this experience to his fellow disciples (Luke 24:34). As a result they have a much more positive attitude toward reports of a resurrection. Paul also mentions the appearance to Peter (1 Cor. 15:5). This appearance probably gave the Eleven the courage to come together again as a group (without Judas and at first without Thomas). At the end of the resurrection day we see them back together for the first time, although the doors are locked for fear of the Jews (John 20:19).

All the disciples are confronted with a detailed explanation from the Scriptures through the story of the *fourth* appearance, to the *travelers to Emmaus.* Jesus appears to these two travelers sometime during the day, perhaps before he appeared to Simon. The report of their experience could not have its effect in Jerusalem until evening because they first had to make the trip back (Luke 24:13–35). This is the fourth appearance of which the apostles receive reports. By now they trust the witnesses to the resurrection because Simon is one of them. The travelers to Emmaus explain that there are even stronger grounds for belief: the Scriptures say that it *had to* happen (Luke 24:35a, cf. vv. 25–27).

One of the travelers to Emmaus is named Cleopas (Luke 24:18). This may have been the husband of Mary the mother of James (Clopas is mentioned in John 19:25), which would make him one of Jesus' uncles (cf. section 5.4).

In the *fifth* and final appearance for the benefit of the unbelieving disciples on this first day of the week, Jesus reveals himself to *the Eleven* (of whom only ten are present) when they gather in the evening (Mark 16:14–18; Luke 24:36–49; John 20:19–23). Their faith is still weak and unstable. Even as he stands before them there is some doubt as to the reality of his physical resurrection. Apparently some of them thought this was only a ghostly, posthumous appearance. So Jesus has to convince them by eating some food and showing them his wounds (Luke 24:37–43; John 20:20). For this appearance see also 1 Corinthians 15:5.

A *sixth* and complementary appearance is to *Thomas* in Jerusalem, one week later. His nonacceptance of the resurrection continues for another week because he was not present on the evening of the first day and refuses to accept the testimony of the others—unless he himself can see and feel the Lord's wounds. In a second appearance to the Eleven in Jerusalem, Jesus conquers this last bit of resistance so that all eleven remaining members of the Twelve are set on the road to faith. The goal of the first appearances, which really should not have been necessary at all, is thereby reached.

17.9.3 Appearances in Galilee

The meeting that Jesus had announced before his death takes place in Galilee *on the mountain* where he met so often with his disciples and where he proclaimed the new constitution for God's people in the Sermon on the Mount. It was here also that he fed the multitudes with only a few loaves of bread and a few fish. The great work will now spread further throughout the world. Many disciples are present here: Paul speaks of more than five hundred brothers (1 Cor. 15:6).

John reports one more appearance *by the Sea of Tiberias* (John 21:1–23), which is accompanied by a miraculous catch of fish and Peter's threefold confession that he really loves Jesus. It is possible that this appearance took place on the morning of the meeting on the mountain and served as an introduction to it. This is supported by the fact that they had not expected Jesus to be there. The disciples are surprised when they realize that it is Jesus who is standing on the shore (John 21:7, 12).

It is not certain whether the *appearance to James*, the brother of Jesus, took place in Jerusalem or in Galilee. Until Good Friday, this James did not play an active role in Jesus' ministry—even Jesus' brothers did not believe in him (John 7:5). While on the cross, Jesus could not put his mother in James's care but had to enlist John to provide her with spiritual support. At the ascension, however, we see that Jesus' brothers are among the circle of believing disciples (Acts 1:14). Between the resurrection and the ascension Jesus has brought his own oldest brother home into his community! There is no detailed description of the privileged personal appearance to James. Paul only touches on it briefly (1 Cor. 15:7). Perhaps Jesus visited his brother in Galilee, in Nazareth, but nothing can be said with certainty. It is also possible that James met the Lord during the first days in Jerusalem.

17.9.4 Farewell in Jerusalem

Paul says that before appearing to him personally on the road to Damascus, the last appearance of the Lord was to "all the apostles" (1 Cor. 15:7b). This was probably the appearance during which Jesus led his disciples—who had returned to Jerusalem at his request—out of the city (Luke 24:50–53) for the ascension (Mark 16:19; Acts 1:4–14). There probably were more appearances. Each source (the four Gospels and 1 Corinthians 15) mentions appearances that are not found in the other sources, so the odds are that we do not have an exhaustive account, even though we are told nothing of the other appearances.

17.10 Ascension

After his resurrection Jesus no longer moves about with his disciples. He occasionally appears to them and speaks with them. The ascension thus no longer brings about a radical change. Jesus' stay elsewhere now becomes permanent and is no longer regularly interrupted by occasional appearances (except for the appearance to Saul!). The ascension is not mentioned by every evangelist in so many words, although it is implied in each overall narrative (especially Matt. 28:16–20; John 21:22–23, 25).

Mark mentions the ascension very briefly (Mark 16:19–20). Only Luke gives a somewhat more detailed account—not in his Gospel (Luke 24:50–51) but in the Book of Acts (1:4–14). Here we are told of the exact time of the ascension: forty days after Easter (Acts 1:3). Luke also describes the other circumstances surrounding this event (Acts 1:9–11).

The ascension took place on the Mount of Olives, a Sabbath day's journey away (Acts 1:12), and thus near Bethphage[5] where the road to Bethany branches off (Luke 24:50). This is exactly where Jesus as the humble king on a donkey's colt began his triumphal entry into the city where he would die for his people. After his Passion and death, this is also the site from which he begins his royal entry into the *heavenly* Jerusalem!

---

5. See my commentary on Mark 11:1 (*Marcus: Het evangelie volgens Petrus*).

Tables

Table 1
Distribution of Narrative Material in the Gospels (Chapter 3)

Period	Matthew	Mark	Luke	John
Birth and Youth	Birth 1–2		Preparation 1 Birth 2:1–39 Youth 2:40–52	Prologue 1:1–18
Ministry of John the Baptist	John the Baptist 3:1–4:11	John the Baptist 1:1–13	John the Baptist 3:1–4:13	John the Baptist 1:19–36 Jesus' ministry before John's arrest 1:37–3:36
Galilean Period	Galilean period 4:12–18:35	Galilean period 1:14–9:50	Galilean period 4:14–9:50	To Galilee 4 In Jerusalem 5 "Bread of Life" discourse 6 In Jerusalem 7:1–10:21
Journey to Jerusalem			From Galilee to Judea 9:51–14:35	In Perea 10:22–11:16
Suffering, Death, and Resurrection	Judea 19:1–20:34 Jerusalem (and Galilee) 21–28	Judea 10:1–52 Jerusalem 11–16	Judea 15:1–19:27 Jerusalem 19:28–24:53	Judea 11:17–57 Jerusalem (and Galilee) 12:1–21:23

Table 2
Birth and Youth in Joseph's House (Chapter 4)

Event	Matthew	Mark	Luke	John
Appearance of Gabriel to Zechariah			1:5–25	
Appearance of Gabriel to Mary			1:26–38	
Mary with Elizabeth			1:39–56	
Birth of John			1:57–80	
Joseph's call	1:1–24			
Birth of Jesus	1:25		2:1–20	(cf. 1:1–18)
Circumcision			2:21	
Visit of the Magi	2:1–12			
Presentation in the temple			2:22–38	
Flight to Egypt	2:13–18			
Return and settlement in Nazareth	2:19–23		2:39	
Twelve-year-old Jesus in the temple			2:40–52	

Table 3
John the Baptist and Jesus (Chapter 6)

Event	Matthew	Mark	Luke	John
Preaching and baptizing by John the son of Zechariah	3:1–12	1:1–18	3:1–17	
Baptism of Jesus	3:13–17	1:9–11	3:21–38	
Temptation in the wilderness	4:1–11	1:12–13	4:1–13	
John's witness to himself and to Jesus				1:19–36
John's disciples follow to Jesus				1:37–53
Miracle at Cana and brief visit to Capernaum				2:1–12
Cleansing of the temple during Passover in Jerusalem				2:13–25
Nicodemus and Jesus				3:1–21
Two baptismal locations: John in Aenon and Jesus' disciples in Judea				3:22–36
Arrest of John the Baptist	4:12	1:14	3:18–20	4:1–3
Jesus goes to Galilee			4:14a	
Journey through Samaria				4:4–42

Table 4
Galilee (I): From the Return to Galilee to the Appointment of the Twelve (Chapter 8)

Event	Matthew	Mark	Luke	John
Arrival in Galilee			4:14b	4:43–45
Preaching in the cities	4:12–17	1:14–15	4:15	
• Son of Capernaum official healed				4:46–54
• Nazareth drives Jesus away			4:16–30	
• Four disciples	4:18–22	1:16–20		
Capernaum				
• Demoniac in synagogue		1:21–28	4:31–37	
• Simon's mother-in-law	8:14–15	1:29–31	4:38–39	
• Many healings	8:16–17	1:32–34	4:40–41	
• Prayer in solitude and beginning of new journey		1:35–39	4:42–44	
The crowds converge	4:23–25			
• Miraculous sign of the catch of fish			5:1–11	
John the Baptist's question	11:2–30		7:18–35	
Jesus is the Lord of the Sabbath				
• Picking heads of grain on the Sabbath	12:1–8	2:23–28	6:1–5	(5:1–47)
• Healing on the Sabbath	12:9–14	3:1–6	6:6–11	
Retreat to the mountain with the crowds	5:1	3:7–12		
Appointment of the Twelve		3:13–19	6:12–16	

Table 5
Galilee (II): From the Sermon on the Mount to the Commissioning of the Twelve (Chapter 9)

Event	Matthew	Mark	Luke	John
Sermon on the Mount	5:2–7:29		6:17–49	
Miracles				
• Leper healed	8:1–4	1:40–45	5:12–16	
• Centurion's servant healed	8:5–13		7:1–10	
• Son of the widow of Nain raised			7:11–17	
The sinful woman			7:36–8:3	
Blasphemy from Jerusalem: through Beelzebub!	12:15–45	3:20–30		
Family visit	12:46–50	3:31–35	8:19–21	
Day of parables	13:1–52	4:1–34	8:4–18	
Following Jesus	8:18–22		(9:57–60)	
Storm at sea	8:23–27	4:35–41	8:22–25	
Demoniac in the Decapolis	8:28–34	5:1–20	8:26–39	
Forgiveness of sins				
• Paralytic in Capernaum	9:1–8	2:1–12	5:17–26	
• Tax collectors and sinners at Levi's house	9:9–13	2:13–17	5:27–32	
• Fasting	9:14–17	2:18–22	5:33–39	
Just believe!				
• Jairus's daughter and the woman with the issue of blood	9:18–26	5:21–43	8:40–56	
• Two blind men	9:27–31			
• Demon-possessed deaf-mute	9:32–34			
• Unbelieving Nazareth	13:53–58	6:1–6		
Commissioning of the Twelve	9:35–11:1	6:7–13	9:1–6	

Table 6
Galilee (III): Preparation for the Passion (Chapter 10)

Event	Matthew	Mark	Luke	John
Herod's suspicions after the death of John	14:1–13	6:14–31	9:7–10	
• Jesus withdraws				
Five thousand fed	14:14–21	6:32–44	9:11–17	6:1–15
• Walking on water	14:22–33	6:45–52		6:16–21
• "Bread of Life" discourse in Capernaum				6:22–71
Healings in Gennesaret	14:34–36	6:53–56		
Attack from Jerusalem: the laws of purity!	15:1–20	7:1–23		
In Tyre and Sidon				
• Canaanite woman	15:21–28	7:24–30		
Return via Decapolis				
• Deaf-mute healed		7:31–37		
• Four thousand fed	15:29–38	8:1–9		
• Asking for a sign	15:39–16:12	8:10–21		
• Blind man in Bethsaida healed		8:22–26		
Around Caesarea Philippi				
• Disciples' confession	16:13–20	8:27–30	9:18–21	
• First announcement of the Passion	16:21–28	8:31–9:1	9:22–27	
Transfiguration	17:1–13	9:2–13	9:28–36	
• Healing of the boy with the evil spirit	17:14–21	9:14–29	9:37–43a	
Second announcement of the Passion: Jesus will be handed over!	17:22–23	9:30–32	9:43b–45	
(Feast of Tabernacles; Adulterous woman; Man born blind; The dying Good Shepherd)				7:1–10:21

Event	Matthew	Mark	Luke	John
Capernaum				
• Temple tax	17:24–27			
• Teaching about serving	18:1–35	9:33–50	9:46–50	
Departure from Galilee	19:1	10:1	9:51	

Table 7
Through Perea and Judea (Chapter 11)

Event	Matthew	Mark	Luke	John
Traveling from Galilee				
Resistance in Samaritan village			9:52–56	
The cost of following Jesus			9:57–62	
Sending out and return of the seventy			10:1–24	
Parable of the Good Samaritan			10:25–37	
Journey to Jerusalem for the Feast				
With Mary and Martha			10:38–42	
Feast of Dedication				10:22–39
Return to Bethany across the Jordan				10:40–42
Bethany across the Jordan				
Teaching on prayer			11:1–13	
Confrontation with the crowds			11:14–36	
Guest of a Pharisee			11:37–52	
Journey through Perea				
Hostility from the Pharisees and teachers of the law			11:53–54	
Teaching the disciples amid the crowds			12:1–13:9	
Healing a woman on the Sabbath			13:10–21	
Does this road lead to salvation?			13:22–30	
Herod threatens, and Jesus decides to go to Jerusalem			13:31–35	11:1–16
Healing a man with dropsy on the Sabbath			14:1–24	
Cost of discipleship			14:25–35	

Event	Matthew	Mark	Luke	John
In Judea				
Raising of Lazarus				11:17–44
Teaching before/after the raising of Lazarus				
• Many parables			15:1–18:14	
• Question of divorce	19:2–12	10:2–12		
• Blessing the children	19:13–15	10:13–16	18:15–17	
• Rich young man	19:16–26	10:17–27	18:18–27	
• Reward for following	19:27–30	10:28–31	18:28–30	
• Parable of the laborers	20:1–16			
Sanhedrin decides to kill Jesus				11:45–53
Hiding in Ephraim				11:54–57

Table 8
The Ascent to Jerusalem (Chapters 12 and 13)

Event	Matthew	Mark	Luke	John
Ascent to Jerusalem				
Third announcement of the Passion	20:17–19	10:32–34	18:31–34	
Position of the sons of Zebedee	20:20–28	10:35–45		
Around the Sabbath				
Blind man outside Jericho			18:35–43	
Staying with Zacchaeus			19:1–10	
Parable of the minas			19:11–27	
Two blind men outside Jericho (incl. Bartimaeus)	20:29–34	10:46–52		
Sunday in Bethany				
Arrival in Bethany	21:1	11:1	19:28–29	12:1
Anointed by Mary	26:6–13	14:3–9		12:2–11
Judas defects	26:14–16	14:10–11		
Monday: Triumphal Entry				
Jerusalem goes to greet Jesus				12:12–13
Jesus rides on a donkey	21:2–7	11:2–8	19:30–35	12:14–16
Cheering crowd accompanies Jesus	21:8–9	11:9–10	19:36	12:17
Meeting and entry	21:10–11		19:37–44	12:18–19
Inspection of the temple		11:11a		
Night in Bethany		11:11b		
Tuesday				
Cursing the fig tree		11:12–14		
Cleansing the temple	21:12–16	11:15–18	19:45–48	
Night in Bethany	21:17	11:19		
Wednesday				
The withered fig tree	21:18–22	11:20–26		
Jesus' authority questioned	21:23–27	11:27–33	20:1–8	
• Parables	21:28–44	12:1–11	20:9–18	

Event	Matthew	Mark	Luke	John
• Arrest thwarted	21:45–46	12:12	20:19	
Parable of the wedding feast	22:1–14			
• Questions to catch Jesus				
(a) Taxes to the emperor	22:15–22	12:13–17	20:20–26	
(b) Resurrection	22:23–33	12:18–27	20:27–40	
(c) Great commandment	22:34–40	12:28–34		
• Counter question: David's Lord?	22:41–46	12:35–37a	20:41–44	
Discourses				
• Warning against the teachers of the law and the Pharisees	23:1–39	12:37b–40	20:45–47	
• The widow's gift		12:41–44	21:1–4	
• About the future	24:1–51	13:1–37	21:5–38	
• The future in parables	25:1–46			
Jesus' response to requests from visiting Greeks				12:20–50
Preparation for death				
• on Jesus' part	26:1–2			
• on the leaders' part	26:3–5	14:1–2	22:1–2	
Thursday				
Preparing for the Passover meal	26:17–19	14:12–16	22:7–13	
Foot washing				13:1–20
Passover; institution of Lord's Supper	26:20–35	14:17–31	22:14–38	13:21–38
Words of Jesus				14:1–17:26
Gethsemane	26:36–46	14:32–42	22:39–46	
Arrest	26:47–56	14:43–52	22:47–53	18:1–11

Table 9
Good Friday (Chapter 16)

Event	Matthew	Mark	Luke	John
Night				
Interrogation by Annas				18:12–14, 19–24
Interrogation by the San-hedrin	26:57–66	14:53–64		
Mocking by the guards	26:67–68	14:65	22:63–65	
Peter's denial	26:69–75	14:66–72	22:54–62	18:15–18, 25–27
Early Morning				
Session of the Sanhedrin	27:1–2	15:1	22:66–23:1	
Judas's remorse	27:3–10			
Pilate's investigation of political charges	27:11–14	15:2–5	23:2–7	18:28–38
• Herod Antipas involved			23:8–12	
Attempt to release Jesus to the people	27:15–22	15:6–13	23:13–21	18:39–40
Pilate's investigation of the Jewish grounds for demanding crucifixion	27:23	15:14	23:22–23	19:3–12a
Jesus mocked by soldiers	27:27–31	15:16–20		19:1–2
Jesus handed over to be crucified	27:24–26	15:15	23:24–25	19:12b–16
Morning				
To Golgotha: Simon the Cyrene	27:32	15:21	23:26–32	
Crucifixion: wine with gall	27:33–44	15:22–32		19:17–24
"Father, forgive"			23:33–38	
Words to Mary and John				19:25–27
Two crucified criminals: "Today you will be with me"			23:39–43	

Event	Matthew	Mark	Luke	John
Noon				
Three hours of darkness	27:45	15:33	23:44–45	
• "Eli, Eli"	27:46–49	15:34–36		
• "I am thirsty/It is finished"				19:28–30
• "Into your hands"	27:50	15:37	23:46	
Jesus' death confirmed				19:31–37
Accompanying events	27:51–56	15:38–41	23:47–49	
Afternoon/Evening				
Anointing and burial	27:57–61	15:42–47	23:50–56	19:38–42

Table 10
Burial, Resurrection, and Ascension (Chapter 17)

Event	Matthew	Mark	Luke	John
Sabbath				
Tomb is sealed and guarded	27:62–66			
Beginning of the First Day				
Angel and earthquake	28:2–4			
Women at the tomb	28:1, 5–8	16:1–8	24:1–11	20:1–2
Soldiers flee	28:11–15			
Peter and John go to the tomb			24:12	20:3–10
Appearances—First Day				
Mary Magdalene and the other Mary	28:9–10	16:9–11		20:11–18
Two unknown disciples		16:12–13		
On the road to Emmaus			24:13–35	
Simon Peter (1 Cor. 15:5)			(24:34)	
Ten apostles (1 Cor. 15:5)		16:14–20	24:36–45	20:19–23
Appearances—Eighth Day				
Appearance to eleven apostles and others, including Thomas				20:24–29
Appearances—Galilee				
Appearance to fishing disciples				21:1–23
Encounter on the mountain (500 persons: 1 Cor. 15:6)	28:16–20			
James (? 1 Cor. 15:7)				
Appearances—Jerusalem				
Ascension (Acts 1:2–11; 1 Cor. 15:7)			24:46–53	

Table 11
Narrative Blocks and Chronological Regressions
in the Synoptic Gospels (Chapter 7)

Event	Matthew		Mark		Luke	
First appearance in Capernaum	4:18–8:17		1:21–2:22		4:14–5:39	
John the Baptist's question		11:2ff.				7:18ff.
Sabbath conflicts				2:23ff.	6:1–7:17	
Sermon on the Mount						
Day of parables						
Paralytic in Capernaum	8:18–9:34					
Levi: discussion about fasting						
Commissioning of the Twelve	9:35–11:1					
Announcements of the Passion						

Bibliography

Aland, K. *Synopsis Quattuor Evangeliorum: Locis parallelis evangeliorum apocryphorum et patrum adhibitis edidit Kurt Aland.* 14th rev. ed. Stuttgart: Deutsche Bibelgesellschaft, 1985.

Barnett, P. W. *Jesus and the Logic of History.* New Studies in Biblical Theology 3. Grand Rapids: Eerdmans, 1997.

Bauer, B. *Christus und die Cäsaren: Die Ursprung des Christentums aus dem römischen Griechentum.* 2d ed. Berlin: Grosser, 1879.

Bauer, J. B. *Die neutestamentlichen Apokryphen.* Düsseldorf: Patmos, 1968.

Becker, J. *Jesus von Nazareth.* De Gruyter Lehrbuch. Berlin: De Gruyter, 1996.

Bellinzoni, A. J., ed. *The Two-Source Hypothesis: A Critical Appraisal.* Macon, Ga.: Mercer University Press, 1985.

Ben-Chorin, S. *Broeder Jezus: De Nazarener door een Jood gezien.* Baarn: Ten Have, 1971.

Benko, S. *Pagan Rome and the Early Christians.* Bloomington: Indiana University Press, 1984.

Berger, K. *Formgeschichte des Neuen Testaments.* Heidelberg: Quelle & Meyer, 1984.

———. *Wer war Jesus wirklich?* Stuttgart: Quell Verlag, 1995.

Best, E., and R. McL. Wilson. *Text and Interpretation: Studies in the New Testament Presented to Matthew Black.* Cambridge: Cambridge University Press, 1979.

Billerbeck, P. "Die Angaben der vier Evangelien über den Todestag Jesu unter Berücksichtigung ihres Verhältnis zur Halakha." In *Kommentar zum Neuen Testament aus Talmud und Midrasch,* by H. L. Strack and P. Billerbeck, vol. 2, *Das Evangelium nach Markus, Lukas und Johannes und die Apostelgeschichte.* Munich: Beck, 1924.

Blinzler, J. *Der Prozess Jesu: Das jüdische und das römische Gerichtsverfahren gegen Jesus Christus auf Grund der ältesten Zeugnisse dargestellt und beurteilt.* 3d ed. Regensburg: Pustet, 1960. (English translation: *The Trial of Jesus: The Jewish and Roman Proceedings against Jesus Christ Described and Assessed from the Oldest Accounts.* Translated by Isabel and Florence McHugh. Westminster, Md.: Newman; Cork: Mercier, 1959.)

———. *Die Brüder und Schwestern Jesu.* Stuttgart: Verlag Katholisches Bibelwerk, 1967.

Blomberg, C. L. *The Historical Reliability of the Gospels.* Leicester, England: Inter-Varsity, 1987.

———. *Jesus and the Gospels: An Introduction and Survey.* Nashville: Broadman & Holman, 1997.

Boer, H. R. *Above the Battle? The Bible and Its Critics.* Grand Rapids: Eerdmans, 1975.

Bovon, F. *Luke the Theologian: Thirty-Three Years of Research (1950–1983).* Translated by K. McKinney. Allison Park, Pa.: Pickwick, 1987.

Brandon, S. G. F. *Jesus and the Zealots: A Study of the Political Factor in Primitive Christianity.* Manchester: Manchester University Press, 1967.

Braun, H. *Jesus: Der Mann aus Nazareth und seine Zeit.* Um 12 Kapitel erweiterte Studienausgabe. Stuttgart: Kreuz, 1984.

Bruce, F. F. *Jesus and Christian Origins outside the New Testament.* London: Hodder & Stoughton, 1974.

Buchanan, G. W. *The Consequences of the Covenant*. Leiden: Brill, 1970.

――――. *Jesus: The King and His Kingdom*. Macon, Ga.: Mercer University Press, 1984.

Bultmann, R. *History of the Synoptic Tradition*. Translated by J. Marsh. Rev. ed. Peabody, Mass.: Hendrickson, 1994.

Cadbury, H. J. "Commentary on the Preface of Luke." In *The Beginnings of Christianity*, edited by F. J. Foakes Jackson and K. Lake, vol. 2, part 1, pp. 489–510. London: Macmillan, 1922.

Carmignac, J. *La naissance des Évangiles Synoptiques*. 3d ed. avec réponse aux critiques. Paris: O.E.I.L, 1984.

Catchpole, D. R. *The Trial of Jesus: A Study in the Gospels and Jewish Historiography from 1770 to the Present Day*. Studia Post-biblica 17. Leiden: Brill, 1971.

Cohn, H. *The Trial and Death of Jesus*. New York: Harper & Row, 1971.

Cullmann, O. *Jesus and the Revolutionaries*. Translated by G. Putnam. New York: Harper & Row, 1970.

De Jonge, M., ed. *L'Évangile de Jean: Sources, rédaction, théologie*. Gembloux: Duculot, 1977.

Delobel, J., ed. *Logia*. Leuven: Peeters, 1982.

Derrett, J. D. M. *Law in the New Testament*. London: Darton, Longman & Todd, 1970.

Drews, A. *Die Leugnung der Geschichtlichkeit Jesu in Vergangenheit und Gegenwart*. Wissen und Wirken 33. Karlsruhe: Braun, 1926.

Eisler, R. *Ièsous Basileus ou basileusas: Die messianische Unabhängigkeitsbewegung vom Auftreten Johannes des Täufers bis zum Untergang Jakobs des Gerechten usw*. Heidelberg: Winter, 1929–30.

Falk, H. *Jesus the Pharisee: A New Look at the Jewishness of Jesus*. New York: Paulist Press, 1985.

Farmer, W. R., ed. *New Synoptic Studies: The Cambridge Gospel Conference and Beyond*. Macon, Ga.: Mercer University Press, 1983.

Feldman, L. H. *Josephus: A Supplementary Bibliography*. New York: Garland, 1986.

Fitzmyer, J. A., and D. J. Harrington. *A Manual of Palestinian Aramaic Texts*. Biblica et Orientalia 34. Rome: Biblical Institute Press, 1978.

Flusser, D. *De Joodse oorsprong van het Christendom: Twee essays*. Amsterdam: Moussault, 1964.

――――. *Jesus*. Translated by R. Walls. New York: Herder & Herder, 1969.

――――. *Tussen oorsprong en schisma: Artikelen over Jezus, het Jodendom en het vroege Christendom*. 2d ed. Hilversum: Folkertsma Stichting voor Talmudica, 1984.

Funk, R. W., and R. W. Hoover, eds. *The Five Gospels: The Search for the Authentic Words of Jesus*. New York: Macmillan, 1993.

Gasque, W. W., and R. P. Martin, eds. *Apostolic History and the Gospel: Biblical and Historical Essays Presented to F. F. Bruce*. Exeter: Paternoster, 1970.

Greijdanus, S. *Hoofddoel en Gedachtengang van Lucas' Evangelieverhaal*. Kampen: Kok, 1922.

――――. *De opwekking van Christus*. Kampen: Kok, 1947.

――――. *Heilige geschiedenis volgens de vier evangelieverhalen: Geboorte van Jezus Christus en aanvang van Zijn publieke optreden*. Goes: Oosterbaan & Le Cointre, 1951.

――――. *De toestand der eerste christelijke gemeente in zijn betekenis voor de synoptische kwestie*. Kampen: Kok, 1973.

Guevara, H. *La resistencia judia contra Roma en la epoca de Jesus*. Meitingen: Meitingen, 1981.

Helms, R. *Gospel Fictions*. New York: Prometheus, 1988.

Hock, R. F., and E. N. O'Neil. *The Chreia in Ancient Rhetoric*. Vol. 1, *The Progymnasmata*. Atlanta: Scholars Press, 1986.

Hoehner, H. W. *Herod Antipas*. Cambridge: Cambridge University Press, 1972.

――――. *Chronological Aspects of the Life of Christ*. Grand Rapids: Zondervan, 1977.

Hoffmann, R. J. *Jesus outside the Gospels*. Buffalo: Prometheus, 1984.

Jeremias, J. *Unknown Sayings of Jesus*. 2d English ed. London: S.P.C.K, 1964.

Juster, J. *Les Juifs dans l'Empire Romain*. Paris: Geuther, 1914.

Kalthoff, A. *Das Christus-Problem: Grundlinien zu einer Sozialtheologie*. Leipzig: Diederichs, 1902.

Klijn, A. F. J., and G. J. Reinink. *Patristic Evidence for Jewish-Christian Sects*. Leiden: Brill, 1973.

Körtner, U. H. J. *Papias von Hierapolis: Ein Beitrag zur Geschichte des frühen Christentums*. Göttingen: Vandenhoeck & Ruprecht, 1983.

Kossen, H. B. *Op zoek naar de historische Jezus: Een studie over Albert Schweitzers visie op Jezus' leven*. Assen: Van Gorcum, 1960.

Kümmel, W. G. *Vierzig Jahre Jesusforschung (1950–1990)*. 2d ed. Edited by H. Merklein. Bonner Biblische Beiträge 91. Weinheim: Beltz Athenäum, 1994.

Kürzinger, J. *Papias von Hierapolis und die Evangelien des Neuen Testaments: Gesammelte Aufsätze, Neuausgabe und Übersetzung der Fragmente, kommentierte Bibliographie*. Regensburg: Pustet, 1983.

Lapide, P. *Israelis, Jews and Jesus*. Translated by P. Heinegg. Garden City, N.Y.: Doubleday, 1979.

Lategan, B. C. *Die aardse Jesus in die prediking van Paulus volgens sy briewe*. Rotterdam: Bronder, 1967.

Lawler, E. G. *David Friedrich Strauss and His Critics: The Life of Jesus Debate in Early Nineteenth-Century German Journals*. New York: Lang, 1986.

Lehmann, M. *Synoptische Quellenanalyse und die Frage nach dem historischen Jesus: Kriterien der Jesusforschung untersucht in Auseinandersetzung mit Emanuel Hirschs Frühgeschichte des Evangeliums*. Berlin: De Gruyter, 1970.

Levin, T. *Fasti Sacri or a Key to the Chronology of the New Testament*. London: Longmans, Green, & Co., 1865.

Lichtenstein, H. "Die Fastenrolle: Eine Untersuchung zur Jüdisch-Hellenistischen Geschichte." *Hebrew Union College Annual* 8–9 (1931–32): 257–351.

Lindeskog, G. *Die Jesusfrage im neuzeitlichen Judentum: Ein Beitrag zur Geschichte der Leben-Jesu-Forschung*. Mit einem Nachwort. Darmstadt: Wissenschaftliche Buchgesellschaft, 1973. (Original edition: Uppsala, 1938.)

Maier, J. *Jesus von Nazareth in der talmudischen Überlieferung*. Darmstadt: Wissenschaftliche Buchgesellschaft, 1978.

Marsh, C. "Quests of the Historical Jesus in New Historicist Perspective." *Biblical Interpretation* 5 (1997): 403–37.

McGrath, A. E. *The Making of Modern German Christology: From the Enlightenment to Pannenberg*. Oxford: Blackwell, 1986.

McHugh, J. *The Mother of Jesus in the New Testament*. London: Darton, Longman & Todd, 1975.

Meier, J. P. *A Marginal Jew: Rethinking the Historical Jesus*. Vol. 1, *The Roots of the Problem and the Person*. New York: Doubleday, 1991.

———. *A Marginal Jew: Rethinking the Historical Jesus*. Vol. 2, *Mentor, Message, and Miracles*. New York: Doubleday, 1994.

Merkel, H. *Die Widersprüche zwischen den Evangelien: Ihre polemische und apologetische Behandlung in der Alten Kirche bis zu Augustin*. Tübingen: Mohr, 1971.

———. *Die Pluralität der Evangelien als theologisches und exegetisches Problem in der Alten Kirche*. Bern: Lang, 1978.

Mokofeng, T. A. *The Crucified among the Crossbearers: Towards a Black Christology*. Kampen: Kok, 1983.

Ogg, G. *The Chronology of the Public Ministry of Jesus*. Cambridge: Cambridge University Press, 1940.

Pelikan, J. *Jesus through the Centuries: His Place in the History of Culture.* New Haven: Yale University Press, 1985.

Pines, S. *An Arabic Version of the Testimonium Flavianum and Its Implications.* Jerusalem: Israel Academy of Sciences and Humanities, 1971.

Reimarus, H. S. *The Goal of Jesus and His Disciples.* Translated by G. W. Buchanan. Leiden: Brill, 1970.

Riesner, R. *Jesus als Lehrer: Eine Untersuchung zum Ursprung der Evangelien-Überlieferung.* Tübingen: Mohr, 1981.

Rist, J. M. *On the Independence of Matthew and Mark.* Cambridge: Cambridge University Press, 1978.

Ristow, H., and K. Matthiae, eds. *Der historische Jesus und der kerygmatische Christus: Beiträge zum Christusverständnis in Forschung und Verkündigung.* 3d ed. Berlin: Evangelische Verlagsanstalt, 1964.

Sabbe, M., ed. *L'Évangile selon Marc: Tradition et rédaction.* Gembloux: Duculot, 1974.

Sanders, E. P. *The Tendencies of the Synoptic Tradition.* Cambridge: Cambridge University Press, 1969.

Schalit, A. "Zu AG 25,9 [On Acts 25:9]." *Annual of the Swedish Theological Institute* 6 (1968): 106–13.

Schillebeeckx, E. *Jesus: An Experiment in Christology.* Translated by H. Hoskins. London: Collins, 1979.

———. *Christ: The Experience of Jesus as Lord.* Translated by J. Bowden. New York: Seabury, 1980.

———. *Interim Report on the Books* Jesus *and* Christ. Translated by J. Bowden. New York: Crossroad, 1981.

Schmithals, W. *Einleitung in die drei ersten Evangelien.* Berlin: De Gruyter, 1985.

Schneemelcher, W. *New Testament Apocrypha.* Rev. ed. Translated by A. J. B. Higgins et al. English translation edited by R. McL. Wilson. Cambridge: Clarke, 1991–92.

Schreckenberg, H. *Bibliographie zu Flavius Josephus.* Leiden: Brill, 1968. (Supplementband mit Gesamtregister. Leiden, 1979.)

Schweitzer, A. *The Quest of the Historical Jesus: A Critical Study of Its Progress from Reimarus to Wrede.* Translated by W. Montgomery. London: Black, 1948.

Schürer, E. *The History of the Jewish People in the Age of Jesus Christ: 175 B.C.–A.D. 135.* New English ed. Revised and edited by G. Vermes, F. Millar, M. Black, and M. Goodman. 3 vols. Edinburgh: Clark, 1973–87.

Sevenster, J. N. *Bultmanniana: Een vraag naar criteria.* Wageningen: Veenman, 1969.

Sherwin-White, A. N. *Roman Society and Roman Law in the New Testament.* Oxford: Clarendon, 1963.

Smith, M. *Jesus the Magician.* 2d ed. Wellingborough: Aquarian Press, 1985. (1st ed., New York: Harper & Row, 1978.)

———. *The Secret Gospel: The Discovery and Interpretation of the Secret Gospel according to Mark.* New York: Harper & Row, 1973.

Sobrino, J. *Christology at the Crossroads: A Latin American Approach.* Maryknoll, N.Y.: Orbis, 1978.

Stein, R. H. *Jesus the Messiah: A Survey of the Life of Christ.* Downers Grove, Ill.: InterVarsity, 1996.

Stoldt, H. H. *History and Criticism of the Marcan Hypothesis.* Translated by D. L. Niewyk. Macon, Ga.: Mercer University Press, 1980.

Strauss, D. F. *The Life of Jesus Critically Examined.* Edited and with an introduction by P. C. Hodgson. Translated from the 4th German ed. by G. Eliot. Philadelphia: Fortress, 1973.

Strecker, G. *Der Weg der Gerechtigkeit: Untersuchung zur Theologie des Matthäus.* 2d ed. Göttingen: Vandenhoeck & Ruprecht, 1966.

Strecker, G., ed. *Jesus Christus in Historie und Theologie: Festschrift für H. Conzelmann.* Tübingen: Mohr, 1975.

Streeter, B. H. *The Four Gospels: A Study of Origins.* London, 1924.

Theissen, G., and A. Merz. *Der historische Jesus: Ein Lehrbuch.* Göttingen: Vandenhoeck & Ruprecht, 1996.

Tuckett, C. M. "Arguments from Order: Definition and Evaluation." In *Synoptic Studies: The Ampleforth Conferences of 1982 and 1983,* edited by C. M. Tuckett, 197–219. Sheffield: JSOT Press, 1984.

Van Bruggen, J. *De oorsprong van de kerk te Rome.* Groningen: De Vuurbaak, 1967.

———. *"Na veertien jaren": De datering van het in Galaten 2 genoemde overleg te Jeruzalem.* Kampen: Kok, 1973.

———. "The Year of the Death of Herod the Great." In *Miscellanea Neotestamentica,* vol. 2, edited by T. Baarda et al., 1–15. Leiden: Brill, 1978.

———. *Ambten in de apostolische kerk: Een exegetisch mozaïek.* Kampen: Kok, 1984.

———. *Wie maakte de bijbel? Over afsluiting en gezag van het Oude en Nieuwe Testament.* Kampen: Kok, 1986.

Verdam, P. J. *Sanhedrin èn Gabbatha.* Kampen: Kok, 1959.

Versteeg, J. P. *Evangelie in viervoud: Een karakteristiek van de vier evangeliën.* Kampen: Kok, 1980.

Vielhauer, P. *Geschichte der urchristlichen Literatur: Einleitung in das Neue Testament, die Apokryphen und die Apostolischen Väter.* Berlin: De Gruyter, 1975.

Vogels, H. J. *St. Augustins Schrift De consensu Evangelistarum unter vornehmlicher Berücksichtigung ihrer harmonistischen Anschauungen.* Freiburg: Herder, 1908.

Wenham, D., and C. L. Blomberg, eds. *The Jesus Tradition outside the Gospels.* Gospel Perspectives 5. Sheffield: JSOT Press, 1985.

Wenham, J. *Easter Enigma: Do the Resurrection Stories Contradict One Another?* Exeter: Paternoster, 1984.

Wieseler, K. *Chronologische Synopse der vier Evangelien: Ein Beitrag zur Apologie der Evangelien und der evangelischen Geschichte vom Standpuncte der Voraussetzungslosigkeit.* Hamburg: Perthes, 1843. (English translation: *A Chronological Synopsis of the Four Gospels.* Translated by E. Venables. 2d ed., rev. and corrected. Bohn's Theological Library. London: Bell, 1877.)

———. *Beiträge zur richtigen Würdigung der Evangelien und der evangelischen Geschichte: Ein Zugabe zu des Verfassers "Chronologische Synopse der vier Evangelien."* Gotha: Perthes, 1869.

Wilken, R. L. *The Christians as the Romans Saw Them.* New Haven and London: Yale University Press, 1984.

Wilkins, M. J., and J. P. Moreland. *Jesus under Fire: Modern Scholarship Reinvents the Historical Jesus.* Grand Rapids: Zondervan, 1995.

Winter, P. *On the Trial of Jesus.* 2d ed. Revised and edited by T. A. Burkill and G. Vermes. Studia Judaica 1. Berlin: De Gruyter, 1974.

Witherington III, B. *The Jesus Quest: The Third Search for the Jew of Nazareth.* Downers Grove, Ill.: InterVarsity, 1995.

Wrede, W. *The Messianic Secret.* Translated by J. C. G. Greig. Cambridge: Clarke, 1971.

Wünsch, D. *Evangelienharmonien im Reformationszeitalter: Ein Beitrag zur Geschichte der Leben-Jesu-Darstellungen.* Berlin: De Gruyter, 1983.

Zahn, T. *Das Evangelium des Lucas.* Leipzig: Deichert, 1913.

General Index

Scripture Index

Old Testament

Old Testament Apocrypha

New Testament

Index of Other Ancient Writings

Christian Writings

Classical Writings

Jewish Writings

Jakob van Bruggen is professor of New Testament at the Theological University in Kampen, Netherlands, where he has taught since 1967. He is the author of more than fifteen commentaries and monographs in Dutch and English, including *The Future of the Bible*. He is the general editor of a major New Testament commentary series published by J. H. Kok, Kampen, Netherlands.